Lecture Notes in Computer Science 7858

Commenced Publication in 1973
Founding and Former Series Editors:
Gerhard Goos, Juris Hartmanis, and Jan van Leeuwen

Alex Galis   Anastasius Gavras (Eds.)

The Future Internet

Future Internet Assembly 2013:
Validated Results and New Horizons

 Springer

Volume Editors

Alex Galis   Anastasius Gavras

Co-Editors

Federico Álvarez   Laurent Lefevre   Danny Raz
Alessandro Bassi   Jasper Lentjes   Gaël Richards
Michele Bezzi   Man-Sze Li   Elio Salvadori
Laurent Ciavaglia   Paul Malone   Susana Sargento
Frances Cleary   Antonio Manzalini   Hans Schaffers
Petros Daras   Volkmar Lotz   Joan Serrat
Hermann De Meer   Henning Müller   Burkhard Stiller
Panagiotis Demestichas   Karsten Oberle   Antonio F. Skarmeta
John Domingue   Noel E. O'Connor   Kurt Tutschku
Theo G. Kanter   Nick Papanikolaou   Theodore Zahariadis
Stamatis Karnouskos   Dana Petcu
Srdjan Krčo   Rahim Rahmani

Acknowledgement and Disclaimer
The work published in this book is partly funded by the European Union under the
Seventh Framework Programme. The book reflects only the authors' views. The Union
is not liable for any use that may be made of the information contained therein.

ISSN 0302-9743   e-ISSN 1611-3349
ISBN 978-3-642-38081-5   e-ISBN 978-3-642-38082-2
DOI 10.1007/978-3-642-38082-2
Springer Heidelberg Dordrecht London New York

Library of Congress Control Number: 2013936977

CR Subject Classification (1998): C.2, D.4.4, D.2, H.3.5, H.4, K.6.5

LNCS Sublibrary: SL 3 – Information Systems and Application, incl. Internet/Web
and HCI

Typesetting: Camera-ready by author, data conversion by Scientific Publishing Services, Chennai, India

Printed on acid-free paper

Springer is part of Springer Science+Business Media (www.springer.com)

List of Editors

Alex Galis
(chief editor) University College London, United Kingdom
a.galis@ucl.ac.uk

Anastasius Gavras
(chief co-editor) Eurescom GmbH, Heidelberg, Germany
gavras@eurescom.eu

Federico Álvarez
Universidad Politecnica de Madrid, Spain
federico.alvarez@upm.es

Alessandro Bassi
Alessandro BassiConsulting, France
alessandro@bassiconsulting.eu

Michele Bezzi
SAP Labs, France
michele.bezzi@sap.com

Laurent Ciavaglia
Alcatel-Lucent, France
laurent.ciavaglia@alcatel-lucent.com

Frances Cleary
Waterford Institute of Technology - TSSG, Ireland
fcleary@tssg.org

Petros Daras
CERTH-ITI, Greece
daras@iti.gr

Hermann De Meer
University of Passau, Germany
hermann.demeer@uni-passau.de

Panagiotis Demestichas
University of Piraeus, Greece
pdemest@unipi.gr

John Domingue
Knowledge Media Institute, The Open University, United Kingdom
john.domingue@open.ac.uk

Theo G. Kanter
Stockholm University, Sweden
kanter@dsv.su.se

Stamatis Karnouskos
SAP Research, Germany
stamatis.karnouskos@sap.com

Srdjan Krčo
Ericsson, Serbia
srdjan.krco@ericsson.com

Laurent Lefevre
INRIA AVALON, LIP Laboratory, Ecole Normale Supérieure de Lyon, France
laurent.lefevre@inria.fr

Jasper Lentjes
Vlastuin, Netherland
j.lentjes@vlastuin.nl

Man-Sze Li
IC Focus, United Kingdom
msli@icfocus.co.uk

Paul Malone
Waterford Institute of Technology - TSSG, Ireland
pmalone@tssg.org

Antonio Manzalini
Telecom Italia, Italy
antonio.manzalini@telecomitalia.it

Volkmar Lotz
SAP Labs, France
volkmar.lotz@sap.com

Henning Müller
University of Applied Sciences Western Switzerland, Switzerland
henning.mueller@hevs.ch

Karsten Oberle
Alcatel-Lucent, Bell Labs, Germany
karsten.oberle@alcatel-lucent.com

Noel E. O'Connor
Dublin City University, Ireland
Noel.OConnor@dcu.ie

Nick Papanikolaou
Hewlett-Packard Laboratories, United Kingdom
nick.papanikolaou@hp.com

Dana Petcu
West University of Timisoara, Romania
petcu@info.uvt.ro

Rahim Rahmani
University of Stockholm, Sweden
rahim@dsv.su.se

Danny Raz
The Technion, Israel
danny@cs.technion.ac.il

Gaël Richards
TELECOM ParisTech, France
gael.richard@telecom-paristech.fr

Elio Salvadori
CREATE-NET, Trento, Italy
elio.salvadori@create-net.org

Susana Sargento
University of Aveiro, Instituto de Telecomunicações, Portugal
susana@ua.pt

Hans Schaffers
Aalto University, Finland
hans.schaffers@aalto.fi

Joan Serrat
Universitat Politècnica de Catalunya, Spain
serrat@tsc.upc.edu

Burkhard Stiller
University of Zurich, Switzerland
stiller@ifi.uzh.ch

Antonio F. Skarmeta
Universidad de Murcia, Spain,
skarmeta@um.es

Kurt Tutschku
Blekinge Institute of Technology, Sweden
kurt.tutschku@bth.se

Theodore Zahariadis
Synelixis/TEI of Chalkida, Greece
zahariad@synelixis.com

Preface

The Internet constitutes the most vital scientific, technical, economic and societal set of infrastructures in existence and in operation today, serving 2.5 billion users. Continuing its development will secure future innovation and prosperity and underpin the sustainable economic growth needed in the future. Future Internet infrastructure research is therefore a must.

The Future Internet Assembly (FIA) is a successful conference that brings together participants of over 150 research projects from several distinct yet interrelated areas in the European Union Framework Programme 7 (FP7). The research projects are grouped as follows:

- The network of the future as an infrastructure connecting and orchestrating the future Internet of people, computers, devices, content, clouds, and things.
- Cloud computing, Internet of Services, and advanced software engineering.
- The public-private partnership projects on Future Internet.
- Future Internet research and experimentation (FIRE).

Researchers and practitioners associated with the Future Internet gather at the FIAs every six months in order to exchange ideas and interact on topics within the above areas.

This publication constitutes the 2013 edition of the annual Future Internet Assembly book, which has been published since 2009. It contains selected program-level results from the European Union FP7 program on the Future Internet, complementing the FIA conferences. The aim is to disseminate the results as widely as possible. Therefore, as with the previous books, the content is freely available on line[1] as well as in print form.

There were 45 submissions (36 submissions from the open call for chapters and 9 invited submissions). Each open call submission was peer-reviewed by 3 editors, while each invited submission was peer-reviewed by 4 editors. The editorial board decided to accept 26 submissions (18 submissions from the open call and 8 invited submissions). Introductions to the sections of the book and cross topics are also provided.

Each chapter presents both FI enabling technologies and their application to at least one of the networked system and service areas. The chapters of this book have been organized in five sections:

---

[1] The previous FIA books can be found on line at
www.springer.com/computer/communication+networks/book/978-3-642-30240-4,
www.springer.com/computer/communication+networks/book/978-3-642-20897-3,
www.booksonline.iospress.nl/ Content/View.aspx?piid=12006 and
www.booksonline.iospress.nl/Content/View.aspx? piid=16465

- Software Driven Networks, Virtualisation, Programmability, and Autonomic Management
- Computing and Networking Clouds
- Internet of Things
- Enabling Technologies and Economic Incentives
- Book Sponsoring Projects Overview

We would like to acknowledge the hard and expert work of the editors of this book. We also would like to voice our appreciation of the European FP7 projects that financially supported this publication as open access: 3DLIFE, CONCORD, FLAMINGO, GEYSERS, iCORE, IoT6, MOBILECLOUD, SMARTENIT, SMARTSANTANDER, and UNIVERSELF.

May 2013   Alex Galis
                                              Anastasius Gavras

Introductions

— Introduction —
Virtualized, Software-Defined and Software-Driven Networks

Kurt Tutschku[1], Panagiotis Demestichas[2], Antonio F. Skarmeta[3], Elio Salvadori[4], Alex Galis[5], and Laurent Ciavaglia[6]

[1] Blekinge Institute of Technology (BTH), Karlskrona, Sweden
kurt.tutschku@bth.se
[2] University of Piraeus, Greece
pdemest@unipi.gr
[3] University of Murcia, Spain
skarmeta@um.es
[4] CREATE-NET, Trento, Italy
elio.salvadori@create-net.org
[5] University College London
United Kingdom, a.galis@ucl.ac.uk
[6] Alcatel-Lucent, France
Laurent.Ciavaglia@alcatel-lucent.com

Introduction

In the mid of the 2000s, contemporary communication and data networks have become *ossified* [1]. This term denotes their inability to be changed and to adapted to new technologies. The standstill happened although the networks were aligned along well-defined layering concepts, which were aiming at extendibility and adaptivity. The ossification of the network was traced to large extends to the missing separation of the data plane and the control plane.

Moreover at the same time, novel software technologies for distributed systems have demonstrated that software-based control concepts for networks can be superior to control paradigms using conventional networking hardware and software. These impressive capabilities were evidenced, for example, by the efficiency of P2P-based file-sharing systems or the quality of HTTP-based video streaming using smart control from server or host side.

The paradigms of *Software-defined* or *Software-driven Networks* have emerged recently as results of the above outlined trends. They are aiming at architecting computer networks that separate and abstract network elements and network resources. These paradigms largely exploit *virtualization technologies* for sharing and aggregation of resources and for decoupling and isolating virtual networking elements. The abstraction of networking elements enables and simplifies *the programmability of networks* based on these concepts. The desired operational features hoped for these new networking architectures are: *a)* higher cost efficiency, *b)* increased networking capabilities and *c)* innovative service offerings.

Challenges

The implementation of these paradigms in real world networks, however, is rather difficult. Their materialization constitute various research and implementation challenges. Amongst others, the challenges comprise the following topics:

- What is the appropriate level of abstraction for network elements and network resources?
- Which functional areas should be described by the abstraction and how do they relate in an architecture to each other?
- How can security be achieved in virtualized networks?
- How can today's network elements be abstracted as future virtual elements and how can these virtual elements be mapped to generic physical network hardware?
- How does the abstraction of virtual network elements relate to future network services and applications?
- How can international standardization organizations support the features of abstraction and programmability?
- How future Internet architecture could be deployed in a transition approach based on virtualization?

Contributions

Chapters contained in this book that address some of the aforementioned challenges include:

- The chapter *"The NEBULA Future Internet Architecture: A Mid-Course Report"* describes a high reliable and trustworthy network architecture which is based on concepts from *Cloud Computing*. The architecture interconnects abstracted network elements which are assumed to be ultra-reliable, such data centers or high performance routers, by programmable interconnections.
- The chapter *"Towards a Secure Network Virtualization Architecture for the Future Internet"* proposes a virtualization architecture where elements refer to each other rather to be just interconnected. The referencing concept enables improved security in virtualized networks.
- The chapter *"Integrating OpenFlow in IMS Networks and Enabling for Future Internet Research and Experimentation"* is on the mapping of real-world network functions onto a virtualized and programable network architecture that uses OpenFlow. The mapping is constituted for the example of the functions of the IP Multimedia Subsystem (IMS), which is used as an essential concept in current public 3G/4G mobile networks.
- The chapter *"Towards an architecture for Future Internet applications"* discusses the relationship of future application and virtualized and programmable networks. It focuses on middleware support to interconnect applications and networks.

- The chapter "ComVantage: Mobile Enterprise Collaboration Reference Framework and Enablers for Future Internet Information Interoperability" presents a framework how mobile applications in enterprise environments can reference data by collaboration. It exploit the concept of *Linked Data*.
- The chapter *"Open the Way to Future Networks – a viewpoint framework from ITU-T"* outlines how the ITU as an international standards organization aims to provide support for the implementation of future virtualized and programmable networks.

Reference

[1] Turner, J.S., Taylor, D.E.: Diversifying the Internet. In: Proc. of IEEE Global Telecommunications Conference 2005 (GLOBECOM 2005) (December 2005)

— Introduction —
Autonomic Management and Operations

Panagiotis Demestichas[1], Alex Galis[2], and Laurent Ciavaglia[3]

[1] University of Piraeus, Greece
pdemest@unipi.gr
[2] University College London, United Kingdom
a.galis@ucl.ac.uk
[3] Alcatel-Lucent, France
laurent.ciavaglia@alcatel-lucent.com

Introduction

During the recent years, new applications and services are offered through different networks and devices over the wider umbrella of Internet. The success of the Internet is verified by the over a billion users world-wide. Of course, the constant development of new applications and services has imposed the respective evolution of the networks, services and technologies. The main goal of the Future Internet (FI) is to establish powerful network infrastructures, so as to support numerous applications and services and the emergence of new business models. To this end, the infrastructure will be highly pervasive consisting of people, smart objects, machines and the surrounding space, and embedded devices (e.g., sensors, RFID tags) that will result in a highly decentralized environment of resources, interconnected by dynamic Networks of Networks. This additional complexity will have to be supported so as to handle the multiple, demanding and changing conditions for the requested QoE/QoS, the maximization of the efficiency of the infrastructures, and their overall management.

Challenges

Autonomic systems, having the ability to self-manage and adapt to given circumstances without external intervention, are seen as the most viable direction for realizing the FI era. Moreover, the autonomic systems also incorporate learning mechanisms, evolving knowledge and establishing a decision making process for handling future situations. More specifically, self-management is essential for fast adaptations to changing situations, while learning can increase the reliability of decisions through knowledge. This feature enables multiple heterogeneous management systems to act on top of a common managed infra-structure in both fixed and mobile Internet, leading to reductions in the OPEX and CAPEX. Autonomic systems call for the design, development and validation of functionality in the area of context acquisition and reasoning, the derivation and evaluation of policies, distributed optimization techniques, and learning for acquiring and sharing knowledge and experience. In the latest years, work has been done with respect to governance, coordination, and support through knowledge of autonomic systems and application areas.

The chapters selected for this FIA book cover the areas of optimization and algorithms, protocols for the Future Internet, management platforms for the autonomic Future Internet, security issues and standardization initiatives for the autonomic management of the Future Internet.

Contributions

Chapters contained in this book that address some of the aforementioned challenges include:

- The chapter *"High Availability in the Future Internet"*, gives a comprehensive overview of Loop-Free Alternates (LFA) and survey the related LFA network optimization methods, pointing out that these optimization tools can turn LFA into an easy-to-deploy yet highly effective IP fast resilience scheme.
- In chapter *"Towards a Minimal Core for Information-Centric Networking"* the concept of information space as a potential solution is introduced, based on the sharing of information and late binding service composition of decoupled entities as the essence of information-centrism. The specified framework is an abstract model without dependencies to low-level implementation details and achieves minimality by leaving naming and content security outside the core. This approach makes the experimentation of new features above and their implementation below faster and provides a possible evolutionary kernel for information-centric networking (ICN).
- In chapter *"Managing QoS for Future Internet Applications over Virtual Sensor Networks"* the way the VITRO routing solution could be employed in various use cases including smart homes/buildings, smart cities, smart business environments and security-related applications is demonstrated. The achieved performance using computer simulation results is evaluated and guidelines for prospective users are provided.
- The chapter *"Design and Implementation of Cooperative Network Connectivity Proxy using Universal Plug and Play"* introduces a new approach to design and implement the cooperative Network Connectivity Proxy (NCP) for reducing energy waste in the ever-growing Future Internet. The NCP allows all registered network hosts to transition into the low power sleep modes and maintains the network connectivity on their behalf. It handles basic net-work presence and management protocols like ICMP, DHCP, ARP etc. on behalf of the sleeping network hosts and wakes them up only when their resources are required. Depending on the network hosts time usage model, the NCP can provide about 60–70% network energy savings.
- In chapter *"Cooperative Strategies for Power Saving in Multi-standard Wireless Devices"* the way cognitive radio and cooperative communication can be

integrated in 4G networks is presented, so as to conduct wireless devices to either perform vertical handover or execute relaying by exploiting their available short range interfaces (e.g., WiMedia, Bluetooth, etc.) to reduce their power consumption, while still enabling the required QoS. Simulation and experimental results validate that 4G wireless devices can double their battery lifetime by adopting the proposed strategies.

- The chapter *"Towards a Socially-aware Management of New Overlay Application Traffic Combined with Energy Efficiency in the Internet (SmartenIT)"* focuses on an incentive-compatible cross-layer network management for providers of over-lay-based application (e.g., cloud applications, content delivery, and social net-works), network providers, and end-users to ensure a QoE-awareness, by ad-dressing accordingly load and traffic patterns or special application requirements, and exploiting at the same time social awareness (in terms of user relations and interests). Moreover, energy efficiency with respect to both end user devices and underlying networking infrastructure is tackled to ensure an operationally efficient management. Incentive-compatible network management mechanisms for improving metrics on an inter-domain basis for ISPs serve as the major mechanism to deal with and investigate real-life scenarios.

- The chapter *"The NEBULA Future Internet Architecture: A Mid-Course Report"* focuses on a future network that enables the vision of cloud computing to be realized. With computation and storage moving to data-centres, networking to these data-centres must be several orders of magnitude more resilient for some applications to trust cloud computing and enable their move to the cloud.

- The chapter *" SmartSantander: Internet of Things Research and Innovation through citizen participation"* presents two novel services that have been implemented in order to bring the Smart City closer to the citizen. The Participatory Sensing service proposed exploits the advanced features of smartphones to make the user part of the ubiquitous sensing infrastructure over which the Smart City concept is built. The Augmented Reality service is connected to the smart city platform in order to create an advanced visualization tool where the plethora of available information is presented to citizens embedded in their natural surroundings.

- In chapter *"Counting the Cost of FIRE – Overcoming Barriers to Sustainable Experimentation Facilities"* the way cost modelling and usage accounting can be used to support operational and sustainability decisions for a federated cloud experimentation facility is demonstrated.

- The chapter *"Towards a Secure Network Virtualization Architecture for the Future Internet"* discusses the Global Virtualization Architecture (GVA) that enables communications between network entities according to the way they refer to each other rather than understanding the constraints of particular networks. The approach is to instantiate a virtual network that is based on identities of network entities and their demands on security and network capabilities.

— In chapter *"Open the Way to Future Networks – a viewpoint framework from ITU-T"* the background and the context of Future Networks' standardization, the results and future plans originated from the initial standardization work performed by ITU-T are presented.

— Introduction —
The Future Internet Cloud: Computing, Networking and Mobility

Dana Petcu[1], Alex Galis[2], and Stamatis Karnouskos[3]

[1] West University of Timişoara, Romania
petcu@info.uvt.ro
[2] University College London, United Kingdom
a.galis@ucl.ac.uk
[3] SAP Research, Germany
stamatis.karnouskos@sap.com

Introduction

Cloud computing has received tremendous attention the last years, both in academia as well as in industry, especially with the deployment of multiple commercially available solutions that foster the basis for a variety of value-added services. In the Future Internet era, the cloud will still have a considerable impact on the way the new infrastructures will be used by the Future Internet envisioned applications. However this attention is moving fast beyond from purely computing-oriented focus (although this will expand), towards covering networking and mobility.

The Future Internet Architecture will integrate the Cloud computing paradigm to a new level encompassing several aspects such as the Cloud of Things, Software Defined Networking, Fog Computing etc. Considerable research efforts are already devoted today to ensure that the amalgamation between new revolutionary network technologies and the Cloud computing is properly exploited in context like data deluge.

Clouds in the Future Internet are expected to come in various forms depending on their stakeholders' needs. Sophisticated capabilities will significantly expand what we today classify under "computing" and for instance real-time analytics on big data will empower a new generation of services and applications. To this direction networking and information exchange will be further enhanced and cross-layer interactions among the billions of interconnected devices, systems and services will be assisted by the Future Internet Cloud paradigm. In that era, mobility will be of key importance and will be supported both in terms of mobile users and their devices, as well as seamless transcoding of sessions among different systems of varying capabilities. The Future Internet Cloud is seen at the heart of the service offering and empowerment in the Future Internet vision.

Challenges

In the Future Internet Cloud, the main concerns raised today will still be a challenge, e.g., aspects related to security, trust, privacy, interoperability and portability. As the Future Internet will stretch the Cloud infrastructure, other aspects such as quality of service, high performance guarantees, dependability, value-added services, data management, analytics, etc. will still need to be addressed in order to assist industry embracement of the Future Internet solutions.

Of special importance is of course the support of the billions of mobile users and the respective apps running in the increasingly heterogeneous devices. Hence the integration with the Internet of Things (an amalgamation described as Cloud of Things) as well as offering value added services on huge amounts of data (Big Data), will foster key challenges that need to be addressed. All these will need to be done with new approaches that guarantee adherence to concerns on security and privacy as well as to industry requirements for lifecycle management of the data and the services.

Networking and efficient interaction with the cloud and its services, as well as cross-cloud interaction (federation of cloud infrastructures) and development of value added services on top will be of pivotal importance. Adding also the seamless provision of service to the mostly mobile devices and users, as well as support for mobility in emerging application areas e.g., smart cities needs to be tackled. Considering also the global sustainability goals, green cloud computing in the Future Internet needs also to be efficiently addressed in a cooperative holistic way.

Contributions

Chapters contained in this book that address some of the aforementioned challenges include:

- The chapter *"Open the Way to Future Networks – a viewpoint framework from ITU-T"* focuses on the Future Network objectives and design goals for further developing technologies and systems. The chapter points out the results and future plans stemming from the initial standardization work performed by ITU-T as well as recommendations for standardization bodies in order to support the Future Networks development.
- The chapter *"The NEBULA Future Internet Architecture: A Mid-Course Report"* is presenting an architecture intended to provide secure and resilient networking to support present and future applications of cloud computing. To this end, reliable routing, data-center interconnections, data plane with policy enforcements, and a control plane for network configuration are investigated.
- The chapter *"Towards a Secure Network Virtualization Architecture for the Future Internet"* analyses different architecture proposals for the Future Internet and subsequently presents an architecture design that fills those gaps

by means of virtualization techniques working together with the overlay network concept. The notion of Virtual Group Networks, which group physical and abstract mobile entities, and focus on the demands in terms of security and network capabilities is introduced.

- The chapter *"Seeding the Cloud: An Innovative Approach to Grow Trust in Cloud Based Infrastructures"* tackles the issues of security, trust and privacy in the cloud. It introduces a network of secure elements (software and hardware elements connected locally with or in pieces of equipment), defining a minimal trusted computing base and allowing an end-to-end virtual security chain from the user to the server where the services are executed or data is stored.

- In the chapter *"Cloud-based Evaluation Framework for Big Data"* a discussion on the challenges that arise when doing benchmarking on big data is depicted. The problem of bringing the algorithms to the data in the Cloud is analysed in conjunction with the particular use cases of segmentation and retrieval of three-dimensional medical images.

- The chapter *"Resource Optimisation in IoT Cloud Systems by using Matchmaking and self-Management Principles"* a proposal to annotate data of monitored cloud performance and user profiles and adapt the management systems to use shared infrastructures and resources to enable efficient deployment of Internet-of-Things services and applications is depicted.

- The chapter *"Contrail: Distributed Application Deployment under SLA in Federated Heterogeneous Clouds"* addresses the challenges of offering reliable Cloud services and how to ensure quality of service and of protection in a federation of Cloud providers. Moreover, a deployment service, for distributed applications, that allows interoperability among the Cloud sites participating to the federation is investigated.

- The experimental studies presented in chapter *"Optimizing Service Ecosystems in the Cloud"* are related to the optimization of service compositions. The service ecosystem is emulated in a multi-site federated Cloud and the study subjects are two optimization models.

Conclusions

In the Future Internet, the Cloud is playing a pivotal role. There are several open challenges, some of which are addressed in the chapters presented in this section. However, significant research is remaining in order to support effectively the Future Internet envisioned applications as well as their infrastructure requirements such as computation (including analytics), mobility and networking.

— Introduction —
The Future Internet of Things

Stamatis Karnouskos[1], Antonio F. Skarmeta[2],
Panagiotis Demestichas[3], and Srđan Krčo[4]

[1] SAP Research, Germany
stamatis.karnouskos@sap.com
[2] University of Murcia, Spain
skarmeta@um.es
[3] University of Piraeus, Greece
pdemest@unipi.gr
[4] Ericsson, Serbia
srdjan.krco@ericsson.com

Introduction

Internet of Things is seen as a key part of the Future Internet vision which will enable real-time interaction with the physical environment. Billions of connected heterogeneous devices, sensing and actuating the physical environment in which they are embedded, and interacting among them or with remote users comprise the foundation of IoT.

More sophisticated approaches go beyond simple communication integration and target more complex interactions where collaboration of devices and systems is taking place. The cross-layer interaction and cooperation is pursued (i) at machine-to-machine (M2M) level where the machines cooperate with each other (machine focused interactions), as well as (ii) at machine-to-business (M2B) level where machines cooperate also with network-based services and business systems (business service focus).

As the Future Internet will be a very complex system of systems, the Internet of Things is expected to enable approaches that tame that complexity via real-time fine-grained monitoring, analytics-assisted decision making, and timely management. To do so, it will have to highly depend on the Future Internet infrastructure and envisioned capabilities in an open and collaborative way. This collaborative way of interactions is expected to lead to emergent behaviours in the Future Internet that, at the end, will better serve the end-users.

Challenges

Realizing the vision of Future Internet of Things requires tackling numerous challenges spanning a range of domains from the technical ones, to the social, design, economics etc. domain, or new area like smart cities. At the same time the traditional issues such as security, trust, privacy, openness, user-friendliness and rapid development still have to be supported.

Connectivity will remain in Future Internet a key aspect. However, the major focus is shifted towards supporting interoperable interactions at multiple layers and among various Internet of Things empowered services, and at the same time support legacy systems. The latter includes also aspects of migration of the current partially networked infrastructure to a fully-connected open system in the Future Internet era. Additionally, complexity management, crowdsourcing, real-time analytics, knowledge capturing and communication, simulation are only some indicative aspects that will need to be investigated as they will impact the next generation of Future Internet enabled applications.

Designing software solutions for the Future Internet of Things, and analysing the impact (e.g. of malfunctions) at system-wide level can be assisted by big data analytics. A new generation of data explorative of tools, as well as sophisticated algorithms considering context specific information at several levels on very large scale systems will need to be designed, developed and piloted. Extracting and understanding the business relevant information under temporal constraints and being able to effectively built in solutions that utilize the monitor-analyse-decide-manage approach for a multitude of domains is challenging.

The high heterogeneity of systems, models, quality of data and associated information, uncertainties as well as complex system-wide interactions, will need to be investigated to identify business opportunities and realize a business benefit. Supporting effectively all stakeholders in the Future Internet Era is a key challenge that we will have to deal with. This implies new business models, information exchange and business collaborations that create added value for all participating stakeholders and that will open new business opportunities.

Contributions

Chapters contained in this book that address some of the aforementioned challenges include:

- The chapter *"Test-Enabled Architecture for IoT Service Creation and Provisioning"* targets the service creation and testing in the Future Internet of Things environment. An architecture design is investigated that extends the existing IoT reference architecture and enables a test-driven, semantics-oriented management of the entire service lifecycle. Future Internet of things challenges addressed include integration, service creating and semantic-enabled interaction.
- The chapter *"A Cognitive Management Framework for Empowering the Internet of Things"* presents a framework that has the ability to dynamically adapt its behaviour, through self-management functionality, taking into account information and knowledge (obtained through machine learning) on the situation (e.g., internal status and status of environment), as well as policies (designating objectives, constraints, rules, etc.). Several Future Internet

of Things challenges such as integration, collaboration, self-X, reliability and efficiency are addressed.

– The chapter *"SmartSantander: Internet of Things Research and Innovation through citizen participation"* shows the applicability of the Future Internet of Things in urban environments. The two examined services i.e., participatory sensing and augmented reality, address challenges towards the added-value and business effect of the Future Internet of Things.

– The chapter *"IoT6 – Moving to an IPv6-based future IoT"* investigates the design and development of a highly scalable IPv6-based Service-Oriented Architecture to achieve interoperability, mobility, cloud computing integration and intelligence distribution among heterogeneous smart things components, applications and services, taking advantage of the IPv6 features. The domain of building automation is chosen to show the feasibility of the approach. The challenges addressed include integration, service-driven interaction, openness and empowerment of applications and services in IPv6 Future Internet of Things era.

– The chapter *"Building modular middlewares for the Internet of Things with OSGi"* investigated how to develop intelligent infrastructures combining various devices through the network by fully utilizing the capabilities of OSGi for development of modular, fine-grained and loosely coupled Java applications. Challenges of the Future Internet of Things addressed include scalability, integration, lifecycle management etc.

Conclusions

The Internet of Things is an integral part of the Future Internet vision. There are numerous challenges that need to be tackled that spawn several domains. Some of the chapters presented in this book go towards depicting how a subset of these challenges can be addressed. It is clear however, that we are still at the dawn of an the Future Internet of Things era and significant research efforts need to be investigated in a well balanced way in order to make sure that the benefits expected can be harvested.

— Introduction —
Enabling Technologies for Infrastructures and Experimentation

Henning Müller[1], Petros Daras[2], and Anastasius Gavras[3]

[1] University of Applied Sciences Western Switzerland (HES–SO), Switzerland
henning.mueller@hevs.ch
[2] Centre for Research and Technology Hellas (CERTH), Greece
daras@iti.gr
[3] Eurescom, Germany
gavras@eurescom.eu

Introduction

This section describes the enabling technologies and infrastructures and experimentation endeavours for the Future Internet. These topics are covered by chapters devoted to (i) network and information–centric network architectures; (ii) cloud–related solutions; and (iii) IoT–related research, the Internet of Things. These three domains are addressed by a multitude of chapters describing currently ongoing projects and results of past projects.

Challenges

The challenges in enabling technologies are diverse. It is clear that the Internet has become omnipresent and the Internet of Things will increase this permanent presence. Many different applications and techniques exist and are currently being tested in various settings. Network and access questions are another challenge discussed by several of the chapters. Energy efficiency of networks and systems is increasingly getting important with big data centres for cloud infrastructures consuming massive amounts of energy. The data centers are necessary for cloud computing, another approach that is currently being used in many applications and in many different ways. Trust and security in clouds are getting important as critical or confidential data are increasingly being stored in clouds.

Contributions

Chapters contained in this book that address some of the aforementioned challenges include:

- The chapter *"An Internet–based Architecture Supporting Ubiquitous Model–driven User Interfaces"* describes how Web technology and the Internet infrastructure make ubiquitous applications a reality. The authors present webinos, a multi–device application platform founded on the Future Internet infrastructure and describe webinos' model–based user interface framework as a means to support context–aware adaptiveness for applications that are executed in such ubiquitous computing environments.
- The invited chapter *"Sustainable Wireless Broadband Access to the Future Internet – The EARTH Project"* gives an overview of the FP7 project EARTH contributions to a sustainable wireless broadband access to the Future Internet. The chapter explains the wide range of areas in which EARTH has and will have significant impact ranging from reinforced leadership of European industry in the field of Future Internet technology, over increase economic efficiency of access infrastructures, global standards, interoperability and European IPRs reflecting federated and coherent roadmaps to accelerated uptake of next generation of network and service infrastructure. Project EARTH was awarded best FIA project at the last Future Internet Assembly that was held in Aalborg, in spring 2012.
- The chapter *"High Availability in the Future Internet"* presents a comprehensive overview of Loop–Free Alternates (LFA) and survey the related LFA network optimization methods, pointing out that these optimization tools can turn LFA into an easy–to–deploy yet highly effective IP fast resilience scheme.
- The chapter *"Design and Implementation of Cooperative Network Connectivity Proxy using Universal Plug and Play"* describes a new approach to design and implement the cooperative Network Connectivity Proxy (NCP) for reducing energy waste. The NCP allows all registered network hosts to transition into the low power sleep modes and maintains the network connectivity on their behalf. Depending on the network hosts time usage model, the NCP can provide about 60–70% network energy savings.
- The chapter *"Towards a Minimal Core for Information-Centric Networking"* proposes an abstract model for information–centric networking (ICN), that allows the bulk of features of current ICN architectures to be expressed as independent extensions to this model. It presents a possible evolutionary kernel for ICN allowing experimentation of new features above and implementation below faster.
- The chapter *"Cooperative Strategies for Power Saving in Multi–standard Wireless Devices"* demonstrates how cognitive radio and cooperative communication can be integrated in 4G networks to reduce their power consumption while still enabling the required QoS. Simulation results validate that 4G wireless devices can double their battery lifetime by adopting the proposed power saving strategies.
- On the second point, the chapter *"Seeding the Cloud: An Innovative Approach to Grow Trust in Cloud Based Infrastructures"* proposes a way to build a secure and trustable Cloud. The idea is to spread and embed Secure Elements on each level of the Cloud in order to build a trusted infrastructure

complying with access control and isolation policies. This chapter presents a trusted Cloud infrastructure based on a Network of Secure Elements (NoSE), and illustrates it through different use cases.

- The chapter *"Optimizing Service Ecosystems in the Cloud"* presents experimental results of the performance of two optimization models in service ecosystems by (i) testing the maturity of existing technology and its suitability for use in Future Internet scenarios, and (ii) investigating the existing infrastructure capabilities.

- The chapter *"Cloud–based Research Infrastructure for Evaluation on Big Data"* describes a cloud–based research infrastructure for evaluating machine learning and information retrieval algorithms on large amounts of data. Instead of downloading data and running evaluations locally, the data are centrally available in the cloud and the algorithms are executed in the cloud, effectively bringing the algorithms to the data.

- The chapter *"Contrail: Distributed Application Deployment under SLA in Federated Heterogeneous Clouds"* presents the challenges of interoperability, performance guarantee, and dependability. It then presents three components: Contrail federation; SLA manager; and Virtual Execution Platform. These components provide interoperability guarantees in a cloud federation and enable deployment of distributed applications over a federation of heterogeneous cloud providers.

- On the third point, the chapter *"Test–Enabled Architecture for IoT Service Creation and Provisioning"* presents the efforts of the IoT.est project to develop a framework for service creation and testing in an IoT environment. The architecture extends the IoT reference architecture and enables a test–driven, semantics–based management of the service lifecycle. Its validation is illustrated through a dynamic test case generation and execution scenario.

- The chapter *"A Cognitive Management Framework for Empowering the Internet of Things"* presents a Cognitive Management framework for the Internet of Things (IoT). The framework dynamically adapts its behaviour, through self–management functionality, based on knowledge of status and policies. It presents a first indicative implementation of the proposed framework, comprising real sensors and actuators. The preliminary results demonstrate high potential towards self–reconfigurable IoT.

- The chapter *"Resource Optimisation in IoT Cloud Systems by using Matchmaking and self–Management Principles"* focuses on integrated IoT cloud service data management based on annotated data of monitored cloud performance and user profiles. It illustrates a cloud service management approach based on matchmaking operations and self–management principles that enable faster distributed service analysis and use the results as mechanisms to control applications and services deployment in cloud systems.

Conclusions

The enabling technologies for the future Internet are manifold. The articles described in this section show several future directions towards innovative uses of computing clouds and an extension of the Internet towards an Internet of things that can have many faces and potential application areas.

— Introduction —
Trust and Security, Economic Incentives, Open Solutions

Burkhard Stiller[1], Man-Sze Li[2], and Hans Schaffers[3]

[1] University of Zürich, Department of Informatics IFI, Communication Systems
Group CSG, Zürich, Switzerland
stiller@ifi.uzh.ch
[2] IC Focus, London, U.K.
msli@icfocus.co.uk
[3] Aalto University, School of Business, CKIR, Espoo, Finland
hans.schaffers@aalto.fi

Introduction

Previous sections of the FIA 2013 book with respect to the Future Internet area
focused on architectures, foundations, and enabling technologies; this part III
ad-dresses the highly relevant dimensions of trust and security, combined with
economic incentives, and open solutions. These three dimensions determine key
enabling aspects in operationally feasible and sensible approaches, which the
Future Internet needs to be supported with rather sooner than later.

While the inter-operation between providers and users (determining the two
very distinct groups of stakeholders in place today and tomorrow) is required
to be either run on a trusted basis, which has to be established by respective
technical means, such as algorithms and system components, the security itself
opens up a large umbrella of aspects, such as authentication, authorization, integrity, privacy, confidentiality, non-repudiation, and trust. Enabling user-driven
policy enforcements and configurations requires a well-balanced selection of such
mechanisms. However, in all cases a system-specific view on any vulnerabilities
and attacks need to be established to under-stand the full risks of operation,
which involves a trusted or un-trusted human.

Only the optimal combination of those aspects, which are application-
dependent at least, and the ease-of-use type of solution will determine a successful deployment of large scale in the Future Internet. However, since only the
right set of incentives will make a pure technology-driven solution operational,
typically, in a commercialized world of services and interactions, economic incentives will enable a viable solution under combined technological and commercial
views. Therefore, the examination and further development as well as implementation of economic incentives for those two groups of stakeholders are a key
condition for a viable Future Internet functionality.

The user plays a crucial role. His and her requirements shall be taken into consideration closely and respective user interfaces are deemed highly ubiquitous.

Last but not least, the openness of such approaches, solutions, mechanisms, and implementations will help accelerate the implementation of technological solutions into a user-acceptable system, which forms the very basic for an advantageous, productive, and finally prosperous Future Internet, since all parameters and settings are openly visible, they may be configured to application needs and per-use specific demands. In that sense the ITU-T's standardization work is considered a valuable path to follow.

Challenges

The recently published FIA 2020 Roadmap [1] presents an interesting analysis of the ongoing importance of trust and security, based on the view of the Future Internet as a complex technical-socio-economic system. As the scale of threats and potential for conflicts and the society's reliance on Internet-based networks for operation of critical infrastructures continues to increase, the management of securities and the development of adequate and also "user-friendly" technologies and solutions remains a challenge over the next decades. A holistic, systems approach to security will be necessary. This will be based on not only intelligent and differentiated measures and robust systems architectures, but also on making the user part of the system secure. This will involve security considerations being automatically taken into account during the software development, with justifiable assurance that the software is secure. It will be possible to dynamically compose and personalize services in a secure way, and customization does not come at a cost to security. Services that are available on the open market will have well defined security properties. Inter-organizational security analysis and management will be possible. There will be good tools and other support for end users to understand security (and privacy) implications of those services they use. The crucial point is that it will be possible for users to make informed choices based on a sound understanding of security and risk; in parallel, users will need to be more empowered with appropriate control over the level of risk, notably through standard, transparent interaction with systems and networks.

Incentives define an economic mechanism to enable an interplay of stakeholders to act in a manner, which gives at best all of them a viable reason to contribute re-sources into a system and to discourage free-riders at the same time, thus, avoiding the use of resources only without commensurate contribution. Incentive mechanisms, such as BarterCast, tit-for-tat, Give-to-Get, or Private Shared History (PSH) in multiple variants, can be divided into two groups – trust-based and trade-based incentive mechanisms: (a) for trust-based incentive mechanisms, all peers are encouraged to act in a way to gain as much trust as possible. While a positive peer's behaviour increases such a trust value, a negative behaviour decreases this value. (b) for trade-based incentive mechanism, resources are exchanged and peers are encouraged to provide in order to consume, thus, a misconduct results immediately in a penalty. With respect to the economic incentives a number of challenges are known today, which include the search for transitive incentive mechanisms in application-independent networking systems, suitable approaches for mapping incentive mechanisms into viable monetary or non-monetized schemes, and especially general and integrated incentive mechanisms for streaming and video-on-demand systems. There are many application level incentive schemes, which are dependent on the business model. Whilst a majority is directly transposed from the bricks-and-mortar world, others leverage the viral effect of the Internet to deliver non-monetary values such as reputation and recommendations.

Finally, the open solutions point of view is associated with a list of challenges linked to the understanding and interpretation of openness from the perspectives of technology, economics/business models, as well as the overall "system" as an ecosystem. At the technology level, developments have focused on increasing interoperability in networks, applications and services, often coupled with considerations for standardization. At the business level, open business models have generated a large volume of scholarship, which is increasingly linked to the notion of open innovation as well as re-appraisal of business values. At the systemic level, the discussion on ecosystems has involved: (a) the development of a wide variety of applications based on a generic technology platform; (b) the development of business partnerships based around a provider's core offering, typically for expanding and/or customizing the functionality of the offering for broadening market reach; and (c) the development of a system of relationships and the supporting infrastructures (technical and business) involving suppliers and customers, potential or actual, that are tightly aligned with those activities, characteristics, objectives, and value proposition of a company. Open solutions viewed through the lenses of an ecosystem are linked to the role of generic technologies in creating markets (as in a); the need to collaborate with a wider range of partners including third party developers, consultants, and channels (as in b), and the emergence of a new type of market and even mode of exchange brought about by Internet and especially Web native companies (as in c). Each of these involves a large set of issues with deep intersections between technology, business, and policy. Research in such areas will need to be intensified and deepened in the coming years.

Contributions

Chapters contained in this book that address some of the aforementioned challenges include:

- The *"The NEBULA Future Internet Architecture"* chapter discusses the future network enabling the vision of cloud computing. In particular, the NEBULA approach presented is organized into three major architectural thrust areas: (a) reliable routing system and data center interconnect, (b) a data plane enabling policy enforcement, and (c) a novel approach to a control plane architecture allowing users to control the network configuration from the edge.

- The chapter *"User Involvement in Future Internet Projects"* addresses user involvement in the Future Internet community. The authors were interested to find out, whether current Future Internet projects support user-led innovation and in this way empower ordinary people, citizens, and non-commercial entities. Thus, to determine actual attitudes and practices of those working in the Future Internet industry toward user-centricity, the approach presented follows a focus group approach.
- The chapter *"An Internet-based Architecture Supporting Ubiquitous Application User Interfaces"* presents the multi-device application platform "webinos" founded on the Future Internet infrastructure and in particular discusses this platform's ability to dynamically adapt application user interfaces to the current delivery context.
- The chapter *"Open the Way to Future Networks – A Viewpoint Framework from ITU-T"* presents major background and the context of Future Networks' standardization by the ITU-T, current results, and future plans originating from the initial standardization work performed, which has resulted by now in initial Recommendations laying out essential directions for subsequent detailed work including further standardization of Future Networks.

Reference

[1] FIA Research Roadmap (June 2012),
   http://fisa.future-internet.eu/index.php/FIA_Research_Roadmap

— Introduction —
Smart Applications and Services in the Future Internet

John Domingue[1] and Stamatis Karnouskos[2]

[1] The Open University, United Kingdom
john.domingue@open.ac.uk
[2] SAP Research, Germany
stamatis.karnouskos@sap.com

Introduction

This is the fifth book capturing the results of the Future Internet Assemblies – the first was published in 2009. In that time we can see that the prominence of applications has increased of that time – there were no application chapters in the first book. This increase is due to two main factors. Firstly, the technologies are maturing over time and are now at a stage where serious industrial deployment is feasible. Secondly, within the early Future Internet Assemblies (FIAs) there was a realization that a wide range of stakeholders needed to be engaged to ensure that we continue to move in a direction which meets Europe's economic and societal needs. Moreover, it is essential that our stakeholder group includes representatives from the important vertical niches such as transport, energy and the public sector. The fact that we now combine Smart Applications and Services into one section highlights the strong connection between these two strands.

The Future Internet can be thought of in many ways. A simple service-centric view is the Internet has three main components: (i) a network to provide connectivity (wired or wireless), (ii) a service layer to expose resources and (iii) an application layer which provides added value for end-users. Within the service layer two main classes of services can be found. Infrastructure services expose core capabilities required for the service layer to function. Typically, these may be related to networking, to managing resource repositories and core SOA function such as service invocation. Higher level services support the creation of business services supplying value to customers typically for a fee. Thus, the service layer acts as a bridge between the low-level network infrastructure and companies enacting a variety of business models to serve the related communities.

Smart applications was a concept which was adopted early on in the FIA series. The notion captured here was that Future Internet technologies enable a new type of application to be constructed. Ubiquitous and high bandwidth connectivity means that in principle applications have access to all required data and resources in real-time as required with geographic distance no longer a barrier. Applications based upon ecosystems of online data and computational resources, developers and users are now emerging where boundaries between both real-world and computational entities and roles are blurred.

The complexity in the Future Internet will increase, as billions of devices, users and service will coexist and interact. In such a sophisticated infrastructure which can be seen as a very complex system of systems, the applications will be the entry point for many users to interact and enjoy its offerings. Future Internet application developers will have to tame the heterogeneity of sources and target end-user devices, in addition to dealing with the utilization of the Future Internet infrastructure offerings such as Cloud Computing, and the Internet of Things. Collaborative approaches may give rise to a new generation of applications and sophisticated services that are user-centric and provide added-value at a fraction of time and cost. However for the latter to happen, several grand challenges still need to be tackled.

Challenges

A world where on the one hand users demand 24/7 access to cheap (or free), easy-to-use, secure, mobile, personalized and context aware applications and on the other where services and applications are provisioned within dynamic, fluid frameworks with no central control, provides many challenges for the Future Internet community. Within this scenario, the components of applications and services are spread over highly inter-connected infrastructures which may be hosted on heterogeneous hardware and software platforms within distinct organisations. In order to fulfil user demands service and application Future Internet technologies need to support a range of non-trivial requirements including:

- On-the-fly discovery – instantaneously finding resources which match new or changing user requirements, within a setting where no uniform description language or vocabulary exists.
- On-the-fly aggregation – automatically or semi-automatically composing components to create a running application requires a number of research problems to be solved.
- Transitivity – passing information related to payments and faults, for example, between just-aggregated systems across institutions and platforms is a significant challenge.
- Interoperability – systems run on a mixture of software and hardware platforms where data and services will differ in syntax, semantics and interaction characteristics. Mediating between these heterogeneities requires more research.
- Seamless substitution – if a service or resource becomes unavailable finding and accommodating a new one, which meets the needs in a seamless fashion, is an important pre-requisite to fulfilling end-user expectations today.

Meeting the above challenges has been a goal for the research carried out in the FIA projects since the begin of FIA.

Contributions

Chapters contained in this book that address some of the aforementioned challenges include:

- The chapter *"Towards an architecture for Future Internet applications"* deals with the needs of applications in the Future Internet Era where multiple devices should be addressed and context information provided by ubiquitous sensors need to be integrated. Here challenges addressed include integration and device-agnostic application development.
- The chapter *"User Involvement in Future Internet Projects"* addresses in a survey the aspect of user-centred development. User involvement is highly valued and expected to maximise the societal benefits of Future Internet applications.
- In chapter *"An Internet-based Architecture Supporting Ubiquitous Application User Interfaces"*, a multi-device application platform founded on the Future Internet infrastructure is presented; the focus is on the model-based user interface framework as a mean to support context-aware adaptiveness for applications that are executed in ubiquitous computing environments such as those envisioned in Future Internet.
- The chapter *"ComVantage: Mobile Enterprise Collaboration Reference Framework and Enablers for Future Internet Information Interoperability"* presents a reference architecture for mobile enterprise collaboration based on linked-data interoperability. Additionally, security, semantic data lifting, business process modelling interoperability and mobile app orchestration enablers are presented with the goal of facilitating trustful and effective inter-organisational collaboration.
- The chapter *"SmartSantander: Internet of Things Research and Innovation through Citizen Participation"* depicts the development of smart city services and applications in the Future Internet era that benefit all stakeholders.

Conclusions

Smart applications and services lie at the heart of the Future Internet. Value added services and innovative applications that will empower their users is one of the key goals for the new global communications platform. The challenges that lie ahead in order to support multi-domain scenarios over an increasingly complex infrastructure should not be underestimated and need to be addressed in a cross-disciplinary manner.

Table of Contents

Internet of Things

Enabling Technologies and Economic Incentives

Book Sponsoring Projects Overview

Software Driven Networks, Virtualisation, Programmability and Autonomic Management

Towards a Socially-Aware Management of New Overlay Application Traffic Combined with Energy Efficiency in the Internet (SmartenIT)[*]

Burkhard Stiller[1], David Hausheer[2], and Tobias Hoßfeld[3]

[1] University of Zürich, Department of Informatics, Communication Systems Group,
Switzerland
[2] P2P Systems Engineering, TU Darmstadt, Germany
[3] University of Würzburg, Institute of Computer Science, Würzburg, Germany
stiller@ifi.uzh.ch, hausheer@ps.tu-darmstadt.de,
hossfeld@informatik.uni-wuerzburg.de

Abstract. The Internet has seen a strong move to support overlay applications, which demand a coherent and integrated control in underlying heterogeneous networks in a scalable, resilient, and energy-efficient manner. A tighter integration of network management and overlay service functionality can lead to cross-layer optimization of operations and management, which is a promising approach as it offers a large business potential in operational perspectives for all players involved. Therefore, the objective of this paper is to present SmartenIT (Socially-aware Management of New Overlay Application Traffic combined with Energy Efficiency in the Internet), which targets at an incentive-compatible cross-layer network management for providers of overlay-based application (*e.g.*, cloud applications, content delivery, and social networks), network providers, and end-users. The goal is to ensure a QoE-awareness, by addressing accordingly load and traffic patterns or special application requirements, and exploiting at the same time social awareness (in terms of user relations and interests). Moreover, energy efficiency with respect to both end-user devices and underlying networking infrastructure is tackled to ensure an operationally efficient management. Incentive-compatible network management mechanisms for improving metrics on an inter-domain basis for ISPs serve as the major mechanism to deal with and investigate real-life scenarios.

Keywords: Economic traffic management, application-layer traffic optimization, inter-cloud communications, social networks, QoE, energy efficiency.

1   Introduction

There are important new applications influencing volume and patterns of Internet traffic and the satisfaction of users [1]. These include cloud computing and applications served, thereby social networks. Additionally, the Future Internet's entertainment use will generate more traffic to come [2]. Finally, the mobile services and respective wireless access network demand is increasing, too [3], resulting in very

---

[*] Invited Paper.

A. Galis and A. Gavras (Eds.): FIA 2013, LNCS 7858, pp. 3–15, 2013.

different communication path quality levels and management tasks. In turn, traffic from such overlay applications on a very dramatically increasing number of devices and end-points (wired and mobile) is continuously exploding [4]. Respective network management and operation frameworks are missing today for heterogeneous technologies and modern applications. New management mechanisms should support effectively scale, agility, stable Quality-of-Experience (QoE), and flexibility, in an integrated set of network and overlay service functionality. This calls for a new traffic management approach, that derives three major pillars of the new SmartenIT project:

- Handling the explosion of traffic of overlay and social network service functionality and respective end-points in the wired and wireless domain, cross-cutting multiple operators' domains in support of combined intra-domain cloud services;
- Proposing an agile network management and operation framework for this case, while addressing a better control of heterogeneous networks and their network functionality and integrating overlay service functionality in support of stable QoE;
- Evaluating the new approach by employing highly distributed mechanisms, optimized control, and energy efficiency aspects.

Under this perspective the remainder of this overview tackles in Section 2 the details of current Internet trends. The challenges emerging from those developments are clarified in Section 3. To enable a viable problem solving, use cases and solution approaches are discussed in Section 4, which lead to the basic requirements design of the systems architecture for SmartenIT in Section 5. Finally, Section 6 draws preliminary conclusions of those plans and next steps to come.

2   Current Trends in the Internet

The introduction of cloud-based services, cloud technologies, and respective stakeholders in a commercialized internetworking world has changed the type and style of traffic generated for and transported within the Internet. This basic change is complemented by well understood effects of overlay services and applications on the network [5]. However, new trends in terms of social network-generated traffic (putting up demands on Internet Service Providers, ISP) as well as energy efficiency requirements (making updates of ISP-internal technology necessary) do affect the transport of ISP traffic in an unknown manner. Thus, depending on certain criteria of optimization (such as QoE, energy efficiency, and traffic profiles) these trends have to be investigated, especially under the new problem of additional stakeholders in the traditional value chain, addressing additionally Cloud Providers (CP), Social Network Providers (SNP), energy-efficient technologies, and constraints.

Overlay Applications. Overlay applications interconnect computers storing and circulating information among each other with no awareness of the topology and state of the underlying transport network infrastructure; some computers also host computational resources to run applications remotely on virtual platforms. Popular overlay applications include, *e.g.*, Content Delivery (CD), Peer-to-peer (P2P), and social networking. Interconnected computers can be personal hosts or end-systems in the user's network edge.

A characteristic of overlay applications is that application endpoints are agnostic of the underlying topology, state, and policy and typically have no detail of where computers they trade content and resources with are physically located. This causes a waste of resources, energy, and revenue for network providers, while degrading the users' QoE and eventually impacting overlay application network providers. This issue is being addressed by Application Providers (AP), who off-load storage of servers and end-systems as well as a user equipment computational burden by moving involved resources into two directions:

- Content Delivery Networks (CDN) move content from origin servers to the end user by disseminating popular contents in caching servers deployed throughout the Internet, shortening the transport path to users and minimizing congestion and server load. Content is retrieved through request routing techniques, such as DNS and HTTP redirect. Likewise, when content is moved across caching servers to fit the social demand, careful decisions need be taken on which content to move, where and when. Akamai (a pioneer in CDNs) operates more than 100,000 caching servers, trying to span the Internet. Other CDNs attempt to CD and provide ISPs with their technology, enabling them to run their own CDN to peer with ISPs having the same CDN technology upon optimizing their local traffic offer, such as Velocix serving Verizon or New Zealand's Orcon. Finally, CDNs are heavily used by social networking providers such as Facebook.
- CPs and APs make movements from the user to the network, by delegating storage and computation burden to the network, which is more valuable for devices with limited resources and access, such as mobile terminals or those located in regions with sparse infrastructure. Clouded applications run over virtual platforms, where actual resources are distributed over several physical machines.

Both CDNs and cloud networks use resources physically located in Data Centers (DC), the meeting point of content and resource movements from and to users. DCs host resources to jointly offer cloud computing, Web services, and CD, *e.g.*, Amazon's Cloudfront CDN. These applications include a selection of physical server/machine(s) to (1) store or get requested content from in a CDN and (2) provide resources requested for a "clouded" application.

On the one hand, CDN or CPs have a too coarse insight into the underlying transport infrastructure as they usually span across several ISP domains. CDNs use request routing to retrieve content and choose the most suitable content location, but lack the visibility on the underlying transport topology that would enable to minimize the routing cost and provide their customers with the best possible QoE. On the other hand, ISPs want to minimize costly transit traffic caused by inter-domain content movements. ISPs running their CD service often need to get the content from other CDNs and to this end need to exchange information to retrieve the "best" location.

Despite numerous proprietary technologies there is no standardized way to distribute infrastructure information to overlay applications or support information exchange between CDNs. One way to do the latter is the use of protocols being specified by the IETF CDNi (CDN interconnection) WG [6]. The IETF ALTO client-server protocol addresses underlay network agnosticity by providing abstracted routing cost information that can be used by the request routing process and any location selection process to comply with the policy of the impacted ISPs. Likewise, orchestration systems for clouded applications, when selecting the location of needed physical resources, have the same need as CDNs selecting locations in different domains. The use of ALTO in CDNi to optimize request routing decisions is being promoted in ALTO and CDNi. The ALTO protocol is seen as "layer cooperative" in that it involves information being provided by one layer to an upper layer through an explicit protocol. Abstraction is definitely the use of an incentive to the owner of the reported network. Further work is needed to (1) extend the ALTO services and information to support CDN and Data Centers based overlay applications, (2) specify ALTO information needed for CDNi, and (3) specify ALTO protocol extensions to ensure provider confidentiality.

The SmartenIT project aims at achieving such a solution as explained in those three topics by enabling a more frequent and dynamic interaction between ISPs and CPs in order to harmonize objectives of each stakeholder and reach, through collaboration, mutually benefiting operation levels. At the same time the incorporation of information from SNPs and QoE feedback from end users will lead to new business relationships between stakeholders. SmartenIT will provide a framework allowing intermediary ISPs to reach specific agreements so as to fulfill requirements of CPs.

Clouds. Clouds (special case of overlay networks) emerged as a major paradigm for the current and the Future Internet [7, 8]: First, CPs see a strong decentralization, such in multiple coordinated data centers, spread across different continents of the world [9]. In turn, different management scopes for CPs with multiple Points-of-Presence (PoP), the distributed DC's cloud infrastructure itself, and the internal management coordination determine the key for an operational and commercial success [10]. Second, CPs largely benefit from economies of scale, since resources, such as storage or CPU power, can be shared among a large number of users. This makes CPs more energy-efficient and less expensive than traditional applications [11, 12]. Third, it simplifies administrative and maintenance tasks (software updates and backups) considerably. Fourth, it permits users to access easily their applications and large amounts of private or public data from different locations and devices.

As a consequence, a large variety of overlay applications (*i.e.* applications served by and/or spanning resources that are scattered in the cloud) already exist, *e.g.*, online office applications like Google documents, data repositories such as dropbox.com, or cloud gaming as offered by OnLive.com. Secondly, the support of those in the wired and wireless access network domain is a commercial must, as end-users expect that.

Today, cloud applications are very popular since they can be accessed from all over the world with different devices. However, cloud and network management methods are limited to technical parameters such as network load or CPU utilization. These criteria are of importance for CPs and ISPs, but have – if at all – a limited importance to end-users. End-users perceive the quality of cloud applications in a different manner. For them, responsiveness and usability are key parameters that decide which applications users like. Cloud computing offers different services and many overlay applications run on top of clouds, where energy-related costs are becoming one of the largest contributors to the overall cost of operating a DC, whereas the degree of DC utilization continues to be very low.

Social Networks. Another important case of overlay networks are Online Social Networks (OSN). In particular, OSNs such as Facebook or Twitter, are today a pervasive part of the Internet and aim to cover the entire digital live of its users in the near future [13, 14, 15]. On one hand, they can be considered as one type of cloud applications, where users organize their social relations, chat, or post their current activities or mood. On the other hand, they deserve high emphasis, since they contain information about user relations, interests, and the popularity of contents available in the Internet, such as movies or songs. Moreover, a significant part of requests for content is placed over SNPs. Facebook remains since 2009 the 3rd largest online video content provider in the US. Hence, based on social relations between Facebook users, one can deduce important observations that have to do with the dissemination patterns of such content in these environments. The structure of OSNs will be exploited for traffic management strategies, like caching or pre-fetching, together with additional useful information stemming from OSNs, *e.g.*, on popularity.

SmartenIT does not only consider OSNs, they will also be used as a source of information about the popularity of specific other cloud applications or content. In this way, OSNs connect user behavior and user expectations to cloud and network management methods. For example, applications that many persons of a specific geographical region in an OSN suggest to their friends will get popular in this area. As a result, allocating cloud storage and processing power in DCs in this region of the world will improve the QoE perceived by users. Thus, SmartenIT will develop interaction mechanisms and paradigms between OSN information and cloud and network management decisions. This tight interaction between management decisions and the information contained in OSNs has not been studied in depth so far, leading to an effective exploitation for traffic management purposes.

3   Challenges Emerging from Internet Trends

These trends in the application domain pose several major challenges for the current structure of the Internet, from a technical and economic point of view [4]:

1st Challenge: Emerging overlay applications, such as cloud applications or OSNs, make traffic management difficult for ISPs, since many of them run on different DCs and ISPs have no influence to which DC a specific user connects to or on which server the user will be served by. Additionally, large ISPs establish their own network management for the transport of all best effort type traffic within their platform under cost optimization constraints. A lack of coordination between ISPs and overlay providers detracts from globally optimized transport paths [16]. Traffic generated by cloud applications will have unpredictable patterns, crossing many and different domains, due to the mobility of cloud users or the distribution of cloud resources. Moreover, the traffic of certain cloud applications may be cacheable, often by different stakeholders, while other traffic is not. Although caching in distributed DCs, in broadband access network nodes, and on user devices improves application performance in many scenarios, the interoperability of caching mechanisms leaves many open issues [6, 16]. Thus, SmartenIT will trade-off between cache-ability and acceptable degradation of performance and QoE, depending on the application [17]. Moreover, SmartenIT will investigate how the coordination can be improved across administration boundaries with different incentives for each involved party.

2nd Challenge: The usability of overlay applications strongly depends on network conditions and Quality-of-Service (QoS) guarantees on the path between the DC and the end-user, which might be controlled by several different ISPs [18]. Furthermore, end-users judge the usability of an application based on their own experience, which is referred to as the QoE. Hence, SmartenIT manages overlay application needs in consideration of crucial QoE. That means that management approaches have to (1) be able to measure or at least estimate the QoE that overlay applications deliver to the end user and (2) use this metric as an important parameter to optimize for. The QoE metric is based on measurable parameters within the network (*e.g.*, packet loss) or at the application layer (*e.g.*, number of stalling events for HTTP-based video streaming). Hence, the QoE metric allows for monitoring the network or the application and later on for evaluating mechanisms developed in SmartenIT with respect to QoE.

3rd Challenge: The variety of often proprietary overlay applications makes it difficult to combine services from different overlay providers to a new service; an example is cloud computing [8, 19]. This implies that application developers need the flexibility to choose already implemented services from different clouds and combine them to provide a new service. Open protocols contain a potential to make the cloud paradigm more powerful [4, 20, 21], however, they are not widely adopted. Thus, SmartenIT addresses composed services from different clouds with new traffic management mechanisms to be influenced by economic criteria and standard requirements, *e.g.*, bandwidth or QoE. It will be important to choose and study overlay applications, which simultaneously have an important impact on network evolution and management, terminals, and user behavior. Such potentially influential applications are, *e.g.*, YouTube, Dropbox, or Facebook. Another viewpoint is related to the commercial market of IPTV applications with Video-on-Demand additions, which are offered by telecommunication service providers and ISPs.

4th Challenge: The trade-off between a cloud computing computational efficiency and the energy consumption also arises with respect to traffic implications. This has to be addressed by a cross-layer management approach [22]. Since users use OSNs to share information on the content they are interested in, the demand for a high-quality content may grow fast. Hence, it is crucial for an innovative CDN to be socially-aware, predict the demand, and avoid resource exhaustion and QoE degradation [23]. However, this may come at a cost due to higher computational complexity or energy consumption. Therefore, SmartenIT applies an energy-efficient traffic management in the context of overlay applications. QoE needs be assessed on a per application basis, since the user-perceived quality of an application depends strongly on the type of application. As a consequence, SmartenIT will define QoE indicators for cloud applications and to derive their power to predict user satisfaction.

5th Challenge: The fact that mobile cloud devices are limited in their battery lifetime and by mobile data caps imposes strict requirements on respective management mechanisms, while considering mobile device's limited battery resources. The energy-efficient access of cloud-based services over Wifi-based ad-hoc networks shows a high potential to reduce traffic in cellular networks, while increasing the download throughput at the same time as reducing the energy consumption despite additional overhead. To be able to estimate energy consumption of different overlay approaches for management of mobile cloud applications, SmartenIT verifies accurate models for the energy consumption of mobile devices, which can simulate overhead introduced by different management approaches.

6th Challenge: Stakeholders of today's and tomorrow's Internet with conflicting interests make decisions that may lead the system into a suboptimal situation. Therefore, traffic management approaches need to provide incentives to stakeholders to support mutually beneficial decisions. Relevant mechanisms address incentives translating either directly or indirectly to an economic benefit arising by the improvement of an index (such as the level of locality or QoS). Therefore, SmartenIT designs solutions that employ appropriate incentive mechanisms to constitute the deployment and use of overlay applications more efficiently.

4   Use Cases and Solution Approaches

For demonstrating how to tackle those emerging challenges, SmartenIT follows a use case driven approach. Selected scenarios show the key potential of the SmartenIT approach for the quality of applications for residential and commercial users, for business opportunities for both ISPs and telecommunication service providers, and for value-added service providers. The final decision on the most important scenario(s) will be based on basic evaluations and a detailed requirements analysis.

Inter-cloud Communication: Three classes of services are offered by clouds: (1) storage, (2) CPU and RAM, and (3) applications. Additionally, an integration of components of (1) and (2) provided by different clouds is possible. The exchange of data between storage and computational resources is performed by the network. Clouds physically connected to different network operators require a multi-domain operation topology and applications may demand for a guaranteed QoS level. Therefore, the exchange of data between storage and computational resources is performed by the network. While setting the connection, QoS/QoE should be taken into account as well as the connection cost, which is depending on the selected route. Some services require an ongoing dynamic allocation of resources due to the migration of virtual machines within the cloud from one physical location to another. Changing locations may require a new connection to be established between new cloud servers, regardless of whether they belong to the same CP or to inter-connected ones. An algorithm for the selection of a new physical location of services or resources in the cloud should take into account the following criteria: (a) data transfer costs, (b) QoS/QoE assurance, (c) service (*e.g.*, MPLS, L2VPN, or L3VPN) availability, (d) service setup costs, (e) network resource availability, and (f) data transfer security. The migration of a service to the cloud offering the same type of resources, but being managed by a distinct provider can be addressed by such an algorithm. This scenario is particularly relevant for the many emerging Virtual DC (VDC) products recently pushed into the market by many network operators, such as Interoute's VDC. In particular, these VDC solutions are attractive for enterprise customers willing to move network services to the (private) cloud. They are becoming an impelling requirement to support services on top of a multi-tenant cloud infrastructure, especially for large enterprise users with many remote offices.

Exploiting OSN Information – Social Awareness: Recently OSNs have become very popular. Facebook currently claims 845 million monthly active users each month, with 250 million photos uploaded daily and 450 million mobile users. User activities in OSNs such as micro-blogging (Twitter) and exchange of photos and videos (Facebook) are responsible for huge portions of the overall Internet traffic [1]. This overlay traffic generated by OSNs implies congestion increase within ISPs and an increase of operating costs, especially for inter-domain traffic. This is in particular the case for video traffic that is induced by OSNs, *e.g.*, if a user posts a link to a video served by a CDN and recommends this video to his friends within the OSN. As a consequence, the structure of OSNs and the information diffusion in OSNs have to be analyzed. Thus, related work and existing measurement data, *e.g.*, for Facebook or Twitter, have to be analyzed in terms of OSN structure and information diffusion. Though a major attribute that characterizes OSNs is the existence of a many meta-information regarding social relationships among their users, *e.g.*, family members and friends (Facebook), colleagues and other professionals (LinkedIn), or people are interested in similar hobbies/activities (MySpace for music bands, songs and video clips, Flickr for photography lovers). The exploitation of such meta-information by ISPs can lead to socially-aware traffic management mechanisms that aim at (1) more sophisticated traffic management, (2) the reduction of traffic load on inter-domain links, and (3) a reduction of operating costs for ISPs. For instance, a video could be cached (pre-fetched) near "friends" of an OSN user, who downloads videos that this user shares with them, while a video containing an interesting lecture could be cached near the users' colleagues. The caching of a video near groups of users that would be interested in it, would allow for an operating cost minimization (avoiding redundant downloads from remote locations). In SmartenIT, the question will be addressed to discover what meta-information can be used, under which circumstances can this information be acquired (*e.g.*, special agreements of OSN providers and the ISPs, incentives of stakeholders), and how to employ traffic management more efficiently for all parties.

5   Requirements for System Design and Architecture Design

The concrete use cases considered in SmartenIT will pose requirements for the system design. In particular, the initial set of requirements, partially discussed above with respect to the approaches for such use cases, will be applied to derive a respective set of architectural components, functions, and interactions, which can generalize those use cases' claims. SmartenIT's preliminary architecture outlines the key properties and functionality of the SmartenIT's approach, each of which span one or multiple domains out of the overlay/cloud domain, the core network domain, and the user/access network domain. Those key properties of SmartenIT's architecture include the three main SmartenIT objectives QoE-/social-awareness, energy efficiency, and incentive-compatibility/ economic efficiency, all of which are equally relevant in all three domains. Key functionality of the overlay/cloud domain (with overlap to the core network domain) includes the overlay management and the cloud traffic management. Likewise, key functionality rooted in the core network domain (with overlap to the overlay/cloud domain) include CD/caching, network traffic management – potentially supported by a Software-defined Networks (SDN)-based approach – and traffic monitoring. Finally, key functionality in the user/access network domain includes the QoS/QoE and mobile traffic management.

QoE-Awareness. The SmartenIT architecture will rely on QoE as one of the key parameters for network and cloud management. This will shift the focus from technical parameters toward user expectations. Mapping between QoS network parameters and the user-perceived service quality, namely QoE, has received a lot of attention in recent years [24]. Development of QoS/QoE models and functions mapping QoS parameters (*e.g.*, packet loss, delay, or jitter) into QoE metrics is promising, which may support the provisioning of services over heterogeneous networks with high and stable QoE. It is, however, not easy, since QoS/QoE mapping models are strongly dependent on application/service types and technical as well as non-technical aspects [25]. SmartenIT will examine QoS/QoE relations for cloud-based service and selected SmartenIT scenarios and applications. Further, ongoing activities in standardization bodies will be followed and utilized, like the proposal for a framework for an opinion model for web-browsing QoE in the ITU-T work group SG12 on "Performance, QoS and QoE", which may be the basis for QoS/QoE mappings and QoE monitoring.

Social-Awareness. Due to the fast propagation of information via OSNs, a growth of content popularity (and application reputation) may occur. *E.g.*, people sharing links to content may cause a rapid increase of demands in some area of the network and a very high load in DCs and networks. As a result, it may be difficult for an ISP to serve all demands efficiently and users may not receive high QoE. Relying on both social- and QoE-awareness, it will become possible to predict such situations and, by proactive reactions, an ISP will be prepared to rapid growth of demands, *e.g.*, by content, server, application replication or reorganization of resources in the cloud.

Economic Efficiency. The shift of computation and data into the cloud has become a key trend in the Internet. With the market approaching perfect competition, the perceived service quality will become an important differentiator between CPs, as the customer is able to choose between different competing providers. For this reason, understanding and managing QoE of end-users provides huge opportunities for CPs to put themselves at an advantage. It enables CPs to observe and react quickly to quality problems, at best before customers perceive them and start churning. From an economic perspective, an optimum QoE has to be achieved while constraining the application to behave as efficient as possible in order to minimize operational costs.

As several QoE evaluation methods exist, they can be classified as subjective tests, objective evaluation, or models. The category of subjective tests encompasses a wide group of methods that involve real users as evaluators. They range from laboratory tests (well prepared experiments in a controlled environment and precisely prepared test scenarios) through crowd-sourcing [26] to test-bed experiments to ask customers a set of questions after using the service (*e.g.*, Skype). A QoE evaluation metric is also the user churn that may be assessed statistically. A second group of QoE evaluation methods is the objective evaluation. These methods do not involve real users. User-perceived quality is approximated on the basis of an examination of selected features of delivered service itself (non-reference methods) or by comparing the source quality to the one received by a customer (full/reduced reference methods).

Finally, QoE models enable the assessment of QoE without involving real users but via examining network conditions (*e.g.*, QoS parameters) and other factors including user device capabilities. Usually such models are not general, but they are closely related to a given service and are tightly connected with its characteristics. They are developed with a support of subjective tests. Once a model, *e.g.*, QoS-QoE, mapping is determined, the QoE may be assessed without involving humans. The advantage of this approach is also that there is no need to examine directly the received content quality itself. For example, [27] proposes a QoE model for YouTube video streaming. With this model, a service provider can monitor QoS parameters (like throughput) and react in advance if their values approach the level that may result in QoE degradation.

Energy Efficiency. The SmartenIT architecture will address the energy-aware dynamic provision of resources based on the consolidation of existing application, while simultaneously addressing under-utilization of servers and in turn reducing energy costs. Thus, energy costs cannot be treated separately from resource provision and allocation. [28] models the problem of minimizing energy consumption of the allocation of resources to networked applications as a Stackelberg leadership game to find an upper bound of energy saving. This model is applied in SmartenIT to a proportional-share mechanism, where resource providers maximize their profit by minimizing energy costs, while users select resources ensuring minimum requirements are satisfied. This mechanism can determine the optimal set of resources, even in realistic conditions considering incomplete information and heterogeneous applications.

6   Summary and Preliminary Conclusions

From the perspective of a multi-stakeholder viewpoint and highly unregulated services market within the Future Internet the management of traffic by respective network and service management mechanisms determines the crucial interface between user demands and service perceptions, networking technology, and operational costs. Thus, SmartenIT's contributions in the clear preparations of the starting point for such investigations indicated that at least two major scenarios will drive the stakeholders' requirements analysis, including conflicting interests, cooperation possibilities, and incentives. This overview has outlined in detail the technical and partially economic basis for a list of optimizations to be considered.

Especially from the perspective of ISPs, APs, and CPs the aim of QoE-awareness is offering a high and stable level of perceived quality to prevent customers' churn and also to increase attractiveness of that offer within overlay or cloud services. Since a high and stable QoE is currently considered crucial for marketability of applications and services, QoE control is desired to enable an advance reaction to imminent quality degradation that would result in user dissatisfaction.

However, many management approaches toward OSNs, overlay service, and QoE management are mainly designed for only a single domain of a single stakeholder. Therefore, their effectiveness suffers from an inherent lack of information exchange between all involved constituents, including service infrastructure (IaaS, PaaS, SaaS), ISPs and telecommunication service providers, and end-users (private and business). To remedy this key problem SmartenIT works on flexible cooperation between stakeholders involved, ultimately enabling every user to (a) access the offered cloud service in any contexts and (b) share content, interact, and collaborate with other users in a dynamic, seamless, and transparent way while maximizing QoE at the same time. As such SmartenIT started the development of QoE-aware network and resource management mechanisms to enable dynamic and proactive QoE support for cloud-based services. Appropriate QoE evaluation methodology and tools will be selected, developed, improved, and used at various stages of SmartenIT solutions development.

Acknowledgements. This work has been performed in the framework of the EU ICT STREP SmartenIT (FP7-ICT-2011-317846). The authors would like to thank the entire SmartenIT team for their discussions and input on major research problems.

References

[1] Cisco: Cisco Global Cloud Index: Forecast and Methodology, 2010-2015, White Paper (2011)

[2] Cisco: Hyper-connectivity and the Approaching Zetabyte Era (2010)

[3] Cisco: Cisco Visual Networking Index: Global Mobile Data Traffic Forecast Update 2010–2015, White Paper (2011)

[4] Stankiewicz, R., Jajszczyk, A.: A Survey of QoE Assurance in Converged Networks. Computer Networks 55(7), 1459–1473 (2011)

[5] Hoßfeld, T., et al.: An Economic Traffic Management Approach to Enable the TripleWin for Users, ISPs, and Overlay Providers. In: Tselentis, G., et al. (eds.) FIA Prague Book "Towards the Future Internet - A European Research Perspective". IOS Press Books Online (2009)

[6] IETF: Content Delivery Networks Interconnection (Active WG), http://tools.ietf.org/wg/cdni/ (last visited February 2013)

[7] Cisco: Cisco Cloud Computing – Data Center Strategy, Architecture and Solutions (2009)

[8] Papazoglou, M.P., van den Heuvel, W.: Blueprinting the Cloud. IEEE Internet Computing 15(6), 74–79 (2011)

[9] Cisco: Cisco Secure Network Container: Multi-Tenant Cloud Computing (2010)

[10] Poese, I., Frank, B., Ager, B., Smaragdakis, G., Feldmann, A.: Improving Content Delivery Using Provider-aided Distance Information. In: 10th Annual Conference on Internet Measurement (IMC), Melbourne, Australia (2010)

[11] Chen, G., et al.: Energy-aware Server Provisioning and Load Dispatching for Connectino-intensive Internet Services. In: 5th USENIX Symposium on Networked Systems Design and Implementation, San Francisco, Calfornia, U.S.A. (2008)

[12] Zhang, Q., Cheng, L., Boutaba, R.: Cloud Computing: State-of-the-art and Research Challenges. Journal of Internet Services and Applications 1(1), 7–18 (2010)

[13] Cha, M., Haddadi, H., Benevenuto, F., Gummadi, K.P.: Measuring User Influence in Twitter: The Million Follower Fallacy. In: 4th International AAAI Conference on Weblogs and Social Media (ICWSM), Washington, D.C., U.S.A. (2010)

[14] Krishnamurthy, B.: A Measure of Online Social Networks. In: 1st International Workshop on Communication Systems and Networks and Workshops (COMSNETS 2009), Bangalore, India (2009)

[15] Gjoka, M., Sirivianos, M., Markopoulou, A., Yang, X.: Poking Facebook: Characterization of OSN Applications. In: 1st Workshop on Online Social Networks (WOSN), Seattle, Washington, U.S.A. (2008)

[16] Haßlinger, G., Hartleb, F.: Content Delivery and Caching from a Network Provider's Perspective. Computer Networks 55(18), 3991–4006 (2011)

[17] Chiu, D., Shetty, A., Agrawal, G.: Elastic Cloud Caches for Accelerating Service-Oriented Computations. In: ACM/IEEE International Conference for High Performance Computing, Networking, Storage and Analysis, New Orleans, Louisiana, U.S.A. (2010)

[18] Hoßfeld, T., Fiedler, M., Zinner, T.: The QoE Provisioning-Delivery-Hysteresis and Its Importance for Service Provisioning in the Future Internet. In: 7th Conference on Next Generation Internet Networks (NGI), Kaiserslautern, Germany (2011)

[19] Bernstein, D., Ludvigson, E., Sankar, K., Diamond, S., Morrow, M.: Blueprint for the Intercloud - Protocols and Formats for Cloud Computing Interoperability. In: 4th International Conference on Internet and Web Applications and Services (ICIW), Venice/Mestre, Italy (2009)

[20] Chieu, T.C., Mohindra, A., Karve, A., Segal, A.: Solution-based Deployment of Complex Application Services on a Cloud. In: IEEE International Conference on Service Operations and Logistics and Informatics (SOLI), Qingdao, China (2010)

[21] Konstantinou, A.V., et al.: An Architecture for Virtual Solution Composition and Deployment in Infrastructure Clouds. In: 3rd International Workshop on Virtualization Technologies in Distributed Computing (VTDC), Barcelona, Spain (2009)

[22] Schulz, G.: Cloud and Virtual Data Storage Networking. Auerbach Publications (2011)

[23] Scellato, S., Mascolo, C., Musolesi, M., Crowcroft, J.: Track Globally, Deliver Locally: Improving Content Delivery Networks by Tracking Geographic Social Cascades. In: 20th International Conference on World Wide Web (WWW), Hyderabad, India (2011)

[24] Fiedler, M., Hoßfeld, T., Tran-Gia, P.: A Generic Quantitative Relationship between Quality of Experience and Quality of Service. IEEE Network 24(2), 36–41 (2010)

[25] Hoßfeld, T., Schatz, R., Varela, M., Timmerer, C.: Challenges of QoE Management for Cloud Applications. IEEE Communications Magazine 50(4), 28–36 (2012)

[26] Hoßfeld, T., et al.: Quantification of YouTube QoE via Crowdsourcing. In: IEEE International Workshop on Multimedia Quality of Experience - Modeling, Evaluation, and Directions (MQoE), Dana Point, California, U.S.A. (2011)

[27] Hoßfeld, T., Schatz, R., Biersack, E., Plissonneau, L.: Internet video delivery in you-Tube: From traffic measurements to quality of experience. In: Biersack, E., Callegari, C., Matijasevic, M. (eds.) Data Traffic Monitoring and Analysis. LNCS, vol. 7754, pp. 264–301. Springer, Heidelberg (2013)

[28] Leon, X., Navarro, L.: Limits of Energy Saving for the Allocation of Data Center Resources to Networked Applications. In: IEEE INFOCOM 2011, Shanghai, China (2011)

The NEBULA Future Internet Architecture*

Tom Anderson[1], Ken Birman[2], Robert Broberg[3], Matthew Caesar[4],
Douglas Comer[5], Chase Cotton[6], Michael J. Freedman[7], Andreas Haeberlen[8],
Zachary G. Ives[8], Arvind Krishnamurthy[1], William Lehr[9], Boon Thau Loo[8],
David Mazières[10], Antonio Nicolosi[11], Jonathan M. Smith[8], Ion Stoica[12],
Robbert van Renesse[2], Michael Walfish[13],
Hakim Weatherspoon[2], and Christopher S. Yoo[8]

[1] University of Washington
[2] Cornell University
[3] Cisco Systems
[4] University of Illinois
[5] Purdue University
[6] University of Delaware
[7] Princeton University
[8] University of Pennsylvania
[9] Massachusetts Institute of Technology
[10] Stanford University
[11] Stevens Institute of Technology
[12] University of California, Berkeley
[13] University of Texas, Austin

1 Introduction

The NEBULA Future Internet Architecture (FIA) project is focused on a future
network that enables the vision of cloud computing [8,12] to be realized. With
computation and storage moving to data centers, networking to these data centers must be several orders of magnitude more resilient for some applications to
trust cloud computing and enable their move to the cloud.

An example application we envision is to use cloud computing as the basis for
a personal health monitoring and advisory service. Sensors, data repositories,
and interactive components could input parameters to the cloud – such as food
consumed and exercise regimen followed. The challenge is in extending such a
service to more advanced inputs and outputs, including real-time data communications to and from medical devices, such as continuous glucose monitors and
insulin pumps. This application requires both high reliability and data privacy,
or, seen from a network security perspective, all of the "CIA" security properties
of Confidentiality, Integrity and Availability.

The NEBULA approach is organized into three architectural thrust areas:
a reliable routing system and data center interconnect (NCore), a data plane
that enables policy enforcement (NEBULA Data Plane, NDP), and a novel approach to control plane architecture (NEBULA Virtual and Extensible Networking Techniques, NVENT) that allows users to control the network configuration
from the edge.

---

* Invited Paper.

A. Galis and A. Gavras (Eds.): FIA 2013, LNCS 7858, pp. 16–26, 2013.

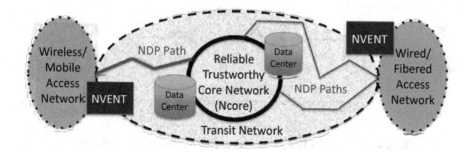

Fig. 1. The NEBULA Future Internet Architecture model

The NEBULA FIA project is characterized by three attributes. First, the architecture is *comprehensive*, in that it addresses a large set of complex and difficult problems. Second, the approach is *completely new*, and therefore in many aspects could not be "extended" or "composed from" any existing work: invention was required before integration could begin. Third, the comprehensive nature of the architecture demanded a *large team with a diversity of skill sets and approaches to sub-problems.*

2 NEBULA as a Network Architecture

A network architecture defines the structure of the network and its components. In NEBULA, we started from the basic position that cloud computing, where computation is performed on large network accessible data centers, would transform networking. Concerns about security properties such as confidentiality, integrity and availability would inhibit the use of cloud computing for new applications unless a new network architecture is designed.

To illustrate what the key challenges are, we discuss our example application – closed-loop control of blood glucose levels for an insulin-dependent diabetic – in a bit more detail. We can presume availability of some devices that already exist, and that the patient is equipped with some of these: a continuous glucose monitor, camera, exercise monitor and insulin pump. The cloud application would determine the current glucose level, monitor what was being eaten, monitor the exercise activity level, and make an insulin infusion recommendation. This application would have strict confidentiality requirements (it is *very* personal healthcare data), integrity requirements (incorrect dosages can be harmful) and availability requirements (a lack of network availability might, at the limit, cause physical harm).

NEBULA addresses these challenges with the three architectural thrust areas named in the introduction. Some basic decisions included the use of packet-switching and a network structure with hosts interconnected by a graph of links and store-and-forward routers. Paths are composed of sequences of links and routers, and will have performance dictated by the capacities of the components

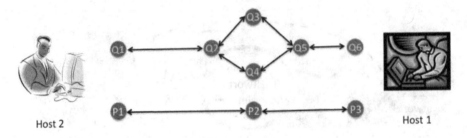

Fig. 2. Host 1 and Host 2 are connected by two physical paths

as well as their current workloads. These are basic properties NEBULA shares with the conventional Internet.

2.1   Today's Internet

However, the Internet makes some additional design decisions that influence its architecture. The first of these is that the routing algorithm attempts to find the *single* best path between two endpoints. The second of these is that the routers use a *best-effort* policy, allowing a packet to reach its destination if possible. Third, routers make *dynamic decisions* about the best path, allowing for unreliable links and routers under the assumption that the network graph is reasonably connected. Finally, the conventional Internet's *evolution occurs at the end-points* (hosts), rather than in the network.

For instance, consider the simple example network in Figure 2. There are nine routers (the red and green balls marked with Ps and Qs), and two interconnected hosts. These could represent either two edge nodes or – more relevant to the NEBULA vision – an edge host and a cloud data center. The red routers have a richer (but more complex) transit network, and the red and green access networks provide redundant access networking. In this network, the Internet would be unable to exploit the redundancy in the paths, and would be unable to enforce any policy (e.g., one related to health care data security and privacy). Diagnosis and policy enforcement would have to be performed at the endpoints.

2.2   NEBULA

NEBULA's support of cloud computing [8,2,12] and highly reliable applications [5] forces it to be different in several respects. First is the realization that data center networks [7] and their interconnection are both different in structure than a conventional Internet and require routers that are far more reliable than today's core routers [8]. Our NEBULA Core (NCore) of ultra-reliable Core routers interconnecting data centers are equipped with new fault-tolerant control software [2]. We exploit path diversity for resilience, and have originated new ways to detect/resist failures [24,18] and malicious attacks [11], including resilient interdomain protocols. In addition, we are examining implications of (and for) resilience solutions on policy and economics.

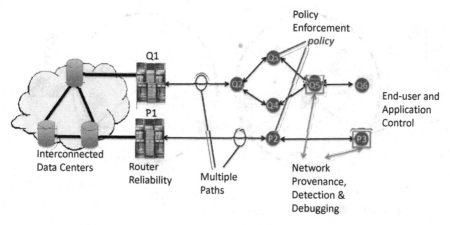

Fig. 3. A NEBULA perspective on the network from Figure 2

Consider Figure 3, a redrawn version of Figure 2 with NEBULA components added; Q3 and Q4 exhibit different security policies. The NEBULA network architecture is resilient: If any single router fails, the application is still left with a usable path it can exploit. Specifically, if Q1, P1, Q6, or P3 fail, access is preserved via P1, Q1, P3, and Q6, respectively. For policy enforcement, if Q3 or Q4's policy is incompatible with the application or the cloud service, either Q4 or Q3 can be used, or the green path can be exploited if it is policy-compliant. Using network provenance [42], failure detection [18,41] and network debugging [20], problems can be rapidly diagnosed and repaired, even while the services continue operating.

3 NEBULA Future Internet Architecture Integration

The first phase of NEBULA required invention of new approaches and elements in areas such as router architecture, data center networking, interdomain networking, network control, and network security. Further, it required work by scholars of regulatory policy and economics seeking to understand the implications of the cloud and NEBULA's changes to networking (including reliable routers and routes chosen with constraints set by flexible policies that reflect desires of parties such as users, cloud providers, internet service providers and web servers).

Ultra-reliable Future Internet Router Example (FIRE): This is the router component [2,10] of NCore. To ease sharing and implementation (see Section 4), an open source implementation is being used, and the team at the University of Delaware has been experimenting with RouteBricks [13] on two high-performance PCs (supplied by Cisco Systems) equipped with 10 Gbps cards.

Ultra-reliable data center or ISP network: This is the data center interconnect to the NCore routers; it is used to access data and compute cycles in the data centers. The interconnect must be ultra-reliable – for example, accesses

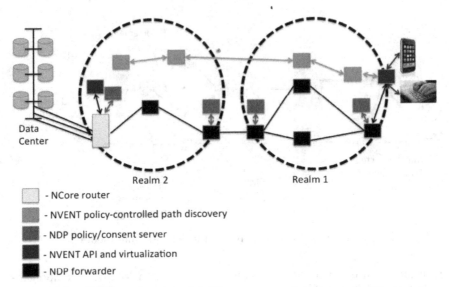

Realm 2   Realm 1

- NCore router

- NVENT policy-controlled path discovery

- NDP policy/consent server

- NVENT API and virtualization

- NDP forwarder

Fig. 4. Illustration of NEBULA Elements as an Integrated Architecture

to the stored glucose records and healthcare data must not fail, and there should be some end-to-end performance isolation [23]. It also makes sense to manage data flows to the NCore routers with a redundant [30] and load-balanced interconnect [33,34,7].

Ultra-reliable Interdomain service: This is primarily focused on the Nebula Data Plane (NDP) and several alternatives we have created [29,31] for its implementation. It is the primary locus for policy issues such as security, privacy, fault-tolerance, and more complex and specialized policies. This is a particular challenge, as the policies must be relevant in spite of a federated structure for NEBULA that we expect to emerge as a result of an emergent marketplace of offered network services.

Policy Control: This is primarily focused on NEBULA Virtual and Extensible Networking Technology (NVENT). It must define an API for service requests [32] – in particular, requests for a specific policy. Approaches [38] developed and matured during Phase I are being melded into an NVENT that provides a service abstraction consistent with our model of network support for the cloud. In particular, the Declarative Networking approach [28] will be used to form networks of policy compliant paths when needed by applications. Since much of the path information is cacheable, discovery can be asynchronous, and path lookup can be very quick. There are also extensive efforts in diagnosis [42,21,1], verification [37,25,35,36,3,41,19], detection [18] and debugging [20].

Economic and Policy Implications of NEBULA: This work [9,40,26,27] is primarily focused on the implications of the NEBULA project on economic and regulatory properties. The Phase I work examined economic implications of dramatically increased router reliability and some of the policy impacts of cloud computing. As we move towards an integrated architecture with policy enforcement, policy and regulatory issues abound. For example, TorIP [29] prevents visibility into packet destinations or content, and the economic and policy implications of this must be understood. Another example is the complex tussle between fine-grained policy enforcement and the desire by some for network neutrality.

A variety of interesting research questions have become apparent. We expect to resolve these as the integration efforts proceed. We briefly discuss two here.

First, the control plane must query policy servers for an ICING-based NDP [31], and the query model of declarative networking must be supported to create policy-compliant routes for the NEBULA control plane. ICING [31] is one alternative for NDP, and ICING enforces policy by having ISPs check the work of other ISPs, while TorIP [29] enforces policy by preventing ISPs from gathering the information needed to do effective policy discrimination. Transit as a Service (TaaS), if used as NDP, uses a third approach to policy enforcement, randomized test packets that cannot be distinguished from regular traffic.

Second, the application interface to specify policy has not been finalized, and the relationship between the policy-enforcing forwarding plane and the NCore routers remains somewhat in flux. We expect to investigate this via the integration of Serval [32] and Declarative Networking [28] that will comprise NVENT.

4   NEBULA Configuration and Operation

If we are to have highly trustworthy networking for the cloud, we must have highly trustworthy interdomain paths, and these in turn require highly reliable *intra*domain paths and services. To realize the latter, we are pursuing enhancements of RouteBricks (to build FIRE), the use of Quagga, and the addition of fault-tolerant protocols for intradomain networking.

Consider two scenarios where the NEBULA architecture's resilience and policy mechanisms would be applied. In Scenario 1, the U.S. Department of Defense wishes to acquire a high-assurance path over the Future Internet, and this path must traverse only trusted networks. Further, since adversaries might choose to attack the path, the network must not only be highly available (i.e., no single point of failure), it must also be DoS-resistant and tolerate Byzantine faults. In Scenario 2, outpatient medical monitoring is performed by software running at a data center; to support this scenario, both high assurance and predictable bandwidth are required.

A variety of goals can be abstracted from these scenarios – for instance, organizations need to be able to contract for end-to-end paths with explicit promises from each organization along the path to convey the traffic, no third party must be able to disrupt the traffic, and so forth. In our view, the model of the Internet being provided by multiple organizations will persist.

For all of this to work, that is, for a user or organization to specify a policy for what it wants from the network, and for a Future Internet Service Provider to specify its policy of what it is willing to provide, the need arises for protocols for the following components: (1) a "name service," by which users locate the services they need; (2) "path advertisements," through which constituent networks gather and convey what each is willing to provide; (3) "assured path provisioning," whereby network resources are sought and bound for use in a given communication; (4) "verifiable data forwarding," whereby traffic is sent on network routes that verifiably comply with the policies of the assured path; and (5) "fault diagnostics," which detects and/or identifies faulty network components.

4.1 Policy Configuration

There is clearly a very large number of possible policies, and these policies come from multiple sources – for example, end-users, their organizations and the ISPs bearing their traffic in the middle of the network. Some applications need path control, some need resource reservations, some need failover guarantees, etc. This requires work at the API level, in NVENT (using Serval [32] as the basis for this API) to determine how a client can ask for certain properties. A second issue is at the protocol level in NVENT, where mechanisms for an ISP advertising its willingness to offer certain properties must be determined.

A policy server will have zero or more policies. The default policy is to drop traffic, sometimes called "deny by default". Policies are assumed to be dynamic (changeable) but we assume they are changed infrequently, and thus are cacheable. In our initial architecture, we expect that users and prototype applications will want policies that are easy to state; for instance, a policy indicating HIPAA compliance could simply be stated as HIPAA=yes. A policy server's policies can be queried by clients and consent servers; a path is constructed from consenting servers.

In choosing paths, the policy logic must not only know which paths are permitted, it must also know which paths are available. This kind of knowledge requires detection support from the network [18].

Some of our work is in the direction of removing the ability for ISPs to discriminate against certain types of traffic (e.g., TorIP), although that might also be accomplished by other means, e.g., regulation or testing. ICING assumes the ability of ISPs to veto paths, which means either delegation of path-granting authority or extra RTTs. Depending on some of those choices, the policy options are somewhat different.

4.2 Path Setup

A user or application specifies policy requirements for the path they wish to use – for instance NEBULA_PATH=HIPAA:AES256:T_BOUND_5. The application specifies a destination or service (see also Section 4.4).

For an ICING-based [31] NDP, when this specification is received, the system checks a cache for a cached compliant path to the destination or service. If such a path is available, try to obtain consent to use the path, perhaps with cached proofs of consent if obtaining consent is expensive. If nothing is cached, or there is no consent for a cached path, the system would iterate requests for consent to consent servers. The end result is that NEBULA will either establish and cache a path, or will fail with an error. For TorIP [29]/TaaS, the assumption is that advertisements will be long-lived; there is no path-veto, so advertisements (in contrast to ICING) are simple and composable, albeit less expressive.

4.3 Forwarding

NEBULA users (either senders, receivers, or service providers) can require that specific network resources be bound to a network path (cf. e.g. Scenario 2 above). To verify compliance, packets can carry secure "markings" of consent, as well as a secure reference to the resources allocated to that connection. This marking strategy might be implemented via Icing's cryptographic "proofs of consent" and "proofs of provenance", or via the cryptographic sealing implied by Onion Routing in TorIP. Below we outline the key steps for the case of verifiable data forwarding in Icing.

Senders mark their packets using the cryptographic tokens included in the proofs of consent they obtained when the connection is established. When processing an incoming packet, an NDP edge router checks whether from the packet's marks it can evince that the packet is "permitted" (it carries proper proof of consent) and "travelled right" (it carries proper proof of provenance). The last check requires that previous routers had updated the "marks" on the packet whenever an ISP ("realm") boundary was crossed. Thus, before forwarding the packet to the next node on the path, an NDP edge router "blesses" the packet (or peels off an onion layer in the case of TorIP).

4.4 Naming

In Serval [32], Service IDs are resolved via a Service Abstraction Layer (SAL). Both TorIP [29] and ICING [31], alternatives for NDP have appropriate solutions for mapping human-readable names into network-usable information. In TorIP a *name server* resolves a name (e.g., `google.com`) to a set of (ISP,ID) pairs. The ID identifies a mailbox where a client can rendezvous with a server or service. A client finds a path connecting ISP-advertised triples. In ICING, DNS is augmented by policy enforcement, by forcing paths to have consenting elements. For example, DNS client resolution of `www.foo.com` requires consenting paths to servers for ".", ".com", "foo.com", etc.

Proofs of Consent (PoCs) are cacheable by clients, so in the common case, only resolving the most specific name would require interaction with consent servers.

5 Conclusions

NEBULA is a Future Internet Architecture intended to provide secure and resilient networking to support present and future applications of cloud computing. At the time of writing, the work on NEBULA is still ongoing, but we have made significant progress in a number of essential areas. NEBULA is a comprehensive architecture, and a number of novel technologies have already been developed for it; however, due to space constraints, we can only give a brief overview of the key building blocks here. For details, we refer the interested reader to the papers we cite below.

Acknowledgments. This work is supported by the U.S. National Science Foundation.

References

1. Aditya, P., Zhao, M., Lin, Y., Haeberlen, A., Druschel, P., Maggs, B., Wishon, B.: Reliable client accounting for hybrid content-distribution networks. In: Proc. NSDI (April 2012)
2. Agapi, A., Birman, K., Broberg, R., Cotton, C., Kielmann, T., Millnert, M., Payne, R., Surton, R., van Renesse, R.: Routers for the Cloud: Can the Internet achieve 5-nines availability? IEEE Internet Computing 15(5), 72–77 (2011)
3. Arye, M., Nordström, E., Kiefer, R., Rexford, J., Freedman, M.J.: A provably-correct protocol for seamless communication with mobile, multi-homed hosts. Technical Report 1203.4042v1, arXiv (March 2012)
4. Birman, K.P., Huang, Q., Freedman, D.: Overcoming the "D" in CAP: Using Isis2 to build locally responsive cloud services. IEEE Internet Computing 12, 50–58 (2012)
5. Birman, K.P.: Guide to Reliable Distributed Systems: Building High-Assurance Applications and Cloud-Hosted Services. Springer (2012)
6. Birman, K.P., Ganesh, L., van Renesse, R.: Running smart grid control software on cloud computing architectures. In: Proc. Workshop on Computational Needs for the Next Generation Electric Grid (April 2011)
7. Bodík, P., Menache, I., Chowdhury, M., Mani, P., Maltz, D.A., Stoica, I.: Surviving failures in bandwidth-constrained datacenters. In: Proc. SIGCOMM (2012)
8. Broberg, R., Agapi, A., Birman, K., Comer, D., Cotton, C., Kielmann, T., Lehr, W., van Renesse, R., Surton, R., Smith, J.M.: Clouds, cable and connectivity: Future Internets and router requirements. In: Proc. Cable Connection Spring Technical Conference (June 2011)
9. Clark, D., Lehr, W., Bauer, S.: Interconnection in the internet: the policy challenge. In: Proc. 39th Research Conference on Communication, Information and Internet Policy (September 2013)
10. Comer, D., Javed, S.: Applying open resilient cluster management (orcm) to a multi-chassis core router. In: Proc. ISCA International Conference on Computers and Their Applications (March 2012)
11. Comer, D., Suingh, P., Vasudevan, S.: Towards a practical and effective BGP defense system. In: Proc. ICICS (January 2012)
12. Comer, D.: A future Internet architecture that supports Cloud Computing. In: Proc. 6th International Conference on Future Internet Technologies (June 2011)

13. Dobrescu, M., Egi, N., Argyraki, K., Chun, B.G., Fall, K., Iannaccone, G., Knies, A., Manesh, M., Ratnasamy, S.: RouteBricks: exploiting parallelism to scale software routers. In: Proc. SOSP (2009)
14. Foster, N., Freedman, M.J., Harrison, R., Monsanto, C., Reitblatt, M., Rexford, J., Story, A., Walker, D.: Language abstractions for software-defined networks. In: Proc. Workshop on Lang. for Distrib. Algorithms (2012)
15. Foster, N., Harrison, R., Freedman, M.J., Monsanto, C., Rexford, J., Story, A., Walker, D.: Frenetic: A network programming language. In: Proc. ICFP (2011)
16. Freedman, D., Marian, T., Lee, J., Birman, K., Weatherspoon, H., Xu, C.: Instrumentation for exact packet timings in networks. In: Proc. Instrumentation and Measurement Technology Conference (May 2011)
17. Ghodsi, A., Sekar, V., Zaharia, M., Stoica, I.: Multi-resource fair queueing for packet processing. In: Proc. SIGCOMM (2012)
18. Gupta, T., Leners, J.B., Aguilera, M.K., Walfish, M.: Exposing network failures to end-host applications for improved availability. In: Proc. NSDI (April 2013)
19. Gurney, A.J.T., Haeberlen, A., Zhou, W., Sherr, M., Loo, B.T.: Having your cake and eating it too: Routing security with privacy protections. In: Proc. HotNets (November 2011)
20. Handigol, N., Heller, B., Jeyakumar, V., Maziéres, D., McKeown, N.: Where is the debugger for my Software-Defined Network? In: Proc. HotSDN (2012)
21. Hong, C.Y., Caesar, M., Duffield, N., Wang, J.: Tiresias: Online anomaly detection for hierarchical operational network data. In: Proc. ICDCS (2012)
22. Hong, C.Y., Caesar, M., Godfrey, P.B.: Finishing flows quickly with preemptive scheduling. In: Proc. SIGCOMM (2012)
23. Jeyakumar, V., Alizadeh, M., Mazières, D., Prabhakar, B., Kim, C.: EyeQ: Practical network performance isolation for the multi-tenant Cloud. In: Proc. HotCloud (2012)
24. Khurshid, A., Kiyak, F., Caesar, M.: Improving robustness of DNS to software vulnerabilities. In: Proc. ACSAC (2011)
25. Khurshid, A., Zhou, W., Caesar, M., Godfrey, P.B.: VeriFlow: Verifying network-wide invariants in real time. In: Proc. HotSDN (2012)
26. Lehr, W.: Measuring the Internet: The data challenge. OECD Digital Economy Papers, No. 194. OECD Publishing (2012)
27. Lehr, W., Clark, D., Bauer, S.: Measuring Internet performance when broadband is the new PSTN. Paper prepared for the "End of PSTN" Workshop at the University of Pennsylvania (May 2012)
28. Liu, C., Ren, L., Loo, B.T., Mao, Y., Basu, P.: Cologne: A declarative distributed constraint optimization platform. Proc. VLDB Endowm. 5(8), 752–763 (2012)
29. Liu, V., Han, S., Krishnamurthy, A., Anderson, T.: Tor instead of IP. In: Proc. HotNets (2011)
30. Liu, V., Halperin, D., Krishnamurthy, A., Anderson, T.: F10: A fault-tolerant engineered network. In: Proc. NSDI (April 2013)
31. Naous, J., Walfish, M., Nicolosi, A., Maziéres, D., Miller, M., Seehra, A.: Verifying and enforcing network paths with ICING. In: Proc. CoNEXT (2011)
32. Nordström, E., Shue, D., Gopalan, P., Kiefer, R., Arye, M., Ko, S.Y., Rexford, J., Freedman, M.J.: Serval: An end-host stack for service-centric networking. In: Proc. NSDI (2012)
33. Popa, L., Krishnamurthy, A., Ratnasamy, S., Stoica, I.: FairCloud: Sharing the network in cloud computing. In: Proc. HotNets (2011)
34. Popa, L., Kumar, G., Chowdhury, M., Krishnamurthy, A., Ratnasamy, S., Stoica, I.: FairCloud: sharing the network in cloud computing. In: Proc. SIGCOMM (2012)

35. Setty, S., McPherson, R., Blumberg, A.J., Walfish, M.: Making argument systems for outsourced computation practical (sometimes). In: Proc. NDSS (February 2012)
36. Setty, S., Vu, V., Panpalia, N., Braun, B., Blumberg, A.J., Walfish, M.: Taking proof-based verified computation a few steps closer to practicality. In: Proc. USENIX Security (2012)
37. Wang, A., Jia, L., Zhou, W., Ren, Y., Loo, B.T., Rexford, J., Nigam, V., Scedrov, A., Talcott, C.: FSR: Formal analysis and implementation toolkit for safe interdomain routing. IEEE/ACM Transactions on Networking (ToN) 20(6), 1814–1827 (2012)
38. Wang, A., Talcott, C., Gurney, A.J., Loo, B.T., Scedrov, A.: Brief announcement: A calculus of policy-based routing systems. In: Proc. PODC (July 2012)
39. Williams, D., Jamjoom, H., Weatherspoon, H.: The Xen-Blanket: Virtualize once, run everywhere. In: Proc. EuroSys (2012)
40. Yoo, C.S.: Cloud computing: Architecturand and policy implications. Review of Industrial Economics 38(4), 405–421 (2011)
41. Zhao, M., Zhou, W., Gurney, A.J.T., Haeberlen, A., Sherr, M., Loo, B.T.: Private and verifiable interdomain routing decisions. In: Proc. SIGCOMM (August 2012)
42. Zhou, W., Fei, Q., Narayan, A., Haeberlen, A., Loo, B.T., Sherr, M.: Secure network provenance. In: Proc. SOSP (October 2011)

Open the Way to Future Networks – A Viewpoint Framework from ITU-T[*]

Daisuke Matsubara[1], Takashi Egawa[2], Nozomu Nishinaga[3],
Myung-Ki Shin[4], Ved P. Kafle[3], and Alex Galis[5]

[1] Hitachi, Japan
daisuke.matsubara.pj@hitachi.com
[2] NEC, Japan
t-egawa@ct.jp.nec.com
[3] NICT, Japan
{nisinaga,kafle}@nict.go.jp
[4] ETRI, Korea
mkshin@etri.re.kr
[5] University College London, United Kingdom
a.galis@ucl.ac.uk

Abstract. Advancements concerning research and development of Future Networks (FNs) technologies have been introduced in recent years, such as network virtualization and software defined/driven network (SDN), information centric networking (ICN), cloud networking, autonomic management, and open connectivity. In this context ITU-T has developed initial Recommendations that lay out the essential directions for subsequent detailed work including further standardization of Future Networks. This paper presents the background and the context of FNs' standardization, the results and future plans originated from the initial standardization work performed by ITU-T.

Keywords: Future Networks, Future Internet, standardization, ITU-T Y.3001.

1 Introduction and Context

In recent years the balance, evolution and relationships between various networking requirements have changed significantly creating the need for new networking systems. These changes include different new equipments and mobile devices connected to the public telecommunication network, significant number of data centers operating with the network representing the realization of cloud computing systems and large number of various sensors, actuators and other "things" connected in the network realizing Machine-to-Machine (M2M) and Internet of Things (IoT) services.

The research community and the telecom industry have made continuous efforts to investigate and develop Future Networks (FNs) technologies and systems. Various technologies such as network virtualization [10] and software defined networking (SDN) [14][17][19][21], cloud networking [13][18][20], information centric networking (ICN) [8], autonomic management [7][11][12], and open connectivity have been

---

[*] Invited Paper.

A. Galis and A. Gavras (Eds.): FIA 2013, LNCS 7858, pp. 27–38, 2013.

examined and developed. Driven by this activity, International Telecommunication Union Telecommunication Standardization Sector (ITU-T) has started the standardization of FNs as networking systems to be deployed roughly in the 2015 - 2020 timeframe. FN standardization was initiated based on two commentary methods of analysis: top down method working from objectives and design goals of FNs, and bottom up method working from individual candidate technologies that are relatively mature.

The result of this analysis has been reflected in Recommendation ITU-T Y.3001 [1][16]. It includes also various candidate technologies as building blocks of FNs as such technologies tend to mature earlier than the overall architecture. For example, network virtualization technology, making use of Network Functions Virtualisation such as SDN [19][21], has already emerged. In addition, some technologies are being investigated in other standards development organizations (SDOs). It is important to understand and benefit from this ecosystem of technologies.

This paper describes the current ITU-T's accomplishments on FN standardization and its underlying concepts.

This paper is organized as follows. The next section provides an overview of FN standardization activities in ITU-T. Next the Recommendation ITU-T Y.3001 that describes the objectives and design goals of FNs is presented. Other FN-related Recommendations and the ITU-T future plan are also presented. A synthesis of related standardization and research activities is presented next. The final section provides concluding remarks.

2   Future Network Standardization in ITU-T

ITU-T Study Group 13 (SG13), a group for network architecture and the lead group for FN standardization in ITU-T, started its activities on FNs in early 2009. Since the discussion of FN was in its very early stage, ITU-T concluded that it is very important to listen to the voice of not only ITU-T members, but also experts including researchers outside of ITU-T. Consequently, Focus Group on Future Networks (FG-FN), a temporary organization open to all experts inside/outside of ITU-T, was established and its activity started in July 2009. It developed deliverables that later were transferred to SG13 and turned into Recommendations ITU-T Y.30xx series.

Recommendation ITU-T Y.3001 [1] – Future Networks: Objectives and Design Goals, describes four objectives and twelve design goals for FNs and as such it presents the first standard definition and description of FNs. The fundamental difference between FNs and other transport networks systems such as those using the Internet Protocol (IP) is the shift from a separate transport and service strata to a packet-based network with service and management-aware characteristics, which is based on shared (virtualized) combined processing, storage and communication / connectivity resources. As such FNs are aimed at a unified infrastructure which connects and orchestrate the future Internet of people, devices, content, clouds, and things.

In this Recommendation, four objectives were identified as essential concerns to which not enough attention was paid in designing current networks. They represent the differential characteristics of FNs when compared with the current networks. The four objectives identified and described in Y.3001 are service awareness, data awareness, environmental awareness, and social and economic awareness. Also twelve design goals were identified as advanced capabilities and features that are necessary for the realization of FNs. Fig. 1 shows the mapping of design goals to the objectives.

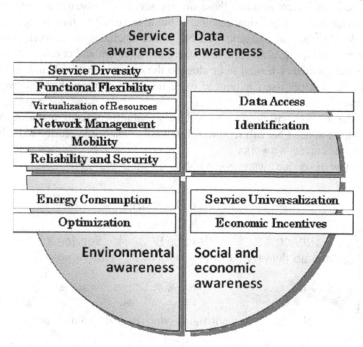

Fig. 1. Four objectives and twelve design goals of Future Networks [1]

2.1   Service Awareness

The number and range of services is expected to explode in the future. Today's network, whose basic design was introduced more than thirty years ago, has supported so far any service using its basic functionality and design. FNs are expected to support not only current services such as Email and web browsing, but also emerging services in an optimal way, by providing additional functionality and flexibility that can accommodate diverse and evolving service requirements.

FNs are aimed to support these services without drastic increases in, for instance, deployment and operational costs. In addition, FNs are required to be flexible and elastic so that they can adapt to new services. For example, if a service requires a certain process to be done inside the network, the network should provision dynamically all managed communication, computing, and storage resources that are needed for that service. Furthermore, these resources may be virtualized to allow flexible deployment and usage by the services.

In order to support diverse services for mobile users including M2M communication devices, advanced mobility features that guarantee sufficient quality of service experience to the users in both homogeneous and heterogeneous mobile environments are needed.

Network and system management will play a significant role in allowing the network to take in and accommodate these diverse services. Network management will need to manage not only physical resources, but also virtual resources located inside the network. Unified management of FNs, which includes in-network autonomic management [7][11][12], is an approach where management and control functions are distributed and located or hosted in or close to the managed network and service elements, and the services itself may need to be managed along with the network in a unified manner.

Finally, the services will need to support the social infrastructure including mission critical services; hence FNs will require substantially enhanced security and reliability compared to the current networks.

An overview of service awareness in FNs is shown in Fig. 2.

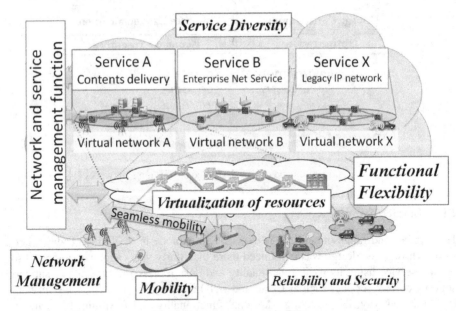

Fig. 2. Service awareness in FNs

A service-aware network is a rich landscape of network services, which can be discovered, negotiated, and contracted with by higher level services at the application level. These services need to be discoverable and describable by attributes such as capacity, throughput, QoS, latency, protocol support, availability, and security in a consistent format. They need to express cost and availability, scalability, and potentially elasticity and support for usage variations. They need to be supported by a negotiation service, which can implement contracts with consumers. FNs are necessary to accommodate these diverse services without a drastic increase in costs of deployment and operation. One method is to enable network operators to control their networks in a unified and programmable manner, and realize multiple isolated and flexible in-networks in order to support a broad range of network services that do not interfere with each other. From this viewpoint, promising technologies includes network virtualization [10][21] and SDN [14], and cloud networking [13][17][18][19][20] technologies.

ITU-T has successfully developed and published Recommendation ITU-T Y.3011 - Framework of Network Virtualization for FNs [2], which is the first Recommendation regarding service awareness in FNs from the perspective of ITU-T. Network virtualization is the process of combining hardware and software network resources and network functionality into a single, software-based administrative entity, a virtual network. Network virtualization involves platform virtualization, often combined with resource virtualization [21]. Network virtualization is also a method that allows multiple virtual networks called Logically Isolated Network Partitions (LINPs) to coexist in a single physical network. In Y.3011, the following eight design principles for realizing network virtualization are presented and investigated.

- Network abstraction: hiding the underlying characteristics of network resources and establishing simplified interfaces for accessing the network resources.
- Isolation: complete separation among the LINPs (e.g., from security and performance aspects).
- Topology awareness and quick reconfigurability: dynamic update of an LINP's capabilities without interruption of operations.
- Performance: avoidance of the performance degradation caused by the virtualization layer or adaptation layer.
- Programmability: programmable control plane and data plane so that users can use customized protocols, forwarding or routing functions in the LINP.
- Management: independent and unified management functions for each LINP.
- Mobility: movement support of virtual resources including users and services.
- Wireless: wireless characteristics support such as limited resource usage, and signal interference.

As the next step of Y.3011, more detailed requirements in realizing network virtualization are being envisaged in a separate Draft Recommendation ITU-T Y.FNvirtreq - Requirements of Network Virtualization for Future Networks, which focuses on virtual resource management, service mobility, wireless virtualization, and candidate protocols and existing requirements for network virtualization.

In addition, SDN technologies are emerging and intensively discussed as one of solutions regarding network virtualization within telecom networks including mobile, data centers, and enterprise networks. Draft Recommendation ITU-T Y.FNsdn - Framework of Telecom Software-Defined Networking (SDN), specifies requirements and use cases for SDN in telecom networks. SDN is defined as a new networking technology, which enables network operators to directly control and manage their networks and resources to best serve their customers' needs by writing simple programs, where controls and data forwarding are decoupled. Its properties include programmable controls, data forwarding abstraction, and virtualization support of the underlying networks infrastructure and resources. ITU-T is planning to collaborate on this topic with other SDOs such as Open Networking Foundation (ONF) and Internet Engineering Task Force (IETF).

2.2   Data Awareness

Current networks are mainly used for accessing and distributing information. To realize this, the networks establish a communication connection between an application process of each terminal (end-host) and exchange data using the connection. The exchange of information in current networks is based on the globally unique location IDs and location based routing as shown in Fig.   3.

However, if identical information objects are placed in multiple locations as expected in FNs, it is not always optimal to access information using globally unique static location IDs. Identical contents may have the same content ID and the content can be accessed via a nearest cache using the content ID based routing as shown in Fig. 3. FNs are aimed at optimizing the handling of enormous amounts of data in a distributed environment with the users enabled to access desired data safely, easily, quickly, and accurately, regardless of their location. In the context of data awareness, "data" is not limited to specific data types such as audio or video contents, but includes all information that is accessible via the network.

In FNs, communication paradigms using IDs other than location IDs is envisaged. FNs aim to support communication using data (or content) IDs. Furthermore, it will support communication using node IDs, application process IDs, etc. These IDs need to be treated separately from location IDs and FNs should support not only separation of end point or node IDs and locators such as specified in Locator/ID Separation Protocol (LISP) and Recommendation ITU-T Y.2015, but also communication using data IDs, service IDs, etc.

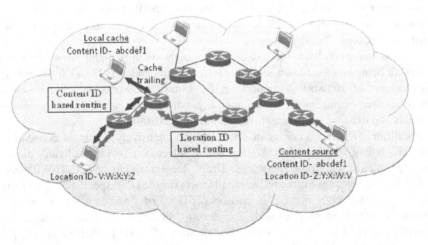

Fig. 3. Data awareness in FNs

Recommendation ITU-T Y.3031 - Identification framework in future networks [4] is part of the series of FN-related Recommendations developed in ITU-T SG13. It complements the FN objectives and design goals specified in ITU-T Y.3001 by developing a new identification framework that would be helpful for intrinsic mobility support and optimal data access. It specifies the identification framework, after giving an analysis of identifiers being used in the current networks and their limitations. It mentions about the overloaded semantic of an IP address as an identifier, a locator and a forwarding tag, and consequent hindrances for mobility and multihoming services.

The identification framework is horizontally positioned between the communication objects (such as user, device, data, and service) and physical networks forwarding data from one place to another. The framework consists of four components: ID discovery service, ID space, ID mapping registry, and ID mapping service. The ID discovery service discovers various types of IDs related to communication objects. The ID space defines and manages various kinds of IDs (e.g., user IDs, data or content IDs, service IDs, node IDs, and location IDs). The ID mapping registry maintains mapping relationships between various types of IDs. The ID mapping service performs mappings of IDs of one type with the IDs of other types. The ID mapping service utilizes the ID mappings obtained from the ID mapping registry to achieve seamless services over heterogeneous physical networks, such as IPv6, IP IPv4, or non-IP networks that may use different protocols and media for forwarding data.

ITU-T is currently working on Y.FNDAN - Framework of Data Aware Networking for Future Networks, which gives an overview of Data Aware Networks (DAN). DAN is a technology, which optimizes handling of enormous amount of data in a distributed environment and enables users to access desired data safely, easily, quickly, and accurately, regardless of their location. In addition, due to the awareness feature of this technology, it enables networks to understand users' requests and to react accordingly in order to support adaptive data dissemination.

The essence of DAN lies in the name-based routing in which the data or the request for the data is routed inside the network not by its location but by its name or ID (i.e., routing and forwarding is based on data ID). It captures many aspects of ongoing research works such as content-centric networking (CCN) [5] and information-centric networking (ICN) [8]. Y.FNDAN will provide general properties and high-level requirements of DAN such as naming, routing, in-network caching, in-network processing, and data security.

2.3   Environmental Awareness

The ratio of carbon dioxide (CO_2) that information and communication technology (ICT) industry produces is two percent of the entire CO_2 emission [15]. This includes CO_2 contribution by PCs, servers, cooling systems, fixed and mobile telephony, local area networks (LANs), office telecommunications and printers.

Internet traffic is growing year by year. It has been predicted that the traffic triples every five years period and will reach 1.3 zettabytes by 2016. Considering the necessity to transmit information via the network, the increase in traffic will mean ever increase in energy consumption; hence the emission of CO_2 will most likely continue to increase. For this reason, FNs aims at minimizing and managing the energy needed to transmit bits in the device-level, equipment-level, and system-level. At the same time, energy can be managed in a better manner by utilizing ICT for various industries such as manufacturing and distribution of goods.

Recommendation ITU-T Y.3021 - Framework of Energy Saving for Future Networks [5] reviews various energy saving technologies and categorizes them into two according to the basic strategy. One is to reduce the network capacity by reducing traffic (e.g., by caching) or peak load shift. The other is improvement of energy efficiency by dynamic control (e.g., clock gating, sleep mode control, etc.) or less power (e.g., LSI fabrication, thermal design, etc.) Then it describes a feedback loop among measurement, control and management as the framework of energy saving.

Also, each ITU-T Recommendation related to FNs has an environmental consideration section that assesses environmental impact of the technology. This is inspired by security consideration section commonly addressed in ICT standards.

There are large numbers of standardization activities that contribute to realize environmental objective of Y.3001. Within ITU-T activities there are Recommendations that defines a power charger specification for mobile terminals to reduce e-waste, assessment methodology for environmental impact of ICT, etc. Many of them are applicable to FNs.

2.4   Social and Economic Awareness

As networks are evolving from just connecting people with common interest to a social infrastructure, service universalization is becoming a key objective in realizing the new networking. The right to have access to a global network will be one of the fundamental rights in the future, and the right should not be limited based on the location of the individual user.

Telecommunication networks have become an essential infrastructure utility that is indispensable to our society, much similar to electricity, gas, and water. For this reason, FNs aims to take into consideration the social and economical aspects when realizing the architecture.

It is also necessary for the network to evolve in a sound and consistent manner. Public networks such as telephony networks have been invested and operated mainly by government-owned companies and have supported and fostered the national industry. Recently private investment has become active and capital market has been introduced in investment and operation of network infrastructure. At the same time, the relationship between the investment model and the profit distribution model has been distorted and it is becoming an obstructive factor for the appropriate development of the market.

FNs should take explicitly into consideration the lowering of the barriers for stakeholders to enter the market and providing a sustainable competitive environment.

Network architecture indirectly but undoubtedly affects society and business by providing the playground for social activity and business. ITU-T Y.3001 is emphasizing that FNs should consider social and economic issues such as the barrier to enter the market or the lifecycle cost for deployment and sustainability, although Y.3001 focuses manly on technical aspect. This is an interdisciplinary issue between technology and policy, which should not be decided by standards, but by the market through competition.

ITU-T started a socio-economic analysis to from a framework called Draft Recommendation ITU-T Y.FNsocioeconomic - Socio-Economic Aware Design of Future Network Technology. Current draft provides a framework to anticipate the socio-economic impact of the technology at technology design time. When a candidate FNs technology is provided, it recommends to take into account the relevant set of stakeholders, tussles emerging among them, and the range of available choices, to anticipate either a stable and incentives-compatible or an unstable outcome resulting from deploying the technology, to identify potential spillover (unwanted) effects from the technology's primary functionality to another functionality, and to help design a technology for FNs that is in-line with the respective socio-economic design goals and objectives.

3   Future Plan

Standardization activities of FNs are gaining momentum. For example, SDN that is closely related to the service-awareness objective is becoming a hot topic in ICT industry. ITU-T SG 13 therefore decided to divide the group involved in standardization of FNs into three groups, first group for service awareness including SDN, second group for data awareness, and third group for environment and socio-economic awareness and short-term realization of FNs. FNs are a huge target, and various areas needs to be discussed for future standardization apart from the draft Recommendations mentioned in the previous sections. One of the most important area is unified management of FNs, which includes in-network autonomic management [7][11][12]. The benefits are the inherent support for self-management features, higher automation and autonomicity capabilities, easier use of management tools and empowering the network with inbuilt cognition and intelligence. Additional benefits include reduction and optimization in the amount of external management interactions, which is a key to the minimization of manual interaction and the sustaining of manageability of large networked systems and moving from a managed object paradigm to one of management by objectives.

The three groups in ITU-T SG 13 are far from enough to cover all these aspects of FNs. And there are many existing and ongoing work in other ITU-T Study Groups and other SDOs. ITU-T will be seeking ways to collaborate with other SDOs considering the technology research and market needs, which is essential task for realizing FNs.

4   Related Research and Standardization and Programs

Fig. 4 shows a chronology of FN related research and development activity along with ITU-T standardization activities for FNs. The NewArch project initiated in 2000 by several US universities and institutes is the ancestor of Future Internet architecture design projects advocating for "clean slate" design approach. It was founded by DARPA (Defense Advanced Research Projects Agency), which was the funding body supporting the initial design of the Internet. The objective of this project was to define a network architecture as "advanced design principles for making use of protocols and algorithms." The 100x100 Clean Slate Project (2000 - 2005) was an NSF (National Science Foundation) - supported collaborative project launched and its slogan was "100Mbps connectivity to 100 million homes" with new technology. The FIND (Future Internet Design) and FIA (Future Internet Architecture) are also funded by NSF. The FIND was a long-term initiative of the NSF NeTS research program and it also focused to the "clean slate" design approach. More than 40 projects were established and four large projects (FIA projects) are generated as the result of FIND. For testing brand new network architecture design through above projects, GENI (Global Environment for Network Innovations) was initiated in 2005 by NSF.

In EU, more than 150 projects clustered as EU Future Internet Assembly (FIA) [6][9] are developing networking systems for the Future Internet.

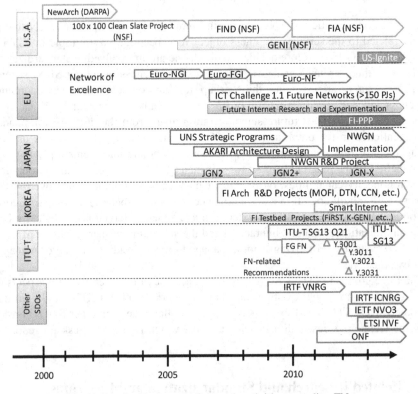

Fig. 4. Standardization and Research activities regarding FNs

Japanese government announced UNS (Ubiquitous Network Society) strategy program in 2005 and AKARI project was initiated in 2006 to design a NeW Generation Network (NWGN) architecture by NICT. It is continuing as one project in NWGN R&D Project. New Generation Network Test beds JGN-X is now under operating with the network virtualization technology.

In Korea, FIArch projects such as Mobile Oriented Future Internet (MOFI), Delay Tolerant Networking (DTN), and CCN were launched in 2007. Future Internet Research for Sustainable Testbed (FiRST) and international federation projects such as K-GENI were initiated in 2008. Korean government has also announced Smart Internet as a first deployment model of Future Internet in 2011.

There are also related standardization activities in other SDOs such as ETSI Network Functions Virtualization (NFV), Open Networking Foundation (ONF), IETF Network Virtualization Overlays (NVO3), Internet Research Task Force (IRTF) Virtual Networks Research Group (VNRG), and IRTF Information-Centric Networking Research Group (ICNRG).

5   Concluding Remarks

ITU-T has developed and published during 2009 - 2012 four important Recommendations: Y.3001, Y.3011, Y.3021 and Y.3031, representing the first standard descriptions of Future Networks. In addition to connectivity services, FNs are characterized by four objectives and twelve design goals. These design goals are advanced capabilities, features, and new network services that are needed together in the realization of FNs. As the standardization work progressed through discussions with various experts in this field, ITU-T was able to capture and identify the key characteristics and important aspects of FNs and specify them in these documents. We believe that these Recommendations will provide sound foundation and appropriate guidance for subsequent FNs realization, standardization, research and development.

Acknowledgment. The authors would like to thank Sangjin Jeong, Hideki Otsuki, Toshihiko Kurita, Martin Waldburger, Alojz Hudobivnik, Naotaka Morita, Hyoung-Jun Kim, and Chaesub Lee for their work and contributions to the ITU-T FN activities. This article was partially supported by the European Union UniverSELF project, National Institute of Information and Communications Technology (NICT), and the ICT Standardization program of Korea Communications Commission (KCC).

References

1. Recommendation ITU-T Y.3001, Future Network Vision - Objectives and Design Goals (2011)
2. Recommendation ITU-T Y.3011, Framework of Network Virtualization for Future Networks (2012)

3. Recommendation ITU-T Y.3021, Framework of energy saving for Future Networks (2012)
4. Recommendation ITU-T Y.3031, Identification Framework in Future Networks (2012)
5. Jacobson, V., Smetters, D.K., Thornton, J.D., Plass, M.F., Briggs, N.H., Braynard, R.L.: Networking named content. In: CoNEXT 2009, Rome (December 2009)
6. Álvarez, F.A., et al.: FIA 2012. LNCS, vol. 7281, pp. 1–252. Springer, Heidelberg (2012)
7. Clayman, S., Clegg, R., Mamatas, L., Pavlou, G., Galis, A.: Monitoring, aggregation and filtering for efficient management of virtual networks. In: IEEE International Conference on Network and Service Management (CNSM) (October 2011)
8. Kutscher, D., Ahlgren, B., Kar, H., Ohlman, B., Oueslati, S., Solis, I.: Information-centric networking. Dagstuhl Seminar (2010)
9. Domingue, J., et al.: FIA 2011. LNCS, vol. 6656, pp. 1–465. Springer, Heidelberg (2011)
10. Galis, A., Denazis, S., Brou, C., Klein, C. (eds.): Programmable networks for IP service deployment, pp. 1–450. Artech House Books (June 2004) ISBN: 1-58053-745-6
11. Clegg, R.G., Clayman, S., Pavlou, G., Mamatas, L., Galis, A.: On the selection of management and monitoring nodes in dynamic networks. IEEE Transactions on Computers (99), 1–15 (2012)
12. Ciavaglia, L., et al.: Realizing autonomics for future networks. In: Future Network and Mobile Summit, Warsaw, Poland (June 2011)
13. Rochwerger, B., et al.: The RESERVOIR model and architecture for open federated cloud computing. IBM System Journal, Special Edition on Internet Scale Data Centers 53(4) (2009)
14. Rubio-Loyola, J., et al.: Scalable service deployment on software defined networks. IEEE Communications Magazine 49(12), 84–93 (2011)
15. http://www.gartner.com/it/page.jsp?id=503867 (visited on December 14, 2012)
16. Matsubara, D., Egawa, T., Nishinaga, N., Shin, M.K., Kafle, V.P., Galis, A.: Towards Future Networks: a viewpoint from ITU-T. IEEE Communication Magazine – Special Issue on Telecommunications Standards (to be published in Q2 2013), http://www.comsoc.org/files/Publications/Magazines/ci/cfp/cf pcommag0313.html
17. Software-Defined Networking – Open Networking Foundation (ONF) (April 2012), http://www.opennetworking.org/images/stories/downloads/white -papers/wp-sdn-newnorm.pdf
18. Openstack - quantum wiki, http://wiki.openstack.org/Quantum
19. SDN Document Library, http://www.sdncentral.com/sdn-document-library/
20. Chapman, C., Emmerich, E., Marquez, F.G., Clayman, S., Galis, A.: Software Architecture Definition for On-demand Cloud Provisioning. Springer Journal on Cluster Computing (May 2011), http://www.springerlink.com/content/m31np5112525167v/, doi:10.1007/s10586-011-0152-0
21. " Network Functions Virtualisation" ETSI White Paper (October 2012), http://portal.etsi.org/NFV/NFV_White_Paper.pdf

Towards a Minimal Core
for Information-Centric Networking

Kari Visala[1], Dmitrij Lagutin[1], and Sasu Tarkoma[2]

[1] Helsinki Institute for Information Technology HIIT /
Aalto University School of Science
`firstname.lastname@hiit.fi`
[2] University of Helsinki
`sasu.tarkoma@cs.helsinki.fi`

Abstract. The question of whether there exists a minimal model for *information-centric networking* (ICN), that allows the bulk of features of various recent ICN architectures to be expressed as independent extensions to the model, is largely unexplored. Finding such *core* would yield more orthogonality of the features, better adaptability to the changing multi-stakeholder environment of the Internet, and improved interoperability between ICN architectures.

In this paper, we introduce the concept of *information space* as a potential solution, which is based on the sharing of information and late binding service composition of decoupled entities as the essence of information-centrism. The specified framework is an abstract model without dependencies to low-level implementation details and achieves minimality by leaving naming and content security outside the core. This approach makes the experimentation of new features above and their implementation below faster and provides a possible evolutionary kernel for ICN.

1   Introduction

There are many clean-slate designs for ICN that aim to fundamentally change the basic suite of protocols used in the current Internet or even replace IP as the waist of the hourglass shaped layered stack of dependent protocols. Such proposals include CCN [1], DONA [2], NetInf architecture [3], and PSIRP/PURSUIT [4]. A survey of ICN research can be found in [5].

These systems try to take advantage of the experience gained from observing the evolution of the current Internet and design features of the architectures not as an afterthought, which has been the case so far [6]. Features like *naming and addressing, security, searching and rendezvous, scoping of data, caching, routing,* and *forwarding* have been integrated in cohesive combinations in these designs.

However, it is difficult for this type of engineered and relatively complex solutions to become popular as the replacement for IP, because a large number of stakeholders have their own heterogeneous, changing requirements for the network. For example, IP can be boiled down to the hierarchical addressing and a packet format, which do not fix other aspects of the network, but have allowed

A. Galis and A. Gavras (Eds.): FIA 2013, LNCS 7858, pp. 39–51, 2013.

a large ecosystem of protocols to be built around the basic framework provided by the simple core.

1.1 Advantages of a Minimal Core

Specifying a **minimal** model, a core for ICN, that allows the above-mentioned network functions to be independently developed as extensions to the core (while they already exploit the advantages of information-centrism), would yield the following three main advantages:

Orthogonality of network functions, which would work synergistically in any combinations. For example, a routing mechanism benefits from caching or a rendezvous function can utilize the security solution etc. A minimal core would also be easier to implement in different environments, including faster prototyping, and its optimizations would be maximally reused by the auxiliary functions depending on the core.

An alternative approach to the ubiquitous core would be to simply specify multiple modular functions independently, but this kind of solution would produce orthogonal concepts only as a coincidence. The separate functions would always be specified relative to something else and it would not be possible to combine them easily, because they have nothing in common. They would not benefit from the *network effect* provided by a core.

The core of the ICN architecture could be compared to the role of lambda calculus for functional programming languages: By mapping higher-level concepts to the minimal core instead of directly implementing them, we can get well-defined, tested, orthogonal semantics as the core specification will be reused and the features work together similar to compatible Lego bricks that can be assembled in various ways. Formal semantics for the core also provide a framework for specification of and reasoning about network functions.

Adaptability to changing environment and requirements by multiple stakeholders is a prerequisite for the formation of a stable evolutionary kernel [7]. Handley's observations on the Internet should not be viewed as a motivation for a new top-down design that tries to cater for everyone, but as an argument of what type of protocol can in general become the ubiquitous glue of the Internet. The view that evolution in open markets determines the deployment of protocols, is further supported by the findings in [8].

Interoperability between different ICN architectures becomes easier, if they can agree on a common core concepts without fixing different monolithic organizations for their functions.

1.2 Design Goals for the Core

In general, there seems to be a trend to move towards more **abstract** interfaces and protocols that allow the applications to modularly express their intent using stable concepts on the level of the application logic and use late binding to the actual protocols used [9]. The model exposed to higher layers should not have dependencies to arbitrary low-level implementation details such as the use of packet switching. For example, a database or a file system, which do not have the concept of a packet, could be used to implement ICN locally.

ICN is often motivated by the need to optimize information dissemination, content security, and the receiver-driven communication pattern that allows the tackling of unwanted traffic. In addition, the high-level functional goal of ICN can be stated to implement a network layer substrate that allows the *information-centric paradigm* (ICP) to be used on the application layer with little "impedance mismatch" between the layers.

We have so far given an argument for the need of an abstract, minimal core for ICN. The remaining contributions of this paper are:

1. The definition of our core in Sect. 4 based on our view on the essence of ICP briefly covered in Sect. 2 and the argument why certain functions such as naming and content security should be excluded from the core in Sect. 3,
2. a concrete, example node architecture explained in Sect. 5, which is not meant to be efficient and realistic implementation, but to support the claim that our approach is feasible, and
3. discussion on how to develop new features on top of the core and what advantages does this have compared to the monolithic approach in Sect. 6.

2 Information-Centrism

A typical ICN architecture supports a communication pattern, where the receiver needs to initiate the communication event by subscribing a named data publication. The granularity of the named entities is more fine grained than hosts identified by IP addresses and the names are location independent. After created, publications are typically immutable associations between their name and content. They do not have a destination like messages, and can be cached and received via multiple routes. ICN is in contrast to the message-based approach, where the sender triggers a (remote) continuation, which may change the state of the destination object and spawn a dialog between the two endpoints.

In many current protocols the roles of the communicating entities are typically coupled at the design time and global invariants are easy to maintain as the degrees-of-freedom of the architecture are limited. These invariants are often not explicitly documented in the code, but exist mostly in the head of the developer as assumptions about how the system works as a whole. For example, a connection abstraction can be built between the endpoints, but already giving an identity to data allows interpretation. The decoupling of the acts of receiving and sending of information in space and time can be taken further by allowing more indirection in the addressing [10] or even interaction between applications that do not share anything in common on the protocol level [11].

The variable part in a communication event, the data, is needed to convey information over the channel. The possible assumptions made about the communication channel form a partial order based on the entailment relation. At the very minimum, some assumptions must be shared about the data itself, e.g. typing information, to make the communication meaningful for the applications.

Even though ICP could be approached symmetrically to message-passing by naming data instead of continuations [12], we choose here to reduce the core functionality to the absolute minimum. The idea is that the core can be extended by new features that add assumptions about the communication channel analogous to the development of transport abstractions. The semantics provided by the network are reflected as metadata publications that can specify, for example, *scopes* under which publications adhere to more specific *distribution strategies*.

Weak core semantics encourage explicit "plumbing" of assumptions about the data as machine-readable metadata, which reduces coupling between communicating entities. This supports dynamic service composition, where loosely coupled applications are independently developed and may only indirectly share the knowledge of some data types. The result is not a top-down framework or a pattern of interaction, where each component has its well-defined place, but the late binding of new functionality based on shared metadata. The goal is to utilize all existing functionality in a system by allowing their combination in new ways not available in fixed configurations.

The components sharing information produce in parallel derivations based on the information already available, similar to the *blackboard* architecture, and solutions emerge dynamically. Information items shared can be interpreted as data or *intentions*, such as *subscriptions*, that instruct the subsequent execution.

> For example, Alice with a digital wallet app for her mobile phone with Near Field Communication capability enters a store that does not support the same protocol for mobile payments. However, the store's WiFi network automatically shares metadata about the store with Alice's phone so that it is able to load from the Internet the necessary helper functions to semantically bridge the information provided by both the wallet app and the store.

We informally characterize the model of computation behind our core as:

1. Distributed, parallel execution based on
2. shared data, metadata, and instructions using
3. the metadata to guide dynamic service composition of decoupled functions.

In addition to the model exposed to higher layers (such as addressing), an internetworking architecture needs to define an interface between networks (e.g. packet format) to allow interoperability between heterogeneous implementations.

3   Naming and Content Security

Naming is a central design element in most of the ICN architectures as it pervades most aspects of the system. Typically, naming and routing designs are coupled. For example, the names may contain restrictions such as hierarchical structure or embedded location information, which make it possible to optimize routing

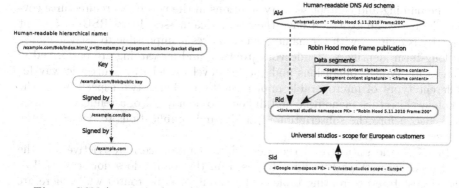

Fig. 1. CCN (on the left) and PURSUIT (on the right) naming side-by-side

based on them. There are also countless other dimensions in which different identifier structures and semantics can be compared such as the lifetime of the identifiers, (im-)mutability of objects, trust model, human-readability etc.

For example, CCN [1] uses opaque, binary objects that have an explicitly specied number of ordered components to name the content chunks hierarchically. These names allow subscriptions that match simple sets of publications and at the same time allow naming of data chunks that do not yet exist.

Another example is the realization of the PURSUIT functional model in [13]. It uses *self-certifying* DONA-like [2] *rendezvous identifiers* (Rids), which are (P, L) pairs. P is the public-key of the *namespace* owner of the identifier and L is a variable length label. CCN and PURSUIT names are shown in Fig. 1.

Both in CCN and PURSUIT, all content chunks can be authenticated with public-key signatures by storing a signature that binds the name and the content in each data packet. The integrity check is possible to do independently for each packet as the PURSUIT Rids contain the public key of the namespace the Rid belongs to. Such identifiers are called *self-certifying*. In CCN, on the other hand, signed data packets are *publicly authenticatable* by containing enough information to allow the retrieval of the public key necessary to verify it. In CCN, the trust model and names are contextual as there does not exist a single entity that everyone trusts for every application. Keys are just CCN data and content can be used to certify other content.

PURSUIT introduces the additional concept of *scope* and every publish operation also determines the scope in which the publication takes place. The scoping of information is orthogonal to the information structures formed by naming schemes and data items refering to other data items. Instead, the scope determines the distribution strategy of the publications inside it. This has the additional benefit that the subscriber can separate its trust on the distribution strategy from the trust on the content. For example, inside untrusted scopes, 3rd party data sources may falsely advertise data that they do not intend to serve in order to cause the data to be unavailable. CCN cannot solve this problem in a general way by using data sources with the credentials from the original publisher as this restricts the use of 3rd party data sources opportunistically.

The naming and content security solutions in the two ICN architectures covered here are different and have their own weaknesses. In PURSUIT, content security is coupled with the names, which makes it impossible to use the names as long-term identifiers. Rendezvous, routing, and forwarding are performed in phases for typical operations and the low-level model leaves little leeway for different types of interoperable implementations. These two aspects make the whole architecture monolithic and difficult to deploy. Also, a rendezvous phase is needed before the subscription of all dynamic publications to determine the correct data source.

In CCN, the structure of the hierarchical namespace is restrictive and the routing of interest packets directly based on the names does not scale well as the largest Internet routing table contains only $4 * 10^5$ routes while there are already $9.5 * 10^7$ generic top-level domains [14]. Also, the subscription of data based on the prefix matching cannot solve locally the problem of the most recent version. CCN tries to incorporate the trust model of SDSI/SPKI for the key management problem of long-term identifiers on the network level, but this type of single solution cannot work for many applications. The lack of global secure identifiers in CCN also increases the complexity of the management of the names at the higher layers. CCN security model does not differentiate the orthogonal concepts of trust to data and trust to the communication channel, which causes availability of data to become a problem, if data is falsely advertised.

Both of the architectures covered here have chosen the naming and content security to be the central design element, maybe following the success of IP, but as the above problems show, the offered solutions cannot satisfy all stakeholders. In the Sect. 4, we present a core for an ICN architecture that does not include these aspects, but allows multiple approaches to naming and content security, that possibly utilize the information-centric problem solving itself, on top of it.

4   Information Space

The abstract, minimal core for ICN, that we define here, does not require any specific API, protocol message format, or a node architecture such as blackboard, but specifies the concept of an *information space* (IS) and its semantics. If a concrete system can be mapped to the concepts of the IS and adheres to its axioms, we say that the system implements the IS. In Sect. 5 we specify an example API and a node architecture, but they are mostly implementation details from the point of view of the core.

4.1   Definition

An IS *trace* is defined to be a six-tuple $(P, R, I, d, i, <)$, where R is a countable set of *receive* events over the whole life time of the IS and I is a countable set of instances of interfaces to the IS. Receive events form the output of the IS. P is a countable set of *publish* events and a pair $(P_c \subset P, I_c \subset I)$ forms the external context of the IS. $d : E \to \mathbb{N}$ (, where $E = (P \cup R)$) is a function that assigns a natural number to each externally observable event of the IS. The contents of the publication related to the event are encoded as this number. Another function $i : E \to I$ maps events to the interfaces in which they took place.

We ground the IS model of distributed computation in the physical concept of spacetime following the *actor model of concurrency* [15]. We assume that each interface of the IS follows its world line and events $e \in E$ occuring at the interface can be assigned a point $L(e)$ on the path of the interface. However, we abstract the physical description into a *strict partial order* relation $<$ over the set of events E. $<$ is intensionally defined to respect the laws given below and it must agree with the causal structure of the spacetime, that is $\forall a, b \in E.a < b \Rightarrow$ there exists a future-directed non-spacelike curve from $L(a)$ to $L(b)$. Different structures for the spacetime can be used here as long as all observers agree on the order of causal connection between two events, which is the case for relativistic frames of reference.

Events must obey the *actor laws* [15]. That is, $\forall e_1, e_2 \in E$ the sets $\{e \mid e_1 < e < e_2\}$ and $\{e \mid e < e_1\}$ are finite. In addition, $\forall x \in I$ the set $\{e \mid i(e) = x\}$ is totally ordered by the relation $<$. For the bare IS, we add one more law:

$$\forall r \in R \, \exists p \in P \, (d(r) = d(p) \land p < r) \quad (No\ publication\ from\ nothing\ (NPN))$$

Finally, we define IS to be a system, whose possible behavior, when run in a given context C, is a set of IS traces. These axioms intensionally describe the IS with weak semantics. The idea is to define subtypes of IS that enrich the structure with additional constructs and axioms that can, for example, apply to a subset of publications, based on the functionality implemented in the network. For example, stronger consistency between publications could be guaranteed for publications inside a given scope.

4.2 Discussion

IS definition is compatible with actor semantics, which means that applications and network elements can be specified as actors attached to the IS. IS can be overlaid on top of multiple implementation technologies by using actors to bridge information relevant to satisfying global semantics between the systems. The creation of new interfaces is outside the scope of this paper, but it can easily be included in the model. Basic IS delivers data only using *best effort* semantics which allows independent failures of parts of the system. This can be seen as a feature for security functions, that may filter unwanted traffic intentionally. An IS does not have a global state, because defining one would impede the scalability of the implementations.

IS can be interpreted to have *one-time-creation* semantics for each publication. Immutability after creation allows cached information to be used safely locally. Implementations can store publications as soft state and automatically garbage collect old data. Whoever wants a publication to persist, must be responsible for keeping it alive. This adheres to the *fate sharing principle* [16].

There is no concept of subcription in the IS, but different kinds of subscriptions are just publications that are routed based on some search ontology specific strategy and resolved to result sets using the late-binding based problem solving

strategy. A high-level query or subscription can be handled in multiple phases
as functions joined to the IS translate publications to other publications of lower
abstraction level, and at some point, the information can trigger an external side
effect such as the forwarding of the information to another node. We claim that
both the CCN and PURSUIT naming can be emulated on top of the IS and
provide evidence for this in Sect. 6 by showing a partial concrete proposal.

The idea is that side-effects external to the IS, such as forwarding of information, are produced by components, that reflect their capabilities in the IS as
metadata. For example, a network description language can be used to describe
the topology and routing algorithm of the network. There is no separate concept
of metadata, but it consists of publications, that refer to other publications.

Compared to Haggle [11], IS does not limit the data model and searching to
information graphs and sets of attributes as we believe that these design choices
will produce a bias in the architecture towards certain applications. Compared
to the NetAPI [9], IS does not specify a concrete API, but an abstract model
based on sharing of information. IS does not assume communication with named
resources, but publications are simply published and received. Specifying an API
instead of information structures is diametrically opposite to the idea of ICP:
In object-oriented paradigm one fixes a stable interface that can have multiple
implementations (construction) with hidden data and in ICP one fixes an al-
gebraic data type, whose elements can be shared and consumed (destruction)
in new ways by new functions. The lack of naming scheme for publications resembles Linda *tuplespace*, but we neither allow removal of data from the IS nor
assume any structure for the data.

5   An Example Node Architecture

As an example, we show a possible language-neutral API that can also be interpreted as link-level protocol, that allow the access to an IS. We call this API an
Universal Information Interface (UII) and it has the following two operations
shown in Haskell-like syntax below:

```
class IS a where
    publish :: a -> Publication -> IO ()
    listen  :: a -> (Publication -> IO ()) -> IO ()
```

An application of the publish function with argument *data* is mapped to the
publish operation $p \in P$ for which $d(p) = data$ and $i(p) = x$, where the API
instance itself is mapped to $x \in I$. The Publication type here is simply a chunk
of binary data. The listen operation registers a callback for receiving publications from the IS and each callback invocation is mapped to a receive operation
of the IS similarly to the publish. All other functionality will be implemented on
top of the IS by publishing and receiving publications. This allows, for example,
extending the core to be able to handle publication of large sets of publications,
when it would be impractical to advertise them individually. In this case, the
application could publish the individual publications dynamically as a response
to certain types of matching subscription publications received.

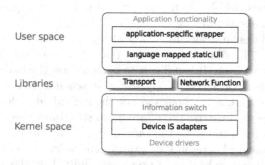

Fig. 2. New transports and network functions can be extended as dynamic libraries over a simple information switch with basic local forwarding semantics

In Fig. 2, an example node architecture, based on a kernel side *information switch* forwarding publications between local components, is shown. The switch itself understands only publications belonging to a simple forwarding ontology. A basic switch could, for example, understand *forwarding directives*, that instruct which interfaces should other publications be sent to. The switch itself could publish a simple map of its interfaces and external helpers would be responsible for mapping higher-level routing protocols to the forwarding directives executed by the switch. Alternatively, the switch can receive the forwarding publications along with the payload publications similar to packet headers. A caching component, for example, could publish a directive to forward everything through it. Even though IC will increase overhead by not exposing low-level optimizations, they would only help with a particular implementation technology.

Devices advertise their metadata and listen to directions via IS adapters attached to the central information switch. The node can be extended by new transports and network functions installed as dynamically linked libraries communicating with the information switch. Each network function implements a new abstraction to the IS, mostly in a layerless fashion and they can be installed on demand, on the fly based on the metadata describing their function. In the diagram, a statically linked, language mapped UII implementation is registered to the local information switch, which implements the kernel sided version of the UII. We assume that the raw UII will not be often exposed to application logic, but specific information ontologies are mapped to easy-to-use wrapper interfaces expressed using the natural idioms of the used language and application domain.

6   Development on Top of the Core

In the ICP, the development of new data vocabularies on top of the core is supposed to be mainly definition of 1. types and ontologies for data and metadata and 2. their semantics based on the framework provided by the IS definition. This is in contrast to the specification of protocol sequences between endpoints with specific roles. For example, instead of specifying a rendezvous architecture as interconnected nodes, we should fix the kind of publication types needed to exchange information about rendezvous.

Avoiding non-local design invariants is not always possible. For example, the efficient operation of a distributed hash table (DHT) is based on the top-down design of its routing algorithm. It is difficult to imagine how the individual nodes could be used as a part of a completely different scheme. Here the reusable pattern is the DHT routing as a whole and not the individual nodes. Therefore, it would be natural to parametrize the information structures used by the DHT to allow other applications to utilize the capabilities of the DHT.

The number of potential interactions grows quadratically as a function of the number of components, which were previously limited by the architectures they were part of. Turning the silent design-time invariants into explicit runtime metadata increases implementation effort upfront, increases overhead, and the modular functionality lacks the immediate security and optimization possibilities offered by monolithic solutions. However, as the amount of information-centric functionality grows past a critical mass, the network effect between the inter-working components may dominate the additional initial cost incurred.

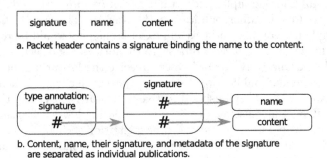

a. Packet header contains a signature binding the name to the content.

b. Content, name, their signature, and metadata of the signature are separated as individual publications.

Fig. 3. Low-level packet format vs. ontology

As a concrete example of how a low-level, non-information-centric, monolithic ICN architecture feature can be translated on top of our core, we use a simplified version of content integrity based on cryptographic signatures of the content. On the top in Fig. 3, we have a supposed packet format, that specifies that the signature of the content is carried in the header of the packet. Below, one possible mapping of this functionality to publication types on top of IC is given. A separate publication is used to store the signature of the content and it contains a cryptographic hash of the payload as a pointer. Similarly, a *run-time type annotation* publication describes the type of the signature publication by referring to it. Two of the above publications need to include the pointer to the data they talk about instead of the tight coupling of a packet format and the associated design-time assumption that the header and payload are connected.

We have now defined the needed publication types without fixing any low-level details such as the use of packet switching. The translated solution has the advantage that new, orthogonal security mechanisms can be simultaneously deployed as *aspects* or the signatures could be completely dropped in some environments. There is also more freedom in the implementation: For example, the signature publications could be mapped back to headers on the wire, or they could as well be cached or transported by some other means. Also, because the signatures are now ordinary publications, they can orthogonally benefit from other functions implemented such as error correction metadata and late-binding based information-centric problem solving. The core-based solutions are also more interoperable, as the security mechanism is specified abstractly and not entangled with the implementation of the core.

6.1   Managing Consistency with Scopes

In the object-oriented paradigm, when the remote state of a service is protected by an interface, the state is easy to keep consistent locally. In the information-centric setting, part of the system state can be shared in the IS as publications interpreted as *factoids*. In the Internet, the source of information can be a malicious party. These reasons contribute to the problem of managing consistency. Transactions are one possible solution to keep a shared state consistent by making the write operations potentially fail. However, this approach is too heavy to be required for all communication. Therefore, we assume that the publish operations always succeed and IC itself does not guarantee any inter-publication relationships. Different types of consistency models can be built on top of the core based on application needs using techniques such as automatic merging.

The basic IS can be enriched with scopes, that each contain a subset of the publications. Scopes can set constraints on their contents based on internal consistency of the data, trust, distribution strategy, or some application logic specific criteria. For example, a distributed algorithm operating on the the data in the IS can produce multiple potential solutions to a problem. Application could then search for the result in the IS and the result of this query could be viewed as one scope containing only the best solution found and related publications consistent with the selected solution. Thus, scopes can be dynamically created by limiting what information is relayed to the application by its request. Scopes can also be represented explicitly as information in the IS and generated by a 3rd party entity, such as a scope implementation in the PURSUIT architecture. For example, a metadata publication could mark which data items belong together.

7   Conclusion

ICN is not just about optimization of information dissemination, but a fundamental change in paradigm providing a natural substrate for information-centric computing. We have shown that basing ICN on a minimal, abstract core has advantages compared to the existing proposals: Using content security as an example of a feature extending the core, we achieved a solution, that does not depend on legacy concepts such as packets and is not entangled in a rigid architecture, but can immediately benefit from the information-centric model.

The benefits of the core still need to be balanced against the increased initial implementation effort, overhead, and the lack of optimization options offered by a monolithic architecture. The manageability of dynamic service composition and the incompatibility of confidentiality with the sharing of information remain open problems even though we sketched an initial solution based on scoping.

References

1. Jacobson, V., Smetters, D., Thornton, J., Plass, M., Briggs, N., Braynard, R.: Networking Named Content. In: ACM CoNEXT 2009 (2009)
2. Koponen, T., Chawla, M., Chun, B.G., Ermolinskiy, A., Kim, K.H., Shenker, S., Stoica, I.: A Data-Oriented (and Beyond) Network Architecture. In: SIGCOMM: Conference on Applications, Technologies, Architectures, and Protocols for Computer Communications, vol. 37, pp. 181–192 (2007)
3. Dannewitz, C., Golić, J., Ohlman, B., Bengt, A.: Secure Naming for a Network of Information. In: 13th IEEE Global Internet Symposium 2010 (2010)
4. Trossen, D., Parisis, G., Visala, K., Gajic, B., Riihijärvi, J., Flegkas, P., Sarolahti, P., Jokela, P., Vasilakos, X., Tsilopoulos, C., Arianfar, S.: PURSUIT Deliverable D2.2: Conceptual Architecture: Principles, patterns and sub-components descriptions. Technical report, PURSUIT (2011)
5. Ahlgren, B., Dannewitz, C., Imbrenda, C., Kutscher, D., Ohlman, B.: A Survey of Information-Centric Networking (Draft). In: Dagstuhl Seminar Proceedings (February 2011)
6. Handley, M.: Why the Internet only just works. BT Technology Journal 24(3), 119–129 (2006)
7. Dovrolis, C.: What would Darwin Think about Clean-Slate Architectures? ACM SIGCOMM Computer Communication Review 38(1), 29–34 (2008)
8. Akhshabi, S., Dovrolis, C.: The Evolution of Layered Protocol Stacks Leads to an Hourglass-Shaped Architecture. In: SIGCOMM 2011 (2011)
9. Ananthanarayanan, G., Heimerl, K., Demmer, M., Koponen, T., Tavakoli, A., Shenker, S., Stoica, I.: Enabling Innovation Below the Communication API. Technical report, University of California at Berkeley (October 2009)
10. Stoica, I., Adkins, D., Zhuang, S., Shenker, S., Surana, S.: Internet Indirection Infrastructure. In: SIGCOMM 2002 (2002)
11. Su, J., Scott, J., Hui, P., Crowcroft, J., de Lara, E., Diot, C., Goel, A., Lim, M.H., Upton, E.: Haggle: Seamless Networking for Mobile Applications. In: Krumm, J., Abowd, G.D., Seneviratne, A., Strang, T. (eds.) UbiComp 2007. LNCS, vol. 4717, pp. 391–408. Springer, Heidelberg (2007)
12. Filinski, A.: Declarative Continuations and Categorical Duality. Master's thesis, University of Copenhagen (August 1989)
13. Visala, K., Lagutin, D., Tarkoma, S.: Security design for an inter-domain publish/subscribe architecture. In: Domingue, J., et al. (eds.) Future Internet Assembly. LNCS, vol. 6656, pp. 167–176. Springer, Heidelberg (2011)

14. Narayanan, A., Oran, D.: NDN AND IP ROUTING - CAN IT SCALE? presentation in ICNRG side meeting, IETF-82, Taipei
15. Hewitt, C., Baker, H.: Laws for Communicating Parallel Processes. In: IFIP 1977 (1977)
16. Carpenter, B.: rfc1958: Architectural Principles of the Internet. Technical report, IETF (June 1996)

Managing QoS for Future Internet Applications
over Virtual Sensor Networks

Panagiotis Trakadas[1,*], Helen Leligou[2], Theodore Zahariadis[2], Panagiotis Karkazis[3],
and Lambros Sarakis[2]

[1] ADAE, Hellenic Authority of Communication Security and Privacy, Athens, Greece
`trakadasp@adae.gr`
[2] Dept. of Electrical Engineering, TEI of Chalkis, Psahna, Greece
`{zahariad,leligou,sarakis}@teihal.gr`
[3] Dept. of Electronic & Computer Engineering, Technical University of Crete, Greece
`pkarkazis@isc.tuc.gr`

Abstract. The integration of Wireless Sensor Networks (WSNs) in the Future Internet has opened new opportunities for novel applications that meet the needs of modern societies. Virtualisation of the available resources and the services offered by WSNs enables their efficient sharing between diverse applications reducing costs. Responding to this challenge, the VITRO project has designed a WSN virtualization architecture that targets to decouple the physical sensor infrastructure from the applications running on top of it. In the concept of Virtual Sensor Network platform, the WSNs are capable of collaborating among each other (even if they belong to different administrator domains or comprise of heterogeneous platforms) to flexibly support service composition and fuel novel application development. To meet the diverse Quality of Service (QoS) requirements imposed by the different applications running on top of the same infrastructure, VITRO has designed, implemented and integrated a routing solution that enables the establishment of different routing paths per application, based on different routing criteria in order to optimize the performance aspect(s) of interest to each application. In this paper, we demonstrate how the VITRO routing solution could be employed in various use cases including smart homes/buildings, smart cities, smart business environments and security-related applications. We evaluate the achieved performance using computer simulation results and provide guidelines for prospective users.

Keywords: wireless sensor networks, virtualization, routing, Quality of Service.

1   Introduction

Future Internet will interconnect trillions of devices, with a significant part being sensor nodes or nodes with sensing capabilities which cater information that enables the development of sophisticated applications towards meeting the needs of modern

---

* Contact information: Dr. Panagiotis Trakadas, ADAE, Hellenic Authority of Communication Security and Privacy, Athens, Greece, `trakadasp@adae.gr`

A. Galis and A. Gavras (Eds.): FIA 2013, LNCS 7858, pp. 52–63, 2013.

societies and citizens. The capability of re-purposing existing Wireless Sensor Networks (WSN) - in order to cope with different tasking functionality beyond the scope of the original sensor design and deployment - and of sharing the network resources can significantly accelerate the development and execution of new applications at significantly lower cost. Responding to this challenge, the notion of Virtual Sensor Networks (VSN) has been introduced, targeting to decouple the physical sensor deployment from the applications running on top of it. In this concept, WSNs are no longer deployed to support a specific service but are capable of collaborating among them towards realizing new services and applications.

The design and development of VSNs are at the center of the VITRO project which has developed a reference architecture [1] to enable the realization of a scalable, flexible, adaptive, energy-efficient and trust-aware Virtual Sensor Network platform. In this architecture, which uses the Internet (IPv6) as the physical bearer between sensor platforms and applications, sensors are deployed by potential (public or private) organizations and can then be used to feed information to applications deployed by other organizations. However, accommodating multiple services with different requirements (e.g. QoS, security) on a shared infrastructure, without predefined resource reservations, jeopardizes the experienced QoS acceptability. For this reason, VITRO has designed a routing solution [2]-[3] that supports QoS differentiation per application and complies with the RPL protocol (Routing Protocol for Low power and lossy networks) which has recently been standardized by IETF [4], providing a formal routing algebra framework for the proper composition of routing metrics.

In this paper, we showcase how the VITRO routing solution can be used to achieve QoS differentiation for applications running over the same WSN infrastructure and how the prospective user should exploit it to optimize the performance metric of interest in different real-life application domains. The rest of the paper is organized as follows: In section 2 we briefly describe the VITRO routing solution. In section 3, we present representative application domains where sensor network virtualization is of benefit and discuss how the VITRO routing solution can be used to achieve the QoS requirements in each use case. We also provide computer simulation results to explore the flexibility of our solution and draw guidelines on the use of the proposed routing framework from prospective users. The simulation results, presented in this paper, have been validated using the integrated VITRO platform. Finally, conclusions are reached in section 4.

2   The VITRO Routing Solution

To maximize exploitation potential, VITRO has decided to use standardized routing protocols as the basis for the design of a routing protocol that meets the needs of the Virtual Sensor Network concept. The so-called IPv6 Routing Protocol for Low power Lossy Networks (RPL) [4] has been standardized by the Routing Over Low power and Lossy networks (ROLL) working group of IETF. RPL provides a mechanism whereby multipoint-to-point traffic from devices inside the Low power and Lossy Network (LLN) is routed towards a central control point, as well as point-to multipoint traffic from the central control point to the devices inside the LLN. RPL constructs Directed Acyclic Graphs (DAG) and defines the rules based on which every node selects a neighbor as its parent in the DAG. To cover the diverse requirements imposed by different applications, ROLL has specified [5] a set of link and node routing metrics and constraints (which can be either static or dynamic), suitable to Low Power and Lossy link Networks that can be used in RPL.

For the construction of the DAG, each node calculates a Rank value and advertises it in the so-called Destination Information Object (DIO) messages. The Rank of a node is a scalar representation of the "location" of that node within a destination-oriented DAG (DODAG). In particular, the Rank of the nodes must monotonically decrease as the DODAG is followed towards the DAG destination (root). Each node selects as parent the neighbor that advertises the minimum rank value. This guarantees loop free operation and convergence. The rank has properties of its own that are not necessarily those of all metrics. It is the Objective Function (OF) that defines how routing metrics are used to compute the Rank, and as such must hold certain properties.

VITRO has proposed specific rules for quantifying five different routing metrics that capture different performance aspects and two different ways (namely the additive and lexicographic approaches) to combine them in composite routing metrics. In [2]-[3], we have also proved (using the well-established by Sobrinho et. al. routing algebra [6]) that the RPL protocol, utilizing the proposed primary and composite routing metrics, converges to optimal paths in a loop-free manner. The proposed routing metrics as well as the affected performance aspect are included in Table 1 [7].

Table 1. The VITRO primary routing metrics and the affected performance aspect

Primary routing metric	Routing operation	Affected performance metric
Hop Count (HC)	Shortest path	Low latency
Expected Transmission Count (ETX)	More reliable link with respect to layer 2 performance	Low packet loss - Low latency
Received Signal Strength Indication (RSSI)	More reliable link with respect to sig-nal strength (does not take into account congestion)	Increased reliability with respect to transmissions successfully received by neighbours, high latency
Packet Forwarding Indication (PFI)	Selection of the most reliable neighbour for forwarding traffic packets	Efficient detection of misbehaving nodes, low packet loss due to misbehaviours
Remaining Energy (RE)	Avoids systematically using the same neighbours for forwarding, leading to energy depletion	Network lifetime elongation

VITRO capitalizes on an important feature of RPL which is the support of different DODAG instances. RPL defines that different DODAG instances can co-exist over the same infrastructure and each instance can be formed based on different routing metrics thus enabling the optimization of different performance aspects. As shown in Figure 1, the infrastructure (shown at the bottom of the figure) consisting of eight (8) nodes is used to form two different VSNs supporting two different applications. Different routing metrics, reflected in different Objective Functions, can be used to guide the construction of each DODAG to optimize different performance aspects. As shown in Figure 1, depending on the supported OFs, each node can participate in one or two VSNs, constructing two separate but concurrent routing graphs. (The objective functions OF0 MRHOF are defined in [8] and [9] respectively.)

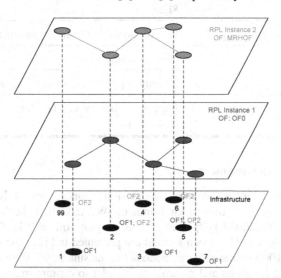

Fig. 1. Two VSN instantiations within the same WSI

3   Applications Exploiting Virtualization of WSNs

As virtualization targets the re-usability of sensing devices for different purposes, it is important to identify the routing metrics (primary or composite) that better match specific application domains. Our aim is to define implementable rules and thus enable effective exploitation of the potential of the VITRO routing solution for a wide set of applications. Thus, further and in-depth investigation on routing metrics composition methods and individual weights for satisfying specific QoS requirements arising from the specific application areas under examination will be presented, supported by results obtained through simulation.

The application domains selected by the VITRO consortium and used to define application and system requirements are included in Table 2. Each application requires either service virtualization, or resource virtualization or service composition or any combination of the previous.

Table 2. Indicative application domains exploiting VSN capabilities

Application Domain	Application
Energy control in public and private buildings	Energy efficient smart schools/buildings
	Energy efficient homes
Traffic control	Traffic light control
	City traffic management through Variable Message Signs
Logistics	Product monitoring in the production to sales chain
Security	Disaster management
	Security in public spaces and buildings
	Baggage proximity checker for security and theft prevention

3.1 Simulation Environment

Before proceeding with the analysis of the simulation results, it is necessary to describe the employed simulation environment. We modelled the VITRO routing solution based on the JSIM [10] open simulation platform and the features of our simulator (available in [11] as open source) are presented in [12]. The network topology consisted of 1000 nodes with one node acting as sink node. We ran several tests with different configurations and parameters in order to capture many characteristics of the network. In detail, tests have been performed for 50, 100, 200 and 500 sessions (number of nodes generating sensing data and sending them to the sink node). This provided the ability to check the network performance under low and high traffic conditions. In all tests, the sensing nodes were kept the same (mainly positioned in the perimeter of the network topology), while the rest of the nodes were randomly placed for each set of tests. Moreover, we ran different tests for several number of misbehaving (either acting maliciously or simply malfunctioning) nodes (50, 100, and 150), uniformly distributed over the network and equally split among a variety of possible misbehaving situations (reduced transmission power, security enabled, missed ACKs, not forwarding packets, etc.). The performance metrics we focused on were latency and packet loss percentage.

3.2 Energy Control in Public and Private Buildings

As energy consumption control is an ultimate priority of our society, applications that collect energy demand information in order to intelligently schedule the energy consumption. The sensors are deployed in buildings (e.g. schools, office buildings and homes) and usually need to detect human and device activities through sensing devices which can be of different technology, possibly initially installed for different reasons (e.g. security). In such situations, VITRO developments offer seamless access to all sensing entities.

For this type of applications, performance optimisation should deal with reducing latency and extending network lifetime to efficiently tackle scalability issues arising in such networks, as the number of nodes may reach thousands in large business environments. Thus, we consider that the routing metric of interest includes composite routing metrics based on either (HC, RE) or (RSSI, RE). For each pair of metrics, we have tested their lexicographical combination and their combination in a weighted sum for different weight values. The results with respect to packet latency for (HC, RE) and (RSSI, RE) combinations are shown in Figure 2.

From Figure 2 it can be observed that, in general, the lexicographic approach incurs less latency, compared to the additive approaches, since path related attributes (namely HC and RSSI) are inspected with absolute priority over RE. Comparing latency values between (HC, RE) and (RSSI, RE) combinations, a non-negligible difference is observed (almost double). This is explained as the path in (RSSI, RE) case is longer and traverses a higher number of nodes. This is because under the RSSI metric, a node prefers as a parent a node being closer (larger value of advertised transmission power) having a direct impact on the length of the traversed path measured in number of hops. Additionally, adopting RSSI as the primary routing metric implies that for the transmission of a message a total number of transmissions in the network is higher than in the case where HC is adopted. As a conclusion, either a lexical (HC, RE) combination or an additive (HC, RE) approach where the RE metric weighting factor will not exceed 0.4 is the optimal choice for this application domain.

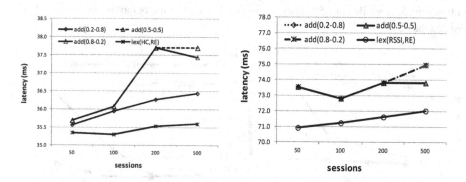

Fig. 2. Simulation results for additive and lexicographic (HC, RE) metric composition on the left and (RSSI, RE) metric composition on the right in terms of latency for 50 misbehaving nodes in the network

3.3   Traffic Control Application Domain

The city traffic management and the traffic light control applications can be considered as representative examples of applications using the same sensing nodes. To manage the city traffic and control the traffic lights, information such as the dynamically changing traffic conditions, the environmental conditions (e.g. temperature, humidity, CO_2 emissions) has to be collected. It is obvious that this type of information is of interest to a great variety of stakeholders/authorities, from municipality to environment related authorities. VITRO makes possible their re-use to save budgets and space in the sidewalk.

In applications such as traffic light control and traffic management through variable message signs, the requirements are quite different from the previous case. More specifically, these applications require a high level of security along with a minimization of latency. Providing traffic control and management requires that measurements and signals must be delivered without delay and with a minimum packet loss percentage. As this is a delay-sensitive application, RSSI is not appropriate. Instead, HC and PFI (which is a security related metric defined in [3] are selected.

The results for different composite metrics of HC and PFI are included in Figures 3 and 4 for 50 and 150 misbehaving nodes respectively. Observing Figure 3, it is obvious that the lexicogaphic combination of PFI and HC results in significantly higher latency and packet loss than all the additive composition metrics approach, because, as it is related solely with neighbour forwarding reliability, it does not manage to guide the construction of a path to the destination. For this reason, we have excluded lex(PFI, HC) from Figure 4.

Comparing the two figures, it is evident, as expected, that the performance degrades as the number of misbehaving nodes increases in terms of both latency and packet loss. For 50 misbehaving nodes, for any number of sessions the latency remains lower than 36ms while for 150 misbehaving nodes the latency reaches the values of 37,5ms. More importantly, the packet loss for 50 misbehaving nodes reamins well below 20% while for 150 misbehaving nodes (called misbehaving nodes), packet loss reaches 23%.

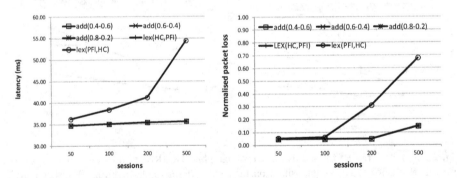

Fig. 3. Latency (left) and packet loss (right) results for additive and lexicographic (HC, PFI) approaches for varying number of sessions in the presence of 50 misbehaving nodes

Apart from the lexicographic (PFI, HC) composite routing metric, the inclusion of PFI in the objective function leads to the efficient detection of misbehaving nodes. It is worth pointing out that the existence of even one misbehaving node on the path, would result in 100% packet loss for all flows traversing this node in the absence of PFI metric. Taking into account PFI, the packet loss is kept below 25% even when

150 misbehaving packet exist in the network and the number of active sessions reach 500 (as shown in Figure 4, right hand side).

The results reveal that any combination of HC and PFI in additive manner leads to stable performance and the weighting factors slightly affect the achieved performance.

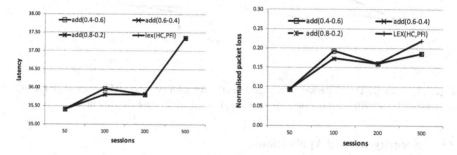

Fig. 4. Latency (left) and packet loss (right) results for additive and lexicographic (HC, PFI) approaches for a varying number of sessions in the presence of 100 misbehaving nodes

3.4   Logistics Applications

The domain of logistics is constantly increasing its indices in Europe with product monitoring being at the focal point of this application area. The automated monitoring of the product saves significant time and hence cost for searching products in wide and distributed even among different cities warehouses.

The applications running on top of the sensing infrastructures require high reliability in an area of dense WSNs and long system lifetime. To meet these requirements, the use of a composite routing metric combining ETX (to minimize retransmissions in this dense environment) and remaining energy (to prolong the network lifetime) is proposed.

The performance results for combinations of ETX and RE routing metrics are depicted in Figure 5. It is observed that the additive approaches perform better than lexicographic ones, for both latency and packet loss performance metrics, even for high traffic cases (high number of active sessions). The observed packet loss is attributed to the absence of a security routing metric (PFI) in the presence of misbehaving nodes. As a result, nodes suppressing data packets cannot be detected and thus, excluded from forwarding. Instead, link reliability as well as distributed energy consumption drives the routing decision. Compared to the previous use case, where link reliability was not taken into account, latency in this case is significantly decreased, as dictated by ETX.

The general remark in this case is that, as the number of sessions increases, both packet loss and latency increase. This occurs, as more sessions result in increased traffic, which is followed by packet collisions causing packet loss.

To reach a conclusion, an additive approach of weighting factors (0.8, 0.2) performs quite well in all cases.

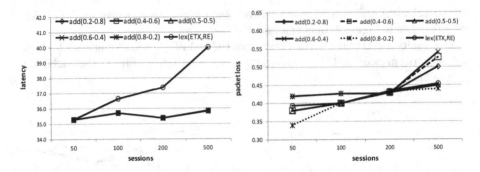

Fig. 5. Latency (left) and packet loss (right) results for additive and lexicographic (ETX, RE) approaches for varying number of session in the presence of 50 misbehaving nodes

3.5   Security-Related Applications

Security in public areas as well as disaster management is a critical application area, where the fundamental criterion is the trust-awareness of the deployed nodes, followed by link reliability maximization. For this reason, in this application domain we consider the combination of PFI and ETX as a suitable proposition. Hence, PFI followed by ETX and RE will be used, considering that the network lifetime in these situations is also important.

The results for combinations of PFI, ETX, RE are depicted in Figures 6 and 7 for 50 and 150 misbehaving nodes respectively. (The lex(PFI, ETX, RE) approach leads to high latency and packet loss as already explained in previous sections and for this reason is left out of our investigation.)

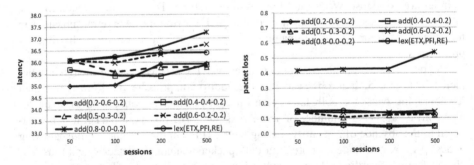

Fig. 6. Latency (left) and packet loss (right) results for additive and lexicographic (PFI, ETX, RE) approaches for varying number of session in the presence of 50 misbehaving nodes

The additive composite routing metric with weights equal to 0.8, 0 and 0.2 respectively, (essentially not inspecting PFI) leads to significantly higher packet loss than any other combination, and is considered not acceptable. For all other more "balanced" solutions, the performance differences are not impressive. However, the weight vector 0.4, 0.4 and 0.2 leads to an optimal performance both in terms of latency and packet loss, performing better than the lex(ETX, PFI, RE) approach.

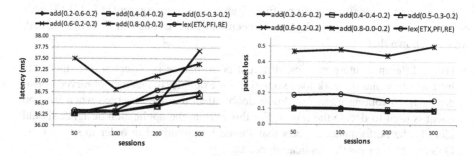

Fig. 7. Latency (left) and packet loss (right) results for additive and lexicographic (PFI, ETX, RE) approaches for varying number of session in the presence of 150 misbehaving nodes

The same qualitative results are observed for 150 misbehaving nodes, as depicted in Figure 7. Again, the additive composition approach with strong weight assigned to ETX and not taking into account PFI (i.e. weight vector equal to 0.8, 0, 0.2) leads to high latency and packet loss. The best performance for both latency and packet loss is observed for the additive composite metric with weight equal to 0.4, 0.4 and 0.2 respectively.

Comparing Figures 6 and 7, we can conclude that the existence of more misbehaving nodes affects mainly the packet loss than the latency. The latency slightly increases as the misbehaving nodes increase (since the traffic has to travel longer paths to avoid misbehaving nodes), while comparing the best packet loss for 50 and 150 misbehaving nodes, a difference of 5% has been measured.

4   Conclusions

In this paper, we have discussed the implications of current networking trends on Wireless Sensor Networks and more specifically, we have focused on the trend to use the deployed WSN infrastructure to support additional (most probably different) applications than the originally targeted. To efficiently implement the Virtual Sensor Networking paradigm over the resource constrained WSN substrate, Quality of Service handling is mandatory.

Although during the last decade large number of routing protocols and an even larger number of routing metrics have been proposed, these have targeted the satisfaction of network and application-specific QoS and operational requirements. In the framework of the VITRO project, we have designed a RPL-based routing solution which enables the construction of different paths between any pair of nodes to be followed by traffic from different applications to better satisfy the QoS needs of each application. To do so, different routing metrics are adopted per application for the definition of the corresponding path. Furthermore, considering that each application may demand the optimization of more than one performance aspect, we have defined routing metric and metric composition approaches that can serve diverse application requirements while guaranteeing convergence to optimal paths.

Based on the formally defined routing algebra formalism, presented in [2]-[3] and-computer simulation results which have been validated through the VITRO testbed, we have shown that:

1. Using different routing metrics, different performance is observed over the same infrastructure and network load scenario. For example, the latency observed considering RSSI routing metric is almost double than the one observed when the hop count is used to decide the routes. For this reason, the application designer should identify the performance aspects that should be optimized in order to support the QoS that better suits the application needs.

2. In case that more than one performance aspects need to be optimized, there are two ways to combine two or more routing metrics: the lexical and the additive approach, where for the additive approach we consider that weight factors can regulate the emphasis placed on each primary routing metric. The additive approach leads to a more "balanced" performance and is thus considered a proper solution for a system designer. The lexical composition approach is suitable in cases when one wishes to optimize two aspects but there is a strict priority of one over the other.

3. For delay sensitive applications, such as the energy consumption control applications, the combination of HC and RE satisfies the QoS requirements. Namely, either a lexical (HC, RE) combination or an additive (HC, RE) approach, where the RE metric weighting factor will not exceed 0.4 is the optimal choice for this application domain.

4. For applications sensitive on security threats and delay performance, such as the traffic control applications over a city, the HC and the trust-related (PFI) metric need to be combined. More specifically, any combination of HC and PFI in additive manner leads to stable performance and the weighting factors slightly affect the achieved performance.

5. For applications sensitive to link reliability, such as the applications targeting the logistics domain (and product localization in large areas), the combination of ETX and RE is suitable with an additive approach (using weighting factors equal to (0.8, 0.2) performs quite well in all cases).

6. Finally, for application sensitive to link reliability and security, as is the case where WSNs are used for security in public areas and disaster management, the trust-related PFI metric has to be combined with ETX (for link reliability) and RE for prolonged network lifetime. In this case, the best performance in terms of both latency and packet loss is observed for the additive composite metric with weight equal to 0.4, 0.4 and 0.2 respectively.

To this end, it is obvious that there is not a "one-fits-all" solution if WSNs are shared between multiple applications with diverse requirements. If the system is lightly loaded and no misbehaving nodes exist, then adopting simply the hop count metric would satisfy all requirements, but this is a rather simplistic approach, contradicting the assumption that the WSN will be shared among multiple applications. On the other hand, combining all the defined routing metrics would result in lack of emphasis on specific performance aspects. Prospective users/designers should take into account the above provided guidelines to achieve their goals.

Acknowledgment. The work presented in this paper was partially supported by the EU-funded FP7 211998 VITRO project.

References

1. Sarakis, L., Zahariadis, T., Leligou, H.C., Dohler, M.: A Framework for Service Provisioning in Virtual Sensor Networks. EURASIP Journal on Wireless Communications and Networking (April 2012), doi:10.1186/1687-1499-2012-135
2. Karkazis, P., Trakadas, P., Leligou, H.C., Sarakis, L., Papaefstathiou, I., Zahariadis, T.: Evaluating routing metric composition approaches for QoS differentiation in low power and lossy networks. In: Wireless Networks. Springer, doi:10.1007/s11276-012-0532-2.
3. Velivasaki, T.-H., Karkazis, P., Zahariadis, T., Trakadas, P., Capsalis, C.: Trust-aware and Link-reliable routing metric composition for Wireless sensor networks. Transactions on Emerging Telecommunications Technologies (October 11, 2012), doi:10.1002/ett.2592
4. IETF, RFC6550. RPL: IPv6 Routing Protocol for Low power and Lossy Networks, http://tools.ietf.org/rfc/rfc6550.txt (accessed November 8, 2012)
5. Vasseur, J.P., et al.: IETF, RFC6551. Routing Metrics used for Path Calculation in Low Power and Lossy Networks, http://tools.ietf.org/html/rfc6551 (accessed November 8, 2012)
6. Sobrinho, J.L.: Algebra and algorithms for QoS path computation and hop-by-hop routing in the Internet. IEEE/ACM Trans. Netw. 10(4), 541–550 (2002)
7. Zahariadis, T., Trakadas, P.: Design Guidelines for Routing Metrics Composition in LLN. draft-zahariadis-roll-metrics-composition-04 (November 23, 2012)
8. IETF, RFC 6552, Objective Function Zero for the Routing Protocol for Low-Power and Lossy Networks, RPL (March 2012)
9. IETF, RFC 6719, The Minimum Rank with Hysteresis Objective Function (September 2012)
10. J-Sim official web site (2005), http://code.google.com/p/rpl-jsim-platform/
11. Karkazis, P., Trakadas, P., Zahariadis, T., Hatziefremidis, A., Leligou, H.C.: RPL Modeling in J-Sim Platform. In: 9th International Conference on Networked Sensing Systems (2012)

High Availability in the Future Internet

Levente Csikor, Gábor Rétvári, and János Tapolcai

MTA-BME Future Internet Research Group
High Speed Networks Laboratory
Dept. of Telecommunications and Media Informatics
Budapest University of Technology and Economics,
Magyar tudósok körútja 2., H-1117 Budapest, Hungary
{csikor,retvari,tapolcai}@tmit.bme.hu

Abstract. With the evolution of the Internet, a huge number of real-time applications, like Voice over IP, has started to use IP as primary transmission medium. These services require high availability, which is not amongst the main features of today's heterogeneous Internet where failures occur frequently. Unfortunately, the primary fast resilience scheme implemented in IP routers, Loop-Free Alternates (LFA), usually does not provide full protection against failures. Consequently, there has been a growing interest in LFA-based network optimization methods, aimed at tuning some aspect of the underlying IP topology to maximize the ratio of failure cases covered by LFA. The main goal of this chapter is to give a comprehensive overview of LFA and survey the related LFA network optimization methods, pointing out that these optimization tools can turn LFA into an easy-to-deploy yet highly effective IP fast resilience scheme.

Keywords: IP Fast ReRoute, network optimization, remote loop-free alternates, reliable networks, protection, failures.

1   Introduction

Current Internet has reached the level of reliability, where Internet and cloud services are widely spreading among users. This gives an increasing push on the service providers to operate the Internet without any interruption and slowly win the trust of most of the potential users. We expect that the reliability of IP networks will further improve in the future, and Internet will become a critical infrastructure for the society. Reliability means that at any given time the connection is ensured throughout the network, and a failure is handled so fast that virtually no packet loss is noticed by the end-users.

Nowadays, not just Internet Service Providers (ISPs) and end-users are concerned, but many other multimedia suppliers started to gain a foothold in this field and broadcast digital content over the IP (Internet Protocol). Moreover, traditional telephony is already being replaced by IP based telephony in order to reduce costs and provide more options, e.g., send text, media and data simultaneously during the phone call. Due to this continuous technical change and digital convergence (collectively referred to as information and communication

A. Galis and A. Gavras (Eds.): FIA 2013, LNCS 7858, pp. 64–76, 2013.

technologies [42]), a huge number of (real-time) multimedia applications use IP network as primary transmission medium, which is the first driving force for a more reliable IP communication infrastructure. Furthermore, not just the scope of contents is growing but the number of the newly connected consumers and terminal equipments as well. The population in the world is currently growing at a rate of around 1.10% per year, and the expected population will be 8 billion in 2025[1]. Today, about two billion people are using the Internet, while six billion people are already a subscriber of some mobile services at the end of 2011 [25]. What is more, in the near future not only human beings will be connected to the Internet all the time, but many machines used day by day will have unique IP addresses and will be accessible from anywhere. This will lead to an emerging communication form, called M2M (Machine-to-Machine), which will likely generate a huge part of total traffic. Moreover, due to the evolution of mobile infrastructure, most of the new users will access all the digital content through their smartphones, increasing the traffic that has to be delivered at the same time. Through the development of already used entertainment services, for instance, television broadcasting and Video on Demand (VoD), two-thirds of the world's mobile traffic will be video by 2016. Note that not just mobile phones account for mobile traffic, since in 2011 the number of mobile-connected tablets reached 34 million, and each tablet generated 3.4 times more traffic than smartphones [10]. Cisco has fore-casted that, if not just mobile users are considered, then *almost 90% of all consumer traffic will account for real-time video broadcasting*, e.g., IPTV, P2P streaming, VoD. Since the improving quality of the content (e.g., High Definition movies, 4K, lossless audio coding) involves a growing size of media streams, the aforementioned proportion will likely grow even further. Necessarily, the Internet has to keep up with these real-time applications, which require continuous and reliable connections. Consequently, if a link or node fails in the network, it does not only cause routing instability, but a whacking portion of the traffic will be lost. Note that low latency is substantial for the standard Internet applications as well [50].

Therefore, high availability has become an all-important factor in operational networks. However, studies over the past decade have shown that the reliability of Internet falls short of the five nines (99.999%) availability, which is readily available in the public-switched telephone network (PSTN) [28]. Note that reliability plays an important role in pure mobile networks too, since an average user will be more satisfied with a constant guaranteed access speed than a, however high, abruptly fluctuating service in densely populated areas [18]. If high availability were always provided, this would open the door for completely new opportunities. For instance, imagine that in the future a qualified doctor could easily and uninterruptedly treat a patient thousands of miles away through remote surgery, by the means of the basic communication network.

Availability in the Internet is severely plagued by component failures that occur frequently due to various reasons, such as physical interruptions, flapping

---

[1] http://www.worldometers.info/world-population/ (accessed in Jan 2013)

interfaces[2], etc. To overcome these issues, the IETF (Internet Engineering Task Force) defined a native IP fast resilience framework, called IP Fast ReRoute (IPFRR [44]), and a basic IPFRR specification called Loop-Free Alternates (LFA [4]). LFA, however, has a substantial drawback in that it cannot protect every possible failure case. Recently, a generalization of LFA has been published, called Remote Loop-Free Alternates (rLFA [5]), which can provide higher protection, but still has limitations evading the possibility to have an ultimate solution. Many IPFRR proposals have appeared to vanquish this, but due to the additional complexity implementation and deployment of these proposals have been rather scarce so far (see Sec. 2 for details). This leads ISPs to rely completely on the only IPFRR scheme available in IP routers today, LFA, and investigate network optimization techniques to adapt their topology to provide the best protection with LFA possible.

The aim of this chapter is to overview the evolution of Internet from reliability perspective. In particular, we focus on the intriguing questions of fast IP resilience. In Section 2, we review former IPFRR proposals and their disadvantages. Afterwards, in Section 3 we show how LFA works and then, in Section 4, we present a deeper analysis of failure case coverage provided by LFA and we discuss how this can be improved with emerging LFA network optimization techniques. We extend these results to the emerging Remote LFA IPFRR specification in Section 5. At last but not least, in Section 6 we conclude our message and sketch up further questions that need to be investigated and solved in the future.

2   Related Work and Background

In operational networks more than 85% of unplanned failures affect only links and almost the half of them are transient [35], i.e., 50% of all failures last less than a minute [23]. In order to reduce the latency and increase the reliability, additional network functionality is essential to recognize the failure and reroute the affected packets rapidly around the failed component.

Formerly, failures were handled by the intra-domain routing protocols, such as OSPF (Open Shortest Path First [38]) or IS-IS (Intermediate System To Intermediate System [24]). After a failure, the information about it was distributed throughout the network so that every router can recalculate the shortest paths with the failed component removed. This process is called re-convergence, and, depending on network size and routers' shortest path calculation efficiencies, it can take between 150 ms and a couple of seconds [30,26]. It is obvious that this is beyond what real-time applications can afford, even if a small delay can be tolerated via buffering.

To overcome these issues, the IETF (Internet Engineering Task Force) defined a framework, called IP Fast ReRoute (IPFRR [44]), for native IP protection in order to reduce failure reaction time to tens of milliseconds. It tries to avoid the global re-convergence with *local rerouting* and *pre-computed detours*, converting

---

[2] A hardware or software failure of an interface can cause the router to announce it alternately as "up" and "down".

the reaction scheme of standard IP networks into faster proactive protection mechanisms [46]. The matter of these approaches is that the router adjacent to the failure tries to solve the problem individually by means of pre-computed alternate routing tables, which are installed long before any failure occurs.

As one of the first approach, a basic specification for IPFRR was defined by the IETF, called Loop-free Alternates (LFA [4]), which is simple, standardized and already available in today's routers [48,27]. In LFA, when a failure occurs, the adjacent router tries to pass the packet to an alternate neighbor, who still has a functioning path to the destination. However, such neighbor does not always exist, evading LFA for providing 100% failure case coverage in every network.

Therefore, in the past few years many IPFRR proposals have appeared, but the majority of them require additional management burden, complexity and non-standard functionality in IP forwarding and routing protocols. Some of them change the traditional IP's destination based forwarding [32,51,16,3], while others use signaling to indicate that a packet is on detour [22,11,1,49,31,33]. On the other hand, there are methods, which use explicit tunneling to avoid the failed components [7,17,36,6]. Proposals in [43,37] have topological requirements, whilst the mechanism proposed in [29] uses a central server to pre-compute forwarding decisions for common failure scenarios and download them into the routers. Accordingly, at the moment none of these proposals is available in IP routers, since they need modifications to the existing protocols, making LFA the only deployable option for ISPs.

In order to improve the level of fast protection provided by LFA, the IETF has published a generalization called Remote LFA (rLFA) [5]. This method provides additional backup connectivity when none can be provided by the basic mechanism. However, even though rLFA can provide higher reliability, it still inherits topology dependence from pure LFA, and thus providing 100% failure case coverage with pure IP remains to be an open question.

3 Providing Fast Protection with LFAs

Probably, the easiest way to understand how basic LFA and remote LFA work, is through an example. Consider the network depicted in Fig. 1, where all links have unit costs. Suppose that node e wants to send a packet to node d' and its default next-hop[3] f is unreachable, since the link between them went down. In this case, e has to find an alternate neighbor, which will not pass the packet back, i.e., which still has a path to the destination unaffected by the failure. Fortunately, node b fulfills this requirement, so e can reroute the traffic destined to d, towards b. Next, suppose that node s wishes to send packets to node d and eventually link (s, a) fails. Now, s can only reach node b. However, since node b has an ECMP (Equal Cost Multiple Path) to node d and it does not know about the failure, it can pass the packet back to s causing a loop. Therefore, this failure case cannot be protected with simple LFA. However, if a tunnel existed between node s and

---

[3] In IP routing, the next router along the shortest path to a destination is called *next-hop*.

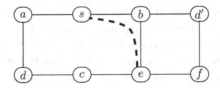

Fig. 1. A sample network topology with uniform link costs. Solid lines mark the IP network topology, while black dashed line marks the tunnel

e (marked by a black dashed line in Fig. 1), then node e, now being an indirect neighbor of s, would become a LFA for d, thereby protecting the link (s, a). Consequently, when a link cannot be entirely protected with local LFA neighbors, the protecting routers try to seek the help of a remote LFA staging point. This repair tunnel endpoint needs to be a node in the network reachable from the source without traversing the failed component. Furthermore, the repair tunnel endpoint needs to be a node from which packets will normally flow towards their destinations without being attracted back to the failed component. These supplementary logical links, used be remote LFA, are provided by tunnels.

Accordingly, after the remote node receives the package, it sends it towards the primary destination. Note that these tunnels are provided by a simple label stack in an MPLS/LDP (Multiprotocol Label Switching/Label Distribution Protocol) [2] enabled network, which is practically relevant nowadays. However, there exist MPLS networks with RSVP–TE (Reservation Protocol–Traffic Engineering) extension, wherein IPFRR is not the only option for fast protection [39,21]. On the other hand, suppose now that node s wants to send a packet to node d', and the link (s, b) fails. Then, (s, b) cannot be protected for a lack of a suitable tunnel since all nodes, whose shortest paths are unaffected by the failure, can only be reached from s through the failed (s, b) itself. This suggests that while the use of rLFA can definitely provide higher protection level than pure LFA, it still does not facilitate full protection for all failure cases in a general.

4   Analyzing and Improving LFA-Based Fast Protection

The most important question concerning LFA is to *analyze how it performs in different network topologies*, what are the fundamental lower and upper bounds of failure case coverage, and *how protection coverage could be improved*.

The authors of [41] made the first steps in this direction, in that they gave a graph-theoretical characterization of LFA protection efficiency. To measure this LFA efficiency in an arbitrary network graph G, the following LFA failure coverage metric is defined [4,41]:

$$\eta(G) = \frac{\#\text{LFA protected source-destination pairs}}{\#\text{all source-destination pairs}} \tag{1}$$

The rLFA failure case coverage $\mu(G)$ can be defined in a similar way.

Table 1. LFA graph extension results for link protection

Topology			Uniform cost		Weighted	
Name	n	m	η_0	Gr_η	η_0	Gr_η
AS1221	7	9	0.833	1	0.809	2
AS3257	27	64	0.946	3	0.923	11
AS6461	17	37	0.919	2	0.933	4
Abilene	12	15	0.56	6	0.56	8
Italy	33	56	0.784	13	0.784	20
Germany	27	32	0.695	5	0.695	12
AT&T	22	38	0.823	6	0.823	13
Germ_50	50	88	0.801	22	0.9	21

The authors in [41] observe that the quintessential worst-case graphs for IPFRR are rings, i.e., cycle graphs wherein all nodes are of degree two [16,8]. In particular, the LFA failure case coverage in an arbitrary 2-connected network is bounded by $\frac{1}{n-1} \leq \eta(G) \leq 1$, and the lower bound is attained for even rings. In a special case, where all links have unit costs, full LFA protection, i.e., $\eta(G) = 1$ can only be reached if every link is contained in at least one triangle[4]. This suggests that complete graphs, chordal graphs [20] and maximal planar graphs have full LFA coverage in the uniform cost case. If arbitrary link costs are taken into account, then the aforementioned condition is even more stricter [41]. However, the latter condition is only sufficient, but not necessary.

As a way of an improvement, the so called *LFA graph extension* problem was also studied in [41], which asks for augmenting the network with the fewest number of new links in order to reach 100% LFA coverage. For example, if the network depicted in Fig. 1 is augmented with 4 new links (namely, (s, d), (b, d), (d, e), and (d', e)), then every link will be contained in at least one triangle, i.e., $\eta(G)$ will be 1.

Unfortunately, adding unit cost links to the network cannot always be afforded by network operators, since it will definitely change at least one shortest path, which might have been previously tweaked with great accuracy to match the needs of the network in terms of load balancing, traffic engineering, etc. [19,47]. In order to prevent this, it was suggested in [41] that the cost of the new link should be larger than the length of the longest shortest path. With this in mind, the example network (Fig. 1) should be augmented with 6 new links with sufficiently high costs in order to attain full protection. Finding the smallest number of additional new links proved a very hard problem, i.e., it is NP-complete [41]. Therefore, an Integer Linear Program (ILP) and an approximating greedy heuristic were developed to solve this problem.

The algorithms were studied in real-world network topologies inferred from Rocketfuel dataset [34] and SNDLib [45]. Succinct results are shown in Table 1,

---

[4] Triangle is a cycle of length 3.

where n denotes the number of nodes, while m indicates the number of links in the network. The initial LFA coverage is marked by η_0, and Gr_η denotes the number of new links added by the greedy heuristic[5] in order to attain full LFA coverage. First observation is that in each link cost case, on average the initial LFA coverage is about 80% and never reaches 100%. For smaller topologies, a few number of new links have to be added to reach full protection, while in larger and sparser networks this number is significantly more. In particular, in the German backbone ca. one fourth of the number of links originally existing have to be added. Additionally, more links are needed for full coverage in weighted networks than in uniform cost graphs. The main conclusion of these results is that some networks readily lend themselves to LFA graph extension, and in many cases adding only 2-4 new links can boost up the LFA failure case coverage close to 100%.

In a subsequent study [40], another improving approach, called the *LFA cost optimization* problem, was examined. The problem asks for finding an optimal cost setting in a network, which produces 100% failure case coverage. This problem proved NP-complete as well. The complexity directly comes from the fact that shortest paths change during the optimization process, therefore it is possible that altering a link cost can provide protection for a certain source-destination pair, but it may eliminate LFAs to other destinations. For instance, consider network depicted in Fig. 1 again and suppose that node c wants to send a packet to node e and the link between them fails. This failure cannot be protected in the current link cost setting, since node d, the only available neighbor of c, will pass the packet back. However, if the cost of the link (c, d) would be, say 4, then d would route the affected traffic to a detour, since its next-hop towards e would be a. By means of this small modification, the initial LFA failure coverage can be improved by 15%. Additionally, it was also proved in [40] that the average node degree Δ plays an important role to determine the attainable upper bound of LFA failure coverage. As a matter of fact, for any connected graph G with $n > 2$:

$$\eta(G) \leq \tfrac{n}{n-1}(\Delta - 2) + \tfrac{2}{n-1} \ .$$

This suggests that in a large but sparse networks (i.e., where $\Delta < 3$), the protection provided by LFA can be very poor.

In order to solve LFA cost optimization problem, a computationally expensive optimal algorithm as well as efficient approximating heuristics were proposed [40,15]. A brief result can be seen in Table 2, where n and m denote the number of nodes and the number of links in the network, respectively. The column Δ indicates the average node degree of the network, while $\eta(G, c)$ marks the initial LFA coverage. At last but no least, $\eta(G, c*)$ represents the LFA coverage reached by cost optimization. One can easily observe that in most cases, chiefly when the average node degree is higher than 3.5, close to perfect LFA coverage can be attained. There were, however, some exceptional topologies where LFA

---

[5] Since the greedy heuristic is faster and it performs almost the same as the ILP, in this paper we concentrated on the greedy approach exclusively.

Table 2. LFA cost optimization results for link protection

Topology				Cost optimization	
Name	n	m	Δ	$\eta(G, c)$	$\eta(G, c*)$
AS1221	7	9	2.57	0.809	0.833
AS3257	27	64	4.74	0.923	1
AS6461	17	37	4.35	0.933	1
Abilene	12	15	2.50	0.56	0.674
Italy	33	56	3.39	0.784	0.944
Germany	27	32	2.94	0.695	0.911
AT&T	22	38	3.45	0.823	0.987
Germ_50	50	88	3.52	0.9	0.966

cost optimization was less appealing. For such networks, combining LFA cost optimization with LFA graph extension could be a viable option.

Since both methods are effective ways of improving LFA coverage in operational networks, the question promptly arises as to what extent the combination of these two approaches can be effective for LFA-based network optimization. However, it is not obvious how these methods should be set together, in particular, how many links should be added and when should cost optimization be executed. The authors in [12] investigated just these questions. They showed by extensive simulations that the combination of the approaches performs the best if we only add 1 new link at a time and then execute a round of cost optimization. These two phases should follow each other until 100% LFA failure case coverage is attained. Their results suggest that the combined algorithm can significantly reduce the number of additional links (on average by more than 50%) necessary for reaching full protection with LFA providing an intermediate solution.

5   Improving Fast Protection with Remote LFA

The wide spectrum of LFA network optimization strategies presented so far provide a rich set of options for operators to choose from, according to their own preference on whether it is economically more feasible to add new links, change link costs, or do both in order to reach high LFA-protection in their network. Nevertheless, in the near future operators should think about upgrading to the remote LFA specification instead, since it has become available in commercial routers [9] and can definitely provide higher protection.

The authors of [13] spearheaded the research to determine the topological requirements and the protection efficiency of remote LFA as well as to find optimization methods to tweak the network for 100% rLFA coverage. They showed that if the implementations support the extended version of rLFA, then every unit cost network is fully protected out of the box. Furthermore, it turned out that, unlike pure LFA, rLFA provides almost full protection in ring topologies [13]. Moreover, there is no 2-edge-connected network, which would not have

Table 3. rLFA graph extension results for link protection

Topology			Uniform cost	
Name	n	m	μ_0	Gr_μ
AS1221	7	9	0.833	1
AS3257	27	64	0.954	1
AS6461	17	37	1	0
Abilene	12	15	0.833	1
Italy	33	56	0.951	2
Germany	27	32	0.882	1
AT&T	22	38	0.8875	2
Germ_50	50	88	1	0

at least 33% of rLFA coverage, while almost the half of the source-destination pairs are protected in every 2-node-connected network.

In order to provide higher protection when rLFA coverage is small, LFA graph extension was adapted from [41] to rLFA. The resultant *rLFA graph extension* problem asks how many links one must add in a real-world network topology to achieve full rLFA coverage. At the moment, it is unclear whether this problem is also NP-complete, although it seems likely that it actually is. The greedy heuristic from [41] was adopted to solve this problem and in [14] more approximating heuristics are examined. A brief view of the results can be found in Table 3, where the notations are the followings: n and m denote the number of nodes and the number of already existing links in the network, respectively. The initial rLFA coverage is indicated by μ_0, whilst Gr_μ marks the number of new links that have to be added to achieve full rLFA protection.

The first observation is that there were two networks, which are initially fully protected, while every other network required less than 3 new links to reach 100% failure case coverage. Furthermore, the number of links have to be added is much less than when only simple LFA capable routers are present, especially, in the Italy and Germ_50 topologies. The results also indicate that on average 3.6 new links are necessary to attain full rLFA protection, while this number is 14.5 in the case of pure LFA.

At the moment, the results for rLFA only cover the case of unit cost networks. A comprehensive investigation of the case of arbitrary cost networks is currently an open problem.

6   Conclusions and Future Work

Due to the increasing number of end-users and real-time services, one of the most important challenges of the future Internet architecture is to be resilient against failures. Since failures occur frequently, IP networks should be able to survive component failures and ensure the service continuity.

In the past few years, a plethora of proposals appeared on how to modify the current IP routers in order to overcome the fast resilience problem, but none of them became industry standard due to their substantial added complexity. As of today, only the Loop-Free Alternates and the Remote LFA specifications have found their ways to operational IP and MPLS/LDP networks, thanks to their simplicity and deployability, and it seems highly unlikely that this situation will change in the future. Since the protection coverage of LFA and rLFA crucially depends on both the underlying network topology and the link costs, the tasks to uncover the intricacies of this dependence as well as to optimize a network for high LFA/rLFA protections have become compelling. This chapter intended to give a comprehensive survey on the state-of-the-art on these pressing problems.

It turned out that there exist many real-world network topologies, where LFA and rLFA can only protect a fraction of possible failures. Fortunately, with LFA and rLFA the protection coverages can be often boosted close to 100% in these networks just by cleverly adding a few new links. However there are still some cases, where LFA/rLFA graph extension cannot be afforded due to limited resources, but in these cases optimizing link costs is still a good approach to increase the coverage. Moreover, the most efficient approach is the combination of the above two. In our experience just adding one or two links and tuning the link costs carefully always resulted in a high increase in failure coverage.

There are still many challenges, which should be solved before it can be attained in most real-world IP networks. In the aforementioned optimization methods the traffic engineering and load balancing issues were not considered at all. Thus, rerouting the traffic after a failure may not results service continuity because some links in the network become congested. Besides, current LFA was developed to protect single failure cases only. As future work we also plan to deal with multiple failures.

With all these in mind, researchers and the industry are facing with an intriguing and complex challenge of converting IP network to a reliable and highly available architecture in the future.

References

1. Amund, K., Fosselie, H.A., Čičic, T., Stein, G., Olav, L.: Multiple routing configurations for fast IP network recovery. IEEE/ACM Trans. Netw. 17(2), 473–486 (2009), doi:http://dx.doi.org/10.1109/TNET.2008.926507
2. Andersson, L., Minei, I., Thomas, B.: LDP specifiaction. RFC 5036 (October 2007)

3. Antonakopoulos, S., Bejerano, Y., Koppol, P.: A simple IP fast reroute scheme for full coverage. In: 2012 IEEE 13th International Conference on High Performance Switching and Routing (HPSR), pp. 15–22 (2012), doi:10.1109/HPSR.2012.6260822
4. Atlas, A., Zinin, A.: Basic specification for IP fast reroute: Loop-Free Alternates. RFC 5286 (2008)
5. Bryant, S., Filfils, C., Previdi, S., Shand, M., So, N.: Remote LFA FRR. IETF DRAFT (December 2012)
6. Bryant, S., Filsfils, C., Previdi, S., Shand, M.: IP fast reroute using tunnels. Internet Draft (2007)
7. Bryant, S., Shand, M., Previdi, S.: IP fast reroute using Not-via addresses. Internet Draft (2010)
8. Čičic, T.: An upper bound on the state requirements of link-fault tolerant multi-topology routing. IEEE ICC 3, 1026–1031 (2006)
9. Cisco Systems: IP Routing: OSPF Configuration Guide, Cisco IOS Release 15.2S - OSPF IPv4 Remote Loop-Free Alternate IP Fast Reroute (downloaded: April 2012)
10. Cisco VNI: Global mobile data traffic forecast update, 2011-2016 (February 2012)
11. Császár, A., Enyedi, G., Tantsura, J., Kini, S., Sucec, J., Das, S.: IP fast re-route with fast notification. Internet Draft (June 2012)
12. Csikor, L., Nagy, M., Rétvári, G.: Network optimization techniques for improving fast IP-level resilience with Loop-Free Alternates. Infocommunications Journal 3(4), 2–10 (2011)
13. Csikor, L., Rétvári, G.: IP fast reroute with remote loop-free alternates: the unit link cost case. In: Proc. RNDM, pp. 16–22 (2012)
14. Csikor, L., Rétvári, G.: On providing fast protection with remote loop-free alternates: Analyzing and optimizing unit cost networks. Submitted to Telecommunication Systems Journal (2013)
15. Csikor, L., Rétvári, G., Tapolcai, J.: Optimizing igp link costs for improving IP-level resilience with loop-free alternates. Computer Communications (2012), doi:10.1016/j.comcom.2012.09.004
16. Enyedi, G., Rétvári, G., Cinkler, T.: A novel loop-free IP fast reroute algorithm. In: Pras, A., van Sinderen, M. (eds.) EUNICE 2007. LNCS, vol. 4606, pp. 111–119. Springer, Heidelberg (2007)
17. Enyedi, G., Szilágyi, P., Rétvári, G., Császár, A.: IP Fast ReRoute: lightweight Not-Via without additional addresses. In: INFOCOM Mini-Conf. (2009)
18. Ericcson Consumer Lab: Smartphone usage experience. Ericsson Consumer Insight Summary Report (2013)
19. Fortz, B., Rexford, J., Thorup, M.: Traffic engineering with traditional IP routing protocols. IEEE Comm. Mag. 40(10), 118–124 (2002)
20. Golumbic, M.C.: Algorithmic Graph Theory and Perfect Graphs, 2nd edn. Elsevier Science (2004)
21. Hock, D., Hartmann, M., Menth, M., Pioro, M., Tomaszewski, A., Zukowski, C.: Comparison of ip-based and explicit paths for one-to-one fastreroute in MPLS networks. Springer Telecommunication Systems Journal, 1–12 (2011), doi:10.1007/s11235-011-9603-4
22. Hokelek, I., Fecko, M., Gurung, P., Samtani, S., Cevher, S., Sucec, J.: Loop-free IP fast reroute using local and remote LFAPs. Internet Draft (February 2008)
23. Iannaccone, G., Chuah, C.N., Mortier, R., Bhattacharyya, S., Diot, C.: Analysis of link failures in an IP backbone. In: ACM SIGCOMM Internet Measurement Workshop, pp. 237–242 (2002)

24. ISO: Intermediate ststem-to-intermediate system (is-is) routing protocol. ISO/IEC 10589 (2002)
25. ITU-T: ICT facts and figures (2011), http://www.itu.int/ITU-D/ict/facts/2011/material/ICTFactsFigures2010.pdf (downloaded: January 2013)
26. Iyer, S., Bhattacharyya, S., Taft, N., Diot, C.: An approach to alleviate link overload as observed on an IP backbone. In: INFOCOM (2003)
27. Juniper Networks: Junos 9.6 routing protocols configuration guide (2009)
28. Kuhn, D.R.: Sources of failure in the public switched telephone networks. IEEE Computer 30(4), 31–36 (1997)
29. Kwong, K.W., Gao, L., Guerin, R., Zhang, Z.L.: On the feasibility and efficacy of protection routing in IP networks. In: INFOCOM, long version is available in Tech. Rep. 2009. University of Pennsylvania (2010)
30. Labovitz, C., Malan, G.R., Jahanian, F.: Internet routing instability. IEEE/ACM Transactions on Networking 6(5), 515–528 (1998)
31. Lakshminarayanan, K., Caesar, M., Rangan, M., Anderson, T., Shenker, S., Stoica, I.: Achieving convergence-free routing using failure-carrying packets. In: Proc. SIGCOMM (2007)
32. Lee, S., Yu, Y., Nelakuditi, S., Zhang, Z.L., Chuah, C.N.: Proactive vs reactive approaches to failure resilient routing. In: INFOCOM (2004)
33. Li, A., Yang, X., Wetherall, D.: Safeguard: safe forwarding during route changes. In: CoNEXT, pp. 301–312 (2009)
34. Mahajan, R., Spring, N., Wetherall, D., Anderson, T.: Inferring link weights using end-to-end measurements. In: ACM IMC, pp. 231–236 (2002)
35. Markopoulou, A., Iannacone, G., Bhattacharyya, S., Chuah, C.N., Diot, C.: Characterization of failures in an IP backbone. In: Proc. IEEE Infocom (March 2004)
36. Menth, M., Hartmann, M., Martin, R., Čičic, T., Kvalbein, A.: Loop-free alternates and not-via addresses: A proper combination for ip fast reroute? Computer Networks 54(8), 1300–1315 (2010), doi:10.1016/j.comnet.2009.10.020
37. Merindol, P., Pansiot, J.J., Cateloin, S.: Providing protection and restoration with distributed multipath routing. In: International Symposium on Performance Evaluation of Computer and Telecommunication Systems, SPECTS 2008, pp. 456–463 (2008)
38. Moy, J.: OSPF version 2. RFC 2328 (April 1998)
39. Pan, P., Swallow, G., Atlas, A.: Fast reroute extensions to RSVP-TE for LSP tunnels. RFC 4090 (2005)
40. Rétvári, G., Csikor, L., Tapolcai, J., Enyedi, G., Császár, A.: Optimizing igp link costs for improving IP-level resilience. In: Proc. of DRCN, pp. 62–69 (October 2011)
41. Rétvári, G., Tapolcai, J., Enyedi, G., Császár, A.: IP Fast ReRoute: Loop Free Alternates revisited. In: INFOCOM, pp. 2948–2956 (2011)
42. Sallai, G.: Defining infocommunications and related terms. Acta Polytechnica Hungarica 9(6), 5–15 (2012)
43. Schollmeier, G., Charzinski, J., Kirstädter, A., Reichert, C., Schrodi, K., Glickman, Y., Winkler, C.: Improving the resilience in IP networks. In: Proc. HPSR (2003)
44. Shand, M., Bryant, S.: IP Fast Reroute framework. RFC 5714 (2010)
45. SNDLib: Survivable fixed telecommunication network design library, http://sndlib.zib.de (downloaded: April 2012)
46. Sterbez, J., Cetinkaya, E.K., Hameed, M.A., Jabbar, A., Qian, S., Rohrer, J.P.: Evaluation of network resilience, survivability, and disruption tolerance: Analysis, topology generation, simulation and experimentation. Springer Telecommunication Systems Journal, 1–32 (2011), doi:10.1007/s11235-011-9573-6

47. Swallow, G., Bryant, S., Andersson, L.: Avoiding equal cost multipath treatment in MPLS networks. RFC 4928 (June 2007)
48. Systems, C.: Cisco IOS XR Routing Configuration Guide, Release 3.7 (2008)
49. Čičic, T., Hansen, A., Apeland, O.: Redundant trees for fast IP recovery. In: Broadnets, pp. 152–159 (2007)
50. Vulimiri, A., Michel, O., Godfrey, P.B., Shenker, S.: More is less: reducing latency via redundancy. In: Hotnets (2012)
51. Zhong, Z., Nelakuditi, S., Yu, Y., Lee, S., Wang, J., Chuah, C.N.: Failure inferencing based fast rerouting for handling transient link and node failures. In: INFOCOM (2005)

Integrating OpenFlow in IMS Networks and Enabling for Future Internet Researchand Experimentation

Christos Tranoris[1], Spyros Denazis[1], Nikos Mouratidis[2],
Phelim Dowling[3], and Joe Tynan[3]

[1] University of Patras, Greece
tranoris@ece.upatras.gr, sdena@upatras.gr
[2] Creative Systems Engineering (CSE) , Greece
n.mouratidis@creativese.eu
[3] TSSG, Ireland
{Pdowling,jtynan}@tssg.org

Abstract. The IP Multimedia Subsystem (IMS) is an architectural framework for delivering IP multimedia services. The appearance of Software Defined Networks (SDNs) concept in the IMS fabric can unleash the potential of the IMS technology which enables access agnostic services including applications like video-conferencing, multi-player gaming, white boarding all using an all-IP backbone. SDN requires some method for the control plane to communicate with the data plane. One such mechanism is OpenFlow which is a standard interface for controlling computer networking switches. This work presents our experience and implementation efforts in integrating OpenFlow mechanisms within IMS. Since this work also is done within the Future Internet Research and Experimentation domain, we also describe how we enabled our infrastructures with experimentation mechanisms.

Keywords: IMS networks, OpenFlow, Software Defined Networking, Future Internet research, Experimentation.

1   Introduction

Experimental networks are built to support experimentally-driven research towards the Future Internet Research (FIRE)[1]. The term experimental networks characterizes diverse communication technologies networks, composed of virtual or physical nodes that allow experimenters to test early prototypes of new protocols, protocol stacks, routing algorithms, services and applications. The main questions regarding the suitability of a testbed to incubate experiments towards the Future Internet are summarized in the capability to support large scale experiments, and to be able to federate with other testbeds. The first prerequisite has been addressed with the introduction of technologies for network virtualization.

OpenFlow was born by the need of experimenting on new technologies, however on commercial grade networks. The OpenFlow technology and the associated OpenFlow Protocol have come to lower the entry-barrier of new ideas application in commercial grade networks. In contrast to the virtual networks technology, OpenFlow

A. Galis and A. Gavras (Eds.): FIA 2013, LNCS 7858, pp. 77–88, 2013.

offers a flexible way of manipulating the routing tables of Ethernet switches. Providing a generic approach to this manipulation, OpenFlow is a technology that allows formation of large testbeds, thus enables large scale experimentation.

In what concerns the second prerequisite, testbed federation has become possible via integration within the context of control frameworks. Such frameworks allowed for testbed resources visualization and provisioning to the experimenters. Nowadays, there are several control frameworks in use, with the most prominent ones being the OMF [2], PII project's Teagle [3][4]. Information exchange between the control frameworks and the underlying testbeds is implemented using particular APIs, such as the Slice-Based Facility Architecture-SFA [5] and the ProtoGENI [6][7].

Building on both enablers of large scale experimentation, the present effort coming from the OpenLab project [8], aims at providing experimenters with more agility concerning exploitation of testbed resources. In particular, we aim at extending experimentation across mixed virtual and physical infrastructure nodes in order to allow running experiments requiring mixtures of pragmatic offerings (e.g. QoS) as well as virtual ones (e.g. non-IP based algorithms). Under the proposed setting, an experimenter may work on a new algorithm using the clean-slate virtual network environment but at the same time can test deployment-related issues such as performance, mapping a set of nodes on physical infrastructure nodes.

As a first step towards this approach, in this paper we present an approach towards OpenFlow deployment in IMS testbeds to be exploited for QoS-based experiments. Section 2 presents why and how we introduced SDN concepts in IMSs, Section 3 provides the implementations to the respective testbeds. Section 4 presents our first approach on enabling these infrastructures for experimentation while section 5 provides some potential experiments. Finally, we conclude our work.

2   Introducing SDN to IMS: Integrating OpenFlow

The IP Multimedia Subsystem (IMS) is an architectural framework for delivering IP multimedia services. It was originally designed by the wireless standards body 3rd Generation Partnership Project (3GPP), as a part of the vision for evolving mobile networks beyond GSM. Unfortunately in many respects it remained just a vision, with sporadic deployments. Operators and Network Providers somehow could not manage to find any compelling reason to re-architect their network by introducing IMS network elements. On the other hand there were no promising applications. But IMSs definitely hold enormous potential and a couple of breakthroughs in key technologies can result in the 'tipping point' of this great technology which promises access agnostic services including applications like video-conferencing, multi-player gaming, white boarding all using an all-IP backbone.[9]

However the last few years the concept of Software Define Networks (SDNs) appeared. SDN decouples the system that makes decisions about where traffic is sent (the control plane) from the underlying system that forwards traffic to the selected destination (the data plane). This architecture allows network administrators to have programmable central control of network traffic without requiring physical access to the network's hardware devices. SDN requires some method for the control plane to communicate with the data plane. One such mechanism is OpenFlow which is a standard interface for controlling computer networking switches. An OpenFlow Controller is able to control network resources in a programmatic manner. These network resources can span routers, hubs and switches, known as a slice, and can be controlled through the OpenFlow Controller. The OpenFlow protocol can manage resources by slicing them in a virtualized manner and that aspect of the OpenFlow protocol can be integrated in an IMS infrastructure.

In the context of the OpenLab[8] project, two IMS testbeds participate in order to offer the IMS technology for further experimentation scenarios, the OSIMS testbed from the University of Patras and the TSSG IMS Testbed. These two testbeds were also used in the Panlab[4] project. Within OpenLab, a goal for these two testbeds is to deploy OpenFlow and SDN characteristics in order to introduce QoS and interconnection features. The OpenFlow Controller will be able to dynamically re-route the traffic to alternate network resources, or a different 'network slice' in cases of congestion or applying QoS in IMS networks through the IMS policy network elements.

3   Enhancements and Implementation on IMS Testbeds

This section describes how OpenFlow is integrated into to IMS testbeds: The OSIMS testbed at University of Patras and a Telco Cloud Testbed at TSSG. The two testbeds participate in the OpenLab project and have adopted proposed federation mechanisms like SFA [5], making thus possible to be included in much more complex and federated experimentation scenarios.

3.1   The UoP OSIMS Testbed

The UoP OSIMS testbed[10] with its current setup is (partially) depicted in Figure 1. The core of OSIMS system is based on the Open Source IMS core of OpenIMS[11]. To ease experimentation on an IMS testbed, OSIMS offer many services available by accessing the Patras Platforms for Experimentation (P2E) portal [10].

OSIMS consists of the following services:

- A Home Subscribe Server (HSS)
- A Serving-CSCF Module (scscf)
- A Proxy-CSCF Module (pcscf)
- An Interrogating-CSCF Module (icscf)
- An OpenSIPS server and a presence server based on OpenSIPS
- A presence server based on OpenSIPS
- An XDMS service for storing directory information
- An Asterisk server for connection to other phone services
- A media server, streaming video channels

80   C. Tranoris et al.

Figure 1 displays also the undergoing extensions on OSIMS testbed, which are based on the considerations presented on section 2 about introducing QoS and OpenFlow on the IMS fabric. To apply QoS in IMS networks two network elements are needed: the Policy Decision Point (PDP) and the Policy Enforcement Point (PEP). The PDP retrieves related policy rules, in response to a RSVP message, which the PDP then sends to the PEP. These are implemented by two IMS components: a Policy and Charging Rule Function (PCRF), and a Policy and Charging Enforcement Point (PCEF).

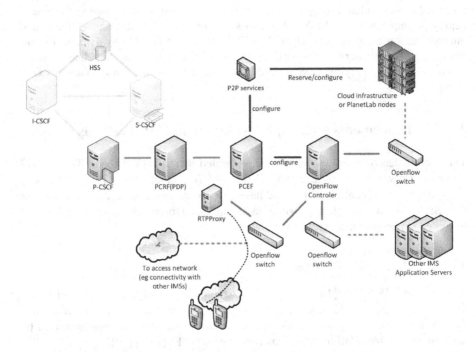

Fig. 1. UoP OSIMS testbed with OpenFlow controller and switches deployed

The P-CSCF is a central IMS core element for SIP signaling. It is the only element that receives information about the user signaling for multimedia sessions. It sends a description of the session the user tries to establish to the PCRF. The PCRF, which plays the role of the PDP, is the element which authorizes the session and does the policy control and flow based charging. PCRF sends through any interface commands to the PCEF. PCEF, which plays the role of PEP, is co-located with the domain gateway and its role is to enforce the policies that the PCRF requires.

In an IMS call flow, the SDP (Session Description Protocol) message is encapsulated within SIP and carries the QoS parameters. The PCRF examines the parameters, retrieves appropriate policies and informs the PCEF for that traffic flow. The advantage of using OpenFlow Controller/OpenFlow switch to the PDP/PEP combination would be the ability to adapt the network flow according to bandwidth changes and traffic.

In OSIMS we installed two open source components of PCRF and PCEF based on the OpenIMSCore. We installed the Floodlight[12] OpenFlow controller while the OpenFlow switches are based on OpenVSwitch[13]. The approach is depicted in Figure 2. We replaced the PCEF with our own functionality in order to communicate with the OpenFlow Floodlight Controller via its RESTful interface. We enhanced the PCEF with a custom API that it is able to identify: i) bandwidth speeds, ii) the network slice which the flows should follow. These will configure our OpenFlow based OpenVSwitches to control network resources, to alternate network slices, or for example connect to cloud resources, to other Application servers or provide connectivity (for example to other IMSs). Using OpenFlow together with policies we will have the ability to dynamically adapt and reroute the network flow according to bandwidth traffic, to an alternate network resource or slice.

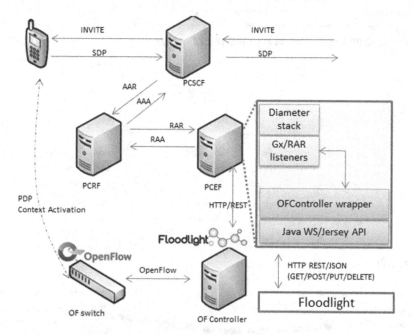

Fig. 2. Openflow integration in OSIMS

Figure 3 and Figure 4 display both what is reported during a video-call between two IMS clients. Figure 3 displays the 8 flows that have been identified that are need in order to establish the call. We need 4 flows for each client. 2 flows are for audio and 2 for video, because they are RTP streams. For each flow there is also an identified Quality of Service Class from the SDP headers, while it is also possible to define the available Bandwidth according to some policies defined within the Policy Control Management service. Figure 4 displays the control panel of the Floodlight Controller, where some static flows are injected through the PCEF component. The figure displays all the flows currently existing in the switch.

Session ID	Flow ID	Source IP	Dest IP	SPort	DPort	BW Up	BW Down	QClass
pcscf.ece.upatras.gr;970477326;3	1,1	150.140.184.212	150.140.189.228	11266	38364	-1	-1	2
pcscf.ece.upatras.gr;970477326;3	1,2	150.140.184.212	150.140.189.228	11267	38365	-1	-1	2
pcscf.ece.upatras.gr;970477326;3	2,1	150.140.184.212	150.140.189.228	32718	60810	-1	-1	1
pcscf.ece.upatras.gr;970477326;3	2,2	150.140.184.212	150.140.189.228	32719	60811	-1	-1	1
pcscf.ece.upatras.gr;970477326;4	1,1	150.140.189.228	150.140.184.212	38364	11266	-1	-1	2
pcscf.ece.upatras.gr;970477326;4	1,2	150.140.189.228	150.140.184.212	38365	11267	-1	-1	2
pcscf.ece.upatras.gr;970477326;4	2,1	150.140.189.228	150.140.184.212	60810	32718	-1	-1	1
pcscf.ece.upatras.gr;970477326;4	2,2	150.140.189.228	150.140.184.212	60811	32719	-1	-1	1

Refresh

Fig. 3. A view of the Policy Control Panel while a video call

☑ Live updates

Floodlight   Dashboard   Topology   Switches   Hosts

Switch 00:00:00:1b:21:cb:fe:44 /150.140.184.227:46428

Connected since Παρασκευή, 15 Φεβρουάριος 2013 11:56:42
Nicira Networks, Inc.
Open vSwitch
1.4.0
S/N: None

Ports (5)

#	Link Status	TX Bytes	RX Bytes	TX Pkts	RX Pkts	Dropped	Errors
3 (vif3.1)	UP	805825718	186666890	5589467	919806	0	0
2 (vif2.1)	UP	433904814	22104052899	5708600	21076123	0	0
12 (vif12.1)	UP	396898599	300101202	1254162	960946	0	0
65534 (pubbr0)	UP	709618900	499557988	6482736	4348733	168844	0
1 (eth1)	UP 100 Mbps FDX	22934861431	1826348201	25207798	9576814	2	0

Flows (12)

Cookie	Priority	Match	Action	Packets	Bytes	Age	Timeout
9007199254740992	0	port=1, xVLAN=-1, prio=0, src=00:14:6a:d5:59:7f,	output	16676	5340443	2765	5 s
45035996273704960	-32768	dest=00:16:3e:4a:06:bf, ethertype=0x0800, proto=6, IP src port=32718, IP dest port=-4726, src=150.140.184.212, dest=150.140.189.228	output 2	0	0	60 s	0 s
45035996273704960	-32768	dest=00:16:3e:4a:06:bf, ethertype=0x0800, proto=6, IP src port=11267, IP dest port=-27171, src=150.140.184.212, dest=150.140.189.228	output 2	0	0	118 s	0 s
45035996273704960	-32768	dest=00:16:3e:4a:06:bf, ethertype=0x0800, proto=6, IP src port=11266, IP dest port=-27172, src=150.140.184.212, dest=150.140.189.228	output 2	0	0	223 s	0 s
45035996273704960	-32768	dest=00:16:3e:4a:06:bf, ethertype=0x0800, proto=6, IP src port=32719, IP dest port=-4725, src=150.140.184.212, dest=150.140.189.228	output 2	0	0	27 s	0 s
45035996273704960	-32768	dest=00:16:3e:4a:06:bf, ethertype=0x0800, proto=6, IP src	output	0	0	148 s	0 s

Fig. 4. The Floodlight web Control Panel with the programmed flows

3.2   The TSSG Testbed

The software implementation for the aforementioned OpenFlow integration in an IMS environment, is based on the OSGI (Open Services Gateway initiative) framework with the use of Maven and PAX. Maven is the build automation tool and OPS4J' PAX's plugin provides the build goals to create, build, manage and deploy OSGI bundles into a contained executable environment. The major benefits of implementing the framework into an OSGI container include effective runtime environment, module life cycle, standard services, and common deployment platform. If the system requires additional resources, OSGI has the ability to distribute modules to other containers via declarative services. Another key feature of the framework is the capability to run modules at distinctive start time levels, permitting the system to categorise functionality into start levels e.g. system debug logging at start level 6, views at start level 5, where core logic modules starting at lower start levels and so on.

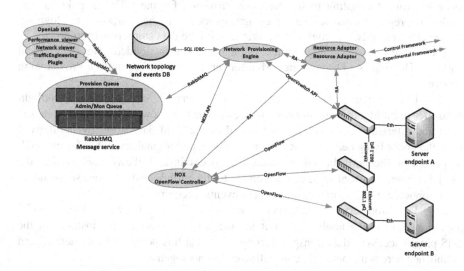

Fig. 5. OpenFlow implementation architecture, queues and protocol flow diagram in TSSG's OpenIMS platform

Further to the components been developed to run control logic in the system, the framework statically deploys elements such as OpenVSwitch, OpenFlow enabled switches and OpenFlow controller parts. These component parts are mostly incorporated in the lower layers of the system where they perform the necessary role in controlling, provisioning and administering underlying network resources. These network elements are the back bone of the data plane and carry out the network path/flow decisions established via the OpenFlow protocol. In this architecture we use OpenVSwitch which provides a native ingress/egress rate limit attribute, with a valuable implementation of the OpenFlow protocol. The OpenVSwitch at the "control plane" performs as a flow filter, flow entry and exit points and additionally provides a platform for transit flows.

At the upper layer there is an API implementation in Java/RabbitMQ that will grant access into the architectures control plane logic and in turn access to OpenFlow which manages network elements. This allows network applications a generic API to the network resources whether it's for topology discovery, slice provisioning, bandwidth provisioning, performance stats, etc. Also in the upper layers, and hosted in the OSGI platform , are the testbed resource adapters, so testers and experimenters alike can provision, evaluate and probe the system for findings.

Bolted onto the system is the capacity for presentence. Here JavaDB ties into the OSGI stack effectively, offering both memory based cache for speed queries and a more permanent read/write location.

The Network Provisioning Engine module, acts as an OpenFlow IMS bandwidth/slice controller that allows the administration of bandwidth or flows that transverse through the underlying communication network. With a flexible implementation of components like RabbitMQ for messaging, JavaDB for both long term and short persistence and Floodlight as an OpenFlow controller, it allows for a loose but robust coupling to the Network Provision Engine. The module has the ability to register and activate message queues for the purposes of logging, performance records, topology views, interact with the data store, provisioning etc.

The network provisioning engine implementation is divided into two logical regions. The first is a Discovering / Monitor service and the second is a Provisioning service:

1.   Discovering / Monitor services: This service will use the Floodlight controller to build a logical network overview. The overview will compose of nodes, links and interfaces, all modelled and stored in the local data store. Events derived from the under lying network, such as node failure, operational state of links, etc., will be passed on the north bound interface for processing and likewise archived in the local database. An event ACL can be applied to the north bound interface so the upper layer application or plugin will only secure events it requires.

2.   Provision services: This service will allow OpenFlow switched nodes to be provisioned, enabling applications outside the network layer in this instance of the IMS plugin access to data transport resources. It is at this point flows are deleted and established across the network, connecting endpoints together.

Operationally the system can have any number for plugins, mimicking a telco north bound interface. Enabling a plugin is as easy as that plugin joining a functional topic in the relevant message queue or queues. One such plugin is the Open IMS plugin, which disseminates network slices from a predefined algorithm set which it contains and on a network topology it has learnt prior. In essence, taking control of the switches flow table to establish a data flow in the network.

4   Enabling for Experimentation

To provide the given testbed setup for experimentation, it is necessary to encode its resources so that they are compatible with the provisioning framework called Teagle. Such encoding is possible by implementing particular XML description tables called Resource Adapters (RA). In Figure 6, we display the concept of the resource adapter

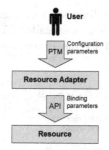

Fig. 6. A Resource Adapter configures a resource through an API

As it is illustrated in Figure 7, a PTM may include several RAs, with each one being dedicated to representing to the Teagle a particular resource or capability of the underlying network. In our realisation we have implemented three RAs, one representing the network setup (VM), another implementing ingress and egress policing rates and bursts (qos_rate_limit), and a third one for sflow monitoring client configuration (sflow). Using the qos_rate_limit RA it is possible to run QoS performance experiments by changing the ingress, egress traffic rates. These RAs have already implemented in OSIMS while in the TSSG testbed is under adaptation and adoption.

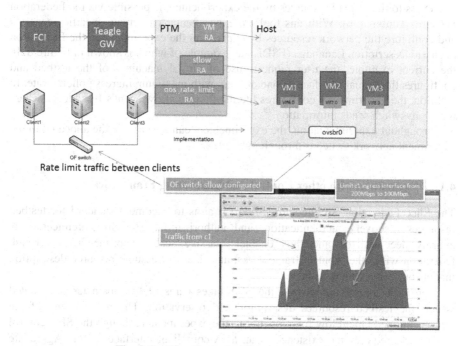

Fig. 7. Enabling the testbed for experimentation

The overall testbed-provisioning framework configuration depicted in Figure 7, is administered by an experiment controller called Federation Computing Interface (FCI) [14][15]. The FCI is used by the experimenters to request and configure resources.

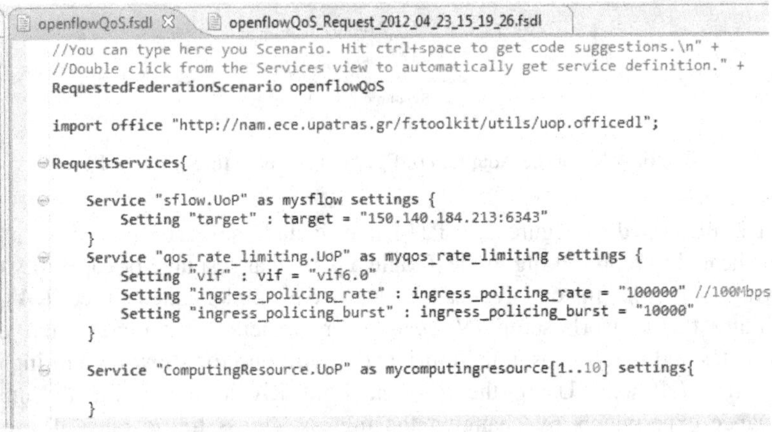

```
openflowQoS.fsdl 🔀      openflowQoS_Request_2012_04_23_15_19_26.fsdl

    //You can type here you Scenario. Hit ctrl+space to get code suggestions.\n" +
    //Double click from the Services view to automatically get service definition." +
    RequestedFederationScenario openflowQoS

    import office "http://nam.ece.upatras.gr/fstoolkit/utils/uop.officedl";

  RequestServices{

        Service "sflow.UoP" as mysflow settings {
            Setting "target" : target = "150.140.184.213:6343"
        }
        Service "qos_rate_limiting.UoP" as myqos_rate_limiting settings {
            Setting "vif" : vif = "vif6.0"
            Setting "ingress_policing_rate" : ingress_policing_rate = "100000" //100Mbps
            Setting "ingress_policing_burst" : ingress_policing_burst = "10000"
        }

        Service "ComputingResource.UoP" as mycomputingresource[1..10] settings{

        }
```

Fig. 8. Requesting and configuring testbed resources

Access to the testbed resources by the experimenters is possible via the Federation Scenario Toolkit [16]. With this tool, an experimenter can create specific scenarios and configure the network resources by expressing the experiments in the Federation Scenario Description Language (FSDL), an example of which is shown in Figure 8. In the current example, the user requests use of virtual machines of the testbed and configures the virtual interface of one of them with maximum ingress policing rate. In addition, the experimenter configures the monitoring sflow agent's IP address, where the openvswitch sends information.

Throughout experimentation, the experimenters can also access the allocated to the experiment network switches through public IPs.

4.1   Integration with other Control and Monitoring Frameworks

The Slice Federation Architecture (SFA) [5] aims to become a standard for testbed resources discovery, authentication, and authorization. The SFA architecture is entirely decentralized and thus enables massive scale experimentation through federation with other control frameworks, and does not assume resource description models but convey them as-is.

Seen as a control framework, the SFA takes cares of two main testbed related issues; the testbed resources description and reservation. The provisioning of the aforementioned OpenFlow functionality to the experimenters though the SFA control framework, requires the existence of an SFA-compliant interface for the Aggregate Manager (AM) within the PTM component. In SFA terminology, components are the offered resources that are independently owned and operated. Components can be organized into aggregates, which are groups of resources owned and administered as an ensemble by some organization. The AM is the domain authority that exposes and controls these resources.

The AM is the point of convergence of the PTM functionality towards the provisioning framework. Thanks to the AM resource specifications testbed resources may become available to the experiments through the SFA control framework. Integration of the PTM component into the SFA framework is done through an implemented SFA compliant API that translates SFA messages into PTM compliant ones and vice versa. The implementation is accomplished by adopting the so called SFAWrapper [17] implemented within the OpenLab project and by enhancing it with our testbed specific entities.

5   Target Experiments/Experimenters

Currently the testbeds were used to experiment with the IMS technology alone. We have envisaged the following usage scenarios that one can execute over such federated infrastructures:

5.1   QoS with Policy Enforcement and OpenFlow Control

Let the experimenter define policies in the PCRF and his IMS Client. Monitor the SIP/SDP message and how the policies are enforced from the OpenFlow Controller to an OpenFlow switch. Experiment with new functionality within the OpenFlow controller.

Expected experimentation results: Telcos can experiment on the results of having an integration of the OpenFlow technology and SDN concepts into their core network prior applying this into their own solutions.

5.2   Prioritizing Traffic between 2 IMS Cores Exchanging Data

In OpenLab we have two IMS Core testbeds and the PlanetLab infrastructure. In such a scenario one can try to define link bandwidth between the two IMS Cores over a best-effort internet connection. Send data between the two networks, but prioritize the SIP traffic. All these while establishing calls.

Expected experimentation results: Having the same link between the two cores, while there is a high demand, the experimenter can monitor how SIP traffic is prioritized over UDP traffic.

6   Conclusions and Future Work

Introducing SDN concepts within the IMS fabric seems to be quite promising as discussed in section 2. Integrating the OpenFlow Protocol to the IP Multimedia network can provide better resource control and advanced QoS support as section 3 presented on the integration within our IMS fabric. We expect also to provide much more interesting applications with these new deployments such as those presented in section 5. Experimenters can benefit by exploiting these new potentials, while not having to deal with complex deployments before they decide to do so. They can test applications and algorithms involving such new technologies by investing less time in preparing and configuring equipment. Finally, for both our testbeds, we plan to provide ready scenarios for certain use cases, to ease experimenters with the learning process of the whole experimentation lifecycle.

Acknowledgments. The research leading to these results has received funding from the European Union's Seventh Framework Programme (FP7/2007-2013) from project under grant agreement n° 287581 – OpenLab.

References

[1]   Gavras, A., Karila, A., Fdida, S., May, M., Potts, M.: Future Internet Research and Experimentation: The FIRE Initiative. ACM SIGCOMM Computer Communication Review 37(3) (July 2007),
        doi:http://doi.acm.org/10.1145/1273445.1273460
[2]   OMF control framework, http://www.mytestbed.net/
[3]   FITeagle, http://fiteagle.org/
[4]   Wahle, S., Tranoris, C., Denazis, S., Gavras, A., Koutsopoulos, K., Magedanz, T., Tompros, S.: Emerging testing trends and the Panlab enabling infrastructure. IEEE Communications Magazine 49(3), 167–175 (2011), doi:10.1109/MCOM.2011.5723816
[5]   SFA, http://svn.planet-lab.org/wiki/SFATutorial
[6]   ProtoGENI, http://protogeni.net/
[7]   National Science Foundation, GENI website, http://www.geni.net
[8]   OpenLab FP7 EU project, http://www.ict-openlab.eu/
[9]   http://gigadom.wordpress.com/2011/10/04/adding-the-openflow-variable-in-the-ims-equation/
[10]   Patras Platforms for Experimentation, http://nam.ece.upatras.gr/ppe
[11]   OpenIMS core, http://www.openimscore.org/
[12]   Floodlight Openflow controler, http://floodlight.openflowhub.org/
[13]   openVSwitch, http://openvswitch.org/
[14]   Tranoris, C., Denazis, S.: Federation Computing: A pragmatic approach for the Future Internet. In: 6th IEEE International Conference on Network and Service Management (CNSM 2010), Niagara Falls, Canada, October 25-29 (2010)
[15]   Federation Computing Interface (FCI), Panlab wiki website (February 12, 2012), http://trac.panlab.net/trac/wiki/FCI
[16]   Federation Scenario Toolkit (FSToolkit) web site (February 12, 2012), http://nam.ece.upatras.gr/fstoolkit
[17]   SFAWrapper, http://sfawrap.info/

Computing and Networking Clouds

Contrail: Distributed Application Deployment under SLA in Federated Heterogeneous Clouds⋆

Roberto G. Cascella[1], Lorenzo Blasi[2], Yvon Jegou[1],
Massimo Coppola[3], and Christine Morin[1]

[1] Inria, Campus Universitaire de Beaulieu, 35042 Rennes, France
{roberto.cascella,yvon.jegou,christine.morin}@inria.fr,
[2] HP Italy Innovation Center, via Grandi 4, 20063 Cernusco Sul Naviglio (MI), Italy
lorenzo.blasi@hp.com
[3] CNR/ISTI "A.Faedo", via G. Moruzzi 1, 56124 Pisa, Italy
massimo.coppola@isti.cnr.it

Abstract. Cloud computing market is in rapid expansion due to the opportunities to dynamically allocate a large amount of resources when needed and to pay only for their effective usage. However, many challenges, in terms of interoperability, performance guarantee, and dependability, should still be addressed to make cloud computing the right solution for companies. In this chapter we first discuss these challenges and then we present three components developed in the framework of the Contrail project: Contrail federation; SLA manager; and Virtual Execution Platform (VEP). These components provide solutions to guarantee interoperability in a cloud federation and to deploy distributed applications over a federation of heterogeneous cloud providers. The key to success of our solutions is the possibility to negotiate performance and security guarantees for an application and then map them on the physical resources.

Keywords: Cloud computing, federation, SLA, QoS, standards, resource management, interoperability, distributed application deployment.

1 Introduction

After decades in which companies used to host their entire IT infrastructures in-house, a major shift is occurring where these infrastructures are outsourced to external operators such as data centers and computing clouds. The growth of interest toward computing clouds is facilitated by virtualization technologies which offer several advantages over traditional data center approach to computing. On the one hand, companies can move their applications to the cloud freeing themselves from the control and management of the infrastructure so that they can focus on the deployed services. On the other hand, companies can rent resources of cloud providers only when needed according to a pay-as-you-go pricing model reducing the cost of the infrastructure. In a nutshell, this paradigm represents a new opportunity for companies and organisations to rely on highly dynamic distributed infrastructures to run applications and services.

⋆ Invited Paper.

A. Galis and A. Gavras (Eds.): FIA 2013, LNCS 7858, pp. 91–103, 2013.

The cloud computing market is in rapid expansion and many cloud providers are flourishing in Europe to offer Infrastructure as a Service (IaaS) services to contrast big players, like Amazon, that have so far dominated. The market opportunities are quite challenging for new IaaS cloud providers, which might have limited resources to offer. They play in a competitive service market where the organisations and companies they want to attract are looking for large pool of resources, as well as for guarantees in terms of the reliability and availability for their services. However the growth of cloud computing may soon be hindered by other factors such as the customers' concerns to be locked-in within a single commercial offer (which reduces the necessary competition between many infrastructure providers), ownership and privacy issues of the data stored in the cloud, and the lack of performance predictability of current clouds. Other major issues are legal requirements for data: they cannot be stored anywhere for legal jurisdiction implication or need to have specific privacy requirements to stick with company or country legislation. These concerns can be summarised in the lack of trust on the clouds with customers being sceptical in the cloud model and in services offered by a cloud provider if no guarantees exist.

A first step to address the users' concerns is to avoid vendor lock-in giving the opportunity to select the most convenient cloud provider based on the application requirements or price of the offer. Interoperability among cloud providers is the only way to challenge vendor lock-in and open the way toward a more competitive market. Moreover, interoperability is a need for small players to enter a market dominated by big cloud providers which can count on a huge number of resources. As such, interoperability becomes even more handy and needed in a multi provider scenario, where customers can protect their investment by counting on a wider number of options to offer their services on top of cloud systems. At the same time, they take full advantage of the elasticity and pay-as-you-go concepts. One way to achieve interoperability is via the adoption of cloud standards or a middleware service that adapts the application to a specific cloud provider. A more comprehensive way to address interoperability is the cloud federation: it can help in hiding the complexity of managing heterogeneous resources and using a multitude of cloud providers at the same time.

However, on top of these federated cloud providers it is of utmost importance to ensure the availability of the computing resources and to provide strict guarantees in terms of quality of service (QoS) and quality of protection (QoP). Users and organizations should have the opportunity to specify these features in a negotiated Service Level Agreement (SLA) and to monitor them at runtime. Deploying applications and services under a SLA will make cloud computing a valid alternative to private data centers responding to the users requirements in terms of availability, reliable application execution, and security.

Few approaches exist so far and they focus more on brokering among cloud providers, ranking them and selecting one based on an objective function [17]. Other approaches focus on creating a level of abstraction to present the resources of cloud providers in a transparent way to the user and then orchestrating the deployment over different cloud providers [4,14,19]. However, to the best of our knowledge, there is no previous work providing a complete solution that tackles interoperability issues, security, and performance guarantees.

Contrail [1] is a European project addressing all these issues to allow a federation of heterogenous clouds to deploy distributed applications under QoS and QoP constraints. Contrail is an open source integrated approach to virtualization, which aims at offering Infrastructure as a Service services (IaaS), services for federating IaaS clouds, and Contrail Platform as a Service services (ConPaaS) on top of federated clouds. In Contrail, the user is relieved from managing the access to individual cloud providers and can focus on specifying the service or application to be automatically deployed over a multitude of heterogeneous providers. The providers can rely on different cloud technologies, exploit different hardware, or offer different types of guarantees.

Contrail offers performance (QoS) and security (QoP) guarantees via SLA enforcement by monitoring the execution of the application, and a scalable management of the computing resources via an interoperable federation. The federation service is the interface with the user, who needs to submit the description of the distributed application to be deployed in the cloud, along with its runtime configuration, and specify the requirements in terms of OVF (Open Virtualization Format specification) [7] and SLA documents respectively. Then, the federation ensures that the providers' resources are utilized as needed for offering a dependable and trustworthy cloud service to customers.

The application is deployed via the Virtual Execution Platform (VEP), a provider-level service supporting federation-level interoperability. The use of VEP allows to deploy a distributed application under the terms of a SLA over the resources of any of the supported IaaS providers, regardless e.g. of the underlying cloud management system. Elasticity of the application is also ensured by monitoring the usage of the resources stated in a negotiated SLA, both within the cloud provider infrastructure and at the federation level.

In this chapter, we present the Contrail federation service, SLA management (negotiation and enforcement) in federated heterogeneous clouds, and the Virtual Execution Platform. The remainder of this chapter is organized as follows. Section 2 highlights the architecture of Contrail software stack and discusses the main services offered. Section 3 presents the cloud federation, a relatively new concept, and the Contrail view and implementation. Section 4 discusses the Contrail project achievements in terms of managing and negotiating Service Level Agreements (SLAs). Section 5 presents the Virtual Execution Platform services and the management of a distributed application. Section 6 concludes this chapter and draws future directions.

2   Contrail Architecture

Fig. 1 depicts the Contrail architecture. The federation layer is the entry-point for users, who register and authenticate to use the Contrail services. The way the Contrail federation is conceived enables seamless access to the resources of multiple cloud providers, avoiding potential vendor lock-in for the end users. It reaches

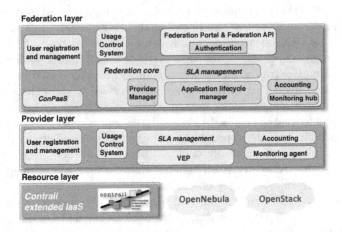

Fig. 1. Simplified vision of the Contrail architecture

a high degree of interoperability by managing private or public cloud providers' resources regardless of the technology implemented or underlying hardware. The Contrail federation enables users to deploy distributed applications on demand on different cloud providers by only interacting with this single component. The federation incorporates in the *Federation core* the necessary functionalities to negotiate SLAs and monitor their enforcement while the application is running. The Federation core, together with its interfaces, is deployed at each *Federation Access Point* (FAP). A Contrail federation is thus made up of distributed, interconnected instances of FAPs and providers. The user submits the description of the application based on the OVF [7] standard format and negotiates the SLAs terms, then the federation selects the most suitable cloud providers based on the resources available, the expressed SLA terms for QoS and QoP, and the reputation of the providers, i.e., matching the level of performance and trustworthiness required by the application. Hence, the federation proceeds to negotiate proper SLA terms with each provider in a transparent way for the users. Contrail technology is able to satisfy the user needs for the deployment of elastic and scalable applications by adding or removing resources in order to satisfy the SLA terms without the need of a new SLA negotiation. Monitoring and auditing are performed during application execution, to ensure that there is no violation of the SLA. Proper authorization and security mechanisms are enforced primarily at the federation layer and then at the other layers to guarantee quality of protection (QoP).

The provider layer implements the business part of a cloud provider: (i) negotiation with the federation and enforcement of the SLA; (ii) resource reservation and application management; (iii) monitoring and accounting. The resource layer is in charge of managing the physical resources of a cloud provider. Contrail does not implement a new IaaS, but leverages the existing ones[1] by adding those functionalities required to provide performance and security guarantees for an application.

In Contrail, each cloud provider runs a copy of the Virtual Execution Platform (VEP) software which in turn seamlessly integrates the provider resources within the Contrail federation. VEP is an open source technology implementing standards that exploits resource virtualization to provide virtualized distributed infrastructures for the deployment of end-user applications independently from the underlying platform: Contrail extended IaaS, OpenNebula or OpenStack[4]. It offers a reliable application deployment platform, which is resilient to operational failures and which ensures that an application is deployed respecting QoS requirements. The degree of interoperability and features that the federation can exploit on each single cloud provider depend on the specific functionalities implemented at the cloud provider level. Interoperability is achieved through the VEP component.

Other relevant services developed in Contrail but not detailed in this chapter are: (i) the Virtual Infrastructure Network (VIN) service which assures the internetworking between Virtual Machines (VMs) of an application and with the public Internet, providing bandwidth reservation capabilities within a data center and isolated environments for an application; (ii) the Global Autonomous File System (GAFS) which guarantees a reliable and highly available storage service for VM images and system logs, and scalable Storage as a Service to cloud users and applications; (iii) self-managed, elastic, and scalable ConPaaS (Contrail PaaS) services [16] which can deploy themselves on the cloud, monitor their own performance, and increase or decrease their processing capacity by dynamically (de-)provisioning instances of the ConPaaS service in the cloud.

The following sections focus on the Contrail components that enable the deployment of distributed applications under the terms of a SLA over a federation of heterogeneous cloud providers. These are (i) the Contrail federation integrating under a common umbrella the resources of different cloud providers relieving the user from the negotiation of the application with each provider; (ii) the SLA component running within the federation core and at the provider layer offering SLA negotiation, management, and enforcement services thanks to the monitoring services; and (iii) the VEP component managing the resources of a cloud provider and offering elastic application deployment within the constraints expressed in a SLA.

3   Federation Concept and Service

A cloud federation is a platform where multiple cloud providers interoperate with each other, creating a service marketplace for users to dynamically match

---

[1] At the time of writing this paper, Contrail extends and supports only OpenNebula whereas OpenStack is future work. The support of non *Contrail extended IaaS* limits the level of control of the resources, thus the type of guarantees that could be offered to a customer.

their needs with the offers from a subset of providers. In addition to the normal service of a federation, the Contrail federation provides state-of-the-art SLA management of QoS and QoP. Contrail also removes most basic user lock-in constraints offering a uniform approach to actor identification, management policies, costs and application description. In the following, we will explain how a federation differs from other interoperation-oriented approaches, and discuss the main features of the Contrail federation.

In the last few years, the cloud market has grown in terms of its IT market penetration, of the number of players in cloud service provisioning and in terms of differentiation of services between the providers. This variegated cloud offer is an opportunity for companies that want to use public clouds for their applications, but also forces to deal with a non trivial comparison and selection problem.

As the cloud market was still taking shape, different proprietary protocols to describe and rent services did imply a certain degree of user lock-in. While on the one hand we now have much more options to choose from (at the IaaS as well as the PaaS and SaaS levels), on the other hand, and despite strong efforts toward standardization and interoperation [2,7,8,15], it has become increasingly complex to choose between semantically equivalent services with different metrics of cost, performance, reliability, security and elasticity. Complexity arises (i) from the need to match the services, and the service quality level descriptions in different languages, with different protocols used to set up, monitor and steer them, as well as (ii) from the need to plan service utilization in order to optimize a user-specific trade-off of the aforementioned metrics, gathering and exploiting information about a multitude of service providers.

Cloud brokering is nowadays the rising approach to address those issues [17], with both open source (DeltaCloud [4,6]) and commercial solutions (CloudSwitch, Enstratus, Rightscale, Kaavo) already being available. Cloud brokers target interoperation between one user application and one provider, only considering multiple cloud interconnection for the restricted case of cloudbursting from the user's private cloud to a public one. Besides, removing API-related lock-in barriers with respect to providers can result in tying up the user to the broker management interface.

The Contrail approach to federations mainly focuses on provider-level integration of infrastructural services (IaaS) including a heterogeneous population of providers of computation, network, and storage services. As opposed to a broker-based approach, the end-user can exploit advanced inter-provider deployment and coordination, even for a single application, and benefit from state-of-the art federated security as well as federation-ubiquitous SLA mechanisms. These features constitute the basis for higher-level services (PaaS, SaaS) and allow to provide standardized guarantees to the platform user. While cloud brokering relies on and fosters a more competitive cloud resource market, Contrail federations also promote *cooperation* among several providers as a way to open new market opportunities, and fully addressing issues (i) and (ii) outlined before.

To this end, the Contrail federation [5] meets several design constraints. *Security* and *decentralization* are key ones: the many Federation Access Points

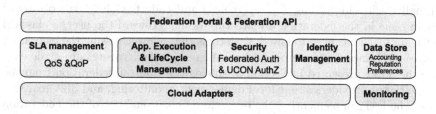

Fig. 2. A Federation Access Point. Each FAP implements the topmost layer of the Contrail abstract architecture, including the Federation Core, its GUI and API.

(FAPs, Fig. 2) implementing the top layer of the Contrail architecture are available to any federation user and can interact with any provider within the federation. Beside leveraging state-of-the-art federated authentication solutions [11] and authorization mechanisms [13], the *Data Store* module of the federation has built-in mechanisms for synchronizing critical data among FAPs. The Data Store provides permanent memory of many information flows (user accounting, reputation monitoring, violation monitoring) each one with its own synchronization policy. Each FAP can be co-located with a cloud provider, making the access to some resources cheaper, but the federation is free to choose resources for an application deployment request from any other provider in the federation, thus completely separating the interests of the cloud provider hosting a FAP and those of the federation/users.

Another key design aim was support for *efficient mapping* of applications under *complex SLA constraints*. The actual mapping of the application over one or more providers is done in the *Application Execution and LifeCycle Management* module (which includes the services of the *Application Lifecycle Manager* shown in Fig. 1), on the ground of several desiderata: the user needs, expressed by the application description and its SLA proposal; information gathered about provider reputation and available resources; the negotiation carried on by the SLA management mechanism. The *SLA management* module inside the FAP architecture is in charge of carrying the topmost level of the hierarchical SLA · negotiation, as described in Section 4, trying to achieve SLA contracts with one or more providers that can overall satisfy the user-proposed SLA.

Application mapping exploits a set of heuristics in order to optimize the user-defined trade-off among application metrics, e.g. balancing economic cost and performance levels. To simplify this task, we employ a software toolkit which translates different parts of the application description (namely OVF files, SLA, deployment information) to and from several standard formats and into an in-memory graph representation. Graph-based optimization algorithms can be applied, and the whole structure can be modified, decomposed and translated in many ways to allow for composite deployment over possibly different cloud providers and SLA contracts. The system is designed to also monitor and control the application execution, to possibly perform resource migration or elasticity management.

Finally, achieving strong *Interoperability* and code flexibility was obviously a main issue in the federation architecture design. Toward the user, a classical REST approach has been followed, with tools that allow accessing the federation services via browser and command line. A great deal of features are made easy since the VEP, presented in Section 5, shields the Contrail federation from the specificities of providers about local deployment, monitoring, and SLA management. The FAP, implementing the operational functionalities of the Federation core (shown in Fig. 1), thus has the task to coordinate (via an extendable set of *cloud adapters*) different federation entities (one or more VEP instances, VIN and GAFS resources) for the sake of a specific application.

4   Service Level Agreements

Different cloud providers may have different interfaces to specify requirements, and not all of them provide automatic quotation for a required user configuration. Interacting with different providers by hand to find the best and cheapest one for a given application is a complex and time consuming task. The Contrail federation SLA Management layer automates this provider comparison and selection task and hides to the final user the complexity of interacting with multiple cloud providers.

The Contrail SLA Management layer allows to express user requirements about application QoS in a uniform way. The same SLA syntax is used by all cloud providers in the federation, enabling it to negotiate with and to compare multiple providers. To enable negotiation interoperability of different cloud providers with the Contrail federation, a SLA Management layer is added to each provider. This layer is able to understand the SLA syntax used by the federation and to automatically create SLA offers which will be proposed to the federation on behalf of the provider.

The model of interaction proposed by Contrail is based on multi-level negotiation of SLAs: a user negotiates a SLA with the Contrail federation, which in turn negotiates with several providers to select the best one that can satisfy all user's needs (see Fig. 3).

The Contrail provider SLA management layer works directly with that specific cloud provider's resources, while SLA management at federation level mediates between the SLA to be agreed with the end user and SLAs to be agreed with different cloud providers. In the negotiation phase the cloud

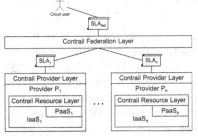

Fig. 3. Multilevel SLA negotiation between user, Contrail federation and multiple cloud providers

user negotiates with the Contrail federation a pre-configured SLA template, over an arbitrary number of rounds, until they both agree on all the terms. On each round the federation SLA Manager provides to the user the best SLA offer for the given application selected after negotiating with multiple providers.

Each SLA offer is composed by multiple terms expressing various QoS guarantees about resources described by an associated OVF descriptor. The price of each resource is also expressed as a SLA term in the offer. The federation SLA Manager compares the SLA offers returned by each provider and then selects the best one with respect to criteria such as price and performance. To compare the offers returned by each provider, each SLA can be represented as a point in a multi-dimensional space: each term will be a dimension in this space. Coordinates of each SLA-point in this space will be defined to be proportional to the value of each term in that SLA. For terms to be maximised, such as the amount of memory of a VM, direct proportionality is used; while for terms to be minimised, such as price, the proportionality relation is inverse. This model allows the definition of a sort of distance between SLA offers and thus supports comparison between them.

The actual comparison between different SLA offers is done according to a prioritised list of criteria defined by the user, such as price, plus the fact that the specific application will be cpu-bound, memory-bound or I/O-bound. Further criteria for the comparison may include the "reputation" of each cloud provider (calculated by the Contrail federation as a function of the number of SLA violation observed) and user's preferences, either positive or negative, as a filter over providers. For example, a user may have registered a list of preferred cloud providers, or another may have specified a list of providers to be avoided.

SLA terms that will be supported by Contrail include specific characteristics defining the configuration of each VM, such as the amount of memory or the number of virtual cores, but also terms that may affect application performance, such as network bandwidth or the possibility to co-locate in the same host different VMs that must exchange large amounts of data, and even terms important at a legal or privacy level, such as the geographical location.

5 Virtual Execution Platform

The Virtual Execution Platform (VEP) [9,10,12] system offers a uniform way of representing and managing the resources of a cloud provider facilitating the tasks of data center administrators and of the Contrail federation, which interacts with heterogeneous cloud providers. Indeed, these providers might have different means to manage VMs or networks, different image formats that can be deployed on a physical host, different interfaces, or different contextualization methods for the physical resources. As such VEP enables the participation of the cloud provider in the federation seamlessly and it does proper VM contextualization and application lifecycle management. Additionally it publishes application events and metrics to the federation and SLA layers for application's monitoring and SLA enforcement.

Due to its capabilities of hiding the complexity of heterogeneous cloud providers, VEP enables interoperability at federation level through its RESTful interface based on the DMTF's Cloud Infrastructure Management Interface (CIMI) [8] standard. The CIMI model defines a framework for the application life cycle management on a cloud provider infrastructure, with applications generated from an Open

Virtualization Format (OVF) document [7]. VEP extends the CIMI API to support both the federation and the deployment of applications under SLA terms.

The Contrail VEP software is part of the business layer of a cloud provider, as depicted in Fig. 1 and it is installed on the provider data center. Nevertheless it could be also used as an external service, in which case it interacts remotely with the IaaS services through its external API.

Very few propositions currently exist to manage the whole application lifecycle at the IaaS level. The advantage of VEP over existing solutions for managing a cloud infrastructure is the integration of the support for SLAs, eg. with respect to VMware vCloud Suite [18], or the use of the OVF standard format for application description, eg. with respect to CompatibleOne [4]. The rest of this section describes the Contrail VEP features that enable the deployment of elastic and distributed applications, described with the OVF standard, on heterogeneous cloud providers and how these applications could be deployed within the constraints expressed in negotiated SLAs.

Standard OVF Support. Contrail and VEP [9] support standard OVF [7] descriptions without any need for extensions, compared to other propositions such as Claudia [3] which require extensions to manage application elasticity. The absence of extensions improves portability as existing OVF applications can be deployed on IaaS cloud providers without any modification.

IaaS cloud providers should guarantee rapid elasticity to dynamically adapt the allocated resources to the application's requirements. Elasticity support and the deployment over multiple cloud providers are facilitated by the VEP support for implicit as well as controlled deployment modes of OVF applications: in implicit mode, all OVF virtual resources are deployed and started; in controlled mode a user can explicitly specify which and how many OVF virtual resources listed in a *deployment document* are to be deployed. The controlled mode is indeed exploited by the Contrail federation for multi-provider deployments: each provider VEP receives a deployment document defining the OVF resources to deploy. This mode is also exploited to manage elasticity: submitting a new deployment document to an existing application adds the resources listed in this document to the application. To improve the dependability of long running applications, the mapping between the OVF description and the deployed virtual resources can be exploited by VEP to take an application snapshot and to package this snapshot in a new OVF document which can be exploited to re-deploy the application, possibly on another provider.

SLA Terms Support. The Contrail federation and the user negotiate the SLA associated to an application, which is then deployed by VEP respecting those negotiated constraints [12]. The SLA support during the deployment is achieved with the definition of the Contrail Constrained Execution Environments (CEEs), which can be derived from a negotiated SLA or made available as templates ready to be instantiated by users. The CEE on which a new application is to be deployed can be specified by the user, the federation acting on behalf of the user, or from default rules. It is possible to deploy multiple applications on the same CEE, for instance applications sharing the same virtual network or storage.

A CEE defines a virtual infrastructure made of resource handlers and constraints where user applications are deployed and managed. Fig. 4 shows the mapping between the resources described in the application OVF document and the CEE resource handlers specifying the constraints which should be respected for the deployment of each resource. Each resource handler specifies the physical resources to be allocated for each virtual resource (virtual machine, storage, or network) instantiated in the infrastructure. Different types of constraints are supported in VEP concerning performance, security, placement or the number of virtual resources which can be allocated. For instance, constraints can specify relations between resources, such as affinity to allocate resources close to each other in order to improve interactions, or anti-affinity to increase dependability, for instance to place virtual machines on different data centers. The CEE also defines the monitoring configurations, which are then used by the provider and the federation to evaluate whether a SLA is enforced.

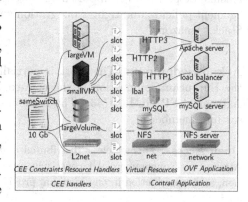

Fig. 4. Constrained Execution Environments and OVF mapping

New deployment requests for additional resources of an application can then be automatically generated by the SLA enforcement services in reaction to performance indicator deviations, or directly requested by the user. Adding new resources to the application does not necessitate any SLA re-negotiation as long as the CEE constraints are respected.

VEP Features. In the previous paragraphs, we have presented the VEP support for SLAs through CEEs and DMTF's OVF standard [7] for application description (without any extension) as well as how VEP deals with elastic applications. Other features of the Contrail VEP not discussed in this section are: partial application deployment to allow multi-provider application deployment from the federation layer; advance reservation to guarantee resource provisioning in the future; application snapshots to improve dependability.

6   Conclusion

The Contrail project provides an open-source integrated approach to virtualization at the IaaS and PaaS levels [1]. This chapter discussed the challenges and the approach in Contrail to address interoperability issues and SLA-aware deployment of distributed applications across a federation of heterogeneous cloud providers. We described the major components of the Contrail architecture and

we outlined the key features and the design of the Contrail federation, SLA
management, and VEP. These components allow dynamic transparent leasing
of resources from multiple sources and ease the user access to cloud services. In
a nutshell, Contrail ameliorates the effectiveness of the pay-as-you go approach
and increases the end-user freedom in the provider selection. Moreover, strong
SLA guarantees support both provider competition (on prices) and collaboration
(provider aggregation) to access new market segments.

Contrail is still under intense development. More advanced policies and mechanisms are planned to support distributed deployment, sophisticated SLA management policies, and tighter integration with other Cloud providers (e.g. Open-
Stack, Amazon).

Acknowledgments. This work is partially funded by the FP7 Programme of
the European Commission in the context of the Contrail project under Grant
Agreement FP7-ICT-257438. The authors would like to thank the Contrail Consortium members.

References

1. Contrail project, http://contrail-project.eu/ code available on, http://contrail.projects.ow2.org/xwiki/bin/view/Main/WebHome
2. Cloud Data Management Interface (CDMI) Version 1.0.2 (June 2012), http://www.snia.org/cdmi
3. Morfeo Claudia, http://claudia.morfeo-project.org/
4. CompaptibleOne, http://www.compatibleone.org/
5. Coppola, M., Dazzi, P., Lazouski, A., Martinelli, F., Mori, P., Jensen, J., John-son, I., Kershaw, P.: The Contrail approach to cloud federations. In: International Symposium on Grids and Clouds (ISGC) (2012)
6. DeltaCloud, http://deltacloud.apache.org/
7. DMTF: Open Virtualization Format Specification (2010), http://www.dmtf.org/standards/ovf
8. DMTF: Cloud Infrastructure Management Interface (CIMI) Model and RESTful HTTP-based Protocol, An Interface for Managing Cloud Infrastructure, v1.0.1 DSP0263 (2012), http://www.dmtf.org/standards/cloud
9. Harsh, P., Dudouet, F., Cascella, R., Jegou, Y., Morin, C.: Using open standards for interoperability issues, solutions, and challenges facing cloud computing. In: 8th International Conference on Network and Service Management (CNSM) (2012)
10. Harsh, P., Jegou, Y., Cascella, R.G., Morin, C.: Contrail virtual execution platform: Challenges in being part of a cloud federation. In: Abramowicz, W., Llorente, I.M., Surridge, M., Zisman, A., Vayssière, J. (eds.) ServiceWave 2011. LNCS, vol. 6994, pp. 50–61. Springer, Heidelberg (2011)
11. IETF OASIS WG: RFC6749 – The OAuth 2.0 Authorization Framework (2012)

12. Jegou, Y., Harsh, P., Cascella, R., Dudouet, F., Morin, C.: Managing OVF applications under SLA constraints on contrail virtual execution platform. In: 8th International Conference on Network and Service Management (CNSM) (2012)
13. Lazouski, A., Martinelli, F., Mori, P.: A prototype for enforcing usage control policies based on XACML. In: Fischer-Hübner, S., Katsikas, S., Quirchmayr, G. (eds.) TrustBus 2012. LNCS, vol. 7449, pp. 79–92. Springer, Heidelberg (2012)
14. mOSAIC Web Site, http://www.mosaic-cloud.eu
15. OGF Consortium OCCI WG (2013), http://occi-wg.org/
16. Pierre, G., Stratan, C.: ConPaaS: a platform for hosting elastic cloud applications. IEEE Internet Computing 16(5), 88–92 (2012)
17. Sundareswaran, S., Squicciarini, A., Lin, D.: A brokerage-based approach for cloud service selection. In: IEEE Fifth International Conference on Cloud Computing (CLOUD) (2012)
18. VMware: VMware vCloud Suite for Cloud Computing & Cloud Management (January 2013), http://www.vmware.com/products/datacenter-virtualization/vcloud-suite/overview.html
19. Wieder, A., Bhatotia, P., Post, A., Rodrigues, R.: Orchestrating the deployment of computations in the cloud with conductor. In: 9th USENIX conference on Networked Systems Design and Implementation (NSDI) (2012)

Cloud–Based Evaluation Framework for Big Data*

Allan Hanbury[1], Henning Müller[2], Georg Langs[3], and Bjoern H. Menze[4]

[1] Institute of Software Technology and Interactive Systems,
Vienna University of Technology, Austria
`hanbury@ifs.tuwien.ac.at`
[2] University of Applied Sciences Western Switzerland (HES-SO), Switzerland
`henning.mueller@hevs.ch`
[3] CIR Lab, Department of Radiology, Medical University of Vienna, Austria
`georg.langs@meduniwien.ac.at`
[4] Computer Vision Laboratory, ETH Zürich, Switzerland
`bjoern@ethz.ch`

Abstract. The VISCERAL project is building a cloud-based evaluation framework for evaluating machine learning and information retrieval algorithms on large amounts of data. Instead of downloading data and running evaluations locally, the data will be centrally available on the cloud and algorithms to be evaluated will be programmed in computing instances on the cloud, effectively bringing the algorithms to the data. This approach allows evaluations to be performed on Terabytes of data without needing to consider the logistics of moving the data or storing the data on local infrastructure. After discussing the challenges of benchmarking on big data, the design of the VISCERAL system is presented, concentrating on the components for coordinating the participants in the benchmark and managing the ground truth creation. The first two benchmarks run on the VISCERAL framework will be on segmentation and retrieval of 3D medical images.

Keywords: Evaluation, Cloud Computing, Annotation, Information Retrieval, Machine Learning.

1 Introduction

Demonstrating progress in data-centric areas of computational science, such as machine learning and information retrieval, requires demonstrating that a new algorithm performs better in its task than state-of-the-art algorithms. However, even though a continuous stream of published papers claim to have demonstrated such improvements, some scepticism remains. Hand [9] discusses the "illusion of progress" in classifier technology, while Armstrong et al. [4] present evidence for "improvements that don't add up" in information retrieval (IR).

Evaluation campaigns and benchmarks aim at quantifying the state-of-the-art by making available tasks and data, and objectively comparing the results

---

* Invited Paper.

A. Galis and A. Gavras (Eds.): FIA 2013, LNCS 7858, pp. 104–114, 2013.

of multiple participants' approaches to performing the set tasks on the provided data. In the area of IR, evaluation campaigns have been run for over 20 years [10]. Current evaluation campaigns include TREC (Text REtrieval Conference)[1], TRECVid (TREC Video Evaluation)[2], CLEF (Cross Language Evaluation Forum)[3], ImageCLEF [14], NTCIR (NII Test Collection for IR Systems)[4], INEX (Initiative for the Evaluation of XML Retrieval)[5] and FIRE (Forum for Information Retrieval Evaluation)[6]. In the area of machine learning, the PASCAL challenges are well known[7], while in the area of medical image analysis, annual challenges are organised as part of the Conference on Medical Image Computing and Computer Assisted Intervention (MICCAI)[8].

However, even with these evaluation campaigns and challenges, a number of causes contribute to the above-mentioned lack of clear improvement:

Data: Even though evaluation campaigns, challenges and other mechanisms lead to the availability of commonly used test datasets "standardised" within communities, these datasets are often not a "realistic" approximation of real-world datasets. Reasons for this are that the datasets are often small so as to simplify dissemination and reduce computation time; are not representative of all of the the variation found in real-world data; or are cleaned in some way to reduce noise and outliers. Furthermore, it is unlikely that a single algorithm will have the best performance on all possible datasets. Concentration on achieving improvements on a few datasets could lead to algorithms highly optimised for these datasets. Alternatively, if many datasets are available, then results could be presented only on datasets for which performance is good. Finally, even though many such datasets are available, proprietary data are still often used in publications.

Algorithms: Source code or even executables for cutting edge algorithms are usually not made available. It is often difficult to re-implement an algorithm based on its description in a paper. This means that comparisons to such an algorithm can only reliably be made on the datasets on which it was tested in the original publication, and it is not possible to judge the performance of this algorithm on new data.

Baselines: New performance results in publications are often compared to a low and little optimized baseline, and not to the state-of-the-art algorithms. This is linked to a certain extent to the difficulty in obtaining or re-implementing state-of-the-art algorithms mentioned in the previous point. However, it could also be linked to the pressure to show some sort of improvement in order to get a paper published. Evaluation campaigns and challenges aim to

---

[1] http://trec.nist.gov/

[2] http://trecvid.nist.gov/

[3] http://www.clef-campaign.org/

[4] http://research.nii.ac.jp/ntcir/index-en.html

[5] https://inex.mmci.uni-saarland.de/

[6] http://www.isical.ac.in/~clia/

[7] http://pascallin2.ecs.soton.ac.uk/Challenges/

[8] http://www.grand-challenge.org has an overview of most MICCAI challenges.

solve this problem, but beyond the single publication incorporating the results of all algorithms submitted, in general little comparison to these results subsequently takes place.

Related to the above points, in the computational sciences in general, there has been recent concern expressed about the lack of reproducibility of experimental results, raising questions about their reliability. The lack of publication of program code has been identified as a significant reason for this [6]. There is currently work underway to counter this situation, ranging from presenting the case for open computer programs [12], through creating infrastructures to allow reproducible computational research [6] to considerations about the legal licensing and copyright frameworks for computational research [18].

Despite these shortcomings, evaluation campaigns do make a significant economic and scholarly impact. TREC, organised by the National Institutes of Standards and Technology (NIST) in the USA, is the longest running IR evaluation campaign and has been running since 1992. A 2010 study of the economic impact of TREC[9] came to the conclusion that "US$16 million of discounted investments made by NIST and others in TREC have resulted in US$81 million in discounted extrapolated benefits or a net present value of US$65 million". This is due to, amongst others, making available evaluation resources at a relatively low cost, developing and publishing evaluation methodologies, encouraging development of improved IR techniques and allowing companies to see which are the most successful techniques to integrate into their products. Recently, the assessments of the scholarly impact based on bibliometric measures have been published for two evaluation campaigns: ImageCLEF [20] and TRECVid [19]. Both papers demonstrate the impact through the high number of citations of papers written as a result of the evaluation campaigns.

The VISCERAL project[10] is developing a cloud-based framework for experimentation on large datasets, with a focus on image analysis and retrieval in the medical domain. Initially, it is aiming to reduce the complexities and barriers to running experiments on huge representative datasets, discussed in more detail in Section 2.

For a benchmark that is run on the VISCERAL framework, the task will be specified and the training data will be placed on the cloud. Participants will program solutions to the task in computing instances (virtual machines) on the cloud, effectively *bringing the algorithms to the data* instead of the more conventional transfer of the data to where the algorithms are. Benchmark organisers will then evaluate the task solutions on an unseen dataset. Over the next two years, two benchmarks for 3D medical imaging will be run: classification of regions of medical images and retrieval of medical images [13]. The benchmarks will be run on a dataset of at least 2TB of radiology images and associated radiology reports. This evaluation framework under development in VISCERAL is presented in Section 3. Finally, Section 4 discusses various considerations for further development of the evaluation framework. Further information on the

---

[9] http://trec.nist.gov/pubs/2010.economic.impact.pdf
[10] http://visceral.eu

VISCERAL project is available targeted at the IR community in [8], and at the medical imaging community in [13].

In other scientific fields such as physics, large Grid networks [5] such as EGI (European Grid Initiative) or previously EGEE (Enabling Grids for E-Science in Europe) [7] have been created for distributed data analysis where several large institutions share large infrastructures in virtual organizations. Still, most Grid middleware is hard to install and many small research groups in computer science do not have the funding to maintain such infrastructures, meaning that this model cannot be transferred to all fields of science and the medical imaging field is an area where this can be problematic [15]. A centralized infrastructure has the advantage of a very low entry level for groups to participate in such a campaign.

2   Challenges in Benchmarking on Big Data

The standard model used by the majority of evaluation campaigns in machine learning follows the following steps, where **O** indicates that the step is performed by the organisers and **P** indicates that the step is performed by the participants:

1. **O**: The organisers define the task to be performed and collect suitable data for the task. The data are divided into a training and test set. Sufficient ground truth for the task is created, where ground truth is required on the training data for training the machine learning algorithms, and required on the test data for evaluating the performance of algorithms by comparing their output to the test data ground truth.
2. **O**: The organisers publish the task information, and make the training data and associated ground truth available for download.
3. **P**: Participants train their algorithms using the training data and ground truth.
4. **O**: At a later date, the test data (without ground truth) is made available to the participants to download.
5. **P**: The participants run their trained algorithms on the test data, and submit the outputs (in a pre-defined format) to the organisers by a specified deadline (usually through an online submission system).
6. **O**: The organisers evaluate the performance of the algorithms on the test data using the corresponding ground truth, and release the results.

For IR benchmarks, the sequence is similar, except that the full set of data (often with some example queries and relevant documents) is released in step 2 for the participants to index in step 3. In step 4, the test queries are released, and the participants must submit the documents returned by each test query in step 5. While it would in theory be possible to provide the ground truth for the relevance of each document to the test queries in step 1, this would in practice require infeasible amounts of human input. In practice, the human input for the relevance judgements is provided in step 6, where relevance judgements are only done on documents returned by at least one algorithm, usually involving a technique such as pooling to further reduce the number of relevance judgements to be made [17].

For applications that in practice involve the processing and analysis of large amounts of data, running benchmarks of the algorithms on representative amounts of data has advantages. Using more data implies that the benchmark data can be more characteristic of the data used in practice, especially in terms of fine features of the data distribution and of the inclusion of outliers. However, running benchmarks on multiple terabytes of data leads to a number of practical problems, including:

Data distribution: Downloading the data through the internet can take an excessive amount of time and is costly. A solution that is often adopted is to send the data to the researchers on hard disks through the postal service. This however requires additional effort on the part of the benchmark organisers and involves higher costs.

Computing power: Not all researchers wishing to participate in the benchmark have sufficient local computing resources (processing and storage capacity) to participate effectively in the benchmark. For some research groups, processing all of the data potentially requires several weeks, while for others several hours may be sufficient.

Comparison of algorithm efficiency: As each participant runs their algorithms on a different infrastructure, comparison of the algorithm efficiency in terms of processing speed is not possible.

Obtaining sufficient ground truth: With more data, correspondingly more ground truth is necessary to make the use of the data advantageous. This means that manual annotation costs increase.

In IR, the largest benchmark datasets available are the ClueWeb datasets. The ClueWeb12 dataset[11] contains 870,043,929 English web pages, with an uncompressed size of 32 TB (5.3 TB compressed). It is distributed on hard drives sent by post.

The high cost of obtaining ground truth can be mitigated in some cases by the use of more cost-effective annotators, such as those available on crowd-sourcing platforms [1,21]. However, this approach is often not suitable for more specialised tasks requiring the annotators to possess expert knowledge.

3   VISCERAL Framework

The VISCERAL cloud-based benchmarking framework currently under development is shown in Figure 1. This represents the envisaged setup for a machine learning benchmark, but an IR benchmark would have a similar setup, with the main change being a single dataset available for indexing. The main components of the framework for managing the benchmark are the *Registration System*, which handles participant registration and management, and the *Analysis System*, which handles the running and analysis of results during the test phase, as

---

[11] http://lemurproject.org/clueweb12.php

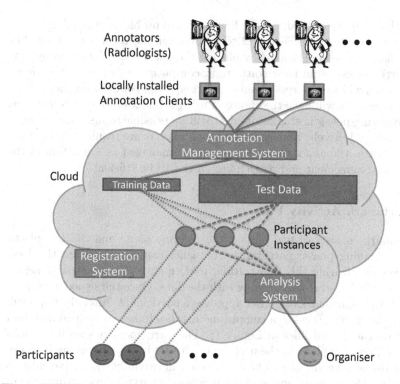

Fig. 1. VISCERAL evaluation framework. The dotted lines represent connections during the training phase, while the dashed lines represent connections during the test phase. Solid lines are connections that exist before and throughout the benchmark.

described in Section 3.2. The *Annotation Management System* coordinates the manual annotation, as described in Section 3.3.

3.1 Cloud-Based Framework

The cloud has innovated a number of aspects of computing, as it provides the appearance of infinite computing resources available on demand, eliminates upfront commitment by cloud users and provides the ability to pay for the use of computing resources on a short-term basis as needed [2]. The abilities necessary for the experimental approach described in this paper are:

- Provide the ability to centrally store and make available large datasets — Cloud providers already provide this service. For example, Amazon hosts public datasets free of charge[12].
- Allow multiple users to process the stored data without requiring the data to be transfered elsewhere — this is done through linking virtual storage drives to computing instances as required. For example, Amazon public datasets are accessed in this way.

---

[12] http://aws.amazon.com/publicdatasets/

The cloud-based framework allows the four practical problems of running benchmarks on big data listed in Section 2 to be overcome to a certain extent. The *data distribution* problem is solved by placing the data in the cloud and by having the participants install their software in computing instances in the cloud. All participants will have access to sufficient *computing power* in the cloud computing instance, and will have the choice of using a Linux or Windows instance. As the computing power is standardised, it will be possible to measure the *algorithm efficency* objectively. Finally, even though experts are required for creating the ground truth, the annotation process can be managed as a function of the inter-annotator agreement and participant entries to be efficient.

3.2   Benchmark Activity Flow

The benchmark consists of two phases, the *training phase* and the *test phase*. During the training phase, potential participants can register using the Registration System. During this registration, participants will be asked to sign a document regulating what can be done with the data. Once the signed document is uploaded, the benchmark organiser approves a participant. After the approval, participants are given access to a computing instance linked to the training data (indicated by the dotted lines in Figure 1). The participant has until the submission deadline to implement the necessary software in the computing instance to perform the benchmark task. The organisers will carefully specify parameters such as output format and naming of the executable files to allow automation of the calling of the programs. Participants will also have the possibility to download a subset of the training data, hence allowing optimisation to be done on local computing infrastructure if this is desired.

After the submission deadline, the Analysis System takes over control of all computing instances from the participants, and participants lose access to their instances. The computing instances are then all linked to the test dataset (indicated by the dashed lines in Figure 1). The Analysis System runs the software, analyses the outputs and computes the performance metrics. These performance metrics are then provided to the participants.

3.3   Manual Annotation

The use of the cloud allows the manual annotation of the data to be effectively controlled, which will be done by the Annotation Management System. As the VISCERAL benchmarks are using radiology image data, expert annotators in the form of radiologists will be used. As the time of such experts is expensive, it is important that the most effective use is made of their time.

The first annotation task, taking place before the begin of the training phase, is the annotation of the training data. The manual annotations will form the *gold corpus* used during the training phase. The radiologists performing the annotation will install a local client that assists in the manual marking of volumes of the images by using semi-automated techniques. The Annotation Management

System will be able to assign images and anatomical structures to specific radiologists to annotate. It will assign part of the images to at least two radiologists so that inter-annotator agreement can be measured, for each annotated structure. This allows the system to measure the quality of the annotation, estimate the ability of the various annotators, and assign "difficult" images having lower inter-annotator agreement to more annotators of higher ability. Since only a part of the overall data will be annotated to form the gold-corpus the choice of cases to annotate is important. Based on the cumulative annotations, the system estimates the information gain expected from a particular case, and assigns those cases where this is maximal. This ensures that the variability represented in the gold corpus is large.

For evaluation of the participants' automatic annotation results on the test set, ground truth annotations are also necessary for this part of the data. Part of these annotations will be created by radiologists as described for the training set. However, due to the huge amount of data in the test set, manual annotation of all of it is infeasible. Therefore, a *silver corpus* approach, such as the one used in the CALBC challenges[13] [16], will be adopted. This silver corpus is built based on voting on the participant submissions. However, the Annotation Management System will also be able to request manual corrections of images for which it appears that the voting is inconclusive.

4 Discussion and Conclusion

The first two benchmarks organised in the VISCERAL framework will work on large scale 3D medical imaging. The first benchmark on segmentation of organs represents a machine learning style of evaluation with separate training and testing datasets, while the second benchmark on retrieval of similar images represents an IR style of evaluation. These first two benchmarks will be run in the style of a classic challenge or evaluation campaign, with a strict submission deadline for algorithms and resulting metrics of the evaluation being released by the organisers simultaneously. The aim is however to automate the process, allowing participants to submit algorithms in computing instances at any time, and to get rapid feedback about the calculated metrics directly from the system. The system could then also store results of all algorithms submitted, allowing effective comparison of a submitted algorithm with state-of-the-art algorithms. However, the willingness of researchers to use such a system allowing direct comparison to state-of-the-art algorithms must be investigated, as initiatives to provide such services have not been well accepted. For example, in the IR community, the EvaluatIR system [3] was hardly used, even though it provided the choice of using it without being obliged to reveal the results obtained to other users.

For the initial two benchmarks run on this cloud-based evaluation framework, participants will have their cloud computing costs funded by project funds of the organisers. However, for sustainability of the framework, further models of

---

[13] http://calbc.eu

financing the participants' computing costs will have to be developed. The simplest is that participants finance their own computing costs, although this will likely disadvantage groups with few financial resources. Alternatively, the cloud service providers could provide computing time to researchers in the form of grants (for example, it is currently possible for researchers to apply for grants in the form of free usage credits from Amazon[14]). Finally, a publicly-funded cloud-based evaluation infrastructure hosting standard datasets could provide subsidised or free access to researchers based on an application scheme.

An important consideration is who should provide this cloud-based evaluation service. Commercial cloud providers are already able to provide it, but it is prudent to avoid "lock-in" of research to a single provider, due to incompatibilities between services provided by different companies. Potentially, a publicly-funded cloud infrastructure would be valuable for running such evaluation experiments in a neutral way.

The proposed infrastructure could also allow evaluation to be conducted on private or restricted data, such as electronic health records or private e-mails, as it is not necessary for the participants to see the test data. However, for researchers, such an approach could be considered unsatisfactory, as researchers would simply obtain metrics on the performance of their algorithms on the data, but not have the possibility to examine why their algorithms performed as they did. Innovative approaches to allow researchers to explore key parts of the private data related to their algorithm performance without revealing private details remain to be developed.

VISCERAL is a solid step toward creating a framework for evaluation of algorithms on large datasets. The framework can be seen as an initial low-level building block of the Innovation Accelerator, as envisioned by van Harmelen et al. [11] as an outline for revolutionising the scientific process.

Acknowledgements. The research leading to these results has received funding from the European Union Seventh Framework Programme (FP7/2007-2013) under grant agreements 318068 (VISCERAL), Khresmoi (257528) and 258191 (PROMISE).

References

1. Alonso, O., Baeza-Yates, R.: Design and implementation of relevance assessments using crowdsourcing. In: Clough, P., Foley, C., Gurrin, C., Jones, G.J.F., Kraaij, W., Lee, H., Mudoch, V. (eds.) ECIR 2011. LNCS, vol. 6611, pp. 153–164. Springer, Heidelberg (2011)

[14] http://aws.amazon.com/grants/

2. Armbrust, M., Fox, A., Griffith, R., Joseph, A.D., Katz, R., Konwinski, A., Lee, G., Patterson, D., Rabkin, A., Stoica, I., Zaharia, M.: A view of cloud computing. Commun 53(4), 50–58 (2010)
3. Armstrong, T.G., Moffat, A., Webber, W., Zobel, J.: EvaluatIR: an online tool for evaluating and comparing ir systems. In: SIGIR 2009: Proceedings of the 32nd International ACM SIGIR Conference, p. 833. ACM (2009)
4. Armstrong, T.G., Moffat, A., Webber, W., Zobel, J.: Improvements that don't add up: ad-hoc retrieval results since 1998. In: CIKM 2009: Proceeding of the 18th ACM Conference on Information and Knowledge Management, pp. 601–610. ACM (2009)
5. Foster, I., Kesselman, C., Tuecke, S.: The anatomy of the Grid: Enabling scalable virtual organizations. The International Journal of Supercomputer Applications 15(3) (summer 2001)
6. Freire, J., Silva, C.T.: Making computations and publications reproducible with VisTrails. Computing in Science & Engineering 14(4), 18–25 (2012)
7. Gagliardi, F., Jones, B., François, G., Bégin, M.E., Heikkurinen, M.: Building an infrastructure for scientific grid computing: status and goals of the EGEE project. Philosophical Transactions of the Royal Society A 363, 1729–1742 (2005)
8. Hanbury, A., Müller, H., Langs, G., Weber, M.A., Menze, B.H., Fernandez, T.S.: Bringing the algorithms to the data: Cloud–based benchmarking for medical image analysis. In: Catarci, T., Forner, P., Hiemstra, D., Peñas, A., Santucci, G. (eds.) CLEF 2012. LNCS, vol. 7488, pp. 24–29. Springer, Heidelberg (2012)
9. Hand, D.J.: Classifier technology and the illusion of progress. Statistical Science 21(1), 1–14 (2006)
10. Harman, D.: Information Retrieval Evaluation. Morgan & Claypool Publishers (2011)
11. van Harmelen, F., Kampis, G., Börner, K., Besselaar, P., Schultes, E., Goble, C., Groth, P., Mons, B., Anderson, S., Decker, S., Hayes, C., Buecheler, T., Helbing, D.: Theoretical and technological building blocks for an innovation accelerator. The European Physical Journal Special Topics 214(1), 183–214 (2012)
12. Ince, D.C., Hatton, L., Graham-Cumming, J.: The case for open computer programs. Nature 482(7386), 485–488 (2012)
13. Langs, G., Hanbury, A., Menze, B., Müller, H.: VISCERAL: Towards large data in medical imaging — challenges and directions. In: Greenspan, H., Müller, H., Syeda-Mahmood, T. (eds.) MCBR-CDS 2012. LNCS, vol. 7723, pp. 92–98. Springer, Heidelberg (2013)
14. Müller, H., Clough, P., Deselaers, T., Caputo, B. (eds.): ImageCLEF – Experimental Evaluation in Visual Information Retrieval. The Springer International Series on Information Retrieval, vol. 32. Springer, Heidelberg (2010)
15. Pitkanen, M., Zhou, X., Tuisku, M., Niemi, T., Ryynänen, V., Müller, H.: How Grids are perceived in healthcare and the public service sector. In: Global Health-Grid: e-Science Meets Biomedical Informatics — Proceedings of HealthGrid 2008. Studies in Health Technology and Informatics, vol. 138, pp. 61–69. IOS Press (2008)
16. Rebholz-Schumann, D., Yepes, A.J.J., van Mulligen, E.M., Kang, N., Kors, J., Milward, D., Corbett, P., Buyko, E., Beisswanger, E., Hahn, U.: CALBC silver standard corpus. Journal of Bioinformatics and Computational Biology 8(1), 163–179 (2010)
17. Sanderson, M.: Test collection based evaluation of information retrieval systems. Foundations and Trends in Information Retrieval 4(4), 247–375 (2010)
18. Stodden, V.: The legal framework for reproducible scientific research: Licensing and copyright. Computing in Science & Engineering 11(1), 35–40 (2009)

19. Thornley, C.V., Johnson, A.C., Smeaton, A.F., Lee, H.: The scholarly impact of trecvid (2003–2009). Journal of the American Society for Information Science and Technology 62, 613–627 (2011)
20. Tsikrika, T., de Herrera, A.G.S., Müller, H.: Assessing the scholarly impact of imageCLEF. In: Forner, P., Gonzalo, J., Kekäläinen, J., Lalmas, M., de Rijke, M. (eds.) CLEF 2011. LNCS, vol. 6941, pp. 95–106. Springer, Heidelberg (2011)
21. Vijayanarasimhan, S., Grauman, K.: Large-scale live active learning: Training object detectors with crawled data and crowds. In: IEEE Conference on Computer Vision and Pattern Recognition (CVPR), pp. 1449–1456 (2011)

Optimizing Service Ecosystems in the Cloud

Usman Wajid, César A. Marín, and Nikolay Mehandjiev

The University of Manchester
{firstname.lastname}@manchester.ac.uk

Abstract. A service ecosystem is a virtual space ideally distributed across networks and geographical areas where vast numbers of services and other digital entities can coexist and converge to form *ad-hoc* solutions. In this paper we present experimental results showing the performance of two optimization models in service ecosystem. We describe the two models and how they operate under service ecosystem conditions. We emulate service ecosystem conditions in a multi-site federated Cloud and test the two models under different scenarios. The experimental results help us to determine strengths and weaknesses of the two optimization models enabling us to make recommendations for their use in different application domains.

1 Introduction

The proliferation of web-based services and rapid adoption of SOA have not only changed the perception of services but in effect also changed the way in which services are offered and consumed. An emerging development in this area is the notion of service ecosystems that can be seen as a virtual space where services and other digital entities interact and form (service-based) solutions at higher levels of granularity to achieve specific objectives. Dynamism is one of the fundamental characteristics of service ecosystem that allows services to appear and disappear at any time thus enabling the creation of ad-hoc solutions composed of various services.

Developing composite service-based solutions involves combining the functionality of multiple services in a unified solution on the basis of several factors, e.g., cost, performance, SLAs, etc. However, an automated approach for service composition may end up with sub-optimal solution (or composition) within service ecosystem because better services may become available soon after a composition was developed or some services in the composition may disappear with key functionality. These and other similar scenarios (e.g. choosing a particular service when the same functionality is offered by a number of services) represent a multi-criteria optimization problem creating the need for composition optimization to determine the best mix of services that can contribute towards the overall goal of the composition.

In this paper we describe two existing optimization models and test suitability of these models for optimizing service compositions in a service ecosystem while taking into account the dynamism of the domain. Building on our earlier research in service-based systems [1, 11] and complex adaptive systems [3, 4], our two service optimization models are characterized as global optimization and local optimization. The first

A. Galis and A. Gavras (Eds.): FIA 2013, LNCS 7858, pp. 115–126, 2013.

one, developed in the European Commission funded SOA4All project (http://www.soa4all.eu), computes the optimization of a service composition from a holistic point of view by analyzing end-to-end connections between composite services together with their non-functional properties [1, 2]. In contrast, the second optimization model called DAEM (Dynamic Agent-based Ecosystem Model) is able to compute local optimizations of service compositions by allowing the one-to-one interactions between service providers and consumers to create emergent service chains providing composite services that are resilient to changes [3, 4].

Both optimization models are computationally intensive, and this impedes their ability to optimize compositions involving a large number of services. To resolve this obstacle and to create necessary conditions for a service ecosystem, we need a suitable infrastructure that allows practical use of the optimizers and supports the dynamism and open nature of our target service ecosystems. The summary requirements to the supporting infrastructure are as follows:

- Multiple Cloud facilities to emulate the conditions for geographically distributing resources and services (i.e. candidate services that can be used in a composition) both manually and dynamically
- Seamless communication across inter- and across distributed sites
- Availability of on-demand computational resources; and
- Monitoring capabilities of computational resources both at runtime and after execution for monitoring data collection.

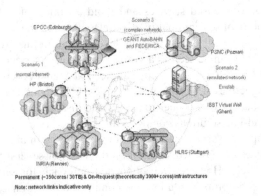

Fig. 1. Multi-site federated Cloud facilities offered by BonFIRE (http://www.bonfire-project.eu/infrastructure)

Based on the above requirements, we have selected the BonFIRE multi-site Cloud infrastructure presented in Fig. 1 (http://www.bonfire-project.eu/) as a suitable facility for running our optimization models.

In this respect, the contribution of this paper is twofold (i) testing the maturity of existing technology represented by two optimization model and its suitability for use in Future Internet scenarios such as service ecosystem, and (ii) investigating the existing infrastructure offerings such as BonFIRE and evaluate its support for Future Internet scenarios.

The rest of the paper is organized as follows: Section 2 presents the details about the two optimization models and the objectives of our tests, Section 3 outlines the design aspects of our experiments, and Section 4 presents a findings of the experiments, Section 5 concludes the paper with recommendations for using optimization models in different application domains and directions for future work.

2   Overview of Optimization Models

Our optimization models were designed to solve optimization problems using different techniques and we characterize the models according to the perspective they use to tackle the optimization problem i.e. globally and locally.

2.1   SOA4All Optimizer

The global model or *SOA4All optimizer* was designed to mainly work with semantic web services. It uses semantic link-based approach [2] for service composition. A semantic link is established between the output and input parameter of two services as a partial link indicating matching functionality. The matching functionality is determined by a matching function [1] that enables the estimation of semantic compatibilities among the descriptions of different services. This matching function is then used to define the quality of data flow in service composition at semantic level. This functional quality estimator is extended by considering non-functional properties of services also known as QoS parameters in the composition. These QoS parameters include Execution Price (i.e. fee requested by the service provider) and Response Time (i.e. expected delay between request and response time). Thus extended, the quality estimator allows the selection of the 'best' pairs of services in a composition. Further details about the optimization model, semantic links and the computation of functional and non-functional quality constraints can be found in [1, 2, 9]

The global optimization model uses this extended quality estimator and comprises the following three components.

- *Genetic Algorithm-based optimizer* a robust combinatorial optimization tool for generating alternative compositions based on different quality weights/criteria.
- *Reasoning engine:* a reasoner for computing the semantic similarities (and matching quality) between composite services.
- *Service repository* for hosting candidate services to be used in the composition.

The above components communicate extensively with each other and can be deployed in a distributed manner.

2.2   DAEM Optimizer

On the other hand, the local optimization model, *DAEM* [3], was developed to test the emergence of service value chains while dealing with unexpected disturbances. It is inspired by ideas from natural ecosystems where local, dynamic interactions are fundamental to the creation of ecosystems [8]. In DAEM links between services are created according to individual input and output matching of two services regardless of how that would affect the overall composition. Thus optimization occurs locally when a service selects another service (from a set of available services) that offers best match for its output. Likewise the other service also tries to selects the service offering best input. As a result a composition emerges from several locally optimized input-output matchings.

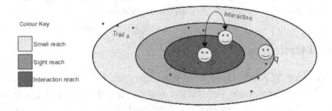

Fig. 2. The DAEM environment sets the rules and necessary conditions for agent interactions

The optimization model contains two types of components.

- *Environment* as a fundamental virtually observable surface where inhabitants (i.e. agents representing services) wander across and encounter others in order to interact. The environment sets the rules for agent interactions as well as mediates agent communication, as shown in Fig. 2.
- *Agent(s)* represent service providers and consumers in the service ecosystem.

Like SOA4All, the above components in DAEM require extensive communication and can be deployed in a distributed manner.

In this respect, the distributed nature of the two optimization models makes them suitable for testing in distributed computational environment.

3   Experimental Design

The experiments concerning both optimization models are designed to solve the problem archetype shown in Fig. 3.

The composition problem shown in Fig. 3 is represented as a service composition process template where various activities (shown by rectangular boxes) are interlinked with connectors (arrows). We choose this template because it contains the basic connectors namely XOR/AND joins and splits and sequence operators.

In the experiments the two optimizers start with a desired process template and select suitable services or agents to perform each activity in the template. The selection is made by matching the description of services (or capabilities of agents in case of

DAEM) with the description of the activities constituting the template. The services or agents are selected from a repository of services or agent clusters, which depending on the deployment configuration can be deployed at the same site as other optimizer components or it can be distributed across different Cloud sites.

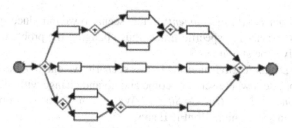

Fig. 3. Composition problem - service composition process template

Once the optimizers associate at least one service with each activity in the template the result is categorized as a non-optimal composition where there is at least one service associated with each activity. The optimizers then try to optimize the composition by replacing already associated services with better candidates using their inherent optimizing techniques. E.g., global optimization generates several alternative compositions and eventually selects the optimal one based on certain factors e.g. functional and non-functional quality of links/connections between composite services.

Whereas, in local optimization agents interact with each other in order to establish preferred provider-consumer chains (for each activity in the process template) that can change when agents find better partners.

Configurations	Scenarios	
	Controlled Environment	Dynamic Environment
One site	Exp1	Exp2
Fixed distribution	Exp3	Exp4

Fig. 4. Configuration and Scenarios used for testing optimization models

In this respect, we designed the experiments concerning the two optimization models to pursue the following objectives.

Objective O1 – To determine the optimal manner of distributing, decoupling and parallelizing the computationally intensive properties of optimization models on a large scale distributed architecture.

Objective O2 - To determine conditions under which both models achieve optimal composition e.g. by running predefined scenarios (involving dynamic changes in deployment configuration, number and properties of services, etc.)

Objective O3 - To analyze the behavior of testbed or Cloud infrastructure (i.e. BonFIRE) by changing dynamically the population size (i.e. number of candidate services or agents) and testing different features offered by the underlying

infrastructure such as how asynchronous interactions between multiple entities are
governed and managed by BonFIRE infrastructure, keeping in view the dynamism.

To achieve the above objectives the experiments are designed to test different
scenarios and also different deployment configurations, as shown in Fig. 4, and
elaborated below:

Scenario I- Controlled Environment: In this scenario we introduce specific changes
to the candidate services at specific times, thus changing the problem the optimisers
are trying to solve one at a time.

Scenario II- Dynamic Environment: In this scenario we emulate the dynamism of a
real service ecosystem where services come and go and change with less control.

Configurations I- One Site: We run each optimiser and
related components in a single BonFIRE site

Configurations II– Fixed Distribution: We distribute the optimisers' components
across different BonFIRE sites.

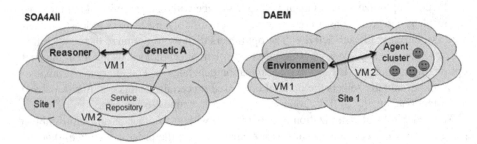

Fig. 5. Design of Exp1 (based on the scenarios and configurations in Fig. 4

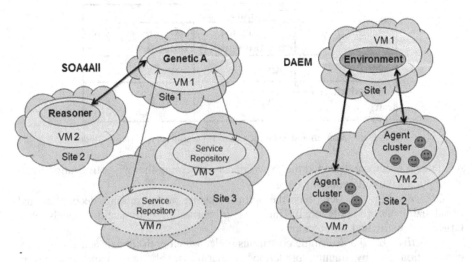

Fig. 6. Design of Exp4 (based on the scenarios and configurations in Fig. 4)

The experiments were specifically designed to allow the study of optimizers in
service ecosystem conditions, such as the effect of distributing optimizer components

on the performance of optimizer, tradeoff between selecting services from one site or various sites and the effect of dynamic changes (in the number and properties of candidate services) on the optimizer outcome. In this respect, based on the combination of scenarios and configurations (from Fig. 4) the experiments range from Exp1 (as shown in Fig. 5) where all components of the optimizers reside at the same BonFIRE site, to Exp4 where the components of the optimizers are scratterd over multi-site BonFIRE Cloud (as shown in   Fig. 1).

4   Experimental Results

We ran 20 simulations for each experiment mentioned in Fig. 4 for each of the optimizers. For each experiment we calculate the median in fixed time intervals. The median was chosen because it does not assume any distribution in the analyzed data.

In each simulation run we first added services to the ecosystem in an incremental manner while consecutively optimizing service compositions. Once we reached an empirical maximum (10,000 service), we semi-randomly changed their service parameters while we carried on with consecutive optimizations. Finally, we reduced the number of services little by little while still optimizing using remaining services. This process was done for both optimizers in order to analyze how the optimization results changed over time by making differentiations in the problem they were optimizing. This emulates the dynamism of service ecosystem which the optimizers do not have control over but have to take into account by consecutive optimizations.

The behavior of the optimizers in service ecosystem conditions is described here.

4.1   Soa4all Is Faster on a Single Site, Whereas DAEM is Faster in a Multi-site Configuration

Our tests reveal the ability of SOA4All optimizer to demonstrate better performance (in terms of time taken to converge to an optimal composition) in a single site deployment configuration i.e., when all components of the optimization model were deployed on different VMs but on the same site.

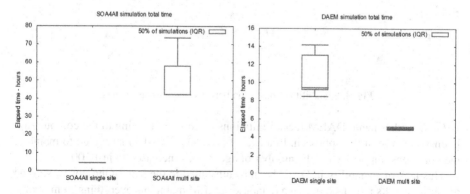

Fig. 7. Performance in different deployment configurations (shown with the help of box plots)

Whereas, contrary to the expected results DAEM demonstrated better performance by taking less time to finish an experiment when deployed in a multi-site configuration i.e. when the environment and agent clusters were deployed on geographically distributed Cloud sites. This behavior is due to an emergent parallelization of component execution. That is, DAEM uses a fixed waiting time (30ms) in between executions in order to allow information to be exchanged between the agents and the environment. In a multi-site configuration, because of the communication delay due to geographic distribution, the environment component starts next execution before receiving all the information. Consequently, it processes the information already received at the same time while it keeps on receiving more. Then after execution it realizes it does not need to wait again because information is already there. Thus it executes again while more information is being received. As a result, there is a parallelization between information transfer and information processing resulting in shorter experiment time than when deployed all in a single site.

In a single site configuration this does not occur because the network is faster thus all the information is received before processing each time. As a result there is a always a waiting time in between executions. This is reflected in Fig. 7.

4.2   Soa4all Is More Scalable than DAEM

Our tests reveal the ability of SOA4All optimizer to be highly scalable without putting too much stress on the underlying infrastructure. As shown in Fig. 8, SOA4All optimizer was tested with up to 10,000 services (i.e. 10,000 candidate services were considered while optimizing the composition template from Fig. 3) without putting too much stress on the infrastructure i.e. in this case memory usage.

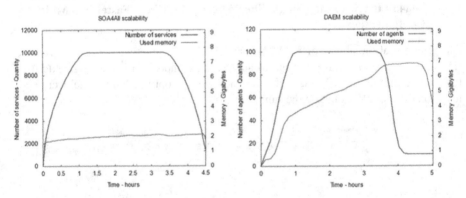

Fig. 8. Scalability comparison between the two optimizers

On the other hand, DAEM faces limitations on this front owing to the computation intensive nature of the approach. In terms of scalability, DAEM struggled to maintain memory consumption when the number of agents was increased to just 100.

This lack of scalability in DAEM can be attributed to the lack of temporary storage of partial results into disk, e.g. in a database. DAEM maintains everything in memory.

4.3   DAEM's Output Is More Stable and Resilient to Changes than SOA4All's

Let us remind the reader that optimizations are consecutive, one immediately after another while in parallel we vary the number of services and their properties to emulate the dynamism of a service ecosystem.

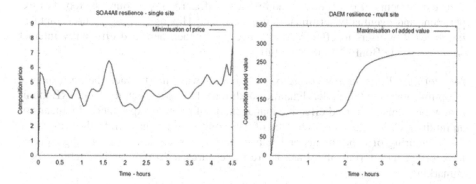

Fig. 9. Comparison of optimizers' output in service ecosystem conditions

The results reveal that SOA4All optimizer's output oscillates frequently without any hints of stabilization. On the other hand, DAEM produces a more stable output regardless of the dynamism of service ecosystem. Fig. 9 depicts these results. In this respect, we can say that DAEM is resilient to changes because it overcomes each consecutive change in the service ecosystem at local level (only changing aspects of the composition that are affected by the change) thus not negatively affecting the final or overall output.

This behavior of DAEM is attributed to the ecosystem properties embedded in it such as agents' short memory which allows the system to absorb any change (new services, removal of services, and change of parameters) and propagate only those that have a positive impact on the agent who detected them. Consequently, a resilient service composition emerges.

4.4   BonFIRE Support for Future Internet Scenarios

Testing the optimization models on BonFIRE also allowed us to test and evaluate various aspects of BonFIRE infrastructure. The evaluation of BonFIRE revealed the following characteristics that contribute towards creating and supporting service eco-system conditions.

Dynamism: A simple way to create service ecosystem conditions for our experiments was to enable dynamism at experiment as well as infrastructure level. That is, dynamism not only referred to the ability of services and other software entities to appear, disappear and change their properties at any time but also to the dynamic fluctuations in the infrastructure offerings such as appearance and disappearance of computational and storage resources. Our experimentation reveal that BonFIRE supports both types of dynamism by i) allowing users to have full control over their experiments, and ii) providing APIs to manage infrastructure resources not only at design time but also at runtime.

Deployment and experiment management: In BonFIRE the initial deployment and management of experiments can be done by using BonFIRE portal that offers a simplistic visual interface for creating experiment, initializing VM instances, allocating computation and storage resources to VMs and deployment of experiments on user specified locations within BonFIRE infrastructure. The portal allow users to manage their experiments at run time e.g. add-remove infrastructure resources, stop-start experiment and eventually terminate the experiment. Having an easy to use graphical interface allow users to effectively manage their experiment and efficiently interact with underlying BonFIRE infrastructure.

Monitoring: Reliable monitoring of experiments was vital to track the performance of optimization models under dynamic conditions. In this respect, the BonFIRE monitoring mechanism allowed effective management of running experiments by means of an intuitive GUI. The visual interface of the monitoring mechanism further simplifies the monitoring of experiments and related activities such as load balancing, service monitoring, monitoring of infrastructure or resource utilization and scalability benchmarking.

Authentication, authorization and cross site communication: Making use of geographically distributed computational and storage resources require certain mechanisms to be in place for seamless authentication, authorization and communication. In BonFIRE the *Identity Manager* offers a single sign-on service for users accessing resources from multiple (geographically distributed) Cloud facilities. The service is also responsible for authentication of software/application components thus allowing different components (residing on different Cloud facilities) to interact without any problem. All Cloud facilities in BonFIRE are connected via a BonFIRE WAN that ensures seamless communication and data exchange (using unique IP addresses) between geographically distributed infrastructure resources.

Overall BonFIRE proved to be a suitable platform for supporting future Internet scenarios that may involve experiments using large number of services, geographically distributed components and requiring on-demand computational and storage resources.

5   Discussion about Related Work

While existing works (e.g. [5, 6]) investigate the QoS and network latency issues in dynamic service composition, they do not particularly focus on issues associated with designing and testing service composition mechanisms in service ecosystem conditions. Further, in [7] a distributed Cloud service composition framework is proposed together with protocols to dynamically select candidate services and form compositions. The service composition protocols support incomplete information about Cloud participants when applying dynamic service selection mechanisms. The main limitations of [7] stem from the scale of the composition scenarios evaluated taking into account small numbers of services and compositions and also the use of desktop based environment instead of a Cloud facility.

In terms of experiments on service ecosystems or similar technologies, [11] proposes an architecture inspired by ecosystems portraying self-adaptation and self-organization to support dynamic scenarios, such as service ecosystems. The approach considers four types of ecosystem entities such as flora and consumers, and niches represented by tuple spaces which function as the interaction interfaces. The entities (agents) have needs and a "happiness" status they try to maximize by fulfilling their needs. Experiments show how the "happiness" levels reach a balanced state at the end of their simulations throughout a set of niches, however this only demonstrate its capacity to converge once to a solution rather than its capacity to deal with continuous changes and dynamism, as we do in this paper.

6   Conclusion

Our experiments provide an opportunity to test the optimization models as well as the Cloud infrastructure in a Future Internet scenario. The results of our experiments reveal interesting characteristics of the optimizers under different scenarios and deployment configurations.

In particular the experiments on BonFIRE helped us to identify the strengths, weaknesses and improvement opportunities of the optimization models, which allow us to make recommendations about the use of optimization models in different application domains.

SOA4All Optimizer: The experimental results reveal that SOA4All optimization is suitable for one-off optimization and/or when unprecedented numbers of services are involved in the composition. This can be case in travel booking applications or financial applications that consider huge number of services before producing a composition that is best suited for the user.

For example, in a travel booking application a user can request a composition of services to represent and automatically perform activities (based on user input/requirements) such as booking airline tickets, travel insurance, hotel reservation, hire car and taxis to and from airport. Up on receiving such a request the SOA4All optimizer can perform the following steps:

- Search the service repository to find suitable services that can perform the user specified activities.
- Select at least one service to perform each of the user specified activity based on the matching the descriptions of the activity and the service. The end result of this step will be a non-optimal composition.
- Starting from a non-optimal composition the optimizer will replace the already associated services with better alternatives while considering the quality of semantic links between the services and other non-functional parameters that affect the overall quality of the composition. This step may involve going through and considering thousands of candidate services for each activity. The end results of this step will be an optimal composition that best suits user requirements.

DAEM: Contrary to the one-off nature of SOA4All optimization, the type of optimization offered by DAEM is suitable for continuous processes as in the case of optimizing traffic infrastructure or complex manufacturing processes.

In the traffic domain the agents in DAEM can represent different entities such as cars, roads and traffic sensors that communicate with each other in order to optimize the overall utilization of the available infrastructure resources.

In future work, we intend to analyze more data that was gathered during the experiments and use the analysis to study further details of our optimizers. The complete analysis will also allow us to make further technological improvements in the implementation of our optimizers and investigate their use in real work applications.

The current implementations of both optimization models are available as open-source resource. BonFIRE is available as an open access multi-site federated Cloud facility (http://www.bonfire-project.eu/involved) for researchers and experimenters to test their applications and technologies.

Open Access. This article is distributed under the terms of the Creative Commons Attribution Noncommercial License which permits any noncommercial use, distribution, and reproduction in any medium, provided the original author(s) and source are credited.

References

1. Lécué, F., Mehandjiv, N.: Seeking quality of web service composition in a semantic dimension. IEEE Transactions on Knowledge and Data Engineering (2010)
2. Lécué, F.: Optimizing QoS-Aware Semantic Web Service Composition. In: Bernstein, A., Karger, D.R., Heath, T., Feigenbaum, L., Maynard, D., Motta, E., Thirunarayan, K. (eds.) ISWC 2009. LNCS, vol. 5823, pp. 375–391. Springer, Heidelberg (2009)
3. Marin, C.A.: Adaptation to unexpected changes: where ecosystems and multiagent systems meet. PhD Thesis. Manchester Business School. The University of Manchester, UK (2010)
4. Marín, C.A., Stalker, I.D., Mehandjiev, N.: Engineering business ecosystems using environment-mediated interactions. In: Weyns, D., Brueckner, S.A., Demazeau, Y. (eds.) EEMMAS 2007. LNCS (LNAI), vol. 5049, pp. 240–258. Springer, Heidelberg (2008)
5. Canfora, G., Di Penta, M., Esposito, R., Villani, M.L.: An approach for QoS-aware service composition based on genertic algorithms. In: GECCO, pp. 1069–1975 (2005)
6. Calinescu, R.: Dynamic QoS Management and Optimization in Service Based Systems. IEEE Transactions on Software Eng. (2011)
7. Gutierrez-Garcia, J.O., Sim, K.-M.: Self-Organizing Agents for Service Composition in Cloud Computing. In: IEEE Second International Conference on Cloud Computing Technology and Science (CloudCom), pp. 59–66 (2010)
8. Green, D.G., Sadedin, S.: Interactions matter-complexity in landscapes and ecosystems. Ecological Complexity 2(2), 117–130 (2005)
9. Lécué, F., Léger, A.: A formal model for semantic web service composition. In: Cruz, I., Decker, S., Allemang, D., Preist, C., Schwabe, D., Mika, P., Uschold, M., Aroyo, L.M. (eds.) ISWC 2006. LNCS, vol. 4273, pp. 385–398. Springer, Heidelberg (2006)
10. Villalba, C., Mamei, M., Zambonelli, F.: A Self-organizing Architecture for Pervasive Ecosystems. In: Weyns, D., Malek, S., de Lemos, R., Andersson, J. (eds.) SOAR 2009. LNCS, vol. 6090, pp. 275–300. Springer, Heidelberg (2010)
11. Lécué, F., Wajid, U., Mehandjiev, N.: Negotiating Robustness in Semantic Web Service Composition. In: Proceedings of IEEE European Conference on Web Services, pp. 75–84. IEEE Computer Society (2009)

Resource Optimisation in IoT Cloud Systems by Using Matchmaking and Self-management Principles

Martin Serrano[1], Danh Le-Phuoc[1], Maciej Zaremba[1], Alex Galis[2],
Sami Bhiri[1], and Manfred Hauswirth[1]

[1] National University of Ireland Galway, NUIG – Digital Enterprise Research Institute,
DERI, Galway, Ireland
`{firstname.lastname}@deri.org`
[2] University College London, UCL – Department of Electronic and Electrical Engineering,
London, U.K.
`a.galis@ee.ucl.ac.uk`

Abstract. IoT Cloud systems provide scalable capacity and dynamic behaviour control of virtual infrastructures for running applications, services and processes. Key aspects in this type of complex systems are the resource optimisation and the performance of dynamic management based on distributed user data metrics and/or IoT application data demands and/or resource utilisation metrics. In this paper we particularly focus on Cloud management perspective – integrating IoT Cloud service data management - based on annotated data of monitored Cloud performance and user profiles (matchmaking) and enabling management systems to use shared infrastructures and resources to enable efficient deployment of IoT services and applications. We illustrate a Cloud service management approach based on matchmaking operations and self-management principles which enable improved distribution and management of IoT services across different Cloud vendors and use the results from the analysis as mechanism to control applications and services deployment in Cloud systems. For our IoT Cloud data management solution we utilize performance metrics expressed with linked data in order to integrate monitored performance data and end user profile information (via linked data relations).

Keywords: Internet-of-Things, Service Platforms, Management, Linked Data, Cloud Computing Systems, Elasticity, Self-Management, Autonomic Management, Cloud Monitoring, Interoperability, Virtual Infrastructures.

1 Introduction

Cloud systems are offering powerful and flexible capabilities for running Internet of Things (IoT) data services and applications by using Internet infrastructure. This capability consists of facilitating service deployment on shared network and computing infrastructure resulting in reduced operational costs [1][2].

Cloud computing offers secure, reliable, scalable and elastic infrastructure operations. Differently from the conventional designs based on hosted and fixed servers solutions, Cloud computing allows a flexible world of options in configuration

A. Galis and A. Gavras (Eds.): FIA 2013, LNCS 7858, pp. 127–140, 2013.

and elasticity in easies expansion of Cloud computing resources as network, storage and computing requirements increase [1][3].

As one of the most prominent challenges in IoT Cloud systems, the control of their resources and the dynamic behaviour of virtual infrastructures rely on their capacity to run computer applications, services and processes independently. A key aspect in this type of complex systems is the performance of dynamic management based on distributed user data metrics, IoT application data demands and resource utilisation metrics (broadly used in managing communications networks). Efficiency of Cloud infrastructures and their autonomic management [4] are research challenges in today IoT Cloud systems [5]. Enabling elasticity of virtual infrastructures as a response to either load balancing protocols or remote monitored data processing is fundamental. In these settings managing Cloud services lifecycle by enabling scalable applications and using distributed information systems and linked data processing in a securely is crucial.

This paper introduces a novel approach for enabling elasticity of IoT Cloud services. The concepts and trends discussed in this paper can be applied to public, private and hybrid Clouds. This paper introduces a Cloud management perspective where integrated IoT Cloud service data management is based on annotated data of monitored Cloud performance and user profiles, enabling management systems to use shared infrastructures and resources to provide efficient deployment mechanism for IoT services and applications. Linked data mechanisms are used in this paper in the context of Cloud service management tools facilitating scalability, enabling efficient management and providing infrastructure control. An experimental testbed implementation using matchmaking requirements and distributed IoT data is illustrated in this paper. This paper briefly analyses and discusses technology trends in the area of Cloud computing and introduces linked data concepts and management principles to understand the advantages linked data offer for enabling matchmaking and services control on IoT Cloud service infrastructures.

This paper is organized as follow: In section 2 we introduce the matchmaking in the Cloud computing context. Section 3 discusses the state of the art related to IoT Cloud services and applications. Section 4 examines challenges and limitations on IoT Cloud computing. Section 5 describes Cloud service matchmaking evaluation and focus on IoT Cloud services. Section 6 describes scalable features about matchmaking and self-management and its benefits when used in IoT Cloud services. Section 7 presents a matchmaking scenario and IoT Cloud service control, from a point of view of on-demand scalability by using resource control by aggregated performance data and distributed computing monitoring. In Section 8 we conclude the paper and discuss future work.

2   Matchmaking for IoT Cloud Systems and Services

The Matchmaking process is an important component of cloud systems. One of its main purposes is to infer unknown preferences from annotated data of monitored performance and user profiles to another. In IoT effective realisation of IoT Cloud service matchmaking will further improve adoption of Cloud computing solutions in this area and provide a consolidated view of the Cloud market enabling cost effective scalability by leveraging Clouds on-demand. IoT Cloud services need to be individually configured by allowing Cloud consumers to choose characteristics of provided Cloud offers. Service descriptions are the core artefacts used in Cloud service matchmaking and the matchmaking results depend largely on the provided service descriptions. IoT Cloud service matchmaking is a crucial part of the solution for self-healing Clouds [6] where alternative vendors are identified on-the-fly and used as replacements for original vendors which no longer satisfy consumer's requirements (e.g., incur higher cost or provide unreliable service). In order to realise this vision, service matchmaking has to operate on quantifiable artefacts suitable for an objective Cloud service ranking. *Service offers* [7] are the most specific, quantifiable, often request-dependent descriptions of Cloud service capabilities.

Details of Cloud services (e.g., the number of available cores, RAM, storage space, etc. in the case of IaaS resources) and service consumer requirements and preferences often change. There is *no one size fits all* Cloud vendor and the ability to determine the best (cheapest, most reliable) Cloud service offer provides a significant business value. Cloud computing vendors offer a great variability in their services. Their services are highly configurable and details of their offers (in the case of IaaS comprised of: availability, price, CPU, RAM, etc.) depend on user requirements. A service might offer an optimal solution for a certain requirements, while for different requirements it might be unavailable (e.g., due to the Cloud's physical location) or be uncompetitive (expensive, unreliable).

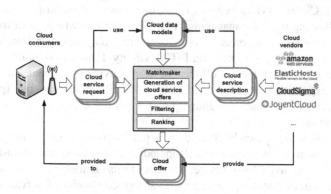

Fig. 1. Cloud computing matchmaking scenario

As shown in Figure 1 we distinguish three types of stakeholders in the IoT Cloud service matchmaking process: consumer (IoT user or vendor), matchmaker (broker) and Cloud vendors (IaaS public Clouds vendors). IaaS Cloud services are described in terms *service descriptions* and service consumers formulate their requirements in *service requests*. Both service descriptions and service requests are communicated to the matchmaker whose role is to provide the best match between the involved parties. Service offers are generated for a specific service request in the matchmaking phase and are often valid for a limited period of time only. The role of the matchmaker is to facilitate generation of Cloud service offers, provide their filtering in order to remove offers that do not satisfy consumers' hard constraints and to finally rank them according to consumers' preferences.

3   Cloud Computing and IoT Services

The convergence of physical infrastructure network resources and computing mechanisms enable virtualization of all types of resources [3][8][9]. IoT as an emergent paradigm is based on the computing realization for heterogeneous infrastructure and the interoperability of diversity of data models. The main benefits of Cloud computing in IoT are: 1) facilitated on-demand service provisioning, 2) pay-as-you-go pricing models and 3) optimisation of shared resources, aspects that are described in Cloud computing systems and that everyday acquire more importance in the IoT domain.

In Cloud computing systems, the owner of the infrastructure is called Cloud vendor. Currently some of the main Cloud vendors are Amazon [5], Salesforce [10] and Google [11] leading the market with their large infrastructures and software portfolios. However increasing popularity of IoT paradigm leads to Cloud computing infrastructure implementations to be most reliable solution for IoT systems which subsidise services in the Cloud with the objective of reducing administration, maintenance and management cost.

IoT Cloud services benefits from Cloud computing by the easy administrative and technological on-demand expansion by running of shared infrastructure and by providing most of the time server applications according with user-oriented demands. Likewise IoT Cloud services benefits from resources on-demand processing, at the same time allowing users for managing processing sessions which, infrastructure can be dynamically assigned to other users or computing purposes, this feature turns on IoT Cloud services as an advantage on IoT Flexibility. Elasticity is an inherent Cloud computing feature that allows for efficient session activation and de-activation that is translated in expansion and reduction of utilized IoT Cloud infrastructure (physical or virtual). Thus elasticity enables scaling up and down IoT Cloud service according to the actual demand.

Cloud services are typically offered in a pay-as-you-go pricing model and are characterized by complex pricing models including time-based, utilization-based, and SLA-based charges. IoT Cloud services benefits of this on demand feature and rely on computing resources that are provided under an agreed Quality of Service (QoS) and Service Level Agreement (SLA). For example, Amazon charges for an instance based on its size and uptime, while allowing for a reduced payment if you pre-pay for a year or 3 years; inbound and outbound network traffic, with reduced pricing and increasing capacity [5]. Amazon also charges for the storage capacity, reliability level, transfer rate, & number of I/O operations performed. Network charges differ also on the basis of the physical location - being free in availability zone, reduced for inter-zone, and full across regions. Load balancing is charged in addition. Amazon also enables users to bid for EC2 spot instances representing computation resources, as such it uses the Cloud infrastructure to enable functionality and scalable services by using the Cloud infrastructure more efficiently.

Recently IoT companies interested in utilizing services in the Cloud have come to realize that Cloud computing can help them to expand their services efficiently and improve the overall performance of their current systems by building up an overlay support system. This provides increased service availability, task prioritization and service load distribution, all based on users' individual requirements and priorities.

4   IoT Data Cloud Challenges and Limitations

In this section we summarize a number of research challenges for IoT Data Cloud. It introduces important issues with respect to improving Cloud management for IoT applications. There are still number of issues preventing a wider adoption of the IoT Cloud computing that are summarized in this section. The Open Data Center Alliance [1] identified interoperability, service catalogues and standard units of measurement as the priorities that the Cloud community needs to resolve. IoT Cloud services are currently described informally, and determining and comparing on the same reference Cloud details (e.g., price per month, CPUs, RAM and storage capacities of the provided infrastructure, etc. in the case of IaaS). IoT Cloud is a time consuming and manual process what prevents Cloud consumers from gaining a consolidated view of the IoT Cloud data market. Figure 2 represent the most important challenges and limitations marked as hype research challenges in Cloud computing (i.e. Multitenancy, Elasticity, Transparency and Service Composition), same problems that IoT domain face up for enabling IoT data service management capabilities.

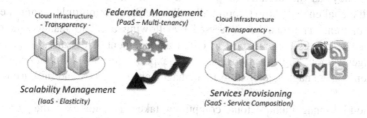

Fig. 2. Cloud Computing Challenges and Limitations

IoT Cloud data services and the use of Cloud infrastructures supporting IoT applications are becoming a common practice in industry (particularly in sensor-related data industry). This is the result of the Cloud economic advantages regarding the initial investment in infrastructure and the cost of outsourcing IoT Cloud data services [12]. Theoretically unlimited scalability of Cloud service provisioning and the simplicity it represents to users operating in the Cloud is attracting more and more businesses to switch to the IoT Cloud data infrastructures and services. The following are key management problems and aspects which would need innovative.

---

[1] http://www.opendatacenteralliance.org

- Real-time scalability of the IoT Cloud services. IoT Cloud services should reflect the current load and actively change the underlying infrastructure to address time-varying demand. Therefore the application is not static anymore and centred around a single IoT Cloud vendor but it can evolve over time across various vendors.
- Scalability of the IoT application. Adding more resources does not necessarily result in increased performance of the application. The challenge in this area is to find proper Cloud scalable application infrastructure as well as to perform predictions regarding application workload. However, Cloud services are commonly referred to as 'infinitely' scalable. That is not the necessary case for IoT, in some situations a collaborative solution of Cloud vendors might be the optimal Cloud implementation in terms of cost, scalability and key performance indicators.
- Optimisation for complex infrastructure and optimisation for complex pricing model, there are many possible options for application architecture. A challenge is to design an optimal architecture to fit Cloud environment and at the same time to optimally use all IoT resources with respect to pricing.
- Security, with the participation of multiple users into the IoT environment, the privacy and security of the information while running processes is crucial. Privacy on IoT Cloud data rely on strong encryption and protection protocols and are guarded by firewalls. However in other IoT security requires more research activities in terms of data protection algorithms and protocols for security and privacy of user identity.
- Multitenancy, as the number of partitioned virtualized resources (or instances) grows the challenge of how to optimally allocate them to multiple tenants become more apparent. This can be addressed by allowing users to manage their own delegated resources – non-expert resource management. This raises a number of challenges including: supporting non-expert resource monitoring and management, managed delegation of management resources and authorities, and auditing.
- IoT Cloud Management, Cloud computing takes advantage of the computing parallelism where by definition it is an attractive feature to optimize the usage of the computing resources and for this reason recently catalogued as green ICT. For IoT Cloud data, this optimisation and management functionality is translated into economic benefit. For this and other economic reasons physical infrastructure has migrated to the Cloud and likewise IoT Cloud data.

The challenges for IoT Cloud data systems are without doubt that must be able to support Clouds system up to their breaking point. In this respect, for example in Cloud elasticity there are two main metrics to be considered: spin-up elasticity (the time response between the t=0 when computing resources request and t+n the time when resource request is running) and spin-down elasticity, (the time response between t=n no longer requiring compute power and no longer paying for it) [13][14].

5   IoT Cloud Service Matchmaking Evaluation

In context of IoT Cloud computing research, we have applied our Service OFFer Discovery (SOFFD) [7] approach to the IaaS Cloud computing domain, made it available online[2] and evaluated it. Service OFFer Discovery (SOFFD) is a generic service search engine for discovering, configuring and selecting highly configurable, search request-dependent services having dynamic properties. It operates on lightweight service description and search request models grounded in RDF and SPARQL which refer to Linked Data vocabularies and datasets in order to foster service description reuse and to facilitate service matchmaking. SOFFD generates request-dependent service offer descriptions tailored to the search request at hand and provides matchmaking against these dynamically generated service offers.

We have described with Linked Data and integrated Cloud services from nineteen IaaS vendors. It has been evaluated by running a series of tests with different search requests and IaaS services. Each request varied by a different in its complexity, specified hard constraints and preferences.

Flexible Cloud search requests (e.g., CPU between 2-4 ECU) enable generation of large number of service offers and required for the optimal search for the best service offers among them. Search requests with fixed properties (e.g., CPU has to be 4 ECU) yield far less service offers, whereas SOFFD allows for the generation of a large number of service offers what plays an important role in finding optimal service offers. For example, fixed search request properties may not yield any results at all whereas flexible search requests are more likely to yield promising results.

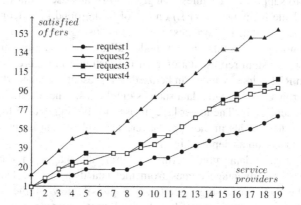

Fig. 3. Generated IaaS Cloud Computing Offers

We show a number of generated service offers for our search requests in Figure 3. As we can see in this Figure, a single search request results in a large number of generated Cloud service offers. SOFFD dynamically generates, filters and ranks a number of Cloud service offers. Cloud service offered by a single vendor

---

[2] http://soffd.deri.ie/

(e.g., Amazon) when evaluated against flexible search request results in a number of possible service offers that SOFFD matchmakes.

SOFFD discovery algorithm scales linearly with a number of generated offers. Evaluation of SPARQL-based hard constraints and calculating ranking takes most of the computational time. We provide IaaS matchmaking results to the service consumer asynchronously what limits perceived time overheads. Our scalability results could be further improved by utilising caching of service offers. Currently SOFFD always generates all possible Cloud service offers for each individual search request.

6   Linked Data and Scalable Cloud Management

In this section we analyse features of Cloud management and infrastructures pointing towards the advantages that linked data can offer when used with the Cloud-based Service management control loop. In Cloud management, in order to apply deployment policies for a service request, the Cloud manager has to check the logs of running services. Traditionally, the logs recorded from running services and computing nodes are processed in the Data Correlation Engine under separated files that need to be loaded to relational tables to be accessed by a rule engine. However, the logs and service requests are fed into Data Correlation Engine in the stream fashion. There are a wide variety of literatures in stream/event processing studied in [15][16] showing that relational database engines do not perform well with continuous processing over log streams. Therefore, the stream/event processing engine should be integrated into the Data Correlation Engine.

In addition, to support the seamless integration of rule-based policy represented as Semantic Web Rule language (SWRL) on top of background knowledge represented in Description Logic with log streams, we propose using linked data model for the Data Correlation Engine. In this unified model, all the data is represented as a graph within the layered system representation as it is illustrated in Figure 4. This graph is composed from RDF triples which can be used to represent data, knowledge base and rules. The upper layer is for static data such as ontologies, schema and business logics which is time-independent. The lower layer is used for linking data of log streams into vocabularies and logic rules in the upper layer. The linked data in the lower layer is called linked data stream as depicted in Figure 4.

The linked stream data model brings several advantages in data correlation operations. The first advantage comes from the data distribution. The graph-based layout gives the data processing operators the global view of the whole dataset. Therefore, the query processor can filter the irrelevant data to a query much earlier than the log-file approach does. Traditionally, the monitoring data recorded in separated log files are partitioned in individual services, processes, etc, thus, cross-correlating the relevant data items among them needs to load all the data into a relational storage before carrying out the correlation.

The push-based and incremental processing model of linked stream processing engines provides much better performance than that of traditional relational database

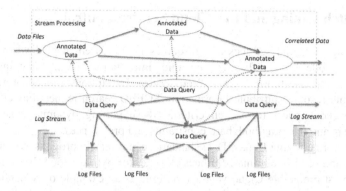

Fig. 4. Cloud Management Service Control Loop

engine. Because a query over the log streams on relation database is performed in pull-based and one-shot fashion whereby any new snapshot of log stream needs the full computation. Thanks to the push-based and RDF triple data model, the log data can be pushed gradually per triples or a set of triples into the Data Correlation Engine. This helps to avoid the overload of matching schema and data loading when receiving large IoT Cloud computing monitoring logs.

To meet the query processing demand of Data Correlation Engine, we have developed and evaluated our Continuous Query Evaluation over Linked Stream (CQELS) engine [16]. This engine can consume very high throughput from log streams and can access large persistent triple storages with millions of triples. The current version can deal with thousands of concurrent queries corresponding to service matching policies registered. The Figure 5 shows initial experiments with stream data processing. Figure 5(a) represent "feed rate" defined as throughput of data consumption (from raw to triples) (10/15 tasks are experiments that have 10/15 concurrent feeding tasks on one node). Figure 5(b) shows the streaming data response with time reference and increase in number of nodes or "feed time" defined as the time spent for loading and transforming a batch of raw data. In summary, more nodes give more capacity to process longer streaming data files and similarly more nodes less result in less time required to satisfy query requests on streaming data.

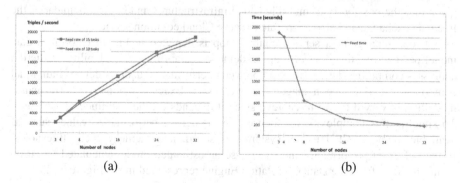

(a)   (b)

Fig. 5. Stream Data Processing Analysis

7   Matchmaking and IoT Cloud Service Control

Matchmaking of Cloud services and resources is addressed in [17] where authors propose a model for reflecting dynamic information (e.g., changing Cloud capabilities, response times, etc.) in Web service descriptions and updating WSDL with dynamic resource attribute information. SOFFD search request model provides more advanced support for search criteria by supporting dynamic generation of service offers and handling both hard constraints and preferences.

Matchmakers utilizing Linked Data standards can be easily provided for third-party integration and used in automated processes (e.g., for hybrid Cloud dynamic scaling using the most preferable Cloud vendor). SOFFD as an example of semantic service matchmaker applied to the Cloud computing area allows consumers to dynamically determine the best available service offers and provide a consolidated view of IaaS market. Matchmaking cannot be achieved using high level service descriptions, as Cloud service properties (e.g., price, provided CPU, RAM, storage, etc. in the case of IaaS) are either offered in bundles or are configurable. Prices of Cloud services are request-dependent and can be dynamic (e.g., price of Amazon EC2 spot instances fluctuate depending on supply and demand). From the point of view of Cloud consumers, matchmaking of Cloud service offers is far more beneficial than operating on the level of high-level Cloud descriptions. Only service offers can satisfy the concrete needs of Cloud consumers.

In Cloud computing, highly distributed and dynamic elastic infrastructures [18] are deployed in a distributed manner to support service applications. In consequence development of management and configuration systems over Internet automatically controlling virtual infrastructures are necessaries [4]. Management operations modifying the service lifecycle control loop and satisfying user demands about quality of service and reliability play a critical role in this complex management process. Cloud computing typically is characterized by large enterprise systems containing multiple virtual distributed software components that communicate across different networks and satisfying secure and personalized service requests [14][19]. The complex nature of these user requests results in numerous data flows within the service components and the Cloud infrastructures that cannot be readily correlated with each other. Ideally data flows can be treated at runtime by correlation engines, given thus the possibility of multiple Cloud infrastructures and beyond boundaries the free data exchange and also cooperate to serve Cloud common services.

A Cloud management service control loop is depicted in Figure 6. From a data model perspective, this control loop on-demand scalability and scalability prediction addresses computing data correlation between performance data models of individual components and service management operations. Exact component's performance modelling is very difficult to achieve since it depends on the multitude of variables. To simplify this complexity we focused the model on performance values such as available memory, CPU usage, system bus speed, and memory cache thresholds. Instead of exact performance model we use an estimated model calculated based on monitored data from the Data Correlation Engine represented in the Figure 6 [20].

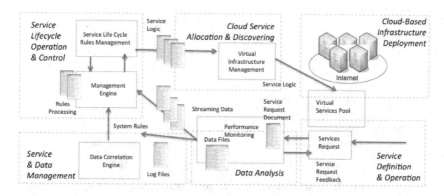

Fig. 6. Cloud Service Management Control Loop

An intermediate solution to efficient service control management is used, the data logs used by the Service Lifecycle Rules Manager is compared and linked with data semantic engineering mechanisms to enable service lifecycle control operations. Result of this linked data operation is named event data model, which is a standardized model and can be used indistinctly in service management or network infrastructure management domains.

These standard data models can be understood by diverse infrastructure and platforms modifying or adapting their performance according to particular applications and systems and pre-defined operation requirements. For example, Management Policies Engine can use the Event data model to define changes and dynamically perform Cloud infrastructure control. Linked data standard model facilitates the dynamic adaptability of the information over infrastructures where other data models are incompatible. The main objective for using this standard linked data model is to modify the performance of the infrastructure satisfying thus general business goals according to the high level rules known as goals and defined into service contracts or service agreements. A service translation is needed in terms of defining the Service Logic that a Virtual Infrastructure Manager can understand.

The data link process provides assurances for interoperability between performance information and the simplistic commands contained in the data models. Further experimentation is being conducted to define service-discovering mechanism by using service allocation protocols.

The approach of using data model translation of the service allocation data model and perform linked data is being considerate as a tentative approach to this complex problem. The Figure 7 shows performance metrics in managing system with virtual infrastructures. Figure 7(a) represents initial experiments with semantic rule-based engine 2SCE [21], CPU usage percentage vs. the number of operations and service rules that has been created and processed by the 2SCE control engine. Figure 7(b) shows memory usage in megabytes vs. the number of operations and service rules when an application or service is using the loaded rules.

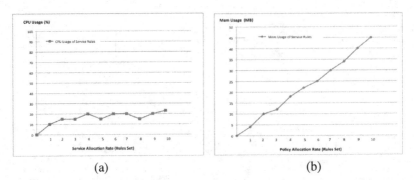

(a)   (b)

Fig. 7. Semantic-Based Rule Engine Performance Analysis

8   Conclusions and Future Work

In this paper we analysed key developments in IoT Cloud data including concepts, trends, challenges and limitations in this emerging area. One of the most important research challenges in IoT Cloud applications and Cloud data systems is the dynamic control of elasticity of the Cloud infrastructure utilizing performance metrics (i.e. logs from computing applications) and user requirements (i.e. annotated data as streaming data analysis).

We have introduced and discussed advancements in terms of using matchmaking and self-management principles in Cloud data added by link data mechanisms and related to IoT systems. Implemented architectural components, in the form of SOFFD prototyped middleware solution have been presented and evaluated as part of proof of the concept process enabling Cloud infrastructure selection. In addition introducing linked data mechanisms allow maximising control of service lifecycle. The concepts presented in this paper can be applied to IoT Cloud applications or Cloud systems.

Further work includes experimentation with service-discovering mechanisms by using service allocation protocols and embedded optimisation methods and algorithms for link data usage in IoT Cloud service management.

Acnowledgements. This work has been partially supported by the European Commission FP7-ICT-2011-7-287305 OpenIoT project[3] and the Universal FP7 project[4]. It is also partially supported by Science Foundation Ireland under grant number SFI/08/CE/I1380 (Lion-II) CSET-DERI Centre for Science, Engineering and Technology - Digital Enterprise Research Institute.

---

[3] OpenIoT Project http://www.openiot.eu
[4] Univerself Project http://www.univerself-project.eu/

References

[1] The Economics of the Cloud,
    http://www.microsoft.com/presspass/presskits/Cloud/docs/
    (online access Wednesday, January 05, 2011)

[2] The 'InterCloud' and the Future of Computing, an interview: Vint Cerf at FORA.tv, the
    Churchill Club, SRI International Building, Menlo Park, CA (January 7, 2010),
    http://www.youtube.com/user/ForaTv#p/search/1/r2G94ImcUuY
    (January 2011)

[3] Rochwerger, B., Caceres, J., Montero, R.S., Breitgand, D., Elmroth, E., Galis, A., Levy,
    E., Llorente, I.M., Nagin, K., Wolfsthal, Y., Elmroth, E., Caceres, J., Ben-Yehuda, M.,
    Emmerich, W., Galan, F.: The RESERVOIR Model and Architecture for Open Federated
    Cloud Computing. IBM Journal of Research and Development 53(4) (2009)

[4] Serrano, J.M.: Applied Ontology Engineering in Cloud Services, Networks and
    Management Systems, 222 pages. Springer Publishers, Hardcover (2012) (to be released
    on March 2012), ISBN-10:1461422353, ISBN-13:978-1461422358

[5] Amazon Web Services, http://aws.amazon.com/

[6] Dai, Y., Xiang, Y., Zhang, G.: Self-healing and Hybrid Diagnosis in Cloud Computing.
    In: Jaatun, M.G., Zhao, G., Rong, C. (eds.) Cloud Computing. LNCS, vol. 5931, pp.
    45–56. Springer, Heidelberg (2009)

[7] Zaremba, M., Vitvar, T., Bhiri, S., Hauswirth, M.: Service Offer Discovery Using Genetic
    Algorithms. In: IEEE European Conference on Web Services, ECOWS (2011)

[8] Chapman, C., Emmerich, E., Marquez, F.G., Clayman, S., Galis, A.: Software
    Architecture Definition for On-demand Cloud Provisioning. Springer Journal on Cluster
    Computing (May 2011), doi:10.1007/s10586-011-0152-0

[9] Clayman, S., Galis, A., Mamatas, L.: Monitoring Virtual Networks. In: 12th IEEE/IFIP
    Network Operations and Management Symposium (NOMS 2010) - International on
    Management of the Future Internet, Osaka, April 19-23, pp. 19–23 (2010),
    http://www.man.org/2010/

[10] Salesforce.com, http://www.salesforce.com/Cloudcomputing/

[11] Google App Engine, http://code.google.com/appengine/

[12] Adoption of Cloud Computing, in Technology, Media & Telecom by askvisory,
    http://askvisory.com/research/adoption-of-Cloud-computing/
    (online access Thursday, February 10, 2011)

[13] Clayman, S., Galis, A., Toffetti, G., Vaquero, L.M., Rochwerger, B., Massonet, P.: Future
    Internet Monitoring Platform for Computing Clouds. In: Di Nitto, E., Yahyapour, R.
    (eds.) ServiceWave 2010. LNCS, vol. 6481, pp. 215–217. Springer, Heidelberg (2010)

[14] Shao, J., Wei, H., Wang, Q., Mei, H.: A runtime model based monitoring approach for
    Cloud. In: IEEE 3rd International Conference on CLOUD 2010, pp. 313–320 (July 2010)

[15] Le-Phuoc, D., Dao-Tran, M., Xavier Parreira, J., Hauswirth, M.: A native and adaptive
    approach for unified processing of linked streams and linked data. In: Aroyo, L., Welty,
    C., Alani, H., Taylor, J., Bernstein, A., Kagal, L., Noy, N., Blomqvist, E. (eds.) ISWC
    2011, Part I. LNCS, vol. 7031, pp. 370–388. Springer, Heidelberg (2011)

[16] Le-Phuoc, D., Quoc, H.N.M., Parreira, J.X., Hauswirth, M.: The Linked Sensor
    Middleware: Connecting the real world and the Semantic Web. In: 9th Semantic Web
    Challenge co-located with ISWC 2011, Bonn, Germany, October 23-27 (2011)

[17] Goscinski, A., Brock, M.: Toward dynamic and attribute based publication, discovery and
    selection for Cloud computing. Future Generation Comp. Syst. 26(7) (2010)

[18] Chapman, C., Emmerich, W., Galn, F., Clayman, S., Galis, A.: Elastic Service Management in Computational Clouds. In: 12th IEEE/IFIP NOMS2010 / International Workshop on Cloud Management (CloudMan 2010), Osaka, April 19-23 (2010)

[19] The Real Meaning of Cloud Security Revealed (online access Monday, May 04, 2009), http://devcentral.f5.com/weblogs/macvittie/archive/2009/05/04/the-real-meaning-of-Cloud-security-revealed.aspx

[20] Holub, V., Parsons, T., O'Sullivan, P., Murphy, J.: Run-time correlation engine for system monitoring and testing. In: ICAC-INDST 2009: Proceedings of the 6th International Conference Industry Session on Autonomic Computing, pp. 9–18. ACM, New York (2009)

[21] Keeney, J., Conlan, O., Holub, V., Wang, M., Chapel, L., Serrano, M.: A Semantic Monitoring and Management Framework for End-to-end Services. In: Proceedings of 12th IFIP/IEEE International Symposium on Integrated Management – IM 2011, Dublin, IE, May 23-27 (2011)

Towards a Secure Network Virtualization Architecture for the Future Internet

Pedro Martinez-Julia[1], Antonio F. Skarmeta[1], and Alex Galis[2]

[1] Department of Communication and Information Engineering,
University of Murcia, 30100, Murcia, Spain
{pedromj,skarmeta}@um.es
[2] Department of Electrical and Electronic Engineering, University College London,
Torrington Place, London WC1E 7JE, United Kingdom
a.galis@ee.ucl.ac.uk

Abstract. In this paper we discuss the Global Virtualization Architecture (GVA) that enables communications between network entities according to the way they refer to each other rather than understanding the constraints of particular networks. Our approach is to instantiate a virtual network that is based on identities of network entities and their demands on security and network capabilities. An entity may be physical e.g. a human user, a device, or any *thing*, or abstract, such as a computer program, service, group, or role. Each entity is identified by a set of attributes so that connections can be 1 to 1, 1 to many, or many to many. We call this a Virtual Group Network (VGN). VGNs are independent of location and device, and their properties may change with time as entities move.

Keywords: Network, Virtualization, Architecture, Security, Future Internet.

1 Introduction

The original Internet model overloads the use of IP addresses as both identifiers and locators. This adds undesirable complexity to the solutions targeting unconsidered scenarios, such as mobility and multi-homing. Such model is also based on host-based end-to-end protocols, meaning that all end systems need to implement the same protocol stack to communicate each other. This significantly reduces scalability as well as the possibility to assume the growing heterogeneity of devices, specially small and low-power smart objects that do not have the same capabilities as high-end servers.

We propose to resolve those problems by separating the network functions into different, uncoupled, and hierarchical scopes. We call it the Global Virtualization Architecture (GVA). On it, access networks have their own protocols and locator spaces, which are specialized for connecting devices to the network. The global transit network, to which access networks are connected, also has a specialized protocol and locator space to deliver information units (packets or messages)

A. Galis and A. Gavras (Eds.): FIA 2013, LNCS 7858, pp. 141–152, 2013.

among access networks. For example, resource-constrained devices may rely into special gateways that implement the network functions they miss in order to allow them interact with any other network entity.

In the GVA model, global communications are implemented by using identifiers that represent network entities, thus achieving the decoupling of location and identification. This permits to provide additional and specialized functionality in the form of network virtualization. Moreover, this approach separates the data and control plane into specialized virtual infrastructures with different network properties. Thus, specific traffic types may be assigned to their own virtual network. This enables, for example, the to treat mobility management exchanges in a different way than data exchanges.

The remainder of this paper is organized as follows. In Section 2 we describe some outstanding architecture proposals for the Future Internet. Then, in Section 3 we analyse the proposals to determine their strengths and weaknesses. In Section 4 we describe how we designed GVA to overcome the limitations shown by analyzed architectures. In Section 5 we discuss the viability of the proposed architecture. Finally, in Section 6 we conclude the paper.

2 Current Architecture Proposals

In this section we give a brief description of the approaches that may resolve the aforementioned problems found in the current Internet. We selected solutions which propose a reasonably complete architecture, separate effectively node identifiers and locators, and resolve the scalability problems.

In TRIAD [6], the authors propose an IPv4 NAT-based architecture in which FQDNs are used as identities, being mapped directly to next hops. Here, routing uses the Name-Based Routing Protocol (NBRP [9]). TRIAD needs to use resolution to reach objects outside their home realm with related scaling problems.

From the solutions that strictly separates identifiers and locators, the Host Identity Protocol (HIP) [26] achieves it by introducing cryptographic host identifiers forming a new global name space as a new intermediate layer between the IP and transport layers. On the other hand, the Locator/Identifier Separation Protocol (LISP) [8] provides routing scalability through a mapping and encapsulation solution to separate global identifiers used by end nodes in their access networks and global locators used to traverse the global transit network (the Internet).

The Heterogeneity Inclusion and Mobility Adaptation through Locator ID Separation (HIMALIS) [18, 23, 25] also follows the separation of identifiers and locators but, in contrast with LISP and HIP, it provides a higher level of routing scalability while providing an independent node identification scheme, which is different from IP and supports sensor networks (e.g. the Internet of Things). It differentiates between local locators (LLOC) and global locators (GLOC), which are correspondingly used in access networks and the global transit network. It therefore includes a new naming scheme for generating host names and IDs.

Mobile Oriented Future Internet (MOFI) [17, 24] is an internetworking architecture that follows the separation of identifiers and locators principle while efficiently supporting envisioned mobile oriented and network diversity environment. MOFI basically pursues ID-based communication. In MOFI, a host is the basic entity that should be identified for communication but can be extended to other objects such as user, contents, etc. Locator for routing in each network is separated from the host ID.

Overlay networks are built on top of other architectures to overcome their limitations. Chord [37] is a decentralised lookup service for mapping keys to nodes, much like a churn-tolerant DHT (Distributed Hash Table), which can be used for routing on flat identifiers (labels). Chord has a fairly good performance and has many improvements, such as LPRS [39]. However Chord has problems to recover from its ring partitioning and lacks security. The architecture proposed by Routing on Flat Labels (ROFL) [5] builds on Chord to provide its benefits to the whole network, removing the necessity of hierarchical addresses in the Internet.

The clean-slate architectures jettison the current Internet. MILSA [29] and Enhanced-MILSA (EMLISA) [28] explore a novel, clean-slate architecture for the Internet, based on the principle of separating identifiers and locators but with other capabilities. They distinguish between realms (organisational areas) and zones (network connectivity areas). MILSA relies on a stable layout of the RZBS (Realm-Zone Bridging Servers), which must be pre-configured. DNS is used for resolving RZBS names (but not for other nodes). Both solutions however lack specific security mechanisms.

The Information-Centric Networking (ICN) raises the role of information to the middle of communications. The EU-funded projects 4WARD [4] and its successor, SAIL [7], are defining an ICN architectural paradigm called Network of Information (NetInf) [3] that extends the concept of identifier/locator split with another level of indirection and decouples self-certifiable objects from their storage location(s). Another EU-funded project, PURSUIT [38], also approach the ICN but proposing a publish/subscribe view where information consumers subscribe to the information they want and information providers "publish" it. Finally, Content Centric Networking (CCN) [16] is an architecture built on named data. It has no notion of host at its lowest level – a packet *address* names content, not location. However, it preserves the design decisions that make TCP/IP simple, robust and scalable.

3   Analysis of Capabilities

In this section we analyse the strengths and weaknesses of the proposals discussed in the previous section, which are HIP, LISP, HIMALIS, MOFI, ROFL, EMILSA, NetInf, PURSUIT, and CCN. For each of them we evaluated its strengths/weaknesses in several aspects by using the following parameters:

- how much architected support for policies they have [A];
- how scalable they are [B];
- how independent they are of the DNS scheme and IP layout [C];

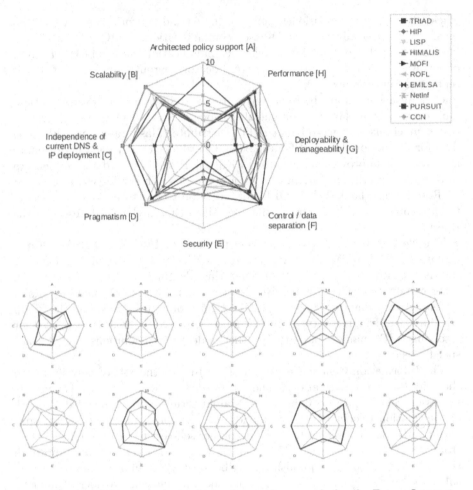

Fig. 1. Results of the strengths analysis of current proposals for the Future Internet. Each aspect has been assigned a value from 0 to 10 for each architecture in the top figure. The bottom figures represent each architecture by its own. It is clear to see that the biggest and less sharp area the better the architecture is.

- how pragmatic they are, as opposed to purely theoretical approaches [D];
- how secure they are [E];
- how much separation they manage to do between control and data flows [F];
- how deployable and manageable they are [G];
- how well they perform [H]

The results of evaluating these parameters are summarised in Figure 1. It shows how all approaches are lacking on security and many of them also lack in policy support. Specifically, even though TRIAD is a fairly complete solution, based on IPv4 and, in principle, quite deployable and scalable, it lacks however an explicit policy framework, and is too dependent on IP addresses being topologically aggregated, and also on nodes following closely the DNS hierarchy.

This deficiency is addressed in HIP and LISP, as also seen in their figures, but they also lack in security, policy support, and independence of IP. Both HIMALIS and MOFI have similar features, as depicted in their diagrams, and share with HIP and LISP the lack on security and policy support. As a totally different architecture, ROFL improves in the independence of IP, pragmatism, and scalability. It also improves in security but neglects the performance and policy support. As it is also a totally different architecture, EMILSA have a good score in policy management, as well as in achieving a good separation between control and data. Its main drawbacks are the need for pre-configuration (placement, population, and management of directory services) and the little security services supported by the architecture. Even though the final three architectures are information-centric, there is a clear separation from NetInf and PURSUIT-/CCN. NetInf has some advancements in security and policy support, being one of the most complete architectures evaluated here. In contrast, PURSUIT and CCN, which are very similar, have many improvements in performance, scalability, pragmatism, independence of IP but, like many other architectures commented above, they lack in security and policy support.

4 Global Virtualization Architecture

The Global Virtualization Architecture (GVA) is designed to overcome the limitations of the current Internet. As shown in Figure 2, it is based on three main functional blocks: 1) A Connectivity Virtualization Layer (CVL) that abstracts the complexity of the underlying networks into different virtualized networks with different properties, like using specialized routing or specific mechanisms for information delivery; 2) An Application and Service Virtualization Layer (ASVL) that manages and offers the Virtual Group Network (VGN) functionality to applications and services; and 3) The Information Infrastructure (I2) that provides the control, management, and security functions as a separated plane to manage the network paths to forward information, the security properties of communications, and support the mobility capabilities.

To offer the benefits of the architecture to the users we defined the VGN concept as a mechanism to build a specific view of the whole network with specific properties and for a specific set of entities. The VGN properties define the security aspects of the communications, the network constraints, etc. Connected entities may be real entities, such as people, software, machines, things, etc. or abstract, such as groups or roles, each represented by its identity with its set of attributes. We emphasise the differentiation of identity and identifier. GVA meets with the ITU-T definition of identity in its X.1250 [12] and the ITU-T definitions for Future Networks [13–15] recommendations.

That said, an identity is the representation of an entity in the form of one or more information elements (attributes) which allow an entity or group of entities to be sufficiently distinguished within context. On the other hand, an identifier

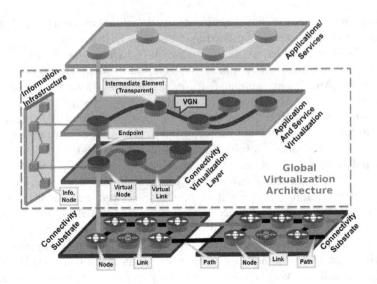

Fig. 2. Architecture Overview

is a piece of data that uniquely identifies something in a particular domain. In a general sense, the ASVL and subsequent communications use identifiers to determine the endpoints of the communication participants and to obtain information from a digital identity if permitted by policies. Nevertheless, they are not used to unambiguously associate an identity to an object over time and space, but rather just at a certain moment and communication event.

We build the CVL on the separation of end-point identifiers (EPID) from network locators (LOC). An EPID is a persistent session-based ID for each network node (entity), which ensures ID-based communication. LOC may be the IP address to which the end-point is attached but it is open to a different address space. End-to-end communication between two end-points will only use their EPIDs, whereas data packets will be delivered to an end point by using the associated LOCs, possibly through one or more transit networks (or even different architectures).

This approach permits GVA to be instantiated on top of any architecture with a smooth evolution path. It abstracts from the network topology to create particular network views for each communication using optimal intermediate elements to transfer information from source to destination. A special entity inside I2, called the Domain Trusted Entity (DTE) [20, 21], has been introduced to each domain and the instances of all domains are joined through the overlay network to build a global trusted infrastructure [22] capable of negotiating the properties of communications, including security.

The VGN model, in conjunction with the I2, supports security and privacy by design, because the information about an entity, which is identified by its identity, will only be given to the allowed entities, as well as cross-layer interactions to enable end-to-end communications including identification of the endpoints.

The identity-based control plane of the I2 provides inter-administrative domain support the federation and building on a trust model that supports end-points and their attributes and identification. Requirements for machine-to-machine communication in self-managing actuator networks, like smart grids, will be covered.

Finally, GVA will inherit proven concepts developed by Identity Management, as well as from locator-identifier and publish-subscribe approaches. New networking scenarios can be instantiated on top of the existing Internet, while providing spotlight examples of new architectural approaches that illustrate the openness to the evolving heterogeneity of the infrastructure and the magnitude of endpoints to validate the approach.

4.1   GVA Features

As a consequence of this design, the GVA operation framework provides a dynamic connectivity model with support for nomadicity and variable reliability through the concept of VGN. It provides a virtual structure within the network allowing arbitrary devices to connect and reconnect to a session. At the same time, VGNs can opt to have a certified level of trust, where the trust level may vary. This solution complements trusted devices and trusted services to provide an overall controllable level of trust for transactions and communication.

GVA supports sustained connectivity for moving endpoints by introducing new protocols and extensions to existing ones. They handle the setting up and tearing down of connections, as well as mobility and nomadicity. General methods known from existing networks will be the starting point to those new protocols developed to manage the complexity of moving endpoints with possibly multiple interfaces and contexts.

The approach to network management and control does not involve network addresses but the identities behind communications. This way, each VGN has specific parameters negotiated by the network and based on *who* is using the network and *what* it can provide. In the same way, when analysing network traffic, it can not be associated to a specific entity, although if permitted by policies, the network can reveal *to whom* messages pertain.

GVA provides an extensible framework through APIs for transport, discovery, name resolution, session control, identity management, security and privacy management will complement the operational framework of GVA and will make it open for new applications and services.

4.2   Functional Blocks

As introduced above and shown by Figure 3, GVA is based on the definition of the CVL as a lower layer functional block, the ASVL as an upper layer functional block, and the I2 as a side plane functional block. Below we detail each component.

The CVL abstracts the specific mechanisms and shape of the underlying networks, such as IPv6, HIMALIS, MOFI, CCN, PURSUIT, etc., to offer a specific

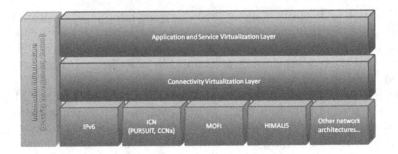

Fig. 3. Functional Blocks of the Architecture

network view that meets with the specific requirements of future communications. The construction of this layer is heavily based on the overlay network concept to support integration of multiple underlying network architectures. It can be seen as a raw arena on which any approach is able to grow without the rigid limitations of current infrastructures, which can also be modelled in different ways to accomplish different communication objectives while being instantiated on top of disjoint and heterogeneous underlying network architectures. In addition, this component permits the underlying network architectures to cooperate and thus offer the best combined functionality to the upper layers and therefore to the users.

Beyond using identifiers, GVA proposes to use attributes that are attached to entities (digital identities). These attributes, such as belonging to a specific group or a specific role within a company, become the handles with which connectivity is established, going far beyond existing approaches, such as the identifier/locator split. ASVL is intended to abstract data communications and thus facilitate to upper layer elements and application clients the access the functionality provided by GVA in the form of VGNs, as described above.

At the identity level, ASVL uses the eXtensible Resource Identifier (XRI) and eXtensible Resource Descriptor Sequence (XRDS) [33]. XRI is used to build the universal identifiers, which are related to identities, resources, and may also be related to VGNs and context identifiers. XRDS is, in turn, used to describe the resources of the endpoints owned by each entity. Thus, the ASVL includes a dynamic but consistent identifier scheme that permits the interaction with other identity management technologies and architectures like SAML [35], Shibboleth [36], and OpenID [32].

All this is achieved by defining context envelopes to wrap communication descriptors (identities of participants, security requirements, environment, etc.). The necessary discovery mechanisms to enable network nodes find each other and know the services they offer is also integrated into the architecture.

I2 is a vertical plane that supports the operations performed by CVL and ASVL. It is intended to abstract ASVL from network complexity by permitting the negotiation of communication parameters (including security) from the identity of their participants, in a secure and isolated manner. Creating this infrastructure is part of our *Security by Design* approach, where security is built into the network infrastructure at the design stage, rather than trying to bolt it on afterwards, which is never an effective or reliable way of managing risks. Therefore, I2 is built with the integration of a security plane, a management plane, and a control plane.

The security plane is built on top of a separate network infrastructure to be totally independent of the underlying network and upper layer architectures. Also, this separation facilitates the fact that data and control messages/packets are separated from the security messages/packets. However, the necessary intermediate elements to build the security plane can be instantiated in the same logical elements or physical equipment as the context control plane.

Finally, communications in GVA are not bound to addresses or identifiers derived from the network attachment point but instead use special context identifiers to identify the VGN endpoint. Thus, a context enclosed in a VGN represents the information that wraps and defines a communication, including the identities of its participants (senders and receivers), the security requirements and parameters, the environment, the communication channel, and the path followed by the information in that channel.

5   Initial Viability Analysis

To get an initial view of the feasibility and viability of GVA we performed a quick study of currently existing solutions to see how they might need to be changed in order to be integrated together to obtain the functionality of some of the components and modules defined in the architecture.

As CVL is primarily built with overlay network mechanisms, we can take advantage of existing approaches like Chord [37], so it is the starting point of our research for this functional block. With this and the storage extension provided by some existing database manager, such as one based on NoSQL like CouchDB, we can have the base to build both the routing table manager and the storage hashing extension modules.

For ASVL we can obtain the functionality of the identity and service discovery by integrating an existing discovery service like those found, for instance, in the SPITFIRE project [31]. Also, the service description module could be instantiated by reusing RDF solutions [19] which provides the necessary service semantics and can be easily integrated with the previous component.

Finally, to build I2 we found many existing solutions. For the mobility and multihoming module, we start by reusing the mechanisms used in other network architectures like Mobile IP [11], HIMALIS [18], or MOFI [17]. The policy engine is provided by a XACML [27] module, like XACML-Light [10], and the topology management can be provided by reusing one of the many existing topology engines. The claims validation service can be based on the credential validation services produced in the TAS3 project, whilst the claims themselves are SAML [35] assertions with holder of key confirmation elements.

6 Conclusions and Future Work

In this paper we analyse different architecture proposals for the Future Internet to know the current gaps and challenges. Then, we introduce GVA, an architecture design that fill those gaps by means of virtualization techniques working together with the overlay network concept. This architecture resolves the previously introduced shortcomings by extensive virtualization and a robust control plane. The separation of identifiers and locators is achieved by the collaboration between CVL and I2, being offered to the user through the ASVL. The global scalability and heterogeneity of underlying architectures is provided by the separation of local and global locators, defining an identity space managed by I2 to address global communications.

We briefly discuss the feasibility of the proposed solution with an initial viability analysis that places the architecture design in terms of other existing architectures, mapping each functional block with other existing architectures, solutions, and infrastructures. Therefore, in future work, we will investigate the relations of the architecture with the main design principles for the Future Internet [30], and how we can improve it by applying them. In particular we would analyse the GVA's realization as part of Software Defined Networks [34] and Network Virtualization Functions [1]. After that we plan to continue the evaluation of the architecture by building a prototype intended to perform extensive experimentation.

Acknowledgments. This work is partially supported by the European Commission's Seventh Framework Programme (FP7/2007-2013) project GN3 and UniverSELF project [2] under grant agreement 257513, by the Ministry of Education of Spain under the FPU program grant AP2010-0576, and by the Program for Research Groups of Excellence of the Séneca Foundation under grant 04552/GERM/06.

References

1. Network Functions Virtualisation White Paper (2012), http://www.tid.es/es/Documents/NFV_White_PaperV2.pdf
2. UniverSELF project (2013), http://www.univerself-project.eu/
3. Ahlgren, B., D'Ambrosio, M., Marchisio, M., Marsh, I., Dannewitz, C., Ohlman, B., Pentikousis, K., Strandberg, O., Rembarz, R., Vercellone, V.: Design considerations for a network of information. In: Proceedings of the 2008 ACM CoNEXT Conference, pp. 1–6. ACM, New York (2008)

4. Brunner, M., Abramowicz, H., Niebert, N., Correia, L.M.: 4WARD: A European perspective towards the future internet. IEICE Transactions on Communications E93-B(3), 442–445 (2010)
5. Caesar, M., Condie, T., Kannan, J., Lakshminarayanan, K., Stoica, I.: Rofl: Routing on flat labels. SIGCOMM Computer Communication Review 36(4), 363–374 (2006)
6. Cheriton, D.R., Gritter, M.: Triad: A scalable deployable nat-based internet architecture. Tech. rep. (2000)
7. Edwall, T., et al.: Scalable and Adaptive Internet Solutions, SAIL (2011), http://www.sail-project.eu
8. Farinacci, D., Fuller, V., Meyer, D., Lewis, D.: Locator/id separation protocol (LISP). Internet-draft, IETF (2012)
9. Gritter, M., Cheriton, D.R.: An architecture for content routing support in the internet. In: Proceedings of the Usenix Symposium on Internet Technologies and Systems (2001)
10. Gryb, O., et al.: XACML Light (2010), http://xacmllight.sourceforge.net
11. Gundavelli, S., et al.: Proxy Mobile IPv6 (2008), http://www.ietf.org/rfc/rfc5213.txt
12. ITU-T: Series X: Data Networks, Open system communications and security. Cyberspace security - Identity management. Baseline capabilities for enhancing global identity management and interoperability. Recommendation ITU-T X.1250 (2009)
13. ITU-T: Y.3001 Recommendation: "Future Network Vision - Objectives and Design Goals" (2011)
14. ITU-T: Y.3011 Recommendation: "New Framework of Network Virtualization for Future Networks" (2011)
15. ITU-T: Y.3021 Recommendation: "New Framework of Energy Saving for Future Networks" (2011)
16. Jacobson, V., Smetters, D.K., Thornton, J.D., Plass, M.F., Briggs, N.H., Braynard, R.L.: Networking named content. In: Proceedings of the 5th International Conference on Emerging Networking Experiments and Technologies (CoNEXT 2009), pp. 1–12. ACM, New York (2009)
17. Jung, H., Koh, S.J.: MOFI: Future internet architecture with address-free hosts for mobile environments. Telecommunications Review 21(2), 343–358 (2011)
18. Kafle, V.P., Inoue, M.: HIMALIS: Heterogeneity inclusion and mobility adaptation through locator id separation in new generation network. IEICE Transactions on Communications E93-B(3), 478–489 (2010)
19. Klyne, G., Carroll, J.J.: Resource Description Framework (RDF): Concepts and Abstract Syntax (2004), http://www.w3.org/TR/rdf-concepts/
20. Martinez-Julia, P., Gomez-Skarmeta, A.F.: A novel identity-based network architecture for next generation internet. Journal of Universal Computer Science 18(12), 1643–1661 (2012)
21. Martinez-Julia, P., Gomez-Skarmeta, A.F.: Using identities to achieve enhanced privacy in future content delivery networks. Computers and Electrical Engineering 38(2), 346–355 (2012)
22. Martinez-Julia, P., Gomez-Skarmeta, A.F., Girao, J., Sarma, A.: Protecting digital identities in future networks. In: Proceedings of the Future Network and Mobile Summit 2011, pp. 1–8. International Information Management Corporation (2011)
23. Martinez-Julia, P., Gomez-Skarmeta, A.F., Kafle, V.P., Inoue, M.: Secure and robust framework for id/locator mapping system. IEICE Transactions on Information and Systems E95-D(1), 108–116 (2012)

24. Martinez-Julia, P., Skarmeta, A.F., Jung, H.Y., Koh, S.J.: Evaluating secure iden-tification in the mobile oriented future internet (mofi) architecture. In: Proceedings of the Future Network and Mobile Summit 2012, pp. 1–8. International Information Management Corporation (2012)
25. Martinez-Julia, P., Skarmeta, A.F., Kafle, V.P.: Research and experimentation with the himalis network architecture for future internet. In: Proceedings of the Future Network and Mobile Summit 2012, pp. 1–8. International Information Management Corporation (2012)
26. Moskowitz, R., Nikander, P.: Host Identity Protocol (HIP) Architecture (2006), http://www.ietf.org/rfc/rfc4423.txt
27. OASIS XACML Technical Committee: XACML: eXtensible Access Control Markup Language (2010), http://www.oasis-open.org/committees/tc_home.php?wg_abbrev=xacml
28. Pan, J., Jain, R., Paul, S., Bowman, M., Xu, X., Chen, S.: Enhanced milsa archi-tecture for naming, addressing, routing and security issues in the next generation internet. In: Proceedings of the International Conference on Communications, pp. 14–18. IEEE, Washington, DC (2009)
29. Pan, J., Paul, S., Jain, R., Bowman, M.: Milsa: A mobility and multihoming sup-porting identifier locator split architecture for naming in the next generation in-ternet. In: Proceedings of the Global Communications Conference, pp. 2264–2269. IEEE, Washington, DC (2008)
30. Papadimitriou, D., Zahariadis, T., Martinez-Julia, P., Papafili, I., Morreale, V., Torelli, F., Sales, B., Demeester, P.: Design principles for the future internet archi-tecture. In: FIA 2012, LNCS, vol. 7281, pp. 55–67. Springer, Heidelberg (2012)
31. Pfisterer, D., Romer, K., Bimschas, D., Kleine, O., Mietz, R., Truong, C., Hase-mann, H., Pagel, M., Hauswirth, M., Karnstedt, M., et al.: Spitfire: Toward a semantic web of things. IEEE Communications Magazine 49(11), 40–48 (2011)
32. Recordon, D., Reed, D.: Openid 2.0: A platform for user-centric identity manage-ment. In: Proceedings of the Second ACM Workshop on Digital Identity Manage-ment, pp. 11–16. ACM, New York (2006)
33. Reed, D., Chasen, L., Tan, W.: Openid identity discovery with XRI and XRDS. In: Proceedings of the 7th Symposium on Identity and Trust on the Internet (IDtrust 2008), pp. 19–25. ACM, New York (2008)
34. Rubio-Loyola, J., Galis, A., Astorga, A., Serrat, J., Lefevre, L., Fischer, A., Paler, A., Meer, H.: Scalable service deployment on software-defined networks. IEEE Communications Magazine 49(12), 84–93 (2011)
35. Security assertion markup language (saml), http://saml.xml.org
36. Shibboleth, http://shibboleth.internet2.edu
37. Stoica, I., Morris, R., Karger, D., Kaashoek, M.F., Balakrishnan, H.: Chord: A scalable peer-to-peer lookup service for internet applications. In: Proceedings of the 2001 Conference on Applications, Technologies, Architectures, and Protocols for Computer Communications, pp. 149–160. ACM, New York (2001)
38. Trossen, D., et al.: Pursuing a Pub/Sub Internet, PURSUIT (2011), http://www.fp7-pursuit.eu
39. Zhang, H., Goel, A., Govindan, R.: Incrementally improving lookup latency in distributed hash table systems. In: Proceedings of the 2003 ACM SIGMETRICS International Conference on Measurement and Modeling of Computer Systems, pp. 114–125. ACM, New York (2003)

Seeding the Cloud: An Innovative Approach to Grow Trust in Cloud Based Infrastructures

Stéphane Betgé-Brezetz[1], Aline Bousquet[3], Jérémy Briffaut[3], Eddy Caron[2],
Laurent Clevy[1], Marie-Pascale Dupont[1], Guy-Bertrand Kamga[1], Jean-Marc Lambert[4],
Arnaud Lefray[2,3], Bertrand Marquet[1], Jonathan Rouzaud-Cornabas[2],
Lamiel Toch[2], Christian Toinard[3], and Benjamin Venelle[1]

[1] Alcatel-Lucent Bell Labs, France
{stephane.betge-brezetz,laurent.clevy,marie-pascale.dupont,
guy-bertrand.kamga,bertrand.marquet,
benjamin.venelle}@alcatel-lucent.com
[2] University of Lyon, LIP Lab, UMR CNRS - ENS Lyon - INRIA - UCB Lyon 5668, France
{eddy.caron,arnaud.lefray,lamiel.toch,
jonathan.rouzaud-cornabas}@inria.fr
[3] ENSI Bourges, LIFO Laboratory, France
{aline.bousquet,jeremy.briffaut,
christian.toinard}@ensi-bourges.fr
[4] Gemalto, France
jean-marc.lambert@gemalto.com

Abstract. Complying with security and privacy requirements of appliances such as mobile handsets, personal computers, servers for customers, enterprises and governments is mandatory to prevent from theft of sensitive data and to preserve their integrity. Nowadays, with the rising of the Cloud Computing approach in business fields, security and privacy are even more critical. The aim of this article is then to propose a way to build a secure and trustable Cloud. The idea is to spread and embed Secure Elements (SE) on each level of the Cloud in order to make a wide trusted infrastructure which complies with access control and isolation policies. This article presents therefore this new approach of trusted Cloud infrastructure based on a Network of Secure Elements (NoSE), and it illustrates this approach through different use cases.

1   Introduction

Cloud Computing is revolutionizing the delivery of information services as it offers several advantages over traditional IT systems mainly in terms of cost-reduction and agility. However, it raises many concerns related to security and privacy which are main obstacles for its large adoption [4].

Moreover, the current situation of Cloud Computing is dominated by the model where the Cloud Service Provider (CSP) defines his terms/conditions and each Cloud User (CU) has to accept them and trust the CSP. Unfortunately, several recent cases of security or privacy breaches [5] showed that CUs should (i) pay attention to how CSPs effectively manage security and privacy within their infrastructures and (ii) be

A. Galis and A. Gavras (Eds.): FIA 2013, LNCS 7858, pp. 153–158, 2013.

part of this management. This point is underlined by key standard [6] or regulation bodies notably in Europe [7]. Indeed, under the EU laws, the CU remains responsible for the collection and processing of sensitive data, even when third parties (i.e., CSP) process these data. Although he has currently no regulatory responsibility, the CSP has however to comply with the contractual obligations required by the CU and therefore has to provide the CU with the necessary features and technologies allowing the protection of the CU sensitive data within his Cloud infrastructure.

Several works are then tackling these Cloud privacy and security issues. Regarding data protection, we can mention the Data Protection as a Service approach [1] or platforms for Cloud privacy management [2]. However, these approaches do not really allow defining a large range of privacy policies and the data privacy protection mechanism needs also to be securely executed so that it should not be corrupted. Regarding the protection of software execution, the use of Secure Elements (SE) is a common solution. A SE can be for example a Trusted Platform Module (TPM) with a secure crypto-processor providing secure storage for cryptographic keys and which can also be used to verify the validity of the software running on a computer [12]. Similarly, Hardware Security Module (HSM), a special type of secure crypto-processor has been used to manage digital keys, and to provide strong authentication to access critical keys for server applications [13]. Several research projects [14] have been launched to define new ways to grow trust in the cloud but not by directly embedding SE (e.g., A4Cloud, TClouds) or using SE (e.g., TECOM) but not tackling how they can build together a cloud Trusted Computing Base.

The European CELTIC+/Seed4C project (Secure Embedded Element and Data privacy for Cloud) [16], presented in this paper, aims to address these key challenges of Cloud security and privacy management. In this Seed4C project, we propose a new approach of cooperative Secure Elements (or "Seeds") allowing the trusted enforcement of a wide range of policy in order to ensure the security properties (confidentiality, integrity, availability) and to protect the privacy of user sensitive data. In order to achieve this, Seed4C aims to tackle various questions and technical challenges such as: What are the critical functions to be supported by these SEs? How to distribute SEs in the infrastructure and provide added value to platform and services? How to address communication between SEs and from SEs to embedding machines? The project is then proposing a technology able to address these challenges and that will be further carried out in use-cases of different domains.

This paper is then structured as follows. In Section 2, we explain the key principles of the Seed4C approach and how it can grow trust for Cloud infrastructures. In Section 3, we illustrate this approach through two examples of use cases respectively in the domains of high performance computing and privacy policy enforcement. Finally, in the conclusion, we discuss the next stages of our work.

2   Seed4C Approach: The NoSE as a Minimal Trusted Computing Base for the Cloud

The Network of Secure Elements (NoSE) is the cornerstone of the Seed4C project. NoSE is then a network of interconnected Secure Elements defining, for the Cloud, a minimal Trusted Computing Base (TCB) (i.e., a minimum set of hardware, firmware, and/or software components necessary for security) [11].

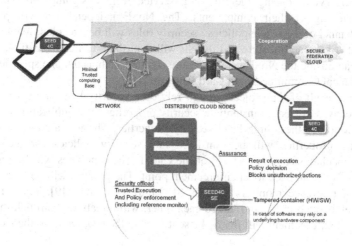

Fig. 1. Seed4C approach based on a Network of Secure Elements ("seeds") deployed within the Cloud infrastructure and offering trustable security and data protection

Secure Elements (SEs) are software or hardware elements that are usually connected locally with/in pieces of equipment. They do not communicate apart with some management services through a dedicated and controlled channel on the overall system or infrastructure. As said, SEs are by definition and construction elements that do not communicate or in a very controlled way. Making them communicate and collaborate to build a Network of Secure Elements that can secure an entire Cloud based infrastructure is indeed a research challenge.

In the Seed4C project, we will introduce deployment and configuration ability at the architecture level. With the NoSE, each Secure Element represents locally the minimal TCB to implement security function and the interconnection of SE makes the minimal TCB for a trusted service on a Cloud infrastructure. The trusted Cloud Computing Base allows connecting different parts of the infrastructure from the access and transport network until the Cloud nodes.

The NoSE allows end-to-end virtual security chain from the user terminal to the high-end server where the services are executed or to the place where data are processed and stored (see Figure 1). One important aspect of the NoSE is proximity. For this purpose, different options of embedment of Secure Element within the Cloud infrastructure will be considered (e.g., SE embedded in a physical Cloud node or rack, SE connected to a node hypervisor, or even software SE embedded in a Virtual Machine). Moreover, as a NoSE is composed of several elements, we can easily envisage that the NoSE will scale accordingly to the Cloud infrastructure or network. Its proximity to the running Virtual Machine or virtualized execution environment will allow correctly checking the environment and giving high assurance. The SE as element of the NoSE will be managed during the equipment lifecycle, for the physical provisioning part, but will be loaded/unloaded of some critical assets (credentials, attributes, etc) through the NoSE protocols. The SE will be accessed by local middleware/services during the life of a service from designing, provisioning & decommissioning of their components. The NoSE independence will provide a separate channel of trust. The policies / security rules will be executed by the different components of the architecture and the SE will contribute to that execution. SEs will communicate inside the NoSE using a secure channel such as the one specified by the ETSI Technical Committee Smart Card Platform [15].

As a first result of the project we will rely on a security language [9] in order to provide a canvas of easy to instantiate security properties. The application developers will be able to use these high level security properties. Through a specific compiler, the security properties will be translated into security policies for the different protection mechanisms at each level of the Cloud. These policies will be transferred through the NoSE to each local enforcement point. The policies will be then enforced by a set of reference monitors such as SE Linux and PIGA [9]. These reference monitors, embedded in SE and linked each other, will collaborate through the NoSE. Evidences of enforcement will finally be sent back to the CU thanks to the NoSE.

3   Examples of Addressed Use-Cases

3.1   High Performance Computing

When one spokes about High Performance Computing (HPC) one thinks about clusters and grids. Nevertheless since few years Cloud Computing offers services for scientists who need high performance computing facilities for their researches. Such intensive computing can use very sensitive data notably in domains as eHealth.

For ensuring the adequate data projection on the computing infrastructure, the software (middleware) which is in charge of communications between scientists and services is then critical. We will use the SOA based middleware DIET developed at ENS Lyon [8]. The principles of DIET are simple and the programming model is based on the GridRPC paradigm. A user sends a request to DIET to know whether a service is available on the platform. If this service exists, he sends the data needed by the service without carrying about where it is located, and finally obtains the results.

Recent developments on the DIET middleware stretch to make it compatible with some CSPs like EC2, Eucalyptus, Nimbus, OpenStack, OpenNebula, etc. Furthermore, DIET was not originally designed to address security problems as confidentiality and integrity. We propose therefore a proof of concept to add security skill to this middleware by leveraging the SE capabilities so that the computation on sensitive data will only be assigned to a trusted node having the adequate security protection. For instance a DIET user in an aerospace company wants to compute a model of an airplane and he does not want the rival companies to know what he does. So his requests and data sent must be confidential (confidentiality) and not allow unauthorized modifications (integrity). Thanks to the SEs embedded both in 1) the servers' daemons which provide services and 2) virtual machines instantiated by these servers, security properties are guaranteed.

3.2   Privacy Policy Enforcement

Another domain that will benefit from the NoSE approach of Seed4C is privacy. Indeed, in the Cloud context, as the CU outsources sensitive data (end-users personal information or enterprise documents such as HR documents on employees, bids, tenders, patents, etc.) to the CSP, the CU should be able to specify some requirements related to access control, data location, retention management, data usage/motion tracking, etc., governing how his data and the related processing must be protected within the Cloud infrastructure of the CSP. Moreover, in order to strengthen the trust between both parties, the CSP must be able not only to enforce the CU data protection requirements all along the data lifecycle but also to prove this enforcement.

For this purpose, we have proposed an approach of multilevel privacy policy enforcement [3] which consists for the CU to express his privacy and data protection requirements as policies applicable at several levels. One can distinguish for instance the *Application-Level* that includes policies governing the end-user or application level actions on CU data and the *Infrastructure-Level* that includes policies governing the CSP components (e.g. storage system, file system) actions on CU data.

In this multilevel policy context, the NoSE concept will be a real chain of trust between the CU and the CSP. Each Policy Enforcement Point either controlled by the CU (*Application-Level Policy Enforcement*) or by the CSP (*Infrastructure-Level Policy Enforcement*) could be executed within or in cooperation with a Secure Element that can among other provide certified information as needed, evaluate policies and generate the tamper-proof traces that can help to prove the fulfillment of the CU data protection requirements.

4   Conclusion

The distributed and dynamic nature of Cloud infrastructures requires thinking differently on how security and assurance are brought to execution elements. The Seed4C project, presented in this article, proposes a new approach called the NoSE (Network of Secure Element). The NoSE can be beneficial in several ways, bringing trust from the infrastructure layer up to the service and application ones.

At this stage, several use-cases have been identified and it is being elaborated the architecture and the abstract model to express policies. The next step is to define how to distribute policies to the NoSE and how the NoSE exchanges information, validates policies, indicates compliance and provides assurance. Moreover, the project has also planned to validate the Seed4C platform using real and large scale distributed infrastructures such as Grid'5000 [10] which can be used to deploy our own Cloud infrastructure with a NoSE. Also different exploitation models will be studied, from the cloud infrastructure operators that control the NoSE up to Over-The-Top scenarios that benefit from the NoSE at lower layers.

Acknowledgements. The authors would like to thank all the Seed4C partners for their valuable contributions. See [16] for more on Seed4C and its consortium.

References

1. Song, D., Shi, E., Fischer, I., Shankar, U.: Cloud Data Protection for the Masses. IEEE Computer Magazine 45(1) (2012)
2. Pearson, S., Shen, Y., Mowbray, M.: A Privacy Manager for Cloud Computing. In: Jaatun, M.G., Zhao, G., Rong, C. (eds.) CloudCom 2009. LNCS, vol. 5931, pp. 90–106. Springer, Heidelberg (2009)
3. Betgé-Brezetz, S., Kamga, G.B., Dupont, M.P., Ghorbel, M.: Privacy Control in the Cloud based on Multilevel Policy Enforcement. In: IEEE 1st International Conference on Cloud Networking (CloudNet 2012), Paris, November 28-29 (2012)
4. Srinivasamurthy, S., Liu, D.Q.: Survey on Cloud Computing Security. In: Proc. Conf. on Cloud Computing, CloudCom 2010 (2010)
5. Rashid, F.Y.: Epsilon Data Breach Highlights Cloud Computing Security Concerns, http://eWeek.com (2011)
6. Jansen, W., Grance, T.: Guidelines on Security and Privacy in Public Cloud Computing. NIST (2011)
7. Article 29 Data Protection Working Party, "Opinion 05/2012 on Cloud Computing", WP 196, Brussels (July 2012)
8. Caron, E., Desprez, F.: DIET: A scalable toolbox to build network enabled servers on the grid. International Journal of High Performance Computing Applications 20(3) (2006)
9. Afoulki, Z., Bousquet, A., Briffaut, J., Rouzaud-Cornabas, J., Toinard, C.: MAC protection of the OpenNebula Cloud environment. In: International Conference on High Performance Computing and Simulation (HPCS), July 2-6 (2012)
10. Bolze, R., et al.: Grid'5000: A large scale and highly reconfigurable experimental grid testbed. International Journal of High Performance Computing Applications 20(4) (2006)
11. NCSC DoD/NIST Orange book Part I section 6.3 (December 1987), http://www.kernel.org/pub/linux/libs/security/Orange-Linux/refs/Orange/OrangeI-II.html#toc6
12. http://www.trustedcomputinggroup.org/resources/trusted_platform_module_tpm_summary
13. http://www.opendnssec.org/wp-content/uploads/2011/01/A-Review-of-Hardware-Security-Modules-Fall-2010.pdf
14. http://cordis.europa.eu/fp7/ict/security/projects_en.html#CLO
15. http://www.etsi.org/deliver/etsi_ts/102400_102499/102484/07.00.00_60/ts_102484v070000p.pdf
16. http://www.celtic-initiative.org/Projects/Celtic-Plus-Projects/2011/SEED4C/seed4c-default.asp

Internet of Things

IoT6 – Moving to an IPv6-Based Future IoT[*]

Sébastien Ziegler[1], Cedric Crettaz[1], Latif Ladid [2], Srdjan Krco[3], Boris Pokric[3],
Antonio F. Skarmeta[4], Antonio Jara[4], Wolfgang Kastner[5], and Markus Jung[5]

[1] Mandat International, Geneva, Switzerland
{iot6,sziegler}@mandint.org
[2] University of Luxembourg, Luxembourg, Luxembourg
latif@ladid.lu
[3] Ericsson, Belgrade, Serbia
srdjan.krco@ericsson.com
boris.pokric@gmail.com
[4] University of Murcia, Murcia, Spain
{skarmeta,jara}@um.es
[5] Vienna University of Technology, Vienna, Austria
{k,mjung}@auto.tuwien.ac.at

Abstract. IoT6 is a research project on the future Internet of Things. It aims at
exploiting the potential of IPv6 and related standards to overcome current
shortcomings and fragmentation of the Internet of Things. The main challenges
and objectives of IoT6 are to research, design and develop a highly scalable
IPv6-based Service-Oriented Architecture to achieve interoperability, mobility,
cloud computing integration and intelligence distribution among heterogeneous
smart things components, applications and services. The present article starts by
a short introduction on IPv6 capabilities for the Internet of Things and information on the current deployment of IPv6 in the world. It continues with a presentation of the IoT6 architecture model and its concept of service discovery.
Finally, it illustrates the potential of such IPv6-based architecture by presenting
the integration of building automation components using legacy protocols.

Keywords: IoT, M2M, IPv6, CoAP, architecture, interoperability, building
automation.

1 Introduction

The Internet of Things is exponentially growing towards an ecosystem interconnect-
ing tens of billions of smart things. Simultaneously, the Internet Protocol version 6
(IPv6) is scaling up the Internet to an almost unlimited number of globally reachable
addresses. IoT6 is a 3 years FP7 European research project on the Internet of Things.
It aims at exploiting the potential of IPv6 and related standards (6LoWPAN, CORE,
COAP, etc.) to address current needs of the Internet of Things, considering how the
IPv6 features like addressing, security, mobility and autoconfiguration could help the
deployment of IPv6 sensor based solution allowing E2E communication on the IoT
ecosystem. Its main challenges and objectives are to research, design and develop a

---

[*] Invited Paper.

A. Galis and A. Gavras (Eds.): FIA 2013, LNCS 7858, pp. 161–172, 2013.

highly scalable IPv6-based Service-Oriented Architecture. Its potential will be researched by exploring innovative forms of interactions such as:

— Information and intelligence distribution.
— Multi-protocol interoperability with and among heterogeneous devices.
— Device mobility and mobile phone networks integration, to provide ubiquitous access and seamless communication.
— Cloud computing integration with Software as a Service (SaaS).
— IPv6 - Smart Things Information Services (STIS) innovative interactions.

The main outcomes of IoT6 are recommendations on IPv6 features exploitation for the Internet of Things and an open and well-defined IPv6-based Service Oriented Architecture enabling interoperability, mobility, cloud computing and intelligence distribution among heterogeneous smart things components, applications and services, including with business processes management tools.

2   IPv6 Capabilities for the Internet of Things

Global Internet human users are currently estimated at 2.4 Billion and are further projected to climb to 3.0 Billion by 2015. More significantly, the number of Internet connected objects has overpassed the number of connected human beings, and is expected to expend far beyond the human population, with 20 to 50 Billion interconnected smart things. Over the last decades, the Internet Protocol version 4 (IPv4) has emerged as the mainstream protocol for networking layer. However, this protocol was not designed for the Internet of Things (IoT) and is inherently limited to about 4 Billion addresses. At the global level, IANA has entirely exhausted its IPv4 addresses allocation on the 3rd Feb 2011; and two out of five RIRs (Regional Internet Registries) have achieved their address allocation limit in April 2011 by APNIC and in August 2012 by RIPE. The Internet Protocol version 6 (IPv6) has been adopted by IANA and the RIRs to overpass the IPv4 limitations and to address the growing demand.   IPv6 provides 2^{128} unique Internet addresses, or 3.4×10^{38} addresses, which corresponds to over 6.67×10^{17} unique addresses per square millimeters of Earth surface. It also provides new features enabling an easier configuration of devices, data streaming compliance, improved security, and effective peer-to-peer connections avoiding Network Address Translation (NAT) barriers. All those elements contribute to turn IPv6 into a natural candidate for the addressing and networking of a globally connected Internet of Things. Many devices are already interconnected through the Internet Protocol, including printers, sensors, lighting, healthcare systems, smart meters, video cameras, TVs and heating control systems. The emergence of IPv6-related standards specifically designed for the IoT, such as 6LoWPAN, CoAP, and CoRE[14][15], has enabled highly constrained devices to become natively IP compliant. IPv6 is being referred to by a growing number of IoT and Machine-to-Machine (M2M) related standards, such as oneM2M, OMA Lightweight M2M, or the IEEE 802.15.4g protocol, which will support Advanced Metering Infrastructure (AMI) for smart cities deployments.

3   IPv6 Worldwide Deployment

The potential of IPv6 to interconnect the future IoT depends on its effective deployment. Thus, it is important to consider its current evolution. Year 2012 has indicated a clear shift towards a global IPv6 deployment across the world. Google has reached 1% of users connecting over IPv6 [1] and over 22% of the top 500 web sites are already IPv6 compliant [2]. In Europe, IPv6 adoption is gaining significant momentum with RIPE NCC having announced its final /8 allocation policy for IPv4 address pool in August 2012. It is reinforced by the European Commission action plan for the deployment of IPv6 [3]. On a percentage basis, Romania is leading the deployment with 8.43% per cent adoption [4] rate followed by France at 4.69%. In North America, IPv6 adoption rate is at 1.97%. It translates into an estimated IPv6 user base of 3.5 million users, the largest base of IPv6 users in the world. In Asia and Pacific, countries like China, Japan and South Korea are proactively supporting the deployment of IPv6 with IoT applications. In March 2000, Japanese Telecommunications Company NTT became the world's first ISP to offer IPv6 services to the public. Millions of smartphones, tablets and other devices in homes, offices and public spaces throughout Japan rely on the country's long-standing IPv6 network. Japan ranking highly at 2.04% user penetration on IPv6. China launched its five-year plan for early IPv6 adoption in 2006. The program, known as the China Next Generation Internet (CNGI) project, has been instrumental in helping the country build the world's largest IPv6 network, which has been showcased at the 2008 Olympic Games in Beijing. Its expansive next-generation network connects millions of devices, users, and security and transportation systems throughout the country. In 2004, South Korea initiated widespread migration, making it one of Asia Pacific's earliest adopters of the next-generation Internet protocol. The policy, established by the Ministry of Information and Communication, required the mandatory upgrade to IPv6 in the public sector by 2010. Indian authorities aim to achieve major transitions on dual stack across the industry by 2017 and plans to achieve complete IPv6 ready status by 2020 [5]. The rest of the Asia Pacific region of Hong Kong ,Singapore, Thailand, Malaysia, Sri Lanka and Indonesia are at a nascent stage of IPv6 adoption and have got started on IPv6 initiatives with mandates for IPv6 transition around 2015-16 timeframes. Africa being a late entrant into the technology landscape also has the advantage of direct IPv6 implementation. According to AfriNIC, IPv4 allocations have been on the decline and countries have started taking up IPv6. Kenya and South Africa are leading in IPv6 allocations. In Latin America, countries such as Brazil, Argentina, Venezuela, Columbia, Chile and Peru are beginning their IPv6 transition.

It results form the current stage, that IPv6 is not fully deployed yet. However, the current evolution tends to provide an extensive worldwide IPv6 network able to address and interconnect an unlimited number of smart things across all the continents.

4   IoT6 Architectural Model

Over the years, a number of projects have specified various versions of IoT architectures, basing them on the specific requirements the projects were addressing (SENSEI

[6], HOBNET [7], iCORE[29], BUTLER [30]etc.) Due to a large heterogeneity of application domains and consequently the requirements, the approaches to the architecture specification differed between the projects resulting in more or less different architectures comprised of a number of components and protocols. The diversity of the architectures was soon recognized by the community as one of the factors limiting the progress in the domain which resulted in more coordinated efforts driven by the IERC (Internet of Things European Research Cluster) aiming at specifying a common, harmonized reference IoT architecture. Significant roles in this effort have the IoT-A and IoT-I projects [8]. The former has extensively analysed IoT application domains to identify requirements and devise a reference architecture model that can be used for specification of reference architectures and architecture instantiations suitable for specific systems. The latter project analysed the IoT-A architecture reference model, compared it to other relevant architectures and validated its applicability in a range of application scenarios [9].

Other important coordinated effort that should be noted is the FI-PPP program and the FI-WARE architecture [10]. There, a detailed architecture of a Future Internet platform has been designed taking into account inputs from numerous European organizations, also covering in the process the IoT functionality as an important aspect of the Future Internet. Further to this, a large and significant effort has been invested in the framework of the ETSI M2M Technical Committee, and more recently oneM2M alliance [11] resulting in corresponding ETSI technical specifications for M2M architecture.

The aim of the IoT6 architecture is to enable a highly scalable IPv6-based Service-Oriented Architecture to achieve interoperability between different communication technologies and interaction with application based services like cloud based services, intelligent information processing, application specific visualization and integration with business processes and workflows. The approach selected towards definition of the IoT6 architecture is to leverage the on-going related activities by extending, enhancing and modifying different architectural components with a particular focus on the communication layer. This focus on the communication layer comes from the project focus on IPv6 as the main integrating point for various IoT devices, underlying technologies as well as higher layer services and applications. The goal was not only to use IPv6 as a pure transport protocol, but to leverage the embedded IPv6 features to enable functions currently implemented using higher layer protocols. This approach complements well other IoT architecture efforts as these mainly focus on higher layers and do not address the details of the communication layer, but usually assume IP or any other communication paradigm.

Having this in mind, based on the requirements analysis of several application domains and similar efforts done in other projects as well as the IoT reference architecture model proposed by the IoT-A project and IoT architectures designed by FI-WARE and ETSI M2M, the initial IoT6 architecture was designed. To a large extent, the IoT6 architecture adopts the existing solutions and provides novel proposals on the communication layer. These proposals facilitate utilization of IPv6 addressing schemes across IoT devices, including those that do not natively support IPv6 and leverage DNS (Domain Name System) functionality to provide resource and service registration and discovery. To that end, service discovery is conducted through the

IPv6 network-based information systems that are already deployed, such as the domain name system with service discovery (DNS-SD). In the same manner, a resource directory serving a local domain can be replaced with a multicast DNS (mDNS), thus providing the required functionality by exploiting and extending the IPv6 functions only [12].

Figure 2 shows the IoT6 architecture model indicating different network domains. IoT devices (sensors and actuators) can be found at the bottom of the architecture stack outlined in Figure 1. There are two distinct types of devices: IoT6 compliant and non IoT6 -compliant or legacy devices. The IoT6 compliant devices can be IPv6-enabled IoT devices or IoT devices based on protocols such as 6LoWPAN and the proposed GLoWBAL IPv6 [13], CoAP [14] and CoRE [15]. protocols. The non-IoT6 compliant devices are based on other, non-IP communication protocols, as well as IPv4-based devices. The non-IoT6 compliant devices require gateways or proxies to be connected to the rest of the IoT6 system in order to adapt the native protocols, functionality and addressing to IPv6 through a transparent mechanism. IoT6 Local Area Network (LAN) provides connectivity mechanisms to IoT devices taking into account their specific protocols and technology and making them available to the rest of the IPv6 powered environment in terms of discovery, access and management. The IoT6 wide area network (WAN) enables the interconnection of multiple IoT6 LANs and IoT6 backend servers and creates the overall IoT6 core infrastructure. This infrastructure offers access to the IoT devices from the application-level layer consisting of different services such as Software as a Service (SaaS), Smart Things Information Service (STIS), Web and mobile applications to mention a few examples [16].

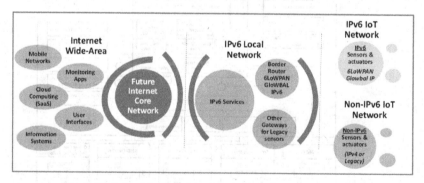

Fig. 1. High-level IoT6 architecture indicating network domains

A more detailed architecture is shown in Figure 2 indicating the component level view. These components take into account the three level of entities indicated in figure 1, covering the upper layer the Internet Wide-Area servies, the middle layer the local IPv6 services like half-gateways, and finally the lower layer the IoT sensor area with the possible integration of legacy system. As can be seen, it builds largely on the ETSI oneM2M and FI-WARE IoT architectures and adds specific solutions on the communication layer. It comprises components from the FI-WARE architectural model as well as service discovery components such as Resource Directory (digrectory), specific protocol adapters accommodating DNS-SD, mDNS, CoAP Resource Directory, and its own IoT6 stack API (discovery API) support. There are distinct types of device (sensor) clusters, namely ETSI M2M clusters, large IPv6 clusters, small IPv6 clusters, RFID clusters, and other clusters (IPv4, proprietary, legacy technologies, etc.). As for the ETSI M2M clusters and others, the existing service discovery mechanism supports CoRE Resource Directory. It is based on DNS-SD and mDNS with appropriate protocol adapters providing the full set of required functionality. The focus of the subsequent analysis related to the service discovery is on the IPv6 sensor clusters using the DNS-SD and mDNS methodology.

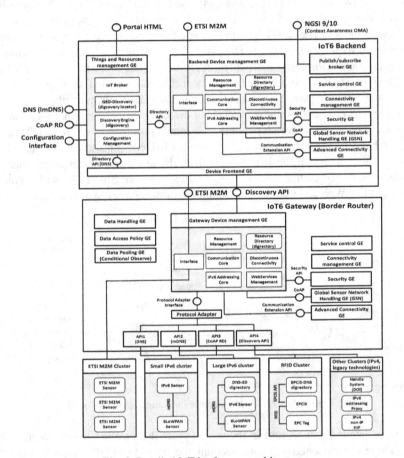

Fig. 2. Detailed IoT6 reference architecture

5   Resources Repository and Service Discovery

A key requirement for any IoT architecture is to provide adequate service discovery and registries. This becomes even more challenging, when it is supposed to encompass the actual heterogeneity of the IoT. IoT6 has designed a concept of *"Digcovery"*, which is illustrated in Figure 3. This presents how the different technologies involved in the Internet of Things ecosystem such as Smart Objects, RFID tags, and legacy devices, are integrated into different directories named *"digrectories"*. These *digrectories* are managed through DNS-queries extended with an elastic search engine in order to make it scalable at the same time it offers a centralized point, called *"digcovery core"*, to manage and discover them.

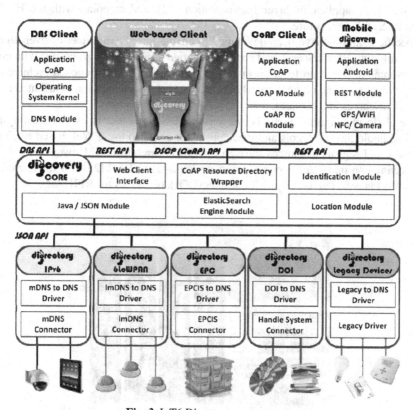

Fig. 3. IoT6 Digcovery ecosystem

All the resources and services are mapped to a common ontology and description, based on existing ontologies and profiles from the IP-enabled Smart Objects Alliance (IPSO) [17, 18], and oBIX from the Building Automation area. It will also consider emerging profiles developed by standardization bodies such as the Open Mobile Alliance (OMA) [19]. These semantic layer interfaces have been integrated into the DNS-SD types, in order to reach a common semantic description accessible through DNS and powered with the universal IPv6 capabilities to carry out the discovery resolution.

This also presents how to interoperate with the discovery architecture through other interfaces different to DNS such as RESTful architecture with data structured in

JSON format. JSON has been chosen for the interoperability with all the resources, since it is considered by the Working Groups from the IETF such as the Constrained Resources (CoRE) Working Group, and the Constrained Management (COMA) Working Group as the most suitable protocol to structure the data for constrained resources, leaving other formats such as XML optional.

The IoT6 architecture uses a RESTful interface based on CoAP [20] developed by the IETF CoRE Working Group. This enables the integration of constrained devices with an overhead of only 4 bytes and a functionality optimized for the observation of resources [21], application-layer fragmentation [22], and mapping with the HTTP-based RESTful architecture.

Specific solutions have been developed to enable look-up and queries over *digcovery*, exploiting ElasticSearch and enabling queries on various *Digrectories* with context awareness, based on location or resource types [ref]. The proposed architecture enables organized and context-based queries over heterogeneous and distributed registries of resources and services.

The platform can use Domain Name Servers (DNS) in order to exploit existing IP-based technologies, protocols and mechanisms. It can also use a Web-based platform to access and register resources through a RESTful architecture. However, the IoT6 architecture can integrate other repositories such as HANDLE [23], for the mirroring of the objects with Digital Object Identifiers (DOI), or EPCIS for RFID tags.

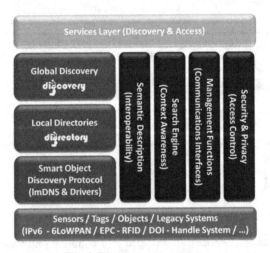

Fig. 4. Digcovery components

6   Building Automation Components Integration

Building automation components constitute a particularly interesting domain of IoT to test an IPv6-based architecture, due to their extensive use of heterogeneous communication protocols. Buildings have to provide supportive conditions for people to work and relax. The underlying demands are best tackled through an appropriate design of the building and its structure as well as technical infrastructure. The task of building automation systems (BAS) is to provide automatic feedback control, central and remote monitoring and access to underlying building services. These building services primarily address the energy intensive areas of heating ventilation and air conditioning (HVAC) and lighting/shading. Besides, dedicated systems for the domains concerning security and safety exist. On the way to intelligent buildings and smart homes, cross-domain integration is of particular relevance. As a next step, it is desirable to integrate existing building automation technologies into an information infrastructure aiming at use case scenarios and applications that are part of the IoT.

Building automation systems follow the well-known automation pyramid with functions dedicated for the field, automation and management level. Meantime, progress in computer engineering progress allows intelligent field devices to take over functions of the automation layer. This has led to a 2-tier architecture of underlying control networks with a field and a backbone layer. While at the field level robust fieldbus networks are deployed, Ethernet and IP communication is already prevalent at the management level.

Over the last three decades, many different protocols for the use in building automation have emerged. Ideally an all-in-one solution that allows total control of all conceivable scenarios within a building would be desired. However, even despite the long timespan of their development, not one specific protocol has yet emerged that covers all relevant domains. Rather, many different protocols co-exist. Some of them aim at the control of multiple domains (e.g. BACnet, KNX, LonWorks), while others exclusively offer tailored functions for a specific area (e.g. lighting: DALI, blinds and shutters: SMI). Another particular class of technologies are wireless standards such as ZigBee, EnOcean, Z-Wave and KNX-RF to name just a few [24].

Integration of this heterogeneity of technologies within the building automation domain is already challenging. A further integration within the future Internet of Things is even a more thrilling task. For the desired interconnection, various approaches can be taken. These have their individual benefits and shortcomings, but all of them aim at providing a homogeneous view on the underlying heterogeneous protocols and systems. While an integration of systems is beneficial in several ways, it is also the case that several challenges still need to be solved on the road to an integrated system. Since the management tier of BAS already provides IP communication, for the integration Web service based approaches seem a reasonable choice. Here OPC Unified Architecture (OPC UA) [25], open Building Information Exchange (oBIX) [26] or Building Automation Control Network / Web Services (BACnet/WS) [27] come into play which either facilitate SOAP or RESTful Web services (or both) for their protocol bindings. These technologies also define and care for information models that can be used for an abstract data representation of the different involved technologies.

Recent research favors the use of RESTful Web services and IPv6 even on most constrained devices and within constrained wireless networks aiming at providing the deepest possible integration and interoperable end-to-end communication within the future Internet of Things. The constrained application protocol (CoAP) together with optimization technologies like 6LoWPAN and EXI allow to deploy sensors and actuators with Web service based protocol stacks.

While Web service interfaces at centralized servers are a feasible solution, within the IoT6 project a solution has been created that combines existing integration approaches with the recent advances for constrained RESTful environments using a protocol stack based on IPv6, CoAP, EXI and oBIX [28]. IPv6 acts a common network layer for end-to-end communication. By means of CoAP, RESTful Web service interface are realized. EXI is used to compress the exchanged XML messages in order to keep the payload of frames exchanged within (wireless) links as low as possible to avoid message fragmentation. Finally, oBIX supports an object model that can be used to model domain specific contracts for different device types. It further provides a standardized XML schema that is required for optimal EXI encoding.

Currently, this protocol stack is deployed within the IoT6 project on one hand on constrained devices and on the other hand on a gateway that offers a central or per-device interfaces based on the protocol stack for existing building automation devices (e.g. KNX, BACnet, ZigBee). These interfaces are then further integrated into the overall IoT6 architecture.

7   Conclusion

After one year of research, IoT6 has demonstrated a good compliance between IPv6 and the various IoT domains requirements, including tags, sensors, building automation, mobile phones and building automation components. A comprehensive IPv6-based architecture for the IoT has been designed and will be tested through practical use cases implementations. IoT6 will continue researching and exploring IPv6 features for the integration of a heterogeneous and fragmented IoT. In parallel, IPv6 starts to be globally deployed across the World and a growing number of IoT and M2M related standards are now clearly referring to IPv6 for their networking layer. It seems to be of good auguries for a possible global convergence and interconnection of the future IoT through IPv6.

References

1. Google IPv6 statistics, http://www.google.com/ipv6/statistics.html
2. According to a study made by Lars Eggert, IRTF Chair– IPv6 Deployment Trends
3. Advancing the Internet: Action Plan for the deployment of Internet Protocol version 6 (IPv6) in Europe, European Commission communication, http://ec.europa.eu/information_society/policy/ipv6/docs/european_day/communication_final_27052008_en.pdf
4. IPv6 Observatory, http://www.ipv6observatory.eu

5. National IPv6 Roadmap Policy version 2, `http://www.dot.gov.in/ipv6` and National Telecom Policy 2012, `http://www.dot.gov.in/ntp/NTP-06.06.2012-final.pdf`

6. SENSEI European research project (Integrating the Physical with the Digital World of the Network of the Future), Pervasive and Trusted Network and Service Infrastructures: ICT-2007.1.1: The Network of the Future, Contract no. 215923, `http://www.sensei-project.eu`

7. Hobnet European research project, `http://hobnet-project.eu`

8. Internet of Things Architecture, IoT-A, `http://www.iot-a.eu`

9. IoT6 European research project, Deliverable D1.5: "IoT6 Reference Model", White Paper (2012), `http://www.iot6.eu`

10. FI-WARE Internet of Things (IoT) Services Enablement, `http://forge.fi-ware.eu/plugins/mediawiki/wiki/fiware/index.php/FI-WARE_Internet_of_Things_(IoT)_Services_Enablement`

11. ETSI M2M Communications, `http://www.etsi.org/website/technologies/m2m.aspx`

12. Jara, A.J., Martinez-Julia, P., Skarmeta, A.F.: Light-weight multicast DNS and DNS-SD (lmDNS-SD): IPv6-based resource and service discovery for the Web of Things. In: International Workshop on Extending Seamlessly to the Internet of Things (2012)

13. Jara, A.J., Zamora, M.A., Skarmeta, A.F.: GLoWBAL IP: an adaptive and transparent IPv6 integration in the Internet of Things. In: MobiWIS 2012, The 9th International Conference on Mobile Web Information Systems, Niagara Falls, Ontario, Canada, August 27-29 (2012)

14. Constrained Application Protocol (CoAP), draft-ietf-core-coap-11 (July 16, 2012), `https://datatracker.ietf.org/doc/draft-ietf-core-coap/`

15. Constrained RESTful Environments (CoRE), `http://tools.ietf.org/wg/core`

16. Kim, S.H., Im, J., Byun, J., Lee, K., Kim, D., Ziegler, S., Crettaz, C., KAIST, Mandat International: Initial IoT6 integrations have been validated with IoT-SaaS integration between Mandat International and RunMyProcess, and STIS integration with KAIST (October 2012)

17. Dunkels, A., Vasseur, J.: IP for Smart Objects, Internet Protocol for Smart Objects (IPSO) Alliance, White Paper, N. 1, IPSO Alliance (2008)

18. Shelby, Z., Chauvenet, C.: The IPSO Application Framework, draft-ipso-app-framework-04, IPSO Alliance, Interop Committee (2012)

19. Tian, L.: Lightweight M2M (OMA LWM2M), OMA Device Management Working Group (OMA DM WG), Open Mobile Alliance - OMA (2012)

20. Shelby, Z., Hartke, K., Bormann, C., Frank, B.: Constrained Application Protocol (CoAP), Constrained Resources (CoRE) Working Group, Internet Engineering Task Force (IETF), work in progress, draft-ietf-core-coap-13 (2012)

21. Li, S.T., Hoebeke, J., Jara, A.J.: Conditional observe in CoAP, Constrained Resources (CoRE) Working Group, Internet Engineering Task Force (IETF), work in progress, draft-li-core-conditional-observe-03 (2012)

22. Shelby, Z.: Embedded web services. IEEE Wireless Communications 17(6), 52–57 (2010), doi:10.1109/MWC.2010.5675778

23. Sun, S., Lannom, L., Boesch, B.: RFC3650 - Handle System Overview. IETF Standards (2003)

24. Kastner, W., Neugschwandtner, G.: Data communications for distributed building automation. In: Embedded Systems Handbook, 2nd edn., vol. 2, pp. 29–34. CRC Press, Boca Raton (2009)
25. OPC Unified Architecture Specification, OPC Foundation (2009)
26. oBIX Version 1.1 Working Draft 06, OASIS (2010)
27. Addendum c to ANSI/ASHRAE Standard 135-2004, BACnet - A data communication protocol for building automation and control networks, American Society of Heating, Refrigerating and Air-Conditioning Engineers (2004)
28. Jung, M., Weidinger, J., Reinisch, C., Kastner, W., Crettaz, C., Olivieri, A., Bocchi, Y.: A transparent IPv6 multi-protocol gateway to integrate Building Automation Systems in the Internet of Things. In: Proceedings of the IEEE International Conference on Internet of Things (iThings 2012), Besancon, France (November 2012)
29. iCORE EU Project, http://www.iot-icore.eu/
30. BUTLER EU Project, http://www.iot-butler.eu

SmartSantander: Internet of Things Research and Innovation through Citizen Participation*

Verónica Gutiérrez[1], Jose A. Galache[1], Luis Sánchez[1], Luis Muñoz[1], José M. Hernández-Muñoz[2], Joao Fernandes[3], and Mirko Presser[3]

[1] Universidad de Cantabria, Santander, Spain
[2] Telefonica I+D, Madrid, Spain
[3] Alexandra Institute; Aarhus, Denmark
{veronica,jgalache,lsanchez,luis}@tlmat.unican.es, jmhm@tid.es,
{joao.fernandes,mirko.presser}@alexandra.dk

Abstract. The Smart City concept relates to improving efficiency of city services and facilitating a more sustainable development of cities. However, it is important to highlight that, in order to effectively progress towards such smart urban environments, the people living in these cities must be tightly engaged in this endeavour. This paper presents two novel services that have been implemented in order to bring the Smart City closer to the citizen. The Participatory Sensing service we are proposing exploits the advanced features of smartphones to make the user part of the ubiquitous sensing infrastructure over which the Smart City concept is built. The Augmented Reality service is connected to the smart city platform in order to create an advanced visualization tool where the plethora of available information is presented to citizens embedded in their natural surroundings. A brief description of the smart city platform on top of which these services are built is also presented.

Keywords: IoT, smart city, augmented reality, participatory sensing.

1 Introduction

Smart cities exploit synergies between the ubiquitous sensing technology and their social components to enhance the quality of life of citizens and to improve the efficiency of the city services. In this sense, the Smart City concept [1] and [2] has typically been associated with an eco-system where technology is embedded everywhere. Thus, the different city services (e.g. traffic, water, sewage, energy, commerce, etc.) are greatly improved by exploiting the interconnected information and actuation capabilities that this technology provides.

However, sometimes this technological environment leads us to disregard the fact that the ultimate aim of the Smart City concept must be the citizens. It is important to avoid focusing only on the technology and missing the engagement of society within this paradigm. Smart cities are not simply those that deploy ICT. They need to combine modern technology with smart new ways of thinking about technologies' role in organization, design and planning. As smart city initiatives are planned, the way that

---

* Invited Paper.

A. Galis and A. Gavras (Eds.): FIA 2013, LNCS 7858, pp. 173–186, 2013.

technology can create new urban user experiences must be envisioned. Thinking about the Smart City as a holistic system and considering the manner in which those new systems can bring in positive behavioural change, needs the citizens to become involved from the very first moment of the city smartening process.

This paper presents architecture that, following Internet of Things (IoT) precepts [3] and [4], enables the creation of a ubiquitous sensing infrastructure within the scope of a Smart City aiming at improving city service efficiency. This architecture tackles the challenges pertaining to infrastructure management and data handling. Moreover, it also defines the necessary middleware that enables seamless access to this infrastructure for the development of value-added services. This latter aspect is what mainly motivates this article as two novel services have been developed on top of an urban deployment in the city of Santander, Spain. The deployment consists of a large-scale IoT infrastructure which supports the provision of impact-generating smart city services, directly perceivable by all the Smart City stakeholders [5].

Augmented Reality (AR) systems have recently emerged as a powerful visualization tool, which augments real world elements with digital information. The proliferation of powerful smartphones has accelerated the adoption of AR in mobile environments too. Several AR-based applications have been developed for Android or iOS devices [6] and [7]. Moreover, a particularly important aspect of the AR is its ability to make the user feel naturally surrounded by the technology, thus providing a perfect eco-system for the user to engage with the Smart City concept. In this paper the AR service that has been developed for improving tourist services is described. In this context, the main insights of the service architecture as well as details of the developed AR mobile application are described.

Moreover, mobile phones have evolved from devices that are just used for voice and text communication to platforms that are able to capture and transmit a range of data types (e.g. image, audio, and location). The adoption of these increasingly capable devices has enabled a pervasive sensing paradigm – participatory sensing [8-10]. Participatory sensing systems encourage individuals carrying mobile phones to explore phenomena and events of interest using in situ data collection and reporting. Pertaining to the Smart City scenario, participatory sensing has a twofold advantage. On the one hand, it expands the sensing capabilities that have been deployed in terms of dedicated sensor networks. On the other hand, it makes the citizens feel part of the Smart City in which they all live. These two features have been addressed through the Participatory Sensing service that is described in this paper. Users' mobile phones serve as yet another sensor feeding physical sensing information, e.g. GPS coordinates, noise, temperature, etc. to the platform. Users can also subscribe to services such as "the Pace of the City", where they can get alerts for specific types of events currently occurring in the city. Finally, users can themselves also report the occurrence of such events, which are subsequently propagated to other users who are subscribed to the respective type of events.

The paper is structured as follows. Section 2 describes the architecture and platform on top of which these services have been developed. Particular emphasis is put on the part of the architecture that deals with the service development framework. In Section 3 the AR and Participatory Sensing services are detailed. Moreover, the service architecture and the implementation insights are thoroughly described. Finally, conclusions are drawn in Section 4.

2   Novel Architecture for Service Provision and Experimentation

The architecture used as reference model for the deployed infrastructure does not solely rely on particular service-specific deployments, but also provides a testbed-like urban experimentation environment for technology and service providers. Although we recognize that the importance of experimentation capabilities in the architecture of a mature smart city of the future may eventually blur, we believe that the early-day Smart Cities will greatly benefit from the capability to experiment towards the development of future services.

The architecture has a three-tiered network approach: IoT node tier, gateway (GW) tier and testbed server tier.

The IoT node tier embraces the majority of the devices deployed in the testbed infrastructure. It is composed of diverse heterogeneous devices, including miscellaneous sensor platforms, tailor-made devices for specific services as well as Radio-Frequency Identification (RFID) and Near Field Communications (NFC) tags. These devices are typically resource-constrained and host a range of sensors and in some cases actuators. Other devices such as mobile phones and purpose-built devices with reasonable computing power (e.g. mobile devices in vehicles), as well as providing wide area communication capabilities, behave as IoT nodes in terms of sensing capabilities and as GW nodes regarding processing and communication capabilities.

The GW tier links the IoT devices on the edges of the capillary network to the core network infrastructure. IoT nodes are grouped in clusters that depend on a GW device. This node locally gathers and processes the information retrieved by IoT devices within its cluster. It also manages (transmission/reception of commands) them, thus scaling and easing the management of the whole network. The GW tier devices are typically more powerful than IoT nodes in terms of memory and processing capabilities, also providing faster and more robust communication interfaces. GW devices allow virtualisation of IoT devices. This enables the instantiation of emulated sensors or actuators that behave in all respects similar to the actual devices.

The server tier provides more powerful computing platforms with high availability and directly connected to the core network. The servers are used to host IoT data repositories and application servers. Server tier devices receive data from all GW tier nodes. As a final step, the concept of federation is supported by the architecture. Servers managing networks located in different physical locations can connect among themselves to allow users of the platforms to transparently access IoT nodes that are deployed in different testbeds.

Fig. 1 shows the high-level architecture consolidated in the SmartSantander project [11] and [12] as well as the main functionalities provided and associated with each of the tiers.

The architecture distinguishes four subsystems, namely management, experimentation, application support and, a transverse one, the Authentication, Authorization and

Accounting (AAA) subsystem. In order to access and interact with these subsystems four interfaces have been defined, named Management support interface (MSI), Experimental Support Interface (ESI), Application Support Interface (ASI) and Access Control Interface (ACI), respectively. For each of the three levels of the architecture, the corresponding functionalities and services associated with the aforementioned four subsystems are implemented.

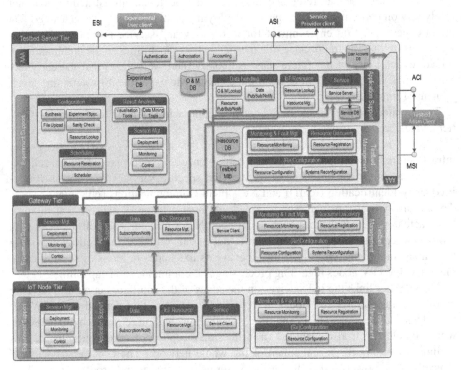

Fig. 1. Platform high-level architecture and building blocks

The Testbed Management subsystem performs three non-trivial management processes, namely: resource discovery, resource monitoring and testbed reconfiguration. The discovery of resources is an essential feature of an IoT platform as it provides support for resource selection according to the user's criteria (for example, sensed phenomena, sensor locality, measurement frequency among others). This essentially entails i) the description of the diversity of IoT resources using a uniform IoT Resource Description Model as well as ii) the generation of these descriptions based on dynamic IoT node registrations, and iii) their lookup based on IoT device attributes, dynamic state and connectivity characteristics. Even under normal operation, the IoT platform is in a constant state of flux: IoT nodes fail, change their point attachment, and join the platform or undergo transition through a number of operation states. Ensuring the correct execution of the IoT testbed's services in the face of such a dynamic environment and guaranteeing the testbed's resilience to failures, requires continuous monitoring of the state of its IoT resources. Finally, on the detection of hardware failures, fault-remediation strategies require that the testbed is reconfigured to omit the faulty nodes from future experimentation or service-provisioning.

The Experiment Support subsystem provides the mechanisms required to support different phases of the experiment lifecycle. During the specification phase, which mainly deals with resource selection (i.e. selection of IoT devices and other testbed resources suitable for execution of desired experiment), the user is supported with adequate functionality enabling exploration of available testbed resources (resources are available during the duration of the experiment) aiming at the selection of those fulfilling (in terms of capabilities offered by selected nodes) the desired properties. Once the selected nodes for a determined experiment are reserved and scheduled, they are wirelessly flashed with the corresponding code image. This flashing procedure, carried out through Multihop-Over-The-Air Programming (MOTAP), enables nodes to be flashed as many times and with as many codes as required. Finally, during the execution phase, the experimenter is empowered with the tools for experiment execution control, experiment monitoring, data collection and logging.

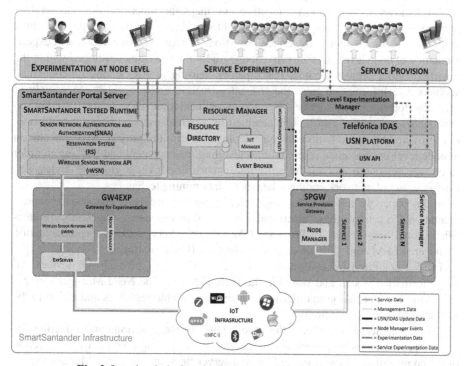

Fig. 2. Low-level platform architecture and implemented modules

Finally, the Application Support subsystem is in charge of providing the functionalities to facilitate the development of services based on the information gathered by the IoT nodes. Besides the storage of the observations and measurements coming from the IoT nodes, its main functionalities relate to the lookup and provision of observations to requesting services by means of a publish/subscribe/notify interaction.

At the IoT node and GW level, subscription, notification and resource management are supported, all information retrieved from them being stored in the server tier in the O&M database. For services taking data retrieved by IoT nodes, the Service client is located in the IoT node tier, whilst for devices acting as GW nodes in terms of communication/processing skills and as IoT nodes providing sensing capabilities, such as mobile phones, the service client is located at GW level. For both cases, information is sent directly from the service client to the service server, storing information in the corresponding database. Finally, information associated with the services is sent from the server tier node to the corresponding Service Provider client through the ASI interface.

Last but not least, the AAA subsystem is in charge of authentication and access control functionalities that are transversally carried out in order to protect all the interaction points that the platform offers to the outside world. This functionality is only carried out at server level in order to grant access to authenticated and authorized experimenters, services providers or testbed administrators.

Fig. 2 shows the low-level architecture that maps the functionalities and services previously described onto specific building blocks. From the user perspective, three main blocks can be identified: service provision, service experimentation and experimentation at node level. Service provision includes the use cases developed within the SmartSantander project, such as Participatory Sensing or AR, among others. These services take information from the IoT infrastructure and process it accordingly to offer the corresponding services. Service experimentation refers to the different experiments/services that can be implemented by external users, utilizing the information provided by the IoT infrastructure deployed within the project. Experimentation at node level implies node reservation, scheduling, management and flashing in order to change behaviour and execute different experiments over a group of nodes, i.e., routing protocol, network coding schemes or data-mining techniques.

In this paper we focus on the description of service provision and service experimentation. To achieve these functionalities, the following main components are identified: Portal Server, Service Provision GW (SPGW), Service-Level Experimentation Manager (SLEM) and Ubiquitous Sensor Network (USN) platform.

The Service Provision GW receives the data retrieved by the deployed devices. All this information is sent and stored in the USN platform. The Node Manager also accesses to this information in order to monitor the available resources and report to the Resource Manager accordingly.

The Portal Server represents the access point to the SmartSantander facility for service providers and experimenters at service level. Through the coordinated action of different building blocks in the GW and server tiers, the Resource Manager keeps the Resource Directory up to date with the available resources within the network

SLEM allows the service-level experimenters (i.e. those running experiments using data provided by deployed nodes) to access data collected from the services. The SLEM allows them to access the USN component providing a number of useful functions for the development of IoT applications and services (e.g. sensor discovery, observation storage, publish-subscribe-notify, etc.). For service providers (i.e. those providing a service with data retrieved by the deployed nodes), data generated by nodes within the network is directly accessed through the USN.

3   Service Provision and Experimentation: Augmented Reality and Participatory Sensing

The process of evolving towards a Smart City concept implies that besides developing infrastructure new services have to be provided. As final recipients of the developed services and applications, users play a very important role in the conception, design and evaluation phases of such services. This user-driven methodology [13] approach allows, in a first stage, the citizens' problems and needs to be understood, then new and innovative solutions that tackle those needs can be designed and developed and finally those solutions can be evaluated. By following this methodology we increase the impact of these applications and services in the cities. This is the case of the two applications described below, that is, AR and Participatory Sensing.

3.1   Augmented Reality Service

In the majority of cities there is a huge amount of information that may be of interest for tourists and citizens but which is not readily accessible because it is so disperse. To avoid that, a new service has been created, unifying the way to access all data sources and presenting them in a context-sensitive, location-aware manner to the end users using AR technology.

Fig. 3. SmartSantanderRA application screenshots

The AR service developed in the SmartSantander project includes information about more than 2700 places in the city of Santander, classified in different categories: beaches, parks and gardens, monuments, buildings, tourist information offices, shops, art galleries, libraries, bus stops, taxi ranks, bicycle hire points, parking lots and sports centres, as shown in Fig. 3. Furthermore, it allows real-time access to traffic and beach cameras, weather reports and forecasts, public bus information and bike hire service, generating a unique ecosystem for end users when moving around the city.

As an illustration of the type of service supported by the SmartSantanderRA application [14], it offers an interactive experience through its "stroll in the city" mode. With the application in this mode, visitors will receive information about specific Points Of Interest (POIs) taking into account their preferences as they stroll around the city. This, in general, enhances the serendipity effect for the application end user. In this sense, they can define their own preferences (language, places to visit, etc.) and have an interactive context-sensitive experience visiting the city, rather than using traditional standalone applications.

The deployment of stickers including Quick Response (QR) codes and NFC tags in strategic places in the urban landscape, see Fig. 4, will provide location-sensitive information (transport service, the cultural agenda, shops, monuments, buildings). These stickers link visitors and citizens to the same information included in the AR Service. Additionally, it complements the SmartSantanderRA app, providing precise information about specific POIs.

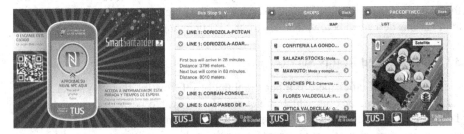

Fig. 4. City guide functionality provided by stickers with NFC technology and QR codes

It is important to note that the AR service has been designed so that the service usage is monitored and the user's behaviour can be analysed, constituting a tool for the creation of new services and experiments within the Smart City context.

3.2   Participatory Sensing Service

Nowadays, social media affect a big part of our lives; around 65% of online adults use social media for personal and professional purposes and 79% of companies currently use or are planning to use social media [15] and [16]. This increase in use of social media by individuals and companies makes the topic very important for research and development of new and innovative services that can serve both the interests of companies and individuals and can create strong relationships among them.

For this reason we have created the Participatory Sensing service, see application appearance in Fig. 5, which aims at exploiting the use of citizens' smartphones to make people become active in observations and data contribution. In this scenario citizens, Santander City Council and the local newspaper "El Diario Montañés" are connected into a common platform where they can report, share and be notified of events happening in the city. As an example, a user walking in the city centre who finds a hole in the pavement can take a picture, write a text and finally share this incidence with other users of the application. The Santander City Council will therefore be notified of the occurrence of the event and proceed accordingly by sending an employee to the location in order to fix this problem. Another example would be when a user reports a road accident; all the other users that are subscribed to this type of event will be notified and can try to avoid driving in this area. By being connected to the Participatory Sensing service, the local newspaper "El Diario Montañés" also enriches this body of knowledge by sharing the daily news information with all the other users of the service. Moreover, the newspaper has created an online information channel called "ElPulsodelaCiudad (Pace of the City)" [17], which provides the citizens with an interface for accessing Participatory Sensing events as well as public transport information, the cultural agenda and sensor values from the SmartSantander IoT infrastructure all on the same website.

Fig. 5. Pace of the City application screenshots

As well as sharing these social-related events, this application periodically samples the values sensed by the smartphones, such as GPS location, acceleration, temperature, humidity, etc. This information is fed into our platform periodically and can be very valuable in the development of new and innovative services.

3.3   Service Component Implementation

Fig. 6 depicts the low-level service provision architecture, showing the interaction between the different components and elements involved in the AR and the Participatory Sensing services. As can be seen, several additional software components are required. SmartSantanderRA mobile applications, AR Server and AR Content Server (ARC Server) can be identified in the AR Service. Besides these, it includes end users with their mobile phones and tags installed in strategic places. Furthermore, two different server components have been developed for the Participatory Sensing Service: the Participatory Sensing Server (PSens Server) and the Pace of the City Server.

Moreover, the USN stores all the data in a common repository, providing an API based on a REST web service for data access. This allows service providers or experimenters to carry out their own developments. In this sense, AR and Participatory Sensing services information can be combined with data collected from the IoT infrastructure in order to create novel and innovative services or experiments.

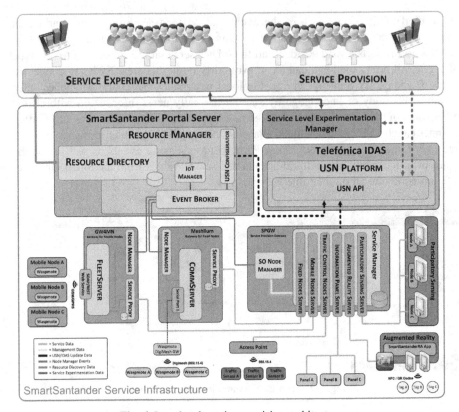

Fig. 6. Low-level service provision architecture

Service Provision Gateway Servers

The PSens Server and AR Server are the bridge between services and the Smart-Santander platform. These components are responsible for registering the mobile nodes in the SmartSantander framework, both PSENS_NODES and AR_NODES, submission of observation messages coming from the applications related to physical sensing, social-related events and retrieval of historical physical sensing information and information generated based on the user behaviour in the AR   scenario.

When starting the application for the first time, the mobile device is registered in the SmartSantander platform through the PSens Server or the AR Server. In the case of successful device registration, they return the generated Universal Unique IDenti-fier (UUID) to the corresponding application. This UUID is stored locally in the mobile phone and will be sent as a parameter in future calls allowing the identification of the device.

Augmented Reality Content Server

The ARC Server is responsible for returning the requested contents to the Smart-SantanderRA application as well as for dynamically generating the mobile web pages. The sequence of actions involving the ARC Server is described below:

i.   Every time the ARC Server receives a request, it communicates to the AR Server, within the Service Provision Gateway, generating messages that will include context information about user behaviour that will enable observations to be sent to the USN.

ii. Once the ARC Server receives a request from the application, it looks for the nearby POIs in its own database, returning the requested information in a unified way, using the ARML v1.0 data format, which is specifically targeted for mobile AR applications.

iii. By reading a NFC tag or QR code, the smartphone sends a request to this server. It will contact legacy systems as well as its own database and return a mobile web page using JQuery Mobile that enhances the mobile web application by integrating HTML5, CSS, JQuery and JQuery UI.

Pace of the City Server

The Pace of the City Server is responsible for handling subscriptions and social-related events. It has its own database with subscriptions and events as well as a PUSH notification component, enabling users to subscribe and unsubscribe to specific types of events. Moreover, it provides a REST service interface with methods to ask about events of a specific type, date, or events nearby the user's current location.

For queries about specific types of events, dates, or even location the mobile applications send the requests to the Pace of the City Server, which retrieves the event information from its local database, matches the events according to the filter and returns the list of filtered events to the application.

SmartSantanderRA Application

SmartSantanderRA is an application for citizens and visitors available on Android and iOS platforms. It combines AR technology with information existing in the City Council legacy systems, creating an interactive experience when walking along the city, rather than using traditional standalone applications or websites.

Once started the application, it presents a main screen with six options (Santander, Tourism, Commerce, Agenda, Transport and Culture), which provide access to information about different areas of interest in the city.

If the user presses on the AR buttons (Tourism, Commerce, Agenda, Transport, Culture), the AR view will be started, creating on the smartphone screen an overlay on the camera feed with nearby POIs filtered by the selected option. If a particular POI is chosen, further information (title, short description, photo and distance to the POI) is displayed. Moreover, the application allows the user to create the route to that place or to show the street view or playing digital content related to the POI (e.g. videos) if it is available. Besides the AR view, the user has the possibility to access such information by placing POIs on the map view or showing and filtering them within the list view.

More than 10.000 users have downloaded the SmartSantanderRA application since 3rd August 2012. During this time, users are actively using the application, on average generating more than 2000 requests per day to the ARC Server. If accessed information is analysed by POI's category, transport reaches 52 per cent of requests, followed by commerce with 28 per cent and tourism with 17 per cent.

Pace of the City Application

The Pace of the City application [18] is available on both Android and iOS platforms. It provides two main functionalities: in the first one the application samples and periodically sends to the PSens Server all the sensor capabilities the smartphone has, which includes: acceleration, temperature, luminosity, noise, battery charge, gravity, pressure, proximity, etc. The second functionality allows the user to create and share the social-related events, subscribe and unsubscribe to specific types of events and to ask about specific events.

Once the application starts, a map view is loaded, in which the user can see his/her current position and, if there are nearby events, they will appear with pins on their location. On the bottom of the screen, five buttons allow the user to: "Add Event" by clicking on this button the user will be able to report an event, the "Events" button allows the user to search for specific events, the filtering can be by event type, date or user location, "My Measures" button allows the user to visualise his historical physical sensing data, "My events" button allows the user to visualise his/her published events and the "Alerts" button allows the user to see his/her current alerts. All the information can be seen either on a map or in a list.

Since November 11th, the application has attracted 4,100 downloads. During this time, the citizens have reported more than 1,200 events. 60 per cent of them have notified the municipal services in order to deal with the corresponding incidence. It is important to note that the use of IOT technology has changed the way the City Council deals with the incidences communicated by the citizens. This has caused a complete reorganization of the municipal services. In this sense, the City Council has improved its response to the citizens, reducing the time to find out a solution for an incidence from 38.5 to 14.2 days in the last two months of 2012. During 2013, this indicator has become even better, taking just 5.71 days on average to solve an incidence within Santander.

4   Conclusions

The smart city scenario provides the different ecosystem stakeholders (municipality authorities, researchers, etc.) with a unique framework for the creation of sustainable cities by means of new services relying on state-of-the-art technologies. However, the risk of an extensive use of technology magnifying the digital gap for those citizens who do not have the required skills cannot be neglected. Aiming at overcoming this risk, when striving for intelligence at the city level to develop the smart city concept, the citizen-centric approach has to be preserved. Furthermore, we believe that the city scenario offers a fantastic possibility to the research community, companies and individuals to explore and research on new technologies, protocols and services. Bearing in mind all these considerations, the project SmartSantander has built a dual-purpose facility, supporting both experimentation and service provision. The infrastructure is suitable to conduct research activity on top of a massive IoT experimental facility with more than 25,000 fixed and mobile devices. Additionally, two citizen-centric services, named AR and Participatory Sensing, have been developed with the aim of intensively involving users in the smart city scenario. The former aggregates the digital information layer made available by the city council and pops it up on citizens' smart phone screens. Additionally, the information implicitly generated by the user is processed by the system with the aim of acquiring knowledge about citizen preferences, mobility patterns and other statistics. The latter makes the concept of the citizen as a sensor a reality. The use of the Participatory Sensing application enables users to report events and incidences and to share them with other users subscribed to the service. Furthermore, there is an option allowing users to enable remote access to some of the physical sensors of his/her mobile terminal, hence helping to provide complementary real-time information about environmental and traffic conditions in different areas of the city.

Of course, the user's privacy always has to be strictly respected in such an interaction, and complete transparency must be provided so citizens are always aware and conscious of the type of information they are contributing with to help create a system that is useful for the community. It is essential for the user to know how to access the option enabled/disabled data sharing, and to be confident that data will be processed in a disaggregated manner, preventing personal information from being bound to retrieved data. Some preliminary surveys show that there is an increasing interest in this type of participatory services, and that a number of people are willing to support them if non-commercial interests can be guaranteed. The first trials have shown that, even with a small proportion of the population taking part in them, data provided through user participation can be extremely useful to complement data gathered from the network of static sensors already deployed throughout the city. This also demonstrates the need for new ways to process and integrate heterogeneous data sources.

Acknowledgements. Although only a few names appear in this paper's list of authors, this work would not have been possible without the contribution and encouragement of the enthusiastic team of the SmartSantander project which has been partially funded by the European Commission under the contract number FP7-ICT-257992.

References

1. Schaffers, H., Komninos, N., Pallot, M., Trousse, B., Nilsson, M., Oliveira, A.: Smart Cities and the Future Internet: Towards Cooperation Frameworks for Open Innovation. In: Domingue, J., et al. (eds.) Future Internet Assembly. LNCS, vol. 6656, pp. 431–446. Springer, Heidelberg (2011)
2. Nam, T., Pardo, T.A.: Conceptualizing smart city with dimensions of technology, people, and institutions. In: Proceedings of the 12th Annual International Digital Government Research Conference, College Park, Maryland, USA, June 12-15, pp. 282–291 (2011)
3. Atzori, L., Iera, A., Morabito, G.: The Internet of Things: A survey. Computer Networks 54(15), 2787–2805 (2010)

4. Vermesan, O., Friess, P., Guillemin, P., Gusmeroli, S., Sundmaeker, H., Bassi, A., Soler-Jubert, I., Mazura, M., Harrison, M., Eisenhauer, M., Doody, P.: Internet of Things Strategic Research Roadmap. In: Vermesan, O., Friess, P. (eds.) Internet of Things - Global Technological and Societal Trends. River Publishers, Aalborg (2011)
5. Galache, J.A., Santana, J.R., Gutiérrez, V., Sánchez, L., Sotres, P., Muñoz, L.: Towards Experimentation-Service duality within a Smart City scenario. In: Proceedings of the 9th International Conference on Wireless On-demand Network Systems and Services, Courmayeur, Italy, January 9-11 (2012)
6. Wikitude Augmented reality browser, http://www.wikitude.com/ (accessed on February 10, 2013)
7. AroundMe, http://www.aroundme.com/ (accessed on February 10, 2013)
8. Campbell, A., Eisenman, S., Lane, N., Miluzzo, E., Peterson, R.: People-centric urban sensing. In: Proceedings of the 2nd International Conference on Wireless Communications, Networking and Mobile Computing, Boston, Massachusetts, USA, September 22-24, pp. 18–32 (2006)
9. Burke, J., Estrin, D., Hansen, M., Parker, A., Ramanathan, N., Reddy, S., Srivastava, M.: Participatory sensing. In: Proceedings of 1st Workshop on World-Sensor-Web: Mobile Device Centric Sensory Networks and Applications, Boulder, Colorado, USA, October 31, pp. 1–5 (2006)
10. Paulos, E., Honicky, R., Hooker, B.: Citizen Science: Enabling Participatory Urbanism. In: Foth, M. (ed.) Urban Informatics: The Practice and Promise of the Real-time City, pp. 414–434. IGI Global (2008)
11. SmartSantander project deliverable D1.1, First Cycle Architecture Specification, http://www.smartsantander.eu/downloads/Deliverables/D1.1.pdf (accessed on February 10, 2013)
12. SmartSantander project deliverable D1.2, Second Cycle Architecture Specification, http://www.smartsantander.eu/downloads/Deliverables/d1.2.pdf (accessed on February 10, 2013)
13. Greenbaum, J.M., Kyng, M.: Design at Work: Cooperative Design of Computer Systems. Routledge (1991)
14. SmartSantanderRA application, http://www.smartsantander.eu/index.php/blog/item/174-smartsantanderra-santander-augmented-reality-application (accessed on February 10, 2013)
15. PewInternet survey, http://pewinternet.org/Reports/2011/Social-Networking-Sites.aspx
16. Harvard Business Review, http://hbr.org/web/slideshows/social-media-what-most-companies-dont-know/1-slide (accessed on February 10, 2013)
17. Pace of the city initiative at El Diario Montañés, http://www.elpulsodelaciudad.com (accessed on February 10, 2013)
18. Pace of the City application, http://www.smartsantander.eu/index.php/blog/item/181-participatory-sensing-application (accessed on February 10, 2013)

A Cognitive Management Framework for Empowering the Internet of Things

Vassilis Foteinos[1], Dimitris Kelaidonis[1], George Poulios[1], Vera Stavroulaki[1],
Panagiotis Vlacheas[1], Panagiotis Demestichas[1], Raffaele Giaffreda[2],
Abdur Rahim Biswas[2], Stephane Menoret[3], Gerard Nguengang[3], Matti Etelapera[4],
Nechifor Septimiu-Cosmin[5], Marc Roelands[6],
Filippo Visintainer[7], and Klaus Moessner[8]

[1] Department of Digital Systems, University of Piraeus, Greece
{vfotein,dkelaid,gpoulios,veras,panvlah,pdemest}@unipi.gr
[2] CreateNet, Italy
{raffaele.giaffreda,abdur.rahim}@create-net.org
[3] Thales Communications, France
{stephane.menoret,gerard.nguengang}@thalesgroup.com
[4] VTT Research Centre, Finland
Matti.Etelapera@vtt.fi
[5] Siemens, Romania
septimiu.nechifor@siemens.com
[6] Alcatel Lucent Bell Labs, Belgium
marc.roelands@alcatel-lucent.com
[7] Centro Ricerche FIAT
filippo.visintainer@crf.it
[8] University of Surrey, Guildford, UK
K.Moessner@surrey.ac.uk

Abstract. This work presents a Cognitive Management framework for empowering the Internet of Things (IoT). This framework has the ability to dynamically adapt its behaviour, through self-management functionality, taking into account information and knowledge (obtained through machine learning) on the situation (e.g., internal status and status of environment), as well as policies (designating objectives, constraints, rules, etc.). Cognitive technologies constitute a unique and efficient approach for addressing the technological heterogeneity of the IoT and obtaining situation awareness, reliability and efficiency. The paper also presents a first indicative implementation of the proposed framework, comprising real sensors and actuators. The preliminary results of this work demonstrate high potential towards self-reconfigurable IoT.

Keywords: Cognitive Management, Composite Virtual Objects, Internet of Things, Stakeholder requirements, User requirements, Virtual Objects.

1 Introduction

The "7 trillion devices for 7 billion people" paradigm as described in [1] yields that the handling of the amount of objects that will be part of the Internet of Things (IoT)

A. Galis and A. Gavras (Eds.): FIA 2013, LNCS 7858, pp. 187–199, 2013.

requires suitable architecture and technological foundations. Internet-connected sensors, actuators and other types of smart devices and objects need a suitable communication infrastructure. At the same time, the lack in terms of management functionality overcome the technological heterogeneity and complexity of the pervasive networks, calls for the definition of mechanisms for enhanced situational awareness. Such mechanisms should provide high reliability through the ability to use heterogeneous objects in a complementary manner for reliable service provision. Moreover energy-efficiency should be enabled through the selection of the most efficient and suitable objects from the set of heterogeneous ones. The sheer numbers of objects and devices that have to be handled and the variety of networking and communication technologies, as well as administrative boundaries that have to be supported require a different management approach. The idea is to enable seamless and interoperable connectivity amongst heterogeneous number of devices and systems, hide their complexity to the users/stakeholders while providing sophisticated services [2].

This work presents a Cognitive Management framework targeted to overcoming this technological heterogeneity and complexity. This framework comprises capabilities to dynamically select its behaviour (managed system's configuration), through self-management functionality, taking into account information and knowledge (obtained through machine learning) on the context of operation (e.g., internal status and status of environment), as well as policies (designating objectives, constraints, rules, etc.). The framework comprises three main levels of enablers, namely the *Virtual Object (VO)*, *Composite Virtual Object (CVO)* and *User/Stakeholder and Service* levels, which are reusable for the realization of diverse applications such as ambient assisted living, smart office (easy meeting), smart transportation, supply chain management [3]. In each layer there are scalable fabrics, which offer mechanisms for the registration, look-up and discovery of entities and the composition of services. Cognitive entities at all levels provide the means for self-management (configuration, healing, optimization, protection) and learning. In this respect, they are capable of perceiving and reasoning on their context/situation (e.g., based on event filtering, pattern recognition, machine learning), and of conducting associated knowledge-based decision-making (through associated optimization algorithms and machine learning).

Virtual objects (VOs) are primarily targeted to the abstraction of technological heterogeneity. VOs are virtual representations of real world objects. (e.g., sensors, actuators, devices, etc.). A CVO is a cognitive mash-up of semantically interoperable VOs that renders services in accordance with the user/stakeholder perspectives and the application requirements. User/stakeholder related objects convey the respective requirements. Such entities are capable of detecting users/group of users' intentions and behaviour, inferring, and eventually acting on behalf of the users. In this respect, there is seamless support to users, which is in full alignment with their requirements (the learning capabilities of the cognitive entities of this layer are applied for acquiring knowledge on user/stakeholder preferences, etc.). Furthermore, this framework comprises three main operations, the *Dynamic Creation of a CVO*, the *Knowledge-based Instantiation of a CVO* and the *Self-healing of a CVO*. The first operation corresponds to the creation of a CVO from scratch, in order to provide the requested service to the users. The second operation enables the reuse of an already existing CVO.

The self-healing operation is responsible for finding the optimal alternative object, when a Real World Object (RWO) is unreachable and through its VO to sustain the CVO's functionality.

The rest of the paper is structured as follows. Section 2 provides an overview of related work regarding the concepts of VOS, CVOs and management frameworks for IoT. Section 3 provides a description of the Cognitive Management framework for IoT, elaborates on the definition of VOs and the mechanisms of the VO level, the CVO management mechanisms and discusses means provided by the User/Stakeholder and Service level. Section 4 focuses on a first implementation of the proposed framework presenting some of the operations that it enables and presents an indicative application example in an ambient assisted living scenario. Finally, a summary of the key points addressed in this work is provided in section 5.

2   Related Work and Paper Contribution

The concept of virtual representations of devices/objects in the scope of the IoT is a key issue in most of the Future Internet, IoT projects and research initiatives. Authors in [3] introduce the concept of the Versatile Digital Item (VDI), which is a package of information about services, people and physical objects, independently of the structure or geographical location of the context. Work in [5] aims at creating an open, business driven architecture that addresses the scalability problems for a large number of globally distributed wireless sensor and actuator networks [6]. Additionally, a platform, which among others aims to transform every device into a web service with semantic resolution, is described in [7]. The platform features a Service Oriented Architecture based on open protocols and middleware, with the aim of transforming every subsystem or device into a web service with semantic resolution.

Virtual representations of Real World Objects (RWOs) are also addressed in [8] with the target to make physical world "information" available for smart services - connecting the physical world with the information world. Smart-M3 [9], a core component of Open Innovation Platform, aims at providing the baseline for a solution to cross-domain and cross-platform interoperability platform and information exchange. Smart-M3 makes it possible to mash up and integrate information among all applications and domains ranging from different embedded domains to the Web.

The concept of the "ucode", an identification number assigned to tangible "physical objects" and "places" is one of the work topics of the Japanese Ubiquitous ID Center [10]. This concept of "ucodes" can also be applied for content and information which do not exist in the real world and for more abstract concepts. One of the most recent works relevant to virtual representations of devices/objects is the concept of the "Web of Things" discussed in [11], where the aim is to integrate RWOs, data and functionality into the Web, instead of exposing these through vertical system designs. More specifically it is suggested that the exploitation of Web technologies is a suitable solution for building applications on top of services offered by smart things.

Regarding research on VOs and CVOs semantics, various activities also address the issue as a means for interoperability. An example work is [12] which aims to investigate unified concepts, methods, and software infrastructures that facilitate the efficient development of applications that span and integrate the Internet and the embedded world.

The framework presented in this work targets a variety of application domains and advanced business processes, while being agnostic of the application domain in which it will be applied, enabling cross-domain re-use of technology and exchange of information. The VO concept is introduced as a dynamic virtual representation of real world/digital objects. Furthermore, the concept of the CVO is introduced, as a collection of information and services from partial digital images of the world and their VOs. The CVO concept leads to intelligent services, fulfilling requirements (also from hidden stakeholders), while details and complexity are hidden from end users. The proposed framework comprises cognitive mechanisms to enable the dynamic creation, invocation, deployment, self-configuration, self-management of VOs, CVOs and services.

3   Cognitive Management Framework for IoT

The Cognitive Management framework for IoT consists of the VO layer, the CVO layer and the User/Stakeholders and Service layers, as already introduced. Figure 1 depicts the aforementioned layers of the proposed Cognitive Management framework. This framework, enables the handling of diverse objects and the functions and services these objects provide. Thus, it will enable the realization of a wider IoT ecosystem which can be exploited by many different types of users and stakeholders (across different application and usage domains). While RWOs may be owned (controlled) by a particular stakeholder, VOs (i.e. the abstractions of real world or digital objects) can be owned (controlled) by particular service providers. In turn, CVOs may be owned (controlled) by yet another provider who adds value by combining different VOs and providing these combinations to users. This hierarchical structure leads to a rather complex eco-system, that opens new opportunities for various stakeholders.

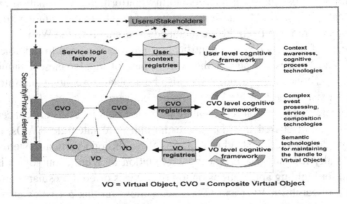

Fig. 1. Layers of the Cognitive Management framework [3]

Furthermore, the Cognitive Management framework will ensure that the complexity of this eco-system will be well hidden from the different players and stakeholders.

3.1 Virtual Objects Level

The world of IoT is characterised by two main features: (i) considerable number of objects that fall within the scope of any IoT application and (ii) inherently unreliable nature of such objects. The purpose of VOs is to efficiently tackle such issues and hide the complexity of the IoT infrastructure. VOs are virtual representations of RWOs and/or digital objects that can enhance IoT, whereby real objects become virtually "always-on". A VO can be dynamically created and destructed, may consist of information, services and is a dynamic object since it has to represent dynamically changing RWOs. Cognitive mechanisms at the VO level enable self-management and self-configuration of RWOs. Moreover, the introduction of cognitive mechanisms will lead to knowledge on how RWOs react to specific situations. Thus, the operation and control of these objects will become more efficient.

The VO level comprises mechanisms that provide awareness about the physical objects presence and relevance. A complete knowledge about physical objects will be necessary to maintain the association between the VOs and the real objects they represent. This knowledge is used to have a constant handle (the VO abstraction) on the best suited physical objects to keep association with, regardless of their mobility or failure of some of the links to them etc. In other words, the VO level comprises mechanisms for monitoring the status/capabilities of physical objects and controlling the various links with physical objects to make sure that the VOs are resilient, even when the associated physical objects might be temporarily unavailable. Another important aspect of this level is optimization from the point of view of resources. In this direction, energy plays an important role in the future IoT applications. Physical objects have varied energy supplies – some of them are battery operated and some are mains/grid powered. It makes sense that VOs representing IoT devices that have high energy supply could take over the tasks rather than VOs that have less supply. In fact, while forming a CVO, VOs need to be selected carefully to get better overall resource (mainly energy but other resources are also considered) profiling. However, while optimizing the resources, dependability of VOs and thus CVOs should also be taken care of. For example, more VOs (in turn more number of hops) could reduce the reliability of a CVO. This is critical for some applications such as health, which require higher reliability.

3.2 Composite Virtual Objects Level

A CVO is a cognitive mash-up of semantically interoperable VOs that renders services in accordance with the user/ stakeholder perspectives and the application/service requirements. Cognitive mechanisms are exploited to enable reuse of existing VOs and CVOs by various applications, potentially also outside the context for which they were originally developed. In this sense, the CVO level encompasses functionalities that allow finding the optimal possible way to deliver the application/service, given:

(i) the requirements coming from the user level; (ii) the capabilities offered by VOs and (iii) existing CVOs' functionality. A CVO is in charge of rendering the requested service, in a manner that is most appropriate with respect to the profile and situation of the user. It is one of the CVO responsibilities to guarantee the availability, performance and dependability of the application, and therefore, of the constituent services. In this respect, the CVO will be in charge of selecting the best VOs (and potentially other CVOs), orchestrating their operation, handling faults, and eventually, releasing the VOs. The selection will be based on the appropriateness of the VO/CVO, e.g., in terms of relevance to the application, situation and profile information and knowledge, and on their status, e.g., in terms of computing, storage, transmission and energy resources. Each CVO will also possess its own (local) cognition capabilities. These derive from learning about the VO existence, behaviour and capabilities as well as monitoring and learning situation aspects that are relevant to the CVO operation. This will be used for optimizing the CVO functionality and the management of the comprised VOs during the CVO life-cycle.

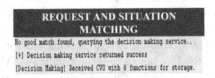

Fig. 2. Request and Situation Matching mechanism

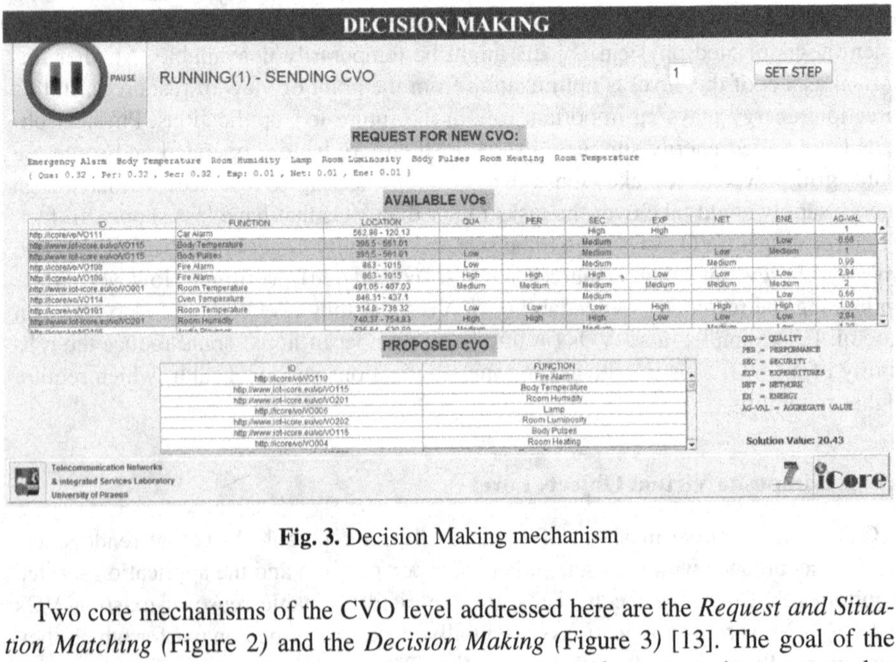

Fig. 3. Decision Making mechanism

Two core mechanisms of the CVO level addressed here are the *Request and Situation Matching* (Figure 2) and the *Decision Making* (Figure 3) [13]. The goal of the *Request and Situation Matching* mechanism is to identify past service requests that match closely enough to the present ones and the situations under which they were issued, so that the task of VO composition from scratch can be avoided under certain circumstances. In order to compare between past and present situations and requests, parameters that describe them have been identified. Request parameters consist of the set of functions and policies requested. Situation parameters consist of the time of day the request occurred, the area of interest, and the available VOs at that time. In order to enhance the filtering process, the requested functions can be matched with approximate ones, e.g. a video capture function can satisfy a requirement for an image capture function. More details on the matching process can be found in [13]. The result of this mechanism is performance gain (mainly in terms of time), as the process of creating a CVO from scratch is more complex. Moreover, reusability of resources is introduced in the system. The *Decision Making* mechanism is triggered by the Request and Situation Matching mechanism. Its objective is to find the optimal composition of VOs that fulfils the requested functions and policies. It receives as input a set of available VOs, a set of functions for each VO, a set of features for these VOs and finally the requested policies. The result of the Decision Making process is the creation and activation of a new CVO. The description of the newly instantiated CVO is recorded in the CVO registry in order to be available for future requests.

3.3   User/Stakeholder and Service Level

From the users/applications perspective, three concepts, i.e. IoT, ubiquitous computing, and ambient intelligence aim at delivering smart services to users [14]. A part of the smartness relies on situation awareness, e.g., service provision according to the needs that exist at the place, time and overall situation. Also, at a societal level, smartness also requires that the needs of diverse users and stakeholders are taken into account. Stakeholders can be the owners of the objects and of the communication means. Different stakeholders that are part of the current Internet environment and will be part of the Future Internet, have interests that may be adverse to each other and their very own criteria on how objects could be used and should be accessed. So, a key challenge that needs to be tackled includes the handling of the diversity of information while respecting the business integrity, the needs and rights of users and of the various stakeholders. At current, the interactions between users/stakeholders and RWOs or "things", are mainly manual. Using these RWOs requires normally manual intervention of the user. The user will need information about how to use a "thing", and how things can be combined for use. This level provides the actual user/service level mechanisms that reside on top of the (C)VOs, and provide the means to leverage the digital representations of RWOs to make IoT applications more cognitive and intention-aware. The User/Stakeholder and Service level comprises mechanisms for the identification of requirements stemming from different types of users, the dependencies they cause, by themselves and across large groups of users, as well as across space and time. Users' and device situation changes, individually or collectively across the user population, time and space, often exhibit certain patterns, and user behaviour and part of the users' intentions could potentially be derived from this.

Moreover, this level comprises mechanisms for the appropriate (automated) analysis of application/service requirements for generating the appropriate service logic and service logic-enabling descriptions for instantiating applications and application-enabling functions in the CVO level.

4   Framework Implementation

4.1   Operation

A prototype of the proposed Cognitive Management framework has been implemented. The current corresponding implementation comprises, apart from software components for the various functional components presented in the previous, a number of actual sensors and actuators. This sub-section provides a high-level view of the implemented framework and presents three main operations this enables, namely dynamic CVO creation, knowledge-based CVO instantiation and self-healing of a CVO.

Dynamic Creation of a CVO. A user requests a service and declares the importance of service/function features, denoted as policies, which should be respected by the system. This request is captured through a User Interface at the Service level and is elaborated, in order to extract the requested functions and defined policies. This information is enriched with the situation parameters (area of interest, time of request) and is forwarded to the Request and Situation Matching mechanism. Moreover, learning mechanisms provide information regarding the user preferences. The Request and Situation Matching mechanism searches for an already existing CVO that can fulfill the request, in the CVO registry (Figure 4). If this reuse of a CVO is not possible, then it forwards the relevant information to the Decision Making, in order to create an optimal composition of VOs, according to requested functions and policies. For this purpose, information on available VO features and provided functions (VO descriptions) are retrieved from the VO registry. Once a CVO is created, the request, associated situation and CVO composition are recorded in the CVO registry, in order to ensure that if a similar contextual situation occurs again, the solution may be retrieved directly. Finally, the created CVO provides the requested service to the user (Figure 5).

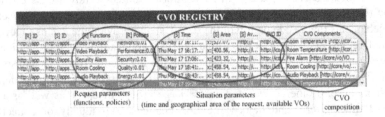

Fig. 4. CVO Registry

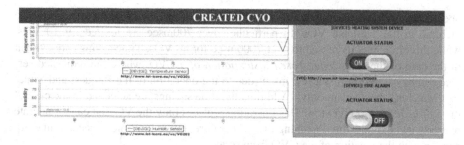

Fig. 5. Created CVO

Knowledge-based Instantiation of a CVO. This process enables the reuse of an already existing CVO. The steps of the previous operation are repeated until the request is received by the Request and Situation Matching component. At this point the service request and situation information can be compared with records in the CVO registry for an adequate match. Past records corresponding to CVO components (VOs) with functions that are unavailable in the current situation (either exact or approximate ones) are filtered out, as they definitely cannot fulfil the service goals. The remaining records are ranked based on a satisfaction-rate similarity metric and the highest ranked one is tested against the similarity threshold. The satisfaction-rate depends on the amount of total requested functions being available as well as their correlations and it is calculated as a score (i.e. sum) of these correlations between the set of the requested and the required CVO functions. Apart from the functions, for the calculation of the overall similarity metric also the rest of the situation and request parameters are taken into account. If the overall similarity metric for an existing CVO equals or exceeds a specific threshold, then this existing CVO can be considered as suitable for a newly issued request. In this way, the CVO level components can apply known solutions as a response to a service request, thus, reducing the time needed for handling of requests from the Service level.

Self-healing of a CVO. The self-healing process enables the detection of a problem in the operation of a used RWO and corresponding VO and dynamic reconfiguration of the corresponding CVO to overcome the problem. This process is triggered when a VO failure is identified due to an RWO becoming unreachable (e.g. due to loss of connectivity of the VO with RWO, RWO hardware failures, etc). A Reconfiguration request is issued from the Request and Situation Matching to the Decision Making component. The Decision Making component then selects the most appropriate VO (and consequently RWO) for replacing the problematic VO. Information on the reconfiguration of the CVO is stored in the CVO registry.

In order to obtain results on the efficiency and scalability of this framework a number of experiments was conducted for different number of available VOs in the area of interest. Figure 6 presents the time required for the Decision Making mechanism to find the optimal composition of VOs, as the number of available VOs increases. As can be observed, while this time increases as the number of VOs increases it remains lower than one second. The ILOG CPLEX OPTIMIZER (CPLEX algorithm) was utilized for the evaluation of this mechanism. Figure 7 depicts the execution times for all operations. As it is expected, the *Dynamic Creation of a CVO* is mostly affected by the increase in the available VOs. In particular, over 700msec are needed for 10 VOs, while this amount is increased to over 7000msec for 50 VOs. Time savings are evident in the case of the *Knowledge-based Instantiation of a CVO*, where the requested service can be offered in just a few msec (due to the operation of the Request and Situation Matching mechanism only). Additionally, time savings are achieved in the case of the *Self-healing of a CVO* too. This operation replaces only the VO that cannot operate properly and exploits the remaining ones. Therefore, minimum time is needed, in comparison with the creation of the CVO from scratch.

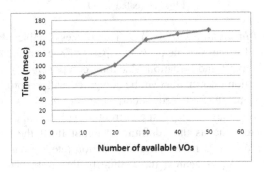

Fig. 6. Decision Making mechanism execution time

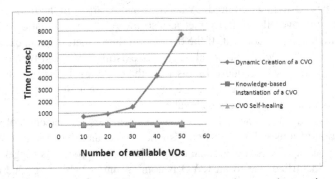

Fig. 7. Execution time of Cognitive management framework operations

4.2   Ambient Assisted Living Example

This sub-section presents an indicative example of how the three operations of the proposed framework can be applied in an Ambient Assisted living scenario. The scenario comprises two different (business) domains; (a) a smart home, where an elderly woman (Sarah) who has opted for an assisted living service lives in, and (b) a medical center, where doctors monitor Sarah's environmental conditions and health status remotely, using the smart objects that exist in smart home. A set of RWOs have been installed in the smart home, comprising of sensors (temperature sensor, humidity sensors, luminosity sensor) that are connected to a Waspmote platform [15] and actuators (namely a fan, a Light Emitting Diode (LED), and a lamp) that are connected to an Arduino platform [16].

First, a doctor through an appropriate user interface (Figure 8) provides a set of application/service requirements, functions and policies (e.g. energy efficiency). At the service level, the set of request and situation parameters are extracted and forwarded to the Request and Situation Matching mechanism, which, in turn, searches in the CVO registry for a previously created CVO that could fulfil the requested application/service. Initially, an appropriate CVO is not found, and the provided parameters are sent to the Decision Making, which will select the most appropriate VOs to satisfy the requirements and policies in the best possible way, and will trigger the creation of a new CVO. The newly created CVO is registered in the CVO registry together with the situation parameters under which it was requested for future reference by the Request and Situation Matching. The doctor, or member of the medical staff, can use the dynamically created CVO to monitor the medical status of Sarah. Feedback regarding the operation of the CVO can be provided and be stored in the CVO registry for future use. Sometime later, another doctor issues a similar request for monitoring Sarah. This request is elaborated at the service level and the derived request and situation parameters are forwarded to the Request and Situation Matching. This time, an already composed CVO that can fulfil the application/service requirements exists in the CVO registry; therefore the Request and Situation Matching proceeds with its immediate instantiation, without the need of triggering the Decision Making mechanism. During the execution of the CVO, one of the used luminosity sensors fails. This is detected by the implemented CVO and the Decision Making mechanism is triggered so as to find alternative luminosity sensor devices that could be exploited (through their corresponding VOs) in order to replace it in the overall CVO, thus ensuring continuity of the service delivery. The CVO is appropriately re-configured.

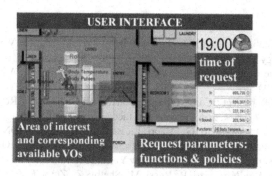

Fig. 8. Graphical User Interface

5   Conclusion

This work described a cognitive management approach to address the huge amount of data, devices and services which the Internet of Things will be comprised of.

The proposed Cognitive Management framework aims to conceal the technological heterogeneity, comprise the perspective of users/stakeholders, and facilitate situational awareness, higher reliability and energy efficiency. The framework comprises three levels of reusable cognitive components, namely the VO level, the CVO level and the User/Stakeholder and Service level. Thus the proposed Cognitive Management framework acts as an open networked architecture that can remove the sector specific boundaries of the early realisations of IoT, and enable a new range of Internet enabled services, which can be integrated with enterprise business processes. Through these features, and by doing work above the levels of the real-world and digital objects, the proposed framework constitutes a unique approach for the efficient integration of the IoT into the service layer of the Future Internet. The paper also presents a first indicative implementation of the proposed framework, comprising real sensors and actuators. The preliminary results of this work demonstrate high potential towards self-reconfigurable IoT.

Acknowledgment. This article describes work undertaken in the context of the iCore project, 'Internet Connected Objects for Reconfigurable Ecosystems' (http://www.iot-icore.eu/). iCore is an EU Integrated Project funded within the European 7th Framework Programme, contract number: 287708. The contents of this publication are the sole responsibility of iCore project and can in no way be taken to reflect the views of the European Union.

References

1. Uusitalo, M.: Global Vision for the Future Wireless World from the WWRF. IEEE Vehicular Technology Magazine 1(2), 4–8 (2006)
2. Weiser, M.: The Computer for the Twenty-First Century. Scientific American, pp. 94–10 (September 1991)
3. FP7-ICT-287708 project iCore (Internet Connected Objects for Reconfigurable Ecosystems), http://www.iot-icore.eu (accessed February 2012)
4. Giusto, D., Iera, A., Morabito, G., Atzori, L., Blefari Melazzi, N.: CONVERGENCE: Extending the Media Concept to Include Representations of Real World Objects. In: The Internet of Things, pp. 129–140. Springer, New York (2010)
5. Castellani, A.P., Bui, N., Casari, P., Rossi, M., Shelby, Z., Zorzi, M.: Architecture and protocols for the Internet of Things: A case study. In: Proc. Pervasive Computing and Communications Workshops (PERCOM Workshops), pp. 678–683 (March 2010)
6. FP7-ICT-215923 project SENSEI (Integrating the Physical with the Digital World of the Network of the Future), http://www.sensei-project.eu (accessed February 2012)

7. Kostelnik, P., Sarnovsky, M., Furdik, K.: The Semantic Middleware for Networked Embedded Systems Applied in the Internet of Things and Services. In: Proc. 2nd Workshop on Software Services (WoSS), Timisoara, Romania (June 2011)

8. ARTEMIS SOFIA project, http://www.sofia-project.eu/ (accessed February 2012)

9. Franchi, A., Di Stefano, L., Tullio, S.C.: Mobile Visual Search using Smart-M3. In: Proc. IEEE Symposium on Computers and Communications (ISCC) (June 2010)

10. Ubiquitous ID Center, http://www.uidcenter.org/ (accessed February 2012)

11. Guinard, D., Trifa, V., Mattern, F., Wilde, E.: From the Internet of Things to the Web of Things: Resource Oriented Architecture and Best Practices. In: Architecting the Internet of Things. Springer (December 2010)

12. De Poorter, E., Moerman, I., Demeester, P.: Enabling direct connectivity between heterogeneous objects in the internet of things through a network service oriented architecture. EURASIP Journal on Wireless Communications and Networking, 61 (2011)

13. Kelaidonis, D., Somov, A., Foteinos, V., Poulios, G., Stavroulaki, V., Vlacheas, P., Demestichas, P., Baranov, A., Rahim Biswas, A., Giaffreda, R.: Virtualization and Cognitive Management of Real World Objects in the Internet of Things. In: Proceedings of The IEEE International Conference on Internet of Things, iThings 2012, Besancon, France (2012)

14. Schonwalder, J., Fouquet, M., Rodosek, G., Hochstatter, I.: Future Internet = content + services + management. IEEE Communications Magazine 47(7), 27–33 (2009)

15. Waspmote, http://www.libelium.com/products/waspmote (accessed February 2013)

16. Arduino, http://www.arduino.cc/ (accessed February 2013)

Building Modular Middlewares
for the Internet of Things with OSGi

Jakub Flotyński, Kamil Krysztofiak, and Daniel Wilusz

Department of Information Technology,
Poznań University of Economics
{flotynski,krysztofiak,wilusz}@kti.ue.poznan.pl

Abstract. The paper addresses an analysis of OSGi in the context of building modular middlewares for the Internet of Things. The Internet of Things (IoT) is an emerging approach to development of intelligent infrastructures combining various devices through the network. OSGi is a framework providing a number of specific mechanisms intended for building modular, fine-grained and loosely-coupled Java applications. Although a number of works have been devoted to OSGi, and several OSGi-based middlewares have been designed for the IoT, they do not thoroughly utilize mechanisms of OSGi. In this paper rich OSGi functions are analysed in terms of development middlewares for the IoT. An example implementation of the system illustrates the presented considerations.

Keywords: Internet of Things, modular, multi-layer, event-based, middleware, OSGi.

1   Introduction

Future Internet is a rapidly evolving phenomena, which significantly influence the business and the society. It incorporates two modern application areas of the networking: the Internet of Things (IoT), and the Service-Oriented Architecture (SOA) [1].

The IoT is a continuously developing concept introduced by MIT Auto-ID Center [2] as an intelligent infrastructure linking objects, information and people via the computer network. The IoT allows for universal coordination of physical resources through remote monitoring and control by humans and machines [3]. Nowadays, the role of the IoT is no more limited only to electronic identification of objects but it is perceived as a way to fill the gap between objects in the real world and their representations in information systems. According to [4] [5], the components of the IoT are participants of business processes seamlessly integrated through independent services.

That is why powerful middleware solutions are required to integrate heterogeneous devices and dynamic services for building complex systems for the IoT. The middleware is a system connecting different components and/or applications [6] in order to build complex layered applications [5]. The objective of the middleware is to hide details of different technologies to avoid dealing with technical, low-level issues [5].

The appropriate middleware solution for the IoT should enable system modularity to permit flexible management of devices and services. To facilitate development of modular, fine-grained and loosely-coupled applications, a few frameworks for Java and

A. Galis and A. Gavras (Eds.): FIA 2013, LNCS 7858, pp. 200–213, 2013.

.NET environments have been designed (e.g., OSGi [7], Jini [8] or MEF [9]). Among these platforms, OSGi (originally Open Services Gateway initiative) is currently the most popular one, supporting a number of specific mechanisms useful for building both desktop and IoT applications.

Although a number of tutorials have been devoted to OSGi, and several middlewares have been designed for the IoT, these works focus mainly on the proposed systems themselves and do not explain how to thoroughly utilize the diversity of OSGi features for building middlewares for the IoT. The main contribution of this paper is an original analysis of OSGi for building applications for the IoT. The considerations are illustrated by an example implementation of a middleware. The system enables integration and management of devices and services in IoT environments with a strong focus on the use of the rich OSGi functionality. Systems built according to the hints given in this paper can be used within secure houses, smart shops, cars, etc. However, it is not possible to describe all mechanisms contained in OSGi very exhaustively. They are explained in detail in the OSGi documentation [7] [16] [17]. In this paper, we explain some of them—the functions especially useful in the context of building systems for the IoT. It has not been our purpose to compare the presented example implementation to other systems proposed in previous works, e.g., in terms of structure or efficiency.

The remainder of the paper is structured as follows. In Section 2, the state of the art in the domain of OSGi-based middlewares is briefly described. Section 3 presents the functionality of the OSGi framework that may be useful during development of IoT systems. Section 4 addresses the requirements for the middleware for the IoT. In Sections 5, 6 and 7, the idea and an example implementation of the system are presented. Finally, Section 8 concludes the paper and indicates possible directions of future works.

2   Middlewares for the Internet of Things

Several middlewares for the IoT have been designed and implemented [10]. In general, these systems often address integration of RFID devices [11] [12] and sensor networks [13], and provide integrated software development environments [14].

In [14] a cooperative web framework integrating Jini into an OSGi-based open home gateway has been presented. The framework connects embedded mobile devices in heterogeneous network and enables discovery and management. Another solution integrating heterogeneous devices has been presented in [13]. The authors utilize the OSGi framework to provide a layer in high level of abstraction for communication with concentrators operating wireless sensors. The Arcada project [12] provides a middleware for management of RFID devices. As a result, a more advanced system dealing with the three characteristics of the IoT (heterogeneity, dynamicity and evolution) has been built upon the previous version [15]. This middleware utilizes OSGi to provide modularity and dynamicity and permits extending the system with hot deployment of components.

3   Selected Mechanisms of OSGi

OSGi [7] [16] [17] is a modular framework for Java applications facilitating software componentization. OSGi supports numerous mechanisms useful for building applications for the IoT, which are described in this section.

3.1 Modularity

OSGi-based Java applications are built from independent and separate modules referred to as bundles. The bundle is a Java project containing packages and classes that may be shared with other bundles as specified in a separated file assigned to the bundle. Bundles have a lifecycle encompassing the following states:

- uninstalled (not included in the application),
- installed (included without satisfied dependencies),
- resolved (stopped but ready to be started),
- active (started),
- transitive states: starting and stopping.

Starting a set of bundles is performed with regard to the dependencies among them but the lifecycles of the particular bundles may be managed independently. This feature is especially useful when some modules must be exchanged without shutting down the entire system (e.g., when new versions of modules are introduced). Once the state of a bundle changes, other bundles may be notified of this fact using the `BundleListener` service handling `BundleEvents`.

3.2 Runtime Configurations

The OSGi `runtime configuration` specifies a set of bundles to be started. Each bundle as well as each `configuration` is assigned an integer specifying a `start level`. Bundles are run in order from the lowest start level to the highest one. While starting the `configuration`, only bundles with `start levels` lower or equal than the `configuration start level` are launched. Such approach facilitates development of applications covering a wide range of functions. Consecutive `configurations` may be super-sets of bundles of their predecessors. `Configurations` with higher start levels can include additional modules implementing extended functionality based on the functionality of bundles contained in `configurations` with lower start levels.

3.3 Configurations of Bundles

Besides configuring the entire application, also individual bundles may be configured. It is performed by the `Configuration Admin Service` that decouples configurations of particular bundles from their source code. Configurations are specified by a set of properties stored, e.g., in files or in a database. Bundles whose configurations are specified by particular properties, implement methods listening for updates of these properties. Such methods properly modify the behaviour of the bundles.

3.4 Console

The OSGi framework has a built-in `console` that can be used to manage bundles and services (e.g., to start and stop them). The `console` is similar to these implemented in widely-used operating systems like Windows and Linux and may be accessed remotely via SSH allowing developers to manage the framework in a flexible way.

3.5 Event-Based Communication

OSGi supports flexible event-based communication among bundles providing one-to-many data exchange in both synchronous (with waiting for handling the event by all interesting modules) and asynchronous modes. OSGi events are broadcasted by the sender and may be filtered by their topics, hence delivered only to proper destination bundles. Using events in OSGi-based applications excludes the necessity of specifying direct dependencies between bundles, thus disabling cycles. The lack of cross-references implies effective implementing of systems working like the Controller Area Network (CAN) bus [18] in which event recipients do not need to be known in advance.

3.6 Local Services

OSGi services are classes implementing Java interfaces. They may be published, discovered and invoked. Services are accessed synchronously and locally (from the same machine). Alike message-passing, invoking services does not require keeping references to bundles containing them. Using the service requires the knowledge of the implemented interface. Customized instances of services are created by the ServiceFactory and cached in the framework. Bundles interested in particular services may be notified of registering, modifying and unregistering them through handling appropriate ServiceEvents in the ServiceListener (likewise Bundle Events handled by the BundleService). To obtain the service reference for a particular interface, the context of a bundle is used as a service repository.

Services are described by metadata specified as a set of properties (e.g., id, description, vendor). The metadata may be changed at any time. Required values of properties may be specified while discovering services using a query language provided by the OSGi framework, e.g., get references only to services from a given vendor, that have been introduced not later than two month ago.

3.7 Web Services

OSGi supports also remote communication between bundles distributed across different platforms. Web services may be implemented using Apache CXF [19] – a reference implementation of the distribution provider component of the OSGi Remote Services Specification [17]. Remote OSGi services can be exported by a Java Virtual Machine and imported by another one. Apache CXF supports both SOAP-based and RESTful web services. Obviously, Apache CXF services may be invoked by any web service clients, enabling flexible and easy integration with other systems.

4   Motivations and Requirements for an OSGi-Based Middleware

OSGi, as a platform designed for building scalable dynamic and modular Java-based systems, may be successfully utilized to develop multi-layer middlewares for the IoT. Although, several works on middlewares for the IoT have been conducted, they do not thoroughly explore the functionality of OSGi in the context of the IoT, instead they mainly focus on the proposed systems – their architectures and functionality. These implementations primarily benefit from OSGi modularity and do not put stress on other rich OSGi features and functions, as well as the way in which the framework can be used for building complex middlewares.

The main contribution of this paper is an analysis how mechanisms of OSGi may be utilized to develop modular, scalable and fine-grained middlewares for the IoT.

The following requirements in terms of modularity, service-oriented architecture and communication between software components and devices have been specified for the proposed middleware to illustrate the robustness of rich OSGi mechanisms described in the previous section.

4.1 Modularity

1. The middleware is fine-grained, based on modules that compose the functionality of devices connected to the environment, e.g., a module responsible for closing a door can first obtain the state of a sensor to check whether the room is abandoned.
2. Complex modules are composed of simpler ones. For instance, close a door and turn on an alarm are the services combined into a complex 'secure the house' service.
3. The modules are loosely-coupled, they can exchange messages in relation one-to-many without keeping direct references, e.g., the service 'secure the house' does not need to know all its sub-modules performing simple actions (like close the door and turn on the alarm) to invoke them.
4. The modules perform actions with regard to the context of the interaction, e.g., the door may be closed only when nobody is inside the room, lights may be switched on only when it is dark outside.
5. Adding, restarting and updating versions of particular modules does not require restarting the entire platform and does not interrupt the work of other modules.
6. Adding new modules to the system that have to cooperate with older modules require neither updating nor restarting the platform, e.g., a new sub-service closing the door of a room should work as a part of the secure the house service regardless of previous modules involved in it.
7. The modules are notified each time when a new module is introduced to the system, e.g., a new thermometer has been added to report the temperature in a room.
8. The system may be started with various configurations of modules. The configurations may be changed dynamically. For instance, first, only modules operating on devices are started; second, interfaces and modules composing the functionality of the devices are started as well.
9. The configuration of particular modules should be decoupled from their source code and managed in a flexible way, e.g., to indicate that a particular number of bulbs should be switched on by a module.

4.2 Service-Oriented Architecture

10. Services are built upon modules that are available for the user through various interfaces, e.g., GUI, web services.

11. The middleware contains a service repository of references to services provided and accessible among the modules. The repository is used for service discovery, e.g., find services responsible for washing dishes.
12. The services are described by a set of properties that may be specified at service discovery, e.g., find services using thermometers that are currently switched on.
13. The middleware may notify the user about some events, e.g., an email is sent always when a temperature in a server room is high.

4.3   Communication with Devices

14. Diverse interfaces of devices incorporated in the middleware should be wrapped with a uniform network interface to enable physical distribution of devices and communication with them in a similar manner, i.e. each device is connected to a proxy hiding its implementation details, e.g., the method of measuring the temperature provided be a thermometer is wrapped with an analogous network service.
15. The interfaces do not limit the functionality of primary device interfaces, at most they change semantics of their invocation, e.g., exchange method invocations with create-read-update-delete (CRUD) services.
16. The devices may be queried by the modules as well as modules may be notified by devices of some events they are interested in. Communication between the modules and the devices is bi-directional, e.g., the thermometer can measure the temperature when invoked by a module, as well as notify interested modules of significant changes on its own.

5   Architecture of the Middleware

Modular Multi-layer Middleware for the Internet of Things (*MOMIT*) has been proposed based on the presented rich OSGi functionality. Functional components of the platform originate from the proposal of S. Bandyopadhyay et al. [10]. In this section, the middleware architecture is presented in detail with regard to the requirements and the OSGi mechanisms depicted in the two previous sections. To provide separation of concerns, the architecture of the system is multi-layer and fine-grained with loosely-coupled components (Fig. 1). It consists of the following layers: the device layer, the business logic layer and the interface layer.

5.1   The Device Layer

It is the bottom layer of the *MOMIT* that incorporates various independent *devices*. In the presented middleware, it is assumed the *devices* communicate with one another through the higher (business logic) layer. In fact, in IoT applications the machine-to-machine (M2M) communication is sometimes a necessary and significant aspect. In such cases the *devices* can communicate directly omitting other system components, but the flexibility of such solution may be limited.

Primarily, the *devices* are accessible through heterogeneous interfaces whose diversity may be a problem while building complex applications that utilize many of the

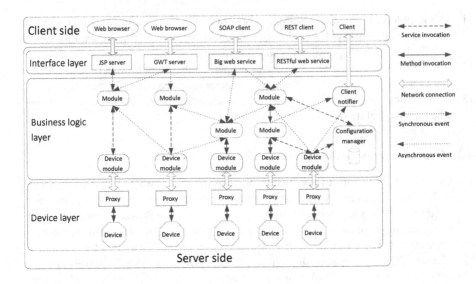

Fig. 1. The *MOMIT* architecture

available devices. To overcome this inconvenience, as well as to enable distribution of the *devices* and making them accessible via the network, each of them is associated with a *proxy*. The *proxies* handle queries from the *business logic layer*, addressed to the *devices*. The *proxies* wrap the *device* interfaces providing a single flexible and uniform interface for all the *devices* within the entire system (Sec. 4, req. 14), e.g., all the *proxies* provide a RESTful interface or all the *proxies* provide a SOAP-based interface. Moreover, the *proxies* do not limit the functionality of the *devices* they wrap. At most, only the semantics of the interfaces can be exchanged (req. 15), e.g., invoking *device* methods is translated to RESTful web service CRUD operations.

For instance, a RESTful web service receives a HTTP PUT request specifying the URI of lights in a room and the value switched on, and translates it into the method invocation lights.switchOn(true). Communication between a *device* and its *proxy* depends on the specificity of the *device* and a particular application in terms of the software and hardware used, and it is not addressed in the *MOMIT* architecture.

Sometimes, it is desirable to inform other system components when specific conditions occur. In such case the communication is initiated by the *proxy* that has detected an event coming from the associated *device*. To satisfy this requirement, the *proxy* includes a web service client that notifies the *business logic layer* of the event (req. 16).

The *Proxies* may be implemented as individual OSGi bundles incorporating network interfaces based on such lightweight platforms as [20] or Apache Tomcat [21].

5.2   The Business Logic Layer

It is the middle layer of the *MOMIT* that utilizes the mechanisms of OSGi very thoroughly. The main purpose of this layer is to combine the functionality of the *devices* into complex services executed with regard to environmental conditions or the context of the interaction between the client and the middleware. Individual elements of the system are described below.

Modules. Primary entities of the *business logic layer* are modules implemented as individual OSGi bundles. Two types: *device* and *service* modules are distinguished. Both types are built according to the service-oriented approach but they are used for different purposes and in different ways.

Device Modules. The device module serves as the *proxy* – it provides a uniform network interface for the *device* (req. 14). Alike *proxies, device modules* do not limit the functionality of the *devices* (req. 15). Every *device module* is associated with exactly one *proxy* and thus with a single *device*.

The *device module* is used to query the *device* via its *proxy*, as well as to allow it to notify other modules in the *business logic layer* of events coming from the associated *device*. In the first case, the *device module* invokes the *proxy* via its web service. In the second case, the *device module* provides a web service (req. 16) invoked every time when data transmission is initialized by the *proxy*. After getting a notification, an OSGi event is broadcasted, and it may be handled by all interested modules in the *business logic layer*. Modules that are not interested in the event, ignore it. Such an approach does not demand that the *Device module* knows all recipients and keeps references to them (req. 3). If a module needs to process an event, its developer should be familiar with this and implement its handling.

All the *device modules* of the *MOMIT* issue OSGi services wrapping the interface of an associated *proxy*. The service is described by a set of properties that depict the *device* and its current state (switched on/off) (req. 12). The services are created by the ServiceFactory and discovered by the context bundle.

When a bundle implementing a *device module* changes its state, a BundleEvent is generated to inform other modules (req. 7). Alike, a ServiceEvents are broadcasted when services have been started or stopped. For instance, from this moment *MOMIT* modules can start/stop invoking the services to which the event is related.

Service Modules. Orchestration of the functions of various *devices* accessible through *device modules* into services (req. 1) is the objective of *service modules*. For instance, a *service module* can use a motion sensor to check whether nobody is inside a room, switch off lights and close the door. Analogously, complex *service modules* may be built upon *device modules*, as well as other *service modules* (req. 2). Implementing complex modules may be performed using OSGi events as well as services created on demand by the ServiceFactory and discovered through the context (req. 11).

In some cases, it may be desirable to notify modules of a new device plugged in/out the system (req. 7). For this purpose, modules interested in new devices should be equipped with the ServiceListener handling events broadcasted when a *Device module* has been started or stopped.

Communication among Modules. Three types of communication among bundles supported in OSGi have been used in the *MOMIT*. In most cases, broadcasting events is used to decouple modules, exempt them from knowing all recipients of the message, exclude cyclic references among bundles, as well as enable one-to-may communication and dynamic adding new modules without updating and restarting the entire system (req. 3, 6). Event-based communication can be utilized in both synchronous and asynchronous modes depending on particular software requirements.

The communication between *service modules* and *device modules* is synchronous and based on OSGi `services`. As described earlier, the `service` is issued by the *device module* and described by `metadata`. Such an approach enables flexible discovery without specified references to other modules. Hence the lack of cycles among bundles.

In some cases, direct method invocations may be used, in particular when the communication between two modules should be effective and synchronous. As this kind of communication requires direct references between the bundles, the destination module should be utilized by few other modules to avoid cycles of dependencies.

Context of the Service Execution. All actions are performed by the *MOMIT* in a particular context determined by variables distributed among the modules, retrieved from devices (e.g., temperature, battery level, etc.), as well as provided by people (e.g., activity results, data obtained from devices not connected to the system). Each variable is a pair *[URI, value]*. Modules connected to particular devices store variables obtained from them on their own, whereas variables coming from other sources may be loaded into modules designed especially for this purpose (e.g., equipped with a database). While storing the context depends on particular modules, accessing it is unified for the entire middleware. Execution of a service that demands a value from the context is preceded by broadcasting a request `event` by the module implementing the service. The `event` contains the *URI* of the required variable. It is handled by modules storing the variable and ignored by others. It is a concern of the software developer to ensure consistency of *URIs* and devices as well as to ensure unambiguous identification of all the variables. After getting a response, the service is performed with regard to the context (req. 4).

Return Channel. In some special cases it is necessary to inform the system administrator about some emergencies, e.g., a tap cannot be turned off or a fridge does not freeze due to a fault. It is permitted by a return channel implemented as a *client notifier* which is a *service module* handling `events` critical for the system reliability, and informing the user if necessary. It is required to implement a web service or to provide an email account on the client side to enable such notifications (req. 13).

5.3   The Interface Layer

It is the top layer of the *MOMIT* providing a multimodal-interface to allow users to utilize system functionality using various clients, e.g., web browser, desktop and web service clients (req. 10). The interfaces encompasses GUI, SOAP-based as well as RESTful web services, but the platform could be also extended with other interfaces such as CORBA or Java RMI. Each interface is implemented within an individual OSGi bundle, thus the interfaces may be added, updated and removed independently without affecting the work of other parts of the system.

All above interfaces enable the client-server interaction. For applications requiring uninterrupted data exchange (e.g., real time streaming), new clients and interfaces could be developed (e.g., based directly on TCP/IP).

6 Management of the Middleware

Management of the middleware includes the three aspects described below.

6.1 Lifecycles of Modules

Management of module lifecycles is performed using the OSGi `console`. It enables adding, restarting and updating modules without restarting the whole middleware (req. 5). Commands related to the lifecycle of bundles may be performed also via Secure Shell enabling remote execution of operating system commands.

6.2 Runtime Configurations

Runtime configurations encompassing different modules (OSGi bundles) may be created depending on requirements for a particular application of the Internet of Thing. Consecutive `configurations` are super-sets of their predecessors and may implement increasingly complex applications (req. 8). For instance, modules with higher start levels (started by higher configurations) implement complex functionality based on modules with lower start levels, which are run in advance. Starting a `configuration` with a given `start level` is performed using the OSGi `console`.

6.3 Configurations of Modules

Configurations of individual modules are managed by the `Configuration Admin Service`. The service is issued by a *configuration manager* service module implemented in the *business logic layer* (req. 9). The *configuration manager* stores configurations in a database and notifies other bundles on updates of the properties. The properties may be changed by using a separate application accessing a database. Such approach enables flexible and centralized management of the *MOMIT* modules.

7 Example Implementation of the Middleware

An example of the *MOMIT* system has been implemented to illustrate the presented idea of the middleware based on the rich OSGi functionality. The system is used at the Departament of Information Technology at the Poznan University of Economics. It is intended mainly for educational purposes and during Internet of Things course. The example implementation is depicted in Figure 2. Below, the system layers are described in detail. The *business logic layer* is comprised of the following modules.

1. `Alarm module` is a *device module* – that composes the functionality of an `alarm switch` through an OSGi `service`. Methods provided by the `alarm switch` are accessible through a RESTful web service issued by an `alarm proxy`. All RESTful web services implemented in the *device layer* of the presented example are based on Restlet [20]. The RESTful web service translates requests from the `alarm module` into the invocations of the `alarm.switchOn(true)` and `alarm.switchOn(false)` methods provided by the `alarm switch`.

2. `Alarm module v2` is an enriched version of the `alarm module` that extends its functionality taking into account whether somebody is inside the room. Two versions of the `alarm module` have been introduced to present the possibility of automatic selection of one of them provided in OSGi.

3. `Door module` is a device module that composes the functionality of a `door locker` through an OSGi `service`. Methods provided by the `door locker` are accessible through the RESTful web service of a `door proxy`. The RESTful web service translates requests from the `door module` into the invocations of the `door.open(true)` and `door.open(false)` methods provided by the `door locker`.

4. `Light module` is a *device module* that composes the functionality of a `light switch` through an OSGi `service`. Methods provided by the `light switch` are accessible through the RESTful web service of a `light proxy`. The RESTful web service translates requests from the `light module` into the invocations of the `lights.switchOn(true)` or `lights.switchOn(false)` methods provided by the `light switch`.

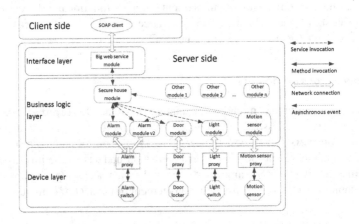

Fig. 2. An example implementation of the *MOMIT*

5. `Motion sensor module` is a *device module* that composes the functionality of a `motion sensor` through an OSGi `service`. Methods provided by the `motion sensor` are accessible through the RESTful web service of a `motion sensor proxy`. The RESTful web service translates requests from the `motion sensor module` into the invocations of the `motionSensor.check()` method provided by the `motion sensor`. The `motion sensor module` can be notified by the `motion`

sensor that somebody is inside the room. To enable such interaction, the `motion proxy` includes a web service client. After receiving such notification, an OSGi `asynchronous event` is broadcasted in the *business logic layer*. The `alarm module v2` handles the event and processes it by suspending the offered OSGi `service`. The second module which handle the event is described below.

6. `Secure the house module` is a *service module* that invokes OSGi `services` provided by the the following device modules: the `alarm module`, the `alarm module v2`, the `light module` and the `door module`. To find an appropriate OSGI `service` issued by an appropriate device, the `secure the house module` specifies service properties while discovering, e.g., to find OSGi `services` responsible for switching the alarm which are currently available in the system. In addition, the `secure the house module` handles the OSGi `asynchronous event` when somebody is inside the room and invokes the OSGi `service` provided by `alarm module v2` instead of the `alarm module`. The `ServiceListener` has been implemented to receive notifications of starting/stopping device modules.

The *interface layer* of the presented example contains a `SOAP web service module` that is integrated into an OSGi bundle using Apache CXF. The `SOAP web service module` provides an interface to allow users to call the service of the `secure the house module` using a web service client. After getting a user request, the `SOAP web service module` broadcasts an OSGi event which is handled only by the `secure the house module`. The `runtime configuration` of the example consists of the following start levels:

1. `Alarm module, alarm module v2, light module`: first, all the device modules and OSGi services issued by them are registered for the further usage.
2. `Secure the house module`: second, the service module and OSGi services issued by it are registered for the further usage for the `SOAP web service module`.
3. `Motion sensor module`: third, this module is registered for the further usage to optionally send an OSGI `event`.
4. `Big service module`: the module enabling an interface to the client is registered.

The proposed example implementation is summarized in Table 1 covering the system requirements satisfied by the considered OSGi mechanisms.

Table 1. Summary of the system requirements satisfied by the OSGi mechanisms

OSGi mechanisms \ System requirements	Modularity	Service-oriented architecture	Communications with devices
Modularity	x	x	x
Runtime configurations	x		
Configurations of bundles	x		
Console	x		
Event-based communication	x	x	x
Local services	x	x	x
Web services		x	x

8 Conclusions and Future Works

In this paper the Modular Multi-layer Middleware for the Internet of Things has been presented. Providing scalable, modular, multi-layer middleware is crucial for development of powerful applications for the IoT. OSGi, that is a framework for building modular desktop Java applications, may be successfully used also in the area of the IoT providing a number of specific mechanisms. Although various middlewares have been proposed, they do not utilize these mechanisms very extensively. The main contribution of this paper is the analysis of the OSGi functionality in terms of building scalable, modular and fine-grained middlewares for the IoT.

Future works include the following aspects. First, the *MOMIT* will be secured through introducing access control both for users and modules of the system. In the first case, the middleware could be extended with a repository of user privileges. In the second case, the event-based communication, in which both senders and receivers are not known in advance, could be secured to protect modules against their malicious counterparts [22], i.e. trusted receivers should be protected against untrusted content sent by a malicious module, content sent by a trusted module should be protected against access of untrusted receivers. Second, the functionality of the devices in the system could be specified by an ontology to enable advanced querying device proxies by the system modules. Furthermore, modules should be notified of updates of some service properties (e.g., a service has been modified to switch off different number of bulbs). Finally, a repository of context properties can be introduced to be queried in order to obtain the value of a particular context property or a reference to this property. In some cases (e.g., frequently read variables), it is eligible to inquire only proper modules to decrease the system load.

References

1. Wilusz, D.: Privacy threats in the Future Internet and the ways of their limitation. In: Kształcenie w zakresie Internetu Rzeczy, Uniw. im. Adama Mickiewicza w Poz, pp. 84–103 (2011); in Polish: Zagrożenia dla prywatności w Internecie Przyszłości i możliwości jej ochrony
2. Ashton, K.: That 'Internet of Things' Thing. RFID Journal (July 22, 2009), http://www.rfidjournal.com/article/view/4986
3. Brock, D.L.: The Elect. Product Code (EPC). A Naming Scheme for Phys. Obj., Auto-ID Center, http://www.autoidlabs.org/uploads/media/MIT-AUTOID-WH-002.pdf (retr. June 8, 2012)
4. Haller, S., Karnouskos, S., Schroth, C.: The Internet of Things in an Enterprise Context. In: Domingue, J., Fensel, D., Traverso, P. (eds.) FIS 2008. LNCS, vol. 5468, pp. 14–28. Springer, Heidelberg (2009)
5. Atzori, L., Iera, A., Morabito, G.: The Internet of Things: A survey. In: Computer Networks, vol. 54, pp. 2787–2805. Elsevier (2010)

6. Eisenhauer, M., Rosengren, P., Antolin, P.: A development platform for integrating wireless devices and sensors into Ambient Intelligence systems. In: Giusto, D., Iera, A., Morabito, G., Atzori, L. (eds.) The Internet of Things. Springer Science+Business, New York (2010)
7. OSGi, http://www.osgi.org/ (retrieved May 26, 2012)
8. Apache River, http://river.apache.org/ (retrieved June 9, 2012)
9. Managed Extensibility Framework, http://archive.msdn.microsoft.com/mef (retr. June 8, 2012)
10. Bandyopadhyay, S., Sengupta, M., Maiti, S., Dutta, S.: A Survey of Middleware for Internet of Things. Communications in Computer and Information Science 162(pt. 2), 288–296 (2011), doi:10.1007/978-3-642-21937-5_27
11. Puliafito, A., Cucinotta, A., Minnolo, A., Zaia, A.: Making the Internet of Things a Reality: The Where X Solution. In: The Internet of Things: 20th Tyrrhenian Workshop on Digital Communications, pp. 99–108. Springer Science+Business Media (2010)
12. Kefalakis, N., Leontiadis, N., Soldatos, J., Donsez, D.: Middleware Building Blocks for Architecting RFID Systems. In: Granelli, F., Skianis, C., Chatzimisios, P., Xiao, Y., Redana, S. (eds.) MOBILIGHT 2009. LNICST, vol. 13, pp. 325–336. Springer, Heidelberg (2009)
13. Vazques, J., Almeida, A., Doamo, I., Laiseca, X., Orduña, P.: Flexeo: An Architecture for Integrating Wireless Sensor Networks into the Internet of Things. In: Corchado, J.M., Tapia, D.I., Jose, J.B. (eds.) 3rd Symposium of Ubiquitous Computing and Ambient Intelligence. ASC, vol. 51, pp. 219–228. Springer, Heidelberg (2009)
14. Chen, Z.-L., Liu, W., Tu, S.-L., Du, W.: A Cooperative Web Framework of Jini into OSGi-based Open Home Gateway. In: Wu, Z., Chen, C., Guo, M., Bu, J. (eds.) ICESS 2004. LNCS, vol. 3605, pp. 570–575. Springer, Heidelberg (2005)
15. Gama, K., Touseau, L., Donsez, D.: Combining heterogeneous service technologies for building an Internet of Things middleware. Computer Communications 35(4), 405–417 (2012)
16. The OSGi Alliance, OSGi Service Platform Core Specification, http://www.osgi.org/Download/File?url=/download/r4v43/osgi.core-4.3.0.pdf/ (retr. May 26, 2012)
17. The OSGi Alliance, OSGi Service Platform Service Compendium, http://www.osgi.org/download/r4v43/osgi.cmpn-4.3.0.pdf (retrieved May 31, 2012)
18. Bosh, R.: CAN Specification Version 2.0, http://www.gaw.ru/data/Interface/CAN_BUS.PDF (retrieved May 26, 2012)
19. Apache CXF, http://cxf.apache.org/ (retrieved May 26, 2012)
20. Restlet, http://www.restlet.org/ (retrieved May 21, 2012)
21. Apache Tomcat, http://tomcat.apache.org/ (retrieved May 21, 2012)
22. Flotyński, J., Picard, W.: Transparent Authorization and Access Control in Event-Based OSGi Environments. In: Information Systems Archictecture and Technology, Service Oriented Networked Systems. Oficyna Wydawnicza Politechniki Wrocławskiej, Wrocław, pp. 197-210 (2011) ISBN 978-83-7493-625-5

Towards an Architecture for Future Internet Applications

Jacek Chmielewski

Poznan University of Economics, Poznan, Poland
chmielewski@kti.ue.poznan.pl

Abstract. A growing number of connected devices and solutions, related to the concept of Internet of Things, makes our environment increasingly smart and capable. However, existing application development processes and tools, designed for single device applications, do not allow to fully address this opportunity and to efficiently create applications that employ multiple devices and use the context information provided by ubiquitous sensors. To address this situation we propose a concept of Device Independent Architecture, which can be used to separate applications from devices and to provide a uniform platform for building smart multi-device applications. The main ideas of the Device Independent Architecture is to move processing from end-devices to a server side (backend) and to introduce a middleware layer that separates applications from devices and supports development of multi-device applications.

Keywords: Internet Architecture, Multi-Device Applications, Device-Independent Applications, Cross-Platform Applications, UI Adaptation, Internet of Things, Internet of Services, Internet Middleware.

1 Introduction

According to current predictions [1], the number of connected devices will reach 30-50 billion in 2020. This is 4 to 6 times more than the estimated world population at that time. On average, every person in the world will be surrounded by 4 to 6 different devices that will be continuously connected to the Internet. This will be not only smartphones and tablets, but also a smart TV [2], a smart fridge and cooker [3], a home automation system with a number of various sensors and actuators, etc. Technology savvy users use more than just one device even today. Usually the set of used devices include a stationary PC or a laptop (at least one at work and sometimes additional at home), a smartphone, a tablet shared with relatives, a game console, a smart TV, etc. Users are more and more surrounded by smart and connected devices. Today these devices are mostly used independently forcing a user to switch contexts and maintain a number of devices with overlapping functionality. In most cases, it is due to applications designed for a single device (platform), which cannot be reused on a different device (platform). Thus, a user is forced to buy and use a similar application on each of his devices (platforms). To fully exploit the smart environment that grows around us, we need new kind of applications: smart multi-device applications.

A. Galis and A. Gavras (Eds.): FIA 2013, LNCS 7858, pp. 214–219, 2013.

A smart multi-device application is an application that uses context information to intelligently adapt its behavior and that can be used on a subset of devices available for a user at a particular moment. The context information describes the situation in which the application is used, so the application may behave accordingly and appear to the user as a 'smart' entity. Usually, the 'multi-device' term means that an application can be used on different devices: on a smartphone, on a tablet, or even on a TV, which is the case of many web applications. However, such application is better described by a term 'cross-platform' application. In our approach, a 'multi-device' application is an application which is capable of employing multiple devices at the same time – for example, a smartphone used as a remote controller for a TV set and a PVR, and as an EPG browser.

This trend poses new challenges to the traditional application development process. Native application development forces developers to target each device specifically, making the development process difficult (different skillset required for each new platform; variable device capabilities) and time consuming (multiple versions of an application targeting different device classes). Therefore, applications shift from end device (native) to the backend (servers, cloud, etc.) using the client-server architecture and sharing resources to support multi-device usage scenarios.

However, it is not the end of application architecture evolution – the future brings new challenges. With new developments in the area of Internet of Things a massive number of new smart and connected devices will appear in the digital ecosystem surrounding a user: a car, a home automation system, a cooker and fridge, a weather station, public displays, various sensors and actuators, etc. It will make application development even more complicated and will open a way for truly multi-device use cases – where a user not only switches from one device to another, but uses multiple devices at the same time for one purpose (the same application). Existing application architectures are not capable of fully supporting the new breed of applications – smart multi-device applications.

2   Device Independent Architecture

To be able to provide applications capable of addressing the large, diverse and fast growing set of end-devices, it is required to build these applications in a way that will make them independent of a particular device and will enable multi-device usage scenarios. This is the goal of the Device Independent Architecture (DIA).

2.1   Device Independence

The idea behind our Device Independent Architecture originates from the Service-Oriented Architecture, where systems are decomposed into atomic services and processes use necessary services without knowing much about systems that provide these services. Similar approach can be used to decompose devices. Each device, be it a laptop, a smartphone, or a smart temperature sensor, provides: resources, services and user interaction channels.

Resources are: processing power (CPU), memory, and storage. Services are providers of context information, such as location, temperature, light intensity and data from other sensors. Input and output user interaction channels are means of communication with a user and include: screen, speakers, vibration, keyboard, mouse or other pointing method, touchscreen, microphone, camera, etc.

One of the main problems of device-independent application development is the diversity of ways in which these resources, services and interaction channels can be utilized by an application. Each operating system or a software platform has its own programing languages and APIs. Even devices of the same class (e.g. Android smartphones and tablets) provide different sets and characteristics of available services and user interaction channels.

Our approach to device independence is to separate the application from a device by using only backend resources (OS and software platform independence), building abstract user interfaces (user interaction channel independence), and providing a middleware layer that wraps all services with a standardized API and adapts application user interfaces to capabilities of available user interaction channels.

Resources can be provided as cloud-based services in the form of a Platform as a Service (PaaS). To maintain device-independence of applications it is not necessary to specify a particular PaaS infrastructure. Each PaaS implementation has its own requirements and API but the selection of a particular PaaS will influence only the choice of a programming language and development patterns. It will not hinder the device-independence of an application developed on the selected platform.

Services cannot exist without a device, but can be exposed using REST GET method (for one time access) or a protocol based on a subscriber/provider pattern (for continuous access). Such a generic protocol ensures proper application—device separation, while maintaining the ability to use data provided by device sensors. Types of data provided by information sources may be described using syntactic and semantic service description languages such as WSDL or USDL [4].

User interaction channels can be divided into output interaction channels provided to applications as data-sinks accepting specific data formats (e.g. visual data for screen, audio data for speakers, etc.) and input interaction channels exposed as services accessible according to a protocol based on the Observer pattern. Again, types of interaction events provided by these services can be described using service description languages.

Such a generic approach to application—device communication enables an application to employ any set of devices that provide services and user interaction channels required by the application. The DIA itself does not impose any requirements on capabilities of devices, suitability of a device depends solely on application requirements. With proper semantic service descriptions a device could expose any services and user interaction channels, including those that will be introduced in the future.

2.2   Multi-device Support

The fact that applications operate on sets of services and user interaction channels, instead of monolithic devices, enables implementation of multi-device scenarios:

- complementary services scenario – application using various services provided by different devices;
- redundant services scenario – application using the same services provided by different devices to get the best possible results (e.g. usually a geolocation service on a smartphone is better than the one on a laptop);
- multi-device UI scenario – application distributing fragments of its UI to separate devices choosing the best composition of available interaction channels.

In our approach, the middleware maintains a register of available services and user interaction channels provided by devices. All actions related to device discovery, authorization and inter-device communication are hidden from an application. What the application sees is a set of services and user interaction channels, not separate devices. When a device becomes available or unavailable the middleware modifies the register accordingly and notifies applications. Therefore, the application may adapt to the new situation.

Also, the middleware layer acts as a user interface proxy, which enables the multi-device application to maintain a single abstract UI description and target multiple end-devices. With additional UI cues embedded in an abstract UI description, it is possible to decide on UI fragmentation and distribute different parts of the application user interface to different devices. Each of such UI fragments is then adapted by the middleware to match capabilities of a target end-device and a final UI is generated and sent to the device. In the reverse direction, user interactions performed at all used end-devices are mapped back by the middleware to appropriate controller actions of the multi-device application. This way, the application developer does not have to care about knowing how many and what devices could be used by a user.

The middleware may also support additional functions such as security or billing. With the Device Independent Architecture, the middleware may act as a device authorization center and device usage policy enforcement point. The security and usage information may influence the set of services and user interaction channels provided to different applications. The DIA architecture may also support or limit the usage of public, shared, and private devices. For example, a usage of public devices may require additional authorization or micropayment and a usage of a shared device may require confirmation by the owner or the current user of the device.

2.3   The Architecture

With DIA, any application may use any subset of the available devices in a way that is transparent for the application development process. The communication between applications and the middleware, and between devices and the middleware, is based on standard protocols, making it easy to support new devices and new applications.

Devices available to a user, that form a personal zone [5] of the user, register with the DIA middleware providing information about the offered services, the available user interaction channels, and – optionally – other information such as usage policy, billing settings, etc. When an application is started, the middleware provides it with information about available services and user interaction channels. The middleware also notifies the application about any changes in the set of services and user interaction channels. Consequently, the application is always aware of the situation and may act accordingly. The application may request a selected service with a standardized API call and respond with an abstract description of a user interface that should be presented to the user. The middleware will forward the service call to a device that provides the service and will use the abstract UI description and embedded UI cues to properly fragment, adapt and distribute the UI to available end-devices. User interactions registered on devices presenting the UI are caught by the middleware, mapped back to appropriate application controller actions, and dispatched to the application closing the user interaction loop.

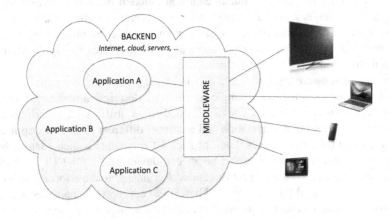

Fig. 1. Device Independent Architecture concept

An early implementation of ideas introduced by the Device Independent Architecture is the ASIS framework [6], which was developed for the IT-SOA project [7] and was also used in e-learning applications [8-9]. Another implementation of DIA concepts related to UI adaptation is being prepared for the UbiqUI project [10].

3   Future Directions

Despite ongoing efforts on defining device-independent or platform-independent cloud services there is no complete framework that could support implementation of smart multi-device applications. The main aim of our current research on the DIA is implementation of a prototype of such a framework. It will be used as a proof-of-concept and will allow analyzing various application scenarios and multi-device issues – including, but not limited, to the following:

- Device discovery and authentication
- Device usage policy
- Services and user interaction channels registration
- Context information modeling and access protocols
- UI abstraction, adaptation and distribution (not only for graphical UI)

- Application catalogs, markets and private application repositories
- User preferences gathering and provisioning methods
- Device usage billing and micropayments

Implementation of such a framework will help to move the focus of IoT research from communication and interoperability issues to applications issues, bringing it closer to final users of IoT solutions. Each of the topics mentioned above is a challenging task on its own. To succeed in this broad field, a coordinated research effort is required. We believe that the concept presented in this chapter provides a solid basis for future research in the field of smart multi-device applications and will eventually ease the burden of developing truly smart applications that efficiently use capabilities of multiple devices.

References

1. Zappa, M.: Envisioning emerging technology for 2012 and beyond, Envisioning Technology (2012), http://envisioningtech.com/envisioning2012/
2. SAMSUNG Smart LED and Plasma TVs Usher in a New Era of Connectivity and Control, Samsung US News Center, http://goo.gl/3pmlb
3. LG smart appliances for 2012 deliver connectivity, efficiency through Smart ThinQ™ technologies, LG Newsroom (2012), http://goo.gl/1sz68
4. Simon, L., Mallya, A., Bansal, A., Gupta, G., Hite, T.D.: A Universal Service Description Language. In: Proceedings of the IEEE International Conference on Web Services, ICWS 2005, pp. 823–824. IEEE Computer Society (2005)
5. Lyle, J., Monteleone, S., Faily, S., Patti, D., Ricciato, F.: Cross-platform access control for mobile web applications. In: Proceedings of the IEEE International Symposium on Policies for Distributed Systems & Networks, pp. 37–44. IEEE Computer Society (2012)
6. Chmielewski, J., Walczak, K., Wiza, W.: Mobile interfaces for building control surveyors. In: Cellary, W., Estevez, E. (eds.) 13E 2010. IFIP AICT, vol. 341, pp. 29–39. Springer, Heidelberg (2010)
7. Chmielewski, J., Walczak, K., Wiza, W., Wójtowicz, A.: Adaptable User Interfaces for SOA Applications in the Construction Sector. In: Ambroszkiewicz, S., Brzeziński, J., Cellary, W., Grzech, A., Zieliński, K. (eds.) SOA Infrastructure Tools - Concepts and Methods, pp. 439–469. Poznań University of Economics Press, Poznań (2010)
8. Walczak, K., Wiza, W., Rumiński, D., Chmielewski, J., Wójtowicz, A.: Adaptable User Interfaces for Web 2.0 Educational Resources. In: Kiełtyka, L. (ed.) IT Tools in Management and Education - Selected Problems, pp. 104–124. Publishing Office of Częstochowa University of Technology, Częstochowa (2011)
9. Walczak, K., Chmielewski, J., Wiza, W., Rumiński, D., Skibiński, G.: Adaptable Mobile User Interfaces for e-Learning Repositories. In: Sánchez, I.A., Isaías, P. (eds.) IADIS International Conference on Mobile Learning, pp. 52–61. IADIS Press (2011)
10. UbiqUI - Ubiquitous mobile user interfaces for industrial monitoring and control applications (2012-2013), http://www.kti.ue.poznan.pl/en/node/3230

ComVantage: Mobile Enterprise Collaboration Reference Framework and Enablers for Future Internet Information Interoperability

Angelika Salmen[1], Tobias Münch[1], Steffen Buzin[1], Jan Hladik[1],
Werner Altmann[2], Conny Weber[3], Dimitris Karagiannis[4], Robert Buchmann[4],
Jens Ziegler[5], Johannes Pfeffer[5], Markus Graube[5], Manuel Carnerero[6],
Oscar López[6], Mikel Uriarte[6], Patricia Órtiz[7], and Oscar Lázaro[7]

[1] SAP Research, SAP AG, Germany
[2] Kölsch and Altmann Software Management and Consulting GmbH, Germany
[3] ISN - Innovation Service Network GmbH, Austria
[4] University of Wien, Austria
[5] Technische Universitt Dresden, Chair for Process Control Systems Engineering,
Germany
[6] NEXTEL S.A, Spain
[7] Innovalia Association, Spain
{angelika.salmen,tobias.muench,steffen.buzin,jan.hladik}@sap.com,
{werner.altmann}@koelsch-altmann.de, {conny.weber}@innovation.at,
{dk,rbuchmann}@dke.univie.ac.at,
{jens.ziegler,johannes.pfeffer,markus.graube}@tu-dresden.de,
{mcarnerero,olopez,muriarte}@nextel.es, {olazaro,portiz}@innovalia.org

Abstract. Future Internet Networked Enterprise Systems demand enhanced collaboration and mobility support. FI technologies are fundamental for increased service differentiation and cost optimisation in manufacturing environments. However, such ICT-based capabilities are not easy to introduce, in particular to SMEs, due to high costs and complexity. To progress in more effective development of value added services based on Web 2.0 principles within a mobile enterprise collaboration context, the complexity of collaboration in terms of information management needs to be leveraged from the end-users. Linked Data (LD) provides a universal and lightweight approach for the collaboration network. However, the elaboration of collaborative business processes based on LD still needs to be properly formulated for FI systems. The aim of this paper is to present a reference architecture for mobile enterprise collaboration based on LD interoperability. Moreover, security, semantic data lifting, business process modelling interoperability and mobile app orchestration enablers are presented to facilitate trustful and effective inter-organisational collaboration.

Keywords: Mobile enterprise collaboration, Future Internet, Linked Data, Industrial Applications, Multi-domain Access Control, Interoperability.

A. Galis and A. Gavras (Eds.): FIA 2013, LNCS 7858, pp. 220–232, 2013.

1   IT Challenges for Collaboration

The manufacturing industry provides over 30 Million jobs throughout the EU as well as employment in various directly associated industries. The industry has further been globalised for the last years and is still expected to increase their collaboration rate. While by 2011 the percentage was about 40%, business outcomes that will depend on parties outside one enterprises control will reach 60% by 2015 [1]. Thus, new requirements emerge for Future Internet Networked Enterprise Systems to meet the manufacturing and service industry demands.

ICT is a key factor for competitive advantage and growth of manufacturing industries due to its impact on productivity and innovation (cf. [2], [3], and [4]. A primary strategic role of ICT in the manufacturing industry is facilitating the collaboration among various organisations involved in industrial supply chains, enabling the efficient flow of information about procurement, inventory, production, delivery, etc. The strategic role of Future Internet technologies for manufacturing industries and supply chain management is highlighted by the fact that two Phase II Use Cases of the FI-PPP; *i.e. cSpace, FITMAN*, deal with specific enablers that will leverage enhanced collaboration processes. ICT in general and Future Internet technologies in particular facilitate the ability to introduce "mass customisation" capabilities, which allow individual end-customers to design and order a product that is uniquely tailored to their preferences. *Cost optimisation* (consequence of improved information flow) and *differentiation* (a consequence of mass customisation) based on ICT capabilities are responsible for the ability of manufacturers to sustain their competitive advantage in contemporary markets.

However, such ICT-based capabilities are not easy to introduce, in particular to SMEs [5], as they involve a high level of cost and complexity. Until now business process optimisation has been focused on centrally organised systems, as business software integrates own core competencies and relations to external partners and their expertise within a closed infrastructure. Although being secure and providing entire control, existing systems are less flexible or dynamic, because of the significant cost of introducing change to existing intra- and inter-organisational processes. Also co-ordination and communication with the partner network is cost intense. Improving the competitiveness of the European industry and striving for future leadership requires innovative approaches that enable lean and agile inter-organisational collaboration. Linked Data [6] in particular provides a universal and easy accessible interface and thus meets the requirements of a lightweight approach for the collaboration network. The provision and **interlinking of data** in the web, being readable for men as well as machines via Linked Data, has proven successful in the public sector. Yet, the elaboration of collaborative business processes based on Linked Data as an add-on to existing business and engineering software for industrial contexts needs to be properly formulated and validated in the context of Future Internet systems.

The EU project ComVantage [18] is elaborating a **product-centric mobile collaboration space** for inter-organisational users including end-customers based on Web 2.0 technologies. ComVantage addresses major challenges comprising the architecture of Future Internet Networked Enterprise Systems [7] facilitating secure multi-domain information access for the Web of Linked Data, coupling of legacy information systems, and provisioning of intuitive and easy to use mobile applications to meet the requirements of the production manufacturing scenarios. The ComVantage **reference architecture** meets the challenge of handling the complexity of heterogeneous data sources [8], while providing lean integration to legacy systems. It provides models and tools to interlink and exploit information on an inter-organisational level, and supports a unified orchestration of and communication between the various technology enablers. One major enabler is **multi-domain secure information access**, which deals with the challenge of handling the complex partner network and provide controlled access to private linked data sources based on authorised user roles, tasks, and multiple devices. To enable scalability of the complex network as well as allow for ad-hoc collaboration, the decision making takes place in a decentralised manner [9]. In addition to the secure access model, the Linked Data approach needs to reflect the underlying **business process models**. Business Process Models are partner specific in the collaboration network and may be based on various BPM languages which also requires a unified communication between these different languages. Therefore, the inter-organisational orchestration of the collaborative workflows needs to be mapped via Linked Data. Finally, ComVantage enablers also deal with **collaboration via mobile devices** to support flexible and location independent applications at the production shop-floor, as well as lightweight approaches suitable especially for small and micro-companies. Moreover, ComVantage enabler aims to transfer well-proved user experiences of single purpose mobile apps towards complex collaboration networks, where the challenge is to orchestrate these mobile apps according to the underlying business workflow and generate easy to use mobile user interfaces.

The chapter is organised as follows. First, ComVantage application areas driving the specification of the technology enablers in the context of the Future Internet are introduced. Next, the reference architecture designed for mobile enterprise collaboration is presented. Then, Section 4 to Section 7, introduce the specific technology enablers proposed by ComVantage in the area of data adaptation, business process modelling, mobile development frameworks and multi-domain linked data access control. Finally, the main conclusions are presented.

2   ComVantage Application Areas in a Nutshell

ComVantage should leverage heterogeneous data interoperability technology enablers for enterprise mobile collaboration. This core idea is illustrated by two exemplary use cases to visualise the ComVantage business value proposition. 1) **Mobile Maintenance** is addressing a temporary, project-based collaboration including SMEs in the automation industry. It faces the challenge to provide a unified interface that handles the technological complexity and vast heterogeneity of data to provide it for the collaboration hub and to exchange information on an inter-organisational level. 2) The second use case is **Customer-oriented Production**. The specific challenge here is to enable the integration of micro-companies and end-customers into the collaboration network. Infrastructure demands on micro-companies to introduce lightweight mobile applications is too large. Furthermore, end-customers are hardly integrated into the production process which hinders creativity and customer satisfaction to a certain extent.

2.1 Mobile Maintenance Scenario

Currently maintenance service companies are spending too much effort and money in finding out which type of error occurred and or which type of spare part and in the end which type of machine expert is needed to repair a special type of machine, that might be world wide installed for different customers. In classical and standard situation maintenance is done in corrective and/or even better in preventive scenarios to avoid too long time slots where the machines are really not available. This situation can be better addressed if information managed by different companies; e.g. machine sensor information, component evaluation tests, maintenance operations performed, etc, could be easily connected and exploited for maintenance purposes. The focus of the ComVantage Mobile Maintenance System is on innovation in the Mobile Maintenance Area, especially in predicting of impending machine defects.

2.2 The Customer-Oriented Production Scenario

A big challenge faced in sectors such as the fashion industry is that design and production processes still are disintegrated with end-customers. No communication channel exists that allows direct interaction with the customer on production level, while at the same time the request for individual products is increasing. As complex and individual products are key for European competitive advantage the gap between companies and their customers is still too large. Potentials such as open innovation or crowdsourcing lie dormant. The objective of this scenario is to refine along the example of Dresscode21, a company offering personalized business shirts, the establishment of the ComVantage prototype for a mobile web shop, i.e. the web shop will focus on mobile devices for customers as well as for the production stakeholders. A further objective of this application scenario is to enhance the competitiveness of SMEs by leveraging a more seamless information exchange among the different suppliers involved within a design and production process. The challenge lies in customers being able to access style recommendation services, shirts designed by the crowd and product information via social media platforms. In parallel, the challenge lies in supporting a highly flexible collaboration space with all interested stakeholders capable of supporting Dresscode21's service, i.e. providing personalized shirts.

3 ComVantage Reference Architecture

As presented in Section 2, to progress in a more effective development of value added services based on Web 2.0 principles within a mobile enterprise collaboration context, demands that the complexity of collaboration in terms of information management is leveraged from the end-users. This vision requires a collaboration network reference architecture to be driven by four main goals:

1. Enterprise data of the collaboration network members remain within existing legacy systems and in the responsibility of the information owner.
2. Enterprise data is leveraged in inter-organizational contexts in a harmonized manner to ease the development and use of collaboration tools.
3. Enterprise data is interlinked among collaboration network members and connected to public data sources to leverage social web added-value.
4. Enterprise and public data are enriched with business process context and embedded into single purpose mobile apps orchestrated to cover complex workflows.

According to the first goal, data is organized in encapsulated domains. Each domain owner enforces his own access control based on local policies. Local access control policies are defined regarding a shared role model that is valid within the whole collaboration network. Furthermore each domain owner specifies which information will be shared with other domains in the collaboration network. Thus, the domain owner keeps full control about his data despite sharing it with external partners. The described features are provided by the Domain Access Server which acts as a single point of access for each domain (see Fig. 1) and offers a HTTP interface for simple GET requests or more complex SPARQL [10] queries to client applications. Usually a domain is represented by an enterprise or a project-based association of enterprises in a collaboration network.

The second goal is addressed by the application of semantic technologies which allow for an abstraction from heterogeneous data source technologies and data models including deviating terminologies. Within each domain a semantic data model of the enterprise environment is created as ontology and is used for the data harmonization within the Data Integration Layer. An adapter for each legacy system will transform syntactic data to RDF [11] and map it to the semantic data model. Client applications are able to access specific information without awareness of concrete data sources or handling of heterogeneous data models. The clients are only aware of the endpoint addresses of each Domain Access Server and the corresponding semantic data model.

The third goal is achieved by utilizing the Linked Data design principles [6]. Linked Data resembles the idea of hyperlinks on the level of machine readable data in order to establish a web of interlinked resources. Foundational aspects to Linked Data are the use of dereferenceable HTTP URIs to identify resources over the web and the use of triple-based notations (RDF) to express semantic statements. The aforementioned semantic data model of each domain is used to derive Linked Data from traditionally syntactic legacy systems within specialized adapters. In order to ease the creation and the retrieval of links across organizational boundaries as well as to public data sources, a mapping between the semantic data models of all connected domains within the collaboration network is provided.

The fourth goal is realized by the use of comprehensive business process models at design time of client applications. ComVantage focuses on mobile applications and implements their main success factors. The most relevant factor is the use of application with very narrow scope and functionality to improve user experience. These single-purpose apps usually cover the processing of one task. In order to support complex workflows within an enterprise, ComVantage offers an advanced app orchestration mechanism to execute individual applications regarding the current workflow step. The dependencies between individual workflow steps, the required resources like view definitions and data invariants are defined in business process models which are used to generate mobile applications with the model-driven development approach. The finally deployed apps contain all the navigation logic and computing tasks of one workflow step as well as the semantic SPARQL queries for requesting information from each domain.

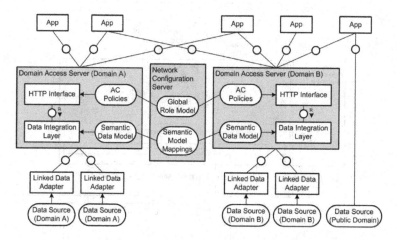

Fig. 1. ComVantage high-level architecture of the collaboration network prototypes

4 Security Model for Linked Data Access Control

Collaboration between different organizations can only be successful if partners can trust each other and be ensured that the information they share remain secure and only authorized users will access the data exposed in the collaboration network. However, within a collaboration environment decision-making is profoundly different from centrally coordinated collaboration. Relying on forming a single domain of trust is no real guarantee that other partners will behave as agreed in the future. Thus, it is essential to define a security approach enabling **policy negotiation, establishment, monitoring and enforcement** for a multi-domain access to linked data sources. In order to guarantee that the information remains private to authorized members only, a dynamic access control model is essential, which supports the most complex combinations of company-based and user-role based rights for access control.

ComVantage security model for decentralised access management to linked data sources is based on the definition of controls for different elements: **(1) Linked Data Units (LDU)**.They are constructed attaching data identifiers and access control policies to data objects. **(2) Linked Data Sets (LDS)**. Aggregate LDU within a domain and specific access control policies. **(3) Linked Data Networks (LDN)**: They are created across domains based on agreements among companies to collaborate in the execution of a particular task-project. Linked Data Units are accessed on the specific enterprise LDN based on the user-role and workflow step being performed.

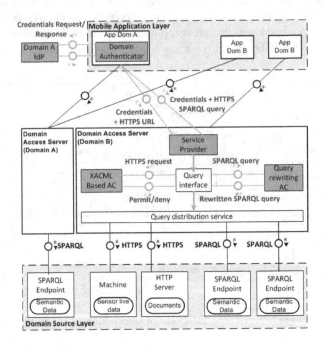

Fig. 2. ComVantage security concept

Access to information takes place at two levels. On one hand, in the domain access server through generic interfaces a request for information is performed. On the other hand, in the data adapters, through specific data interfaces, data is invoked. The security concept should therefore ensure that the queries in the system are compliant with the security policies and that the LDS published by each company and shared through specific LDN, remain accessible only to those partners. ComVantage, as depicted by Fig. 2, proposes a multi-tiered security approach to enhanced role-based multi-domain access control for linked data with two controls: **(1) Domain Access Server Control** is in charge of the first access control level, authorizing only authenticated users who present a security token as well as required personal attributes and role to be granted. At this level SPARQL query rewriting is performed, augmenting the original query with specific security checks to be taken in account by each of the final Endpoint enforcers in the second level. **(2) Data Layer Control** is located at a lower level controlling the executing of the queries on the data sources. This security level, is organised by means of an intelligent structuring of information, which enables the implementation of delegated access controls based on ad-hoc yet traceable information sharing.

5   Semantic Data Lifting

Section 3 highlighted the importance of offering a universal, easily accessible interface for various kinds of information that is compliant with legacy systems. Therefore, ComVantage enablers should facilitate integration of data without semantic information contained in legacy systems with the semantic data model. This functionality, also referred to as *semantic lifting*, is performed by the Linked Data adapters shown in Figure 1. These adapters have to be as unique as the data sources they connect with and their underlying data models. In the ComVantage application areas, these sources range from standard database management systems to highly specific proprietary data management middleware. This demonstrates the versatility of ComVantage Linked Data based approach for integration and collaboration.

5.1   Linked Data Adapter for Databases

The first linked data adapter is driven by the customer-oriented production use case and enhances a standard SQL database system for. In order to semantically lift this data and make it available for collaboration, it is necessary to transform the database entities (like customers, orders, or products) into RDF entities referenced by a unique URI; to assign these objects to their respective RDFS classes; and to transform each line of a table into a set of RDF triples, where columns containing foreign keys are represented by object properties (i.e. they connect two URIs), whereas columns containing literal values are mapped to data properties (i.e. they connect a URI with a literal). This transformation is done using the D2RQ platform [12]. D2RQ reads data from a relational database, converts it into RDF using a set of rules (which logically contain the semantics of the database) and exports this data in RDF or HTML format. It also offers a SPARQL endpoint for queries. Figure 3 shows the RDF graph resulting from this transformation. Here, the oval shapes stand for RDF classes, the diamonds for individuals, and the rectangles for literal values, like text and numbers. Some of the relations between these entities come from the *Friend of a Friend (FOAF)*[1] and vCard[2] ontologies. The benefit of this translation is that instead of the proprietary data model from the database, vocabularies are used some of which are global standards. Even for proprietary vocabularies, a user can dereference

---

[1] http://www.foaf-project.org
[2] http://www.w3.org/2006/vcard/ns

the URIs in order to find out the meaning of the term. The knowledge contained implicitly in the database structure is made explicit and available to application developers.

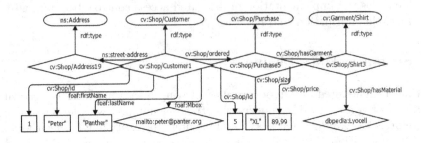

Fig. 3. Semantically lifted database content

5.2   Linked Data Adapter for Real-Time Sensor Data Middleware

The second LD adapter is driven by the RST[3] mobile maintenance application area. This one has more sophisticated demands for its LD integration concept since the maintenance use cases require access to *live* sensor data. The update intervals of these sensor readings are often in the magnitude of milliseconds; thus pushing this data into a triple store is not practical. So a component that transforms the sensor readings into RDF on-the-fly is needed.

In order to access live data, the mobile maintenance application, which runs on a mobile device, accesses the LD server. The server returns a semantic description of the relevant machines, which also contains references (URIs) of the sensor readings. If such a link is dereferenced, the LD server contacts the LD adapter to obtain the current reading. The LD adapter accesses the middleware controller using RST's *Gamma* protocol. The return value is transformed into RDF and reported back to the LD server, so that it can be displayed by the mobile maintenance application.

6   The ComVantage Modelling Framework

Section 3 has highlighted the relevance of business process modelling in the technological context given by Linked Data and mobile app support. This has to be supported by modelling methods able to bridge the business vision with its technological requirements. For this, the ComVantage modelling method has been designed, based on a meta-modelling framework described in [13]. The framework defines a modelling method through its three building blocks: (a) **A modelling language** specifying modelling constructs, their syntax and semantics (grouped in model types addressing specific problems see Figure 4); (b) **A modelling**

---

[3] http://www.rst-automation.de

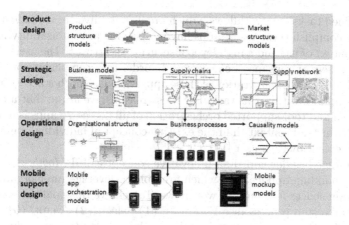

Fig. 4. The ComVantage modelling method stack, version 1.0 [18-D3.1.1]

procedure comprising steps and guidelines to be followed towards the modelling goals; **(c) Mechanisms and algorithms** specifying functionality to be implemented in modelling tools (such as model transformation, visualization, querying and simulation).

A first version of the modelling method specification is shown in Figure 4 for a layered stack of its model types. It has a wider scope than the modelling requirements suggested by Section 3, as it targets the generic context of supply chain management, supporting a modelling procedure comprising the following high level steps: **(1) Product structure / feature design** with a mapping on needs and goals captured from existing market structure research; **(2)** Product features suggest roles required by the production process, which are the basis for **strategic designs**: the business model (according to the e3 value language [14]), the enterprise-level supply network and the product-level supply chain (expressed according to standard frameworks like SCOR [15] [16] or VRM [17]); **(3) At operational level**, business processes can be modelled and mapped on resources of various types: human, hardware, information resources and mobile apps. **(4)** Further on, **mobile app orchestration and abstract designs** can be modelled to express mobile IT support requirements. This layer is involved in the model-driven approach from Section 3 and it relies on: (a) an RDF vocabulary for exporting diagrammatic models in a linked data format; (b) graph rewriting rules for deriving app orchestration from the business process models. (c) a process stepping mechanism to support employee training regarding execution and app support for business processes.

7   Intuitive and Trustful Mobile Collaboration

ComVantage strives to bridge the gap between current state of the art mobile apps and industrial environments. In contrast to complex monolithic applications, apps are affordable, small and fast to develop. However, in the professional area, there are predefined tasks and workflows, which are usually diverse, variable and complex. To accomplish these tasks, apps have to provide proven usability in the industrial context of use and a high level of security and trust to the users. Furthermore, whole sets of apps may be necessary in order to accomplish a complex task showing the need for orchestration of these apps with one another according to the defined workflows within this task. For these reasons, we argue that a common, model-based and tool-supported orchestration of all necessary apps is more feasible in the industrial context than the existing concept of individual app selection and management by each user [19].

ComVantage has developed an innovative concept called *Mobile App Orchestration* for building applications which are able to leverage inter-organizational collaboration spaces for complex workflows. To achieve this goal the concept relies on a three step process (see Figure 5): **(1)** Select, **(2)** Adapt, **(3)** Manage. *Select and Adapt* steps are executed at design time while *Manage* reaches into run time. During selection, apps are selected from a repository (*App Pool*) according to the workflow that is supported. The App Pool contains *Generic Apps* which support a certain task type, e.g. list browsing, diagram analysis but need to be adapted to the use context before they satisfy the needs for industrial usage.

Then the apps are *adapted* to the context of use, taking the data model, ontologies and access rights into account. Basic adaptation is achieved by parameterizing the app's data acquisition (e.g. a SPARQL template), setting a style sheet and choosing app parameters. Selected and adapted apps are installed during the *manage* step on a mobile device with the navigation design derived from the workflow model. On the device a run-time component loads the navigation design and manages inter app communication, switching and data access.

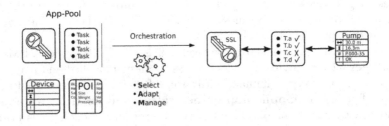

Fig. 5. ComVantage Mobile App Orchestration Concept

8   Conclusions

This chapter has presented the ComVantage reference architecture to meet business and IT challenges for efficient mobile enterprise collaboration in customer-oriented production and mobile maintenance scenarios. The set of collaboration use cases have demonstrated the need for a solution that can facilitate a secure task-driven exchange of product-centric information among different enterprises for the mobile worker. To support such innovative applications, a semantically lifted linked data solution has been proposed that is also supported by a multi-tier linked data access control concept for multi-domain operation. The chapter discussed the benefits of enhanced modelling frameworks for dynamic business collaboration and introduced the concept of Mobile App Orchestration for trustful and intuitive introduction of mobile apps into industrial environments.

Future research directions beyond the ComVantage project should focus on more effective policy management frameworks for efficient View management that derive into optimized inferring processes and data view maintenance. Moreover modelling tools may be turned into knowledge acquisition tools capable of exposing captured knowledge as Linked Data structures. In this direction, meta-models exported as Linked Data can be used to bridge the gap betwwen prescriptive metamodelling and descriptive ontology engineering. Finally, along with the increasing exploitation, more and more Generic Apps will become available for orchestration, which calls for sophisticated tools for App Pool management.

References

1. Gartner Says the World of Work Will Witness 10 Changes During the Next 10 Years (August 4, 2010), http://www.gartner.com/it/page.jsp?id=1416513
2. OECD. Policy Responses to the Economic Crisis: Investing in Innovation for Long-Term Growth. OECD report (June 2009), http://www.oecd.org/dataoecd/59/45/42983414.pdf
3. EU 2020, http://ec.europa.eu/eu2020/index_en.html
4. Digital Agenda (2010), http://ec.europa.eu/information_social/digital-agenda/index_en.html
5. Lazaro, O.: Future Internet and SMEs, FInES Task Force, Brussels (October 12, 2012), http://www.fines-cluster.eu
6. Berners-Lee, T.: Linked Data (2006), http://www.w3.org/DesignIssues/LinkedData.html
7. Angelucci, D., Missikoff, M., Taglino, F.: Future Internet Enterprise Systems: A Flexible Architectural Approach for Innovation. In: Domingue, J., et al. (eds.) Future Internet Assembly. LNCS, vol. 6656, pp. 407–418. Springer, Heidelberg (2011)
8. Pettenati, M.C., Ciofi, L., Pirri, F., Giuli, D.: Towards a RESTful Architecture for Managing a Global Distributed Interlinked Data-Content-Information Space. In: Domingue, J., et al. (eds.) Future Internet Assembly. LNCS, vol. 6656, pp. 81–90. Springer, Heidelberg (2011)
9. Bezzi, M., Trabelsi, S.: Data Usage Control in the Future Internet Cloud. In: Domingue, J., et al. (eds.) Future Internet Assembly. LNCS, vol. 6656, pp. 223–231. Springer, Heidelberg (2011)
10. Prud'hommeaux, E., Seaborne, A.: SPARQL Query Language for RDF (2008), http://www.w3.org/TR/rdf-sparql-query

11. Klyne, G., Carrol, J.: Resource Description Framework (RDF): Concepts and Abstract Syntax (2004), http://www.w3.org/TR/rdf-concepts
12. D2RQ homepage, http://d2rq.org
13. Karagiannis, D., Kühn, H.: Metamodelling platforms. In: Bauknecht, K., Tjoa, A.M., Quirchmayr, G. (eds.) EC-Web 2002. LNCS, vol. 2455, p. 182. Springer, Heidelberg (2002)
14. Gordijn, J., Akkermans, H.: E3-value: Design and Evaluation of e-Business Models. IEEE Intelligent Systems 16(4), 11–17 (2001)
15. Bolstorff, P., et al.: Supply Chain Excellence. AMACOM, New York (2007)
16. The Supply Chain Council, http://supply-chain.org/
17. The Value Reference Model, http://www.value-chain.org/en/cms/?1960
18. The ComVantage project - public deliverables page, http://www.comvantage.eu/results-publications/public-deriverables/
19. Ziegler, J., et al.: Beyond App-Chaining: Mobile App Orchestration for Efficient Model Driven Software Generation. In: 17th IEEE International Conference on Emerging Technologies and Factory Automation (in Press)

Test-Enabled Architecture for IoT
Service Creation and Provisioning

Suparna De[1], Francois Carrez[1], Eike Reetz[1,2], Ralf Tönjes[2], and Wei Wang[1]

[1] Centre for Communication Systems Research (CCSR), University of Surrey, Guildford, UK
{S.De,F.Carrez,Wei.Wang}@surrey.ac.uk
[2] Faculty of Engineering and Computer Science, University of Applied Sciences Osnabrück,
Germany
{E.Reetz,r.toenjes}@hs-osnabrueck.de

Abstract. The information generated from the *Internet of Things* (IoT) potentially enables a better understanding of the physical world for humans and
supports creation of ambient intelligence for a wide range of applications in different domains. A semantics-enabled service layer is a promising approach to
facilitate seamless access and management of the information from the large,
distributed and heterogeneous sources. This paper presents the efforts of the
IoT.est project towards developing a framework for service creation and testing
in an IoT environment. The architecture design extends the existing IoT reference architecture and enables a test-driven, semantics-based management of the
entire service lifecycle. The validation of the architecture is shown though a
dynamic test case generation and execution scenario.

Keywords: Internet of Things, Architecture, Automated Test Derivation,
Semantic IoT Services.

1   Introduction

A dynamic *Service Creation Environment* (SCE) that gathers and exploits data and
information from the heterogeneous sources can help to overcome the technological
boundaries and dynamically design and integrate new services and business opportunities for the *Internet of Things* (IoT). Rapid service creation and deployment in IoT
environments requires a large number of resources and automated interpretation of
environmental and context information. Moreover, the mobility of resources and the
dynamicity of the environment necessitate integration of test-friendly description
capabilities in the development and maintenance of services from the beginning. Integrating service oriented computing mechanisms and semantic technologies to create a
semantic service layer on the top of IoT is a promising approach for facilitating seamless access and management of the information from the large, distributed and heterogeneous sources. The application of semantics to enable automated testing of the IoT
services can reduce the time to deployment, while context-aware service adaptation
can support deployed services to respond to environmental changes. In this paper, we
present an architecture for service creation and testing in an IoT environment, which

A. Galis and A. Gavras (Eds.): FIA 2013, LNCS 7858, pp. 233–245, 2013.

has been developed as part of the *IoT Environment for Service Creation and Testing* (IoT.est)[1] EU ICT-FP7 project.

The IoT-Architecture (IoT-A)[2] EU ICT-FP7 project has proposed an *Architectural Reference Model* (ARM) [1] for the IoT, which identifies the basic IoT domain concepts and the functional components of a *Reference Architecture* (RA). Our contribution is the adoption and application of these principles in order to develop a coherent architecture for self-management and testing of IoT services. This is illustrated by mapping the identified functionalities within IoT.est into the IoT-A ARM, while also including extensions for IoT-enabled testing. Our second contribution is the implementation of the architecture representing a concrete example for a dynamic test case generation and execution scenario.

2   Related Work – IoT-A ARM

The ARM involves identification, use and specification of standardized components, understanding the underlying business models and deriving protocols and interfaces. The ARM is envisaged as a combination of a *Reference Model* (RM) and a RA. The RM aims at establishing a common understanding of the IoT domain with a set of models identifying the main concepts of the IoT, their interactions and constraints. It also serves as a basis of the RA. The RM, detailed in [1], includes, in particular, a *Domain Model* (DM) as a top-level description of IoT concepts and an *Information Model* (IM) explaining how IoT information is going to be modeled. The DM identifies the concepts of entities, resources and services as important actors in IoT scenarios. A short description of the concepts can be found in Table 1.

The RA aims at guidelines, best practices, views and perspectives that can be used for building fully interoperable concrete IoT architectures and systems. Once the RA is defined, it can be used by multiple organizations to implement compliant IoT architectures in specific application domains. The RA, through a functional view, provides the key *Functional Groups* (FG) potentially needed by any concrete IoT architecture, as shown in Fig. 2 (square rectangles in light blue).

The Application FG describes the functionalities provided by applications that are built on top of an implementation of the IoT-A architecture. The IoT Business Process Management FG provides an environment for the modeling of IoT-aware business processes which can be executed in the process execution component. Orchestration and access of IoT Services to external entities and services is organized by the Service Organization FG. It provides a set of functionalities and APIs to expose and compose IoT Services so that they become available to external entities and can be composed by them. The *Virtual Entity* (VE) FG contains functionality to associate VEs to relevant services as well as a means to search for such services. When queried about a service of a particular VE, this FG will return addresses of the services related to this

---

[1]   IoT.est: IoT Environment for Service Creation and Testing (http://ict-iotest.eu/iotest/).
[2]   IoT-A: Internet of Things Architecture (http://www.iot-a.eu/public).

particular VE (through the VE Resolution component). The corresponding associations between a VE and services that can be relevant to the VE are derived and maintained by the VE and IoT service monitoring component. The IoT Service FG provides the functionalities required by services for processing information and for notifying application software and services about events related to resources and corresponding VEs. The IoT service component defines service descriptions. The IoT service resolution component stores and retrieves information about a service and can be used to insert and update service descriptions, retrieve stored descriptions and provide the address of a given service. The Device FG provides the set of methods and primitives for device connectivity and communication.

The Management FG is tasked with efficient management of computational resources, with the *Quality of Service* (QoS) Manager ensuring the consistency of the expressed QoS requirements and the Device Manager setting a default device configuration and firmware upgrades. The Security FG ensures that aspects of security functions are consistently applied by the different FGs.

3 Requirements

Most of the requirements (function and non-functional) identified by IoT.est come from scenario analysis and are mapped to various categories (see below). Specific requirements related to the service life-cycle have also been also identified. After introducing the IoT.est requirements, we will show how the IoT-A ARM takes them into account.

3.1 IoT Requirements

We start talking about IoT when objects of the *Real World* (RW objects) have the capability to interact and cooperate with each other and/or when users can interact with those RW objects. Important aspects of IoT are therefore sensor and actuator technologies that allow to interact with RW objects or the environment and which alternatively can provide RW objects with perception capabilities. Many scenario-driven requirements in IoT.est cover this intrinsic characteristic of IoT. Other requirements specifically deal with the heterogeneous nature of IoT and have lot of impacts upon the architecture of IoT.est. Finally when facing a potentially extremely high number of objects and therefore sensors, actuators and tags, an IoT architecture must provide very powerful and efficient tools for discovering the entities that can be used to create an IoT service.

3.2 Requirements for Knowledge-Based Service Lifecycle Management

To support automated, dynamic IoT service creation and provisioning, the architecture should meet both design-time and run-time requirements. The design-time is understood as service creation time that splits into modeling and development phases.

To ease service creation a semantics-based knowledge-driven approach is suggested. The semantic descriptions represent the knowledge about reusable service components and their composition to complex services in a machine interpretable way to allow automated inference while being explicit, i.e. linked to a human-readable knowledge base, to ease maintenance. The descriptions must allow representation of *Service Level Agreements* (SLAs) to support business contract enforcement, service states such as *Quality of Service* (QoS), *Quality of Information* (QoI) and definition of business and technical roles related to authorization and service lifecycle management. Definition of usage conditions to allow trigger mechanisms in case of failure conditions is also a required characteristic of service descriptions.

To overcome the semantic gap between the sensor data and the IoT enabled business processes, the system must be able to collect low level sensed data and process it to high level information. This requires methods for knowledge based composition of the processing chain including reusable components for data aggregation, sensor fusion, pattern recognition, event detection and reasoning. The SCE must be run-time environment agnostic. It should allow specification of patterns and run-time constraints that match user goals. This requires methods for component capability representation and component discovery.

Run-time aspects cover service provisioning that can be subdivided into service deployment and service execution. Each phase of the service life cycle has to be supported by the corresponding test, monitoring and self-adaptation mechanisms. If one of the components in the system fails, the system should identify and provide alternative components. This imposes high demands on the time constraints of any knowledge-based approach. This requires methods for pre-computed fall back solutions and look ahead approaches.

3.3   Requirements for Test-Driven Service Creation

From a test perspective, the knowledge based life cycle management approach offers the ability to (semi-) automate the derivation of tests from the semantic service description. The semantic service description needs to contain detailed information about the service interface description; the IoT resource interface description and information about the desired SLA and the required meta-data for service provisioning (e.g., resources of desired service run-time environment). *Input Output Precondition Effects* (IOPE) are commonly known as the information required for describing the functional behavior of the service interfaces. For automated test derivation it is required that the IOPE information are stored in the semantic description. Contrary to classical web service testing approaches, the heterogeneity of possible involved IoT resources require a detailed description how to communicate with them.

The involvement of IoT resources changes how testing can be applied to these semantically described services: risk of costs and real world affects results in the requirement to execute the *System Under Test* (SUT) in a controllable environment (sandbox) to assure correct behavior before deploying the SUT in the real world.

3.4 Comparison of Reviewed Architectures against Identified Requirements

In this section we give an overview of the most important requirements from IoT.est per category (architecture, semantic, testing, service composition) and show how they relate to IoT-A requirements.

- *Architecture, Interoperability, Scalability, Portability:* Most of the requirements covered in this category come from the scenario analysis and are covered by IoT-A. Worth noting are heterogeneity (device, technologies, access), semantic support (see below), sensing and actuation support, support for monitoring and management (covered by the Management FG in IoT-A), security (generally compliant with IoT-A Security, Trust and Privacy model). In IoT-A, interoperability, Scalability and Portability (and also Security) are considered as qualities of the system and are described as *Perspectives* following the terminology of Rozanski *et al.* [2]. The ARM provides a large set of Design Choices which give the architectures a large number of options in order to fulfill any targeted quality of the IoT system.
- *Semantics:* In IoT-A, semantics is handled mainly in the IM of the RM, where it is explicitly shown that entities like Devices, Resources and Services are associated with Service Descriptions. How to handle the Semantic aspect of those descriptions is left to the designer, but IoT-A strongly recommends the use of RDF or OWL. Semantic registration and look-up are equally considered in IoT-A and are part of the Functional Decomposition. In IoT-A VE (corresponding to *Entity of Interest* (EoI) in IoT.est) may be described semantically as well. IoT-A requirements do not consider testing activities as part of the model so few IoT.est requirements on this specific topic are not explicitly covered;
- *Service Composition:* The set of requirements in this category are either relating to the SCE design and non-functional requirement (which is beyond the level of detail of the ARM), or describing some aspects of Service Composition that are implicitly covered by the Semantic or finally directly linked to the testing requirements which are not covered by the ARM;
- *Testing:* Majority of the requirements in this category are very much testing-specific and are –as expected- not considered in IoT-A. Some requirements go very precisely in the content of Service Description specifying e.g. bandwidth constraints, pre- and post-test actions, while IoT-A is only proposing a general scheme for modeling such descriptions as part of the IM;
- *Other:* Some requirements relating to role–driven or –based activities access control and confidentiality or specific security technologies are compatible with the Security and Privacy model of IoT-A. Finally, technologies pertaining to SOA-related requirements are also compatible and handled by the ARM (e.g. compatibility with WS-*, RESTful technologies).

4 Architecture

4.1 Architecture for IoT Service Creation and Provision

The architecture has to support the heterogeneity of the current IoT infrastructures and has to bridge the gap between low-level IoT services and high-level business

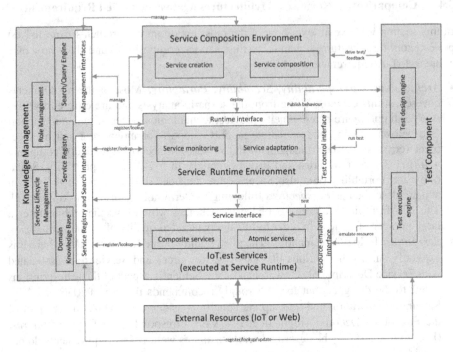

Fig. 1. Architecture for IoT Service Creation and Provision

services. Fig. 1 shows the IoT.est architecture for IoT service creation and provision-ing. The objectives of the six major architectural components are summarized as follows:

The *Knowledge Management* (KM) component is responsible for registration, sto-rage, search and query of the (IoT-based) service descriptions as well as some man-agement tasks. The semantic service descriptions are stored in distributed service registries. The *Service Composition Environment* (SCE) allows end users to compose IoT based services in a semi-automated way based on business goals. A service de-sign GUI facilitates the service creation with operations to build workflows and to edit data flows. It supports the entire service composition life-cycle, from supporting the process specification through elaboration of process and template expansions to the discovery and binding of service endpoints as activities within the processes. The *Service Runtime Environment* (SRE) enables provisioning of IoT enabled business processes. It is related to the deployment and execution phases of the service life-cycle. The SRE monitors context and network parameter (e.g. QoS) and initiates automated service adaptation in order to fulfill SLAs. The *Test Component* (TC) man-ages the derivation and execution of tests of the semantically described services. The test derivation is triggered by the SCE. It fetches the service description from the Registry and search/query engine where it also stores information about its test re-sults. It handles the testing of the service in a controllable instance of the SRE, a so called Sandbox Instance, and emulates the external Resources. The IoT.est Services component represents the collection of the IoT services and reusable service components. Since the target is to allow IoT specific services to be described, annotated and bound in a uniform manner, the term service is generic and not linked to any fixed options regarding the protocol, input/output format or any other specific SLA details. The External Resources are those not designed and developed within the proposed architecture. The resources can be services which can be discovered and used with IoT based services for service composition.

4.2   Reverse Mapping with Respect to IoT-A Domain Model

The list of concepts developed in IoT.est is at a lower level of detail than IoT-A. Obviously, concepts like resources, sensors, actuators are present but they are considered as 'External Resources', as the project it-self tends to focus on the service layer. Even if not developed here, the UML Domain Model from the IoT.est perspective would be compatible with the IoT-A DM. It would however feature a smaller number of main "concepts" but more sub-class entities (as many IoT-A concepts fall under the 'external resource' umbrella).

The list of main concepts used for the IoT-A / IoT.est DM can be found in Table 1:

Table 1. Mapping between IoT-A and IoT.est concepts

IoT-A Concept	Definition	IoT.est counterpart
User	The user of a service	User / Application
Physical Entity (PE)	Any 'things' in the real world including e.g. locations	Things
Virtual Entity (VE)	Representation of PEs in the digital world	Entity of Interest
Augmented Entity (AE)	Composition of VE and PEs. They are the 'Things' in IoT	n/a
Devices	Are used to mediate between PEs and VEs. Sensors, actuators and tags are typical devices	External resource
Resources	Resources are software components that encapsulate devices (resources can be quite Hardware dependent)	External resource
Services	Services offer standardized interfaces to the Resources	IoT service

IoT.est introduces the notion of Network Emulation and Resource Emulation that are used for encapsulating Resources in a black box for testing purpose. Those concepts are not present in the IoT-A DM. In the same way, the DM does not consider 'interface' as a concept at the current stage of its development.

4.3   Extension against IoT-A Reference Architecture

The proposed IoT.est architecture extends the IoT-A RA to include testing, run-time monitoring and adaptation as well as knowledge based service life-cycle management. Fig. 2 shows the major extensions and mapping to the IoT-A RA:

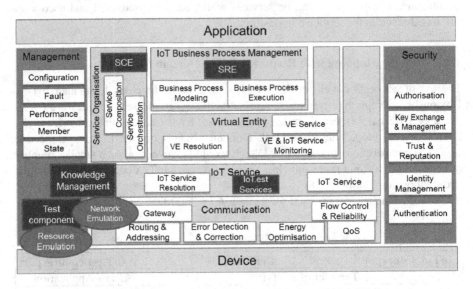

Fig. 2. Mapping of IoT.est functional blocks to IoT-A RA

The proposed framework defines a new functional block, the *Test Component* (TC), which can be situated as an additional component within the IoT-A Management FG. Based on a SOA approach, each IoT resource is wrapped by an atomic IoT service, which may be composed to more complex IoT services. TC also includes IoT Resource Emulation (to insert data transmissions from emulated resources into the SUT) and Network Emulation (to change the network connection behavior), which are defined at design time. Moreover, before deployment in the live system, the service is tested in a sandbox environment.

The KM component maps to the IoT Service FG with its service registration, search and query capabilities. Additionally, it maps to the Management FG with its lifecycle and role management functionalities. The IoT-A IoT Service FG also captures the IoT.est Services component, encompassing description and annotation of both atomic and composite services. The IoT.est SCE Component offers the same functionalities as the Service Organisation FG. The SRE functionalities map to the IoT Business Process Management FG, including built-in monitoring and adaptation capabilities to cope with the dynamics of IoT environments. A service starts monitoring the *Key Performance Indicators* (KPIs) once contracted. If the service SLA is violated, it may be necessary to trigger some adaptation actions to correct the deviations. Service Adaptation provides the necessary functionality (such as reconfiguration, re-assignments and/or temporary work-around) to resolve the problem and get the service back to a normal operational state as efficiently as possible.

5   IoT.est Architecture Building Blocks

As a focused contribution to the identified requirements for a test-driven SCE, in this section, we concentrate on the Knowledge Management and Test Components of the proposed architecture.

The Knowledge Management block is based upon the IoT.est description ontology which is designed as the semantic description framework for the proposed architecture. It provides a light-weight modular framework for describing different aspects such as resources, test and services and is detailed in [3]. The services and resources are linked not only to the concepts in the domain knowledge base but also to other existing sources on the Semantic Web. The Service Description Repository is implemented as a distributed store which hides the complexity of distributed query processing from applications. It exposes management interfaces for service description registration, update, lookup, removal and discovery. The Search/Query Engine consists of two major sub-components: service search and service recommendation. The search procedure is primarily based on a logic based approach (e.g., using the SPARQL language [4]) and enables users to generate expressive and effective logical queries in combination with the distributed repository mechanism. To find the most appropriate service instances in the context of the applications, e.g., service composition, an effective service recommendation function is implemented based on factors such as the users' needs and tasks, application context, and possibly the trustworthiness of the underlying IoT resources. Lifecycle Management provides means to the other modules to update all the information related to the service lifecycle, such as status updates For example, a service that has passed the validation tests consequently can be certified; the change of the lifecycle status of the service includes other information that proves that the service has passed all the tests. Role Management provides the typical operations that allow to create, update, delete or modify roles and to associate and describe the functionality that the user role is allowed to access. For example, an integration tester will be able to certify tests; but not a software developer.

Test Component: Due to the real world interaction and the lack of control of components involved in atomic and composite services, tests cannot be executed in a production environment. Therefore, the SUT will be placed in a so called sandbox, which emulates the target environment as realistically as possible – not only functionally, but also from a real world, e.g., network and resource oriented, point of view. To overcome current time and resource intense approaches we propose a code insertion methodology, which can be derived from the semantic description of the IoT based service [5]. The Test Execution Engine (TEE) controls the environment and executes the test cases. The test creation process is triggered by the SCE and the resulting test cases can be selected to be executed or modified based on expert knowledge. A detailed description of the testing approach can be found in [6]. The Test Design Engine (TDE) creates test cases for new and changed services and prepares their execution.

The test cases are described with the standardized Test Control Notation Version 3 (TTCN-3) [7] language. The test cases are enriched with test data generated based on the IOPE conditions of the semantic service description. A Test Case Compiler produces executable code from the test cases. The TEE is the central component to coordinate the test flow and takes care of the test execution and executes the SUT under controlled and emulated conditions of the target environment. The sandbox ensures that the SUT can be executed in a test environment and can be manipulated during the test execution. In addition, the separation between the TEE and the sandbox offers the ability to execute the tests in a distributed manner. The SUT interfaces are connected with the TEE and a network emulation interface and this enables that each message from or to the SUT can be manipulated in terms of delay and packet loss to evaluate the robustness. Run-time behavior changes are made by the execution runtime emulation that ensures the identification of potential SLA violations. The strict isolation of the SUT within the sandbox is realized by the resource emulation interface, which encapsulates interfaces to external Web Services or IoT resources.

6   Case Study

The concept of (semi-) automated test derivation is based on the machine interpretable semantic service description. The procedure of functional testing is explained using a simple example service. The goal of the service is to switch on the heating when the user approaches home. A *DistanceEvent* starts the service and the current distance is stored. On a *TimerEvent* a second distance is measured and the heating is switched on if the second distance is smaller than the first distance. Heating switch off can be realized by the user request *TurnOff* (cf. Figure 3(b)). In order to accomplish this, the service has to communicate with an external service to identify the user distance and communicate with the heater to switch it on.

For testing a behavior model of the service and an emulation of its interfaces to external services (i.e. distance measure) and IoT resources (i.e. heating) is required. The automated modeling of the service behavior and its interfaces is described as follows: *Derivation of behavior model:* The behavior model of the service is based on an extended *Finite State Machine* (FSM) that has input functions as transitions and an attached complex data model. Automated derivation of the behavior model exploits the combination of various knowledge, including business process description, semantic service description, and service grounding (e.g., full interface description and binding information). The objective of the model is to describe the service behavior for the test purpose in an abstract way. This paper suggests the use of rules (employing Rule Interchange Format Production Rule Dialect (RIF) [8]) to ease the formulation of the service transitions, i.e. preconditions and effects, by the tester. The steps to derive the service model are as follows: 1) state variables and their range of validity are identified (based on data types, or based on preconditions) 2) preliminary states are identified based on partitions of the state variable (e.g. precondition *distanceToHome <10 km*), 3) the input and output functions are determined based on reserved words in the rule descriptions and, 4) transition pre- and post-states are identified. The resulting extended FSM is shown in Figure 3 (b) (without the data model). It shows, for example, that if the service is in the state *DISCOVERY*, the state is left by calling the input function *Calculate* either resulting in the post-state *HEATING* if the condition (distance1>distance2) is true, or in the post-state *INITIAL* otherwise.

Emulation of external services: To test the service in isolation, the connection to external (web-) services needs to be emulated. For messages from the SUT to external services the methods are encapsulated and if the SUT is in emulation mode, it sends the request via a RESTful interface to the emulation component. In this example, the resource emulation interface is capable of inserting the desired distances (*distance1* > *distance2* and *distance1* < *10 km*) into the SUT.

Emulation of IoT resources: The access to IoT resources is emulated like the call to/from external services. Therefore the IoT interface is encapsulated also inside the SUT itself (cf. Figure 3(a) and [9] for more details). Two main steps are required to make use of this approach: 1) insert code based on the interface description and 2) create the behavior model in a similar manner as with the service interface. The inserted code enables a generic communication with the SUT and allows emulating the IoT resource behavior with data insertion. The inserted code consists of: 1) a singleton Test Controller class which stores the SUT mode (e.g. emulation mode), 2) a resource emulation interface, and 3) the encapsulation of methods that are communicating with IoT resources. The resource emulation interface handles all data insertions from emulated IoT resources and invokes the overloaded methods within the SUT.

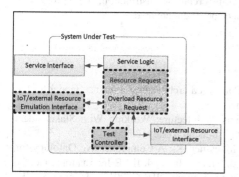 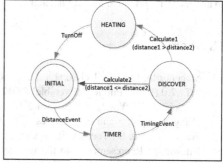

(a) IoT Resource Emulation Interface   (b) Simplified Finite State Machine

Fig. 3. IoT Resource Emulation Concept and Simplified Finite State Machine

With the creation of the resource emulation interface and the SUT model, the concrete test cases can be created. Based on the desired test coverage (here state-based for presentability) paths searching algorithms extract test cases from the extended FSM employing termination conditions to avoid endless loops. In this example, the resulting test cases involve the paths from the INITIAL state to the HEATING state. The created test cases are coded with the TTCN-3 language. The TTworkbench [10]

244 S. De et al.

controls the test execution: The test execution starts with initialization of the service and the emulation components. Then the test case execution engine initiates the *DistanceEvent* by inserting a *distance1 < 10 km* into the SUT via the resource emulation interface. After the timer event has occurred, the *distance2 < distance1* is also inserted into the SUT. The reaction of the service ("turn heat on" message, intercepted by the overloaded methods inside the SUT) indicates the correct behavior of the service.

7 Conclusions

The concept of IoT services that are able to expose capabilities of their corresponding resources defines the paradigm of service-oriented computing in IoT. The mobile, unreliable, and capability-constrained nature of such resources make the IoT services different from most existing legacy services on the Web. In this paper, we have proposed a semantics-oriented test-driven architecture for a dynamic service creation environment for the IoT that addresses these issues in a coherent fashion. After deriving the generic and test-driven requirements placed on such an architecture, we mapped the envisioned building blocks to the IoT-A ARM in order to show compatibility with known IoT reference architectures. We also briefly present an implementation of the architecture components with an automated test generation case study.

Open Access. This article is distributed under the terms of the Creative Commons Attribution Noncommercial License which permits any noncommercial use, distribution, and reproduction in any medium, provided the original author(s) and source are credited.

References

1. Magerkurth, C. (ed.): Deliverable D1.4 – Converged architectural reference model for the IoT v2.0 (IoT-A Public Deliverable) (2012)
2. Rozanski, N., Woods, E.: Software Systems Architecture: Working With Stakeholders Using Viewpoints and Perspectives, 2nd edn. Addison-Wesley (2005)
3. Wang, W., De, S., Toenjes, R., Reetz, E., Moessner, K.: A Comprehensive Ontology for Knowledge Representation in the Internet of Things. In: 11th IEEE International Conference on Ubiquitous Computing and Communications (IUCC 2012), Liverpool, UK, pp. 1793–1798 (2012)
4. W3C, SPARQL Query Language for RDF, W3C Recommendation (2008)
5. Wei, W. (ed.): D2.2 - Report on Reference Architecture For IoT Service Creation and Provision (IoT.est Public Deliverable) (2012)
6. Reetz, E.S., Kümper, D., Lehmann, A., Tönjes, R.: Test Driven Life Cycle Management for Internet of Things based Services: A Semantic Approach. In: The Fourth International Conference on Advances in System Testing and Validation Lifecycle (VALID 2012), pp. 21–27 (2012)
7. ETSI. The Testing and Test Control Notation Version 3 (TTCN-3). European Standard (ES) 201 873 (2002/2003), http://www.ttcn-3.org

8. RIF Production Rule Dialect, 2nd edn. (W3C Recommendation),
   `http://www.w3.org/TR/rif-prd/`
9. Reetz, E.S., Kuemper, D., Moessner, K., Tönjes, R.: How to Test IoT Services before Deploying them into Real World. In: Proc. 19th European Wireless Conference (EW 2013), Guildford, UK (2013) (accepted for publication)
10. Testing Technologies - Products, `http://www.testingtech.com/products/ttworkbench.php`

Enabling Technologies and Economic Incentives

Sustainable Wireless Broadband Access to the Future Internet - The EARTH Project[*]

Dietrich Zeller[1], Magnus Olsson[2], Oliver Blume[1], Albrecht Fehske[3],
Dieter Ferling[1], William Tomaselli[4], and István Gódor[2]

[1] Alcatel-Lucent
[2] Ericsson
[3] Technical University of Dresden
[4] Telecom Italia

Abstract . In a world of continuous growth of economies and global population eco-sustainability is of outmost relevance. Especially, mobile broadband networks are facing an exponential growing traffic volume and so the sustainability of these networks comes into focus. The recently completed European funded Seventh Framework Programme (FP7) project EARTH has studied the impact of traffic growth on mobile broadband network energy consumption and carbon footprint, pioneering this field. This chapter summarizes the key insights of EARTH on questions like "How does the exploding traffic impact the sustainability?", "How can energy efficiency be rated and predicted?", "What are the key solutions to improve the energy efficiency and how to efficiently integrate such solutions?" The results are representing the foundation of the maturing scientific engineering discipline of Energy Efficient Wireless Access, targeting the standardisation in IETF and 3GPP, strongly influencing academic research trends, and will soon be reflected in products and deployments of the European telecommunications industry.

1   Introduction

This chapter gives an overview of the FP7 project EARTH contributions to a sustainable wireless broadband access to the Future Internet. Hence, it summarizes the results of common work of the EARTH consortium obtained during the project duration from January 2010 until July 2012 [1].

The Europe 2020 strategy [2] of the European Union aims towards Smart, Sustainable and Inclusive Growth for Europe. In all these areas ICT (Information and Communication Technologies) are broadly considered as the lever to enable this growth. For instance, the Smart2020 report [3] stated that ICT can lead to emission reductions by 15% in 2020 compared to the emissions resulting from "business as usual".

A key part of the ICT infrastructure is represented by the Internet evolving to the Future Internet. The access to the Future Internet will be dominated by wireless devices. Already now most European citizens witness how much the Internet and mobile access to the Internet transforms their ways to live. But this is just the beginning

---

[*] Invied Paper.

A. Galis and A. Gavras (Eds.): FIA 2013, LNCS 7858, pp. 249–271, 2013.

towards the envisaged society by Europe 2020. All these developments results in an explosive traffic growth, illustrated in Fig.1, which challenges the sustainability of networks.

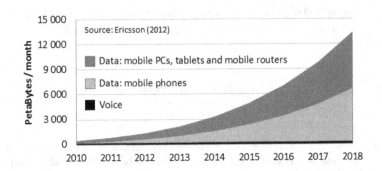

Fig. 1. Evolution of Mobile Data Traffic per Month up to 2018

Obviously, this growth is accompanied by an increased energy consumption of mobile networks, with a corresponding increase in the carbon footprint of the networks. Therefore telecommunication networks and in particular mobile networks have the tendency to increasingly contribute to global energy consumption. And this increase comes at a period where energy prices are extremely volatile and have resumed their upward trend. Rising energy costs have led to a situation where they are a significant part of network operation costs. In fact, operator's OPEX figures indicate that their energy costs are nowadays comparable to their personnel costs for network operations. All this clearly shows that the sustainability of network growth is at risk. But a sustainable growth of networks is the prerequisite that they can play their key role in enabling Smart, Sustainable and Inclusive Growth. So it is pivotal that methods are found ensuring the sustainable growth.

This context was the starting point for the EARTH project [1], a concerted effort with 15 partners from industry, SME and academia addressing improvements of the energy efficiency of mobile communication infrastructure. The project was guided by the ambitious overall goal to derive solutions that together in an Integrated Solution decrease the network energy consumption by 50% without degrading quality of service. The saving is understood as the saving a network deployment having the EARTH solutions in place would have compared to a deployment without these solutions. Both deployments are assumed to be subjected to identical traffic demands.

With this EARTH was addressing the call of EU Commissioner Viviane Reding on ICT industry for intensified efforts to reduce its carbon footprint by 20% as early as 2015 for tackling climate change [4].

In the subsequent sections we first present an analysis of the socio-economic impact of the traffic growth and the EARTH targeted savings. Then we present the EARTH methodology to evaluate the impact of different solutions on the network energy consumption. After presenting solutions on the radio and network level the EARTH approach to integrate solutions efficiently into Integrated Solutions is presented. The validation of the theoretical results by tests of prototype implementations under realistic conditions is described before the chapter is concluded with a summary.

2   Socio-Economic Impact Analysis

EARTH has developed a methodology that allows to accurately quantify the overall global carbon footprint of mobile communications in the period 2007 – 2020 considering the complete network lifecycle. We identify the energy consumption of global RAN (radio access network) operation as a main contributor and further investigate the potential impact of EARTH technologies on RAN energy consumption in several scenarios.

The model is based on detailed life cycle analysis of network equipment as well as models and data on development of mobile traffic volumes, number of base stations, and subscribers globally. We consider all generations of cellular mobile networks including all end-user equipment accessing the networks, all business activities of the operators running the networks, and the use of fixed network resources as a result of data traffic generated by mobile network users. Estimates on the number of mobile subscriptions, traffic volumes, and network infrastructure are based on projections from analysts Gartner and ABI Research and extrapolated for the period 2015 to 2020 as part of the EARTH project. For more details we refer to [5].

Over the last decade, the energy consumption of RAN equipment has already decreased by about 8% per year. This average annual improvement can be attributed to the technology scaling of semiconductors, as well as to improved radio access technologies. Consequently, this 8% per year improvement scenario is taken as a reference throughout the study and referred to as "continuous improvements".

2.1   Global Carbon Footprint of Mobile Communications

- According to the projection (see Fig.2), the overall carbon footprint of mobile communications increases almost linearly until 2020 with annual increase of 11 Mto CO_2e, equivalent to the annual emissions of 2.5 million EU households. The emissions in 2020 amount to more than 235 $MtoCO_2$e, corresponding to more than one third of the present annual emissions of the entire United Kingdom. Relative to 2007, the overall carbon footprint will increase by a factor of 2 until 2014 and a factor of 2.7 until 2020. In the event that only minor efficiency improvements of base station sites and end-user equipment occur, the footprint could even increase more than threefold. In contrast, the footprint of the ICT sector as a whole is expected to increase by a factor of only 1.7 during the same 13-year period.
- While RAN operation was by far the largest contributor in 2007, mobile device manufacturing will develop an equal share in the overall carbon footprint in 2020. The reason for this is that smartphones and laptops represent an actively increasing fraction of the devices accessing the network — a trend driven by the demand for advanced wireless services and applications, especially video. Compared to regular

phones, smartphones and laptops have carbon footprints almost two times and ten times higher, respectively.

- From 2007 to 2020, the annual data traffic volume per mobile subscription is expected to increase substantially from 0.3 GBytes/year up to 100 GBytes/year. The rather moderate linear increase in global footprint compared to the vast exponential increase in traffic volume is made possible by 1) strong increase in network capacity through small cells, 2) increasing spectral efficiency and bandwidths in future mobile standards, and 3) already existing unused capacity.
- An estimated number of 100 million femto cells in 2020 will consume about 4.4 TWh/year, which is less than 5% of that estimated for the global RAN operation in 2020. We infer that the total carbon emissions due to femto cells are comparably small and become significant only if their number approaches the order of 1 billion or more globally.
- The carbon footprint due to manufacturing and operation of M2M communication devices will be small, even for a vast number of existing devices in 2020. Here, only the actual modem part is allocated to be a part of the mobile network.

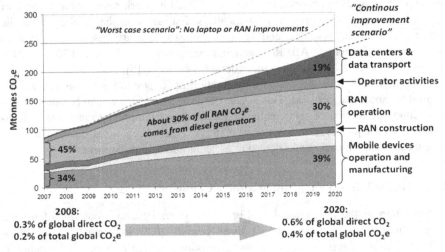

Fig. 2. Global carbon footprint of mobile communications in CO_2e projected until 2020

2.2 RAN Energy Consumption and the Potential Impact of EARTH Technologies

As discussed above, a major source of CO_2e from the network part of mobile communications is from the electrical power used for operation of the base stations (BS) in the RAN. Focusing on this topic we derived the following observations (see Fig.3):

- In the reference case of 8% improvements in efficiency per year, the RAN energy increases by about 28% in 2020 compared to 2012 (Scenario "Improvements 8% p.a." in Fig.3).

- Assuming all base stations deployed in the period 2013-2020 use 50% less electricity (the target of EARTH) RAN operation will increase only slightly compared to its 2012 value - despite the anticipated growth in traffic demand (Scenario "New technologies" in Fig.3). The 50% reduction must be seen as per-site-average due to the combined effects of improved hardware as well as better use of the equipment through improved radio resource management, smarter deployment, and other improvements of the EARTH integrated solution.
- A significant reduction of RAN operation energy for 2020 is possible if innovations are also implemented in already installed base stations, e.g. through software updates, and site modernization (Scenario "Large swap of equipment" in Fig.3). Here, we assume a progressive swap-out of almost 40 percent of globally installed equipment, where old sites are replaced by state-of-the-art equipment during the period 2013 to 2020.

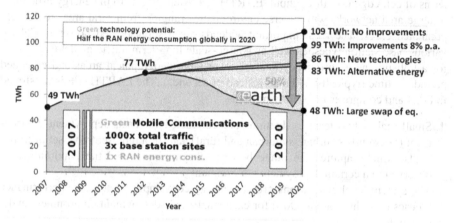

Fig. 3. Global RAN electricity consumption in TWh per year projected until 2020 for different scenarios of technology adoption

In summary, our analysis demonstrates that network operators should focus on savings in RAN operation. A 50% reduction in energy consumption per site yields significant energy savings under realistic assumptions on technology adoption. It shows that with the saving target of EARTH it would be possible to keep the total power consumption of RANs flat after 2012, despite the expected exponential traffic growth. Application of EARTH solutions to the BSs deployed before 2012 would even enable to revert the growth in RAN power consumption experienced between 2007 and 2012.

3   Energy Efficiency Evaluation Framework (E³F)

When the project started, no widely accepted methodology existed in the mobile industry and academia to quantify the energy efficiency of a wireless network. Metrics and measurement specification for the energy efficiency of individual base stations had been specified by the standard body ETSI [6]. However, for a large-scale network, like a national deployment of an operator this is much more difficult to achieve. Nevertheless, GSMA has recently provided a framework for the assessment and comparison of energy efficiency of large deployed networks in the field [7]. The limitation of this benchmarking service is in the assessment of saving potentials. Which parts or functions of the network are the main consumers and how much impact would certain improvements, e.g. in hardware or network management, achieve? EARTH has undertaken the effort to fill the methodology gap for predicting gains in efficiency in theory and in simulations and to build best practice advise for characteristic network scenarios.

The EARTH Energy Efficiency Evaluation Framework (E^3F) [8] takes as starting point the well-known radio network assessment methodology of the Third Generation Partnership Project (3GPP), which is focused on small-scale scenarios and provides results in terms of system throughput, quality of service (QoS) metrics, and fairness in terms of cell edge user throughput. EARTH has extended this to the energy efficiency of large area networks with diverse environments ranging from rural areas to densely populated cities. The most important addends are a sophisticated power model for various base station types, as well as a large-scale long-term traffic model that allows for a holistic energy efficiency analysis over large geographical areas and extended periods of time (typically 24 hours instead of seconds). The EARTH E^3F is illustrated in Fig.4 and comprises the following steps:

1. Small-scale, short-term evaluations are conducted for each deployment environment (dense urban, urban, suburban and rural) and for a representative set of traffic loads, which captures the range between the minimum and the maximum load observed in a certain deployment environment.
2. The system level evaluations provide energy consumption and other performance metrics (e.g. throughput, QoS) for each small-scale deployment environment and a certain traffic load.
3. Given the daily traffic profile of a certain deployment environment, the power consumption over a day is generated by weighted summing of the short-term evaluations.
4. Finally, the mix of deployment environments that quantify the area covered by cities, suburbs, highways and villages, yield the global set of the large-scale system energy consumption.

The EARTH E^3F has found application in the work of ETSI TC EE on defining how to compute "Network Energy Efficiency" [9]. Also the E^3F is already well adopted by the scientific community (e.g. in the Green Touch initiative [10]).

3.1 Small-Scale Short-Term System-Level Evaluations

System level simulations, requiring a lot of computation resources, are not feasible on the global scale and can only be executed for individual scenarios ("snapshots"). Further, studying snapshots, the E^3F enables to identify the most critical contributions to the global network and to study the best improvement strategy for each scenario individually.

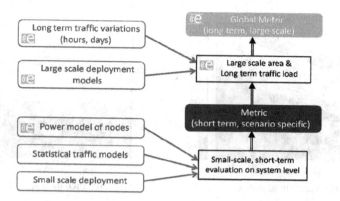

Fig. 4. EARTH Energy Efficiency Evaluation Framework (E^{3}F)

Statistical traffic models (e.g. FTP file download or voice over IP calls), as well as specific small-scale deployment scenarios (e.g. urban macrocell consisting of 57 hexagonal cells with uniformly distributed users), constitute small-scale short-term system-level evaluations (bottom block in Fig.4). These evaluations are carried out by a system-level simulation platform, augmented by a model capturing the BS power consumption.

3.2 Power Model

The BS power model constitutes the interface between the component and system levels, which allows the quantification of how energy savings on specific components enhance the energy efficiency at the network level. The characteristics of the components largely depend on the BS type, due to constraints in output power, size, and cost. These heterogeneous characteristics mandate a power model that is tailored to a specific BS type.

Fig.5 shows power functions for typical macro and pico base stations (BS). A BS consists of multiple transceivers (TRXs), each of which serves one transmit antenna element. A TRX comprises a power amplifier (PA), a radio frequency (RF) small-signal TRX module, a baseband (BB) engine including a receiver (uplink) and transmitter (downlink) section, a DC-DC power supply, an active cooling (CO) system, and a power supply (PS) for connection to the electrical power grid. In the model the power consumption of the various TRX parts are analysed and combined to the total input power, as illustrated in Fig.5.

Examination of the BS power consumption as a function of its load reveals that mainly the PA scales with the BS load. However, this scaling over signal load largely depends on the BS type. While the power consumption P_{in} is load-dependent for macro BSs, the load dependency of pico BSs is negligible. The reason is that for low power nodes the PA accounts for less than 30% of the overall power consumption, whereas for macro BSs the PA power consumption amounts to 55–60% of the total. Other components hardly scale with the load in contemporary implementations.

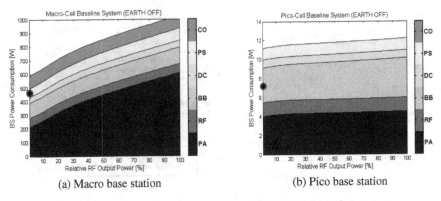

(a) Macro base station   (b) Pico base station

Fig. 5. Base station power model (State of the Art)

The power model has been published both in high level [8] and in detail [11] and has found widespread use in the literature of energy efficiency calculations. Furthermore it has been introduced into 3GPP standardization [12].

3.3 Traffic Model

The E^3F methodology captures the traffic demand by modelling the subscriber density, the data rates of their devices and their daily activity patterns. The traffic model is based on the UMTS Forum's mobile traffic forecast [13].

The model considers different deployment types: dense urban, urban, rural and suburban areas. The basic parameters of the model are depicted in Fig.6. In Europe, these constitute about half the total area and their population densities are such that highly populated areas only cover a few percent of Europe. More than half of the area is so sparsely populated that there basically is no economic case for LTE deployment. These areas are neglected in the model.

The expected traffic volume per subscriber is increasingly dominated by mobile broadband subscribers. Essentially, the traffic model represents a range equivalent of continuous heavy usage of high-definition video streaming with display resolutions of 1280×720 pixels (720p HD) and "light" usage of intensive web browsing. Due to the diminishing share of voice traffic, voice subscribers are not included in our model.

The resulting traffic demand in dense urban areas at peak hours yields between 83 Mb/s/km^2 for 20% heavy users and 276 Mb/s/km^2 for 100% heavy users. For urban and rural deployments the traffic demand is computed using up to 7 times lower activity levels and up to 30 times lower population density. Note that usually several operators share the traffic so that the range of traffic demand scenarios to be used in the small scale system level simulations spans 0.1-100 Mbps/km^2.

Fig.6(c) shows potential energy saving resulting from traffic adaptive energy consumption, i.e., serving lower traffic should require lower energy.

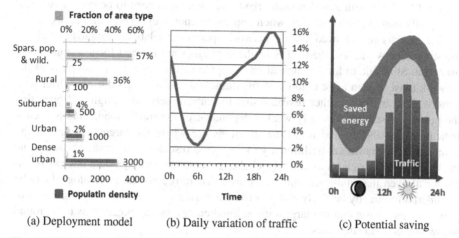

(a) Deployment model (b) Daily variation of traffic (c) Potential saving

Fig. 6. E3F traffic model parameters: *population density, fraction of area types, daily variation of traffic* and potential savings resulting from traffic adaptive energy consumption

3.4   Metrics

Different energy intensity metrics provide dissimilar perspectives on the energy consumption. For expressing the energy saving in access networks the power per area unit metric, in [W/m^2], is the primary choice by EARTH. The energy per bit metric, in [J/bit], and the power per subscriber metric, in [W/sub], make up useful complementary metrics. Whereas the power per area unit metric focuses on the total energy consumption and the saving potential at a given traffic scenario, the energy per bit metric provides a figure on the bit delivery energy efficiency and is useful rather for comparing scenarios with long-term exponential traffic growth. The power per subscriber metric is easily observed in real networks, and offers stability over long time periods, which makes it a suitable candidate for energy consumption measurement in real networks.

3.5   Application of E^{3}F: Where Is the Energy Saving Potential?

One of the first activities in the project was to carry out a situation analysis, i.e., to assess the energy efficiency of a typical mobile broadband network and thereby identify the most important improvement areas to focus on. The purpose of this analysis was to answer questions such as where and when energy is consumed in a typical radio access network. For this, the E^{3}F was used to analyse the power consumption of a European LTE reference network, operating at 2 GHz.

The obtained results reveal that the energy intensity in urban areas is nearly 10 times higher than for rural areas, due to the higher density of base stations. However, the aggregation of E^{3}F reveals a roughly equal impact of rural and urban areas on the total energy consumption because rural areas are by far dominating area wise, c.f. Fig.6(a). This indicates that both urban and rural areas need to be considered, and are equally important to consider, when improving energy efficiency of a network.

The analysis also showed that the network operates at relatively low load levels. In the studied network, less than 10 % of the subframes are utilized for transmission of user data. Still, due to local temporal and geographical variations certain parts of the network must serve a large number of simultaneously active users during shorter time periods. The analysis further revealed that for current network design and operation the power consumption is only weakly dependent of the traffic load. This is a clear indication that the no and low load situations are where the largest energy saving potential is. Furthermore, traditionally radio access research both in the academy and the industry have been focused on the challenge to achieve as high data rates as possible for a given maximum transmission power. Therefore current technologies can be considered to already be fairly energy efficient during transmission. This further supports the conclusion that the largest unexplored energy saving potential is to be found in low and no load situations.

The potential of the non-transmitting scenario depends strongly on the considered time scale. Considering a traditional O&M time scales of 15 minutes there may not be many periods, if any, without any transmissions at all. However, LTE scheduling decisions are made per ms, i.e. per every LTE subframe; when addressing this time scale instead, the possibility for idle subframes becomes considerable, even in fairly loaded cells, something that was seen in the analysis in [8].

4   Hardware Solutions and Radio Interface Techniques

4.1   Hardware Solutions

Several hardware solutions have been defined as energy efficiency enabling techniques for base station components. Adaptability to signal level or traffic load is the key approach for energy efficient operation of base stations. This means that hardware or software solutions can decide and adjust their configuration following the traffic load variation in order to minimize the power consumption. New power-saving features take benefit by the non-uniform load distribution over the day and the short-term signal characteristics.

Investigating the base stations radio equipment aspects, a distinction is done between components for macro-cell and small-cell base stations due to the different origins and their relative weight of power consumption, c.f. Section 3.2.

The energy adaptive transmit path, defined for macro-cell base station, integrates several sub-components (see Fig.7) enabling the component deactivation and adjustment of their operating points in medium and low load situations. The digital signal processing unit (DSPU) represents the digital transceiver part and controls the energy adaptation of the other analogue transmitter components. The conversion module allows the deactivation of some of its components, controlled by the DSPU, for minimizing the power consumption when no signal is transmitted. The highest amount of power saving is achieved by the adaptive power amplifier which allows the adaptation and deactivation of power amplifier stages in correlation with the signal level. This is supported by the adaptive power supply by assuring the reconfiguration of supply voltages.

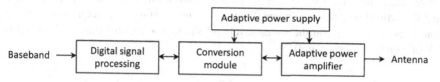

Fig. 7. Block diagram of a transmit system for macro-cell base stations

The component adaptation is strongly correlated to the signal level variation, synchronized with the LTE signal pattern. The power performance of the transmit system is defined by power characteristics showing the consumed power related to the signal load, the instantaneous level of the transmitted signal related to the maximum RF output power defined for transmission. The expected benefit is determined by comparing these characteristics with a state-of-the-art characteristic, which does not consider the proposed concepts. Measured power characteristics of the transmitter are presented in Fig.8, plotted against signal load.

Eight different operating points (OP) show a power reduction of up to 23% at low signal level, while the deactivation of components (CD) provides 55% instantaneous power savings, always compared to OP1 considered as state-of-the-art reference. The determined deactivation and reactivation transition times of 3 μs respectively 10 μs are short enough to allow for applying the CD feature in time slots of 2 or 3 successive LTE symbols.

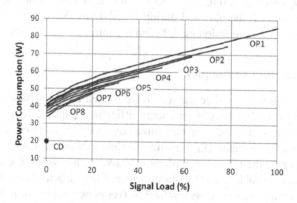

Fig. 8. Power consumption of a transmit system with 20 W of max. average output power

Solutions for small-cell base stations to optimize the energy efficiency or to support power management are included in all sub-components, from baseband engine to antenna interface by means of energy efficient and/or energy adaptive solutions.

Flexible energy aware baseband signal processing algorithms are mainly beneficial in up-link at low signal loads and offer an overall power reduction of about 13% of traffic load dependent improvement. For an adaptive conversion module, flexibility of different building blocks has been introduced and lead to a traffic load dependent power efficiency improvement of 30% on average through SiNAD (signal-to-noise-and-distortion) adaptation and time/frequency duty-cycling. The reduction of power consumption depends on the signal level and shows maximum values of 58% below 5% of signal load (see Fig.9).

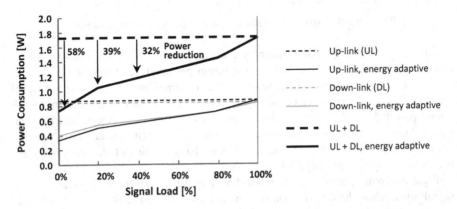

Fig. 9. Power consumption of a dual-antenna pico-cell base-station conversion module

The energy adaptive power amplifier implements the operating point adjustment and component deactivation features similar to the power amplifier of the macro-cell base station. It allow power reductions up to 55% at low signal load while up to 80% efficiency improvement can be obtained during deactivation. Such a component can be easily connected to the conversion module and is controlled via a simple interface.

4.2   Radio Interface Techniques

Radio interface techniques utilize the features provided by the hardware solutions in order to save energy. The benefit on energy efficiency improvement due to energy adaptive component features can be maximized by applying interface solutions acting in time and frequency domain. **Duty-cycling in time** groups the transmitted data over time, by maximizing the time-slots without effective transmission. It exploits the energy saving potential of hardware features which allow deactivating components in time slots of no transmission. **Duty-cycling in frequency** targets to reduce the spectral occupation and the resource elements and thus reduce the power of the transmitted signal. It exploits the energy saving potential of hardware features which adapt their operation for maximum energy efficiency to the level of transmitted signals.

Duty-cycling in time combined with deactivation of components enables discontinues transmission in time domain, called **cell DTX**. It can be realized in some different versions:

- **Micro DTX** is the most straight-forward version. It exploits component deactivation during empty symbols in between transmission of cell-specific reference symbols (CRS) in the current LTE standard.
- **MBSFN-based DTX** is also possible within the current LTE standard. It builds on dynamic allocation of MBSFN (multicast broadcast single frequency network) subframes when possible. The energy saving potential is higher compared to micro DTX as MBSFN subframes show longer time intervals of no signal transmission.
- **Short DTX** assumes that no CRSs are transmitted, something that is not supported by current standards but discussed for future releases. The energy efficiency potential is higher compared to the previously mentioned methods, as deactivation can be performed during several successive sub-frames of no transmission.
- **Long DTX**: Exploits component deactivation during time periods of 10ms or longer. It provides the highest energy efficiency potential in situations of low average traffic load.

Duty-cycling in frequency is applied in combination with the adaptation of component operation mode to the signal level, exploiting the energy efficiency potential at low and medium traffic load situations:

- **Bandwidth Adaptation (BW)** is based on the adjustment of the bandwidth to the required traffic load. Depending on traffic load the bandwidth can be stepwise downscaled so that lower numbers of physical resource blocks (PRBs) are allocated. Also less reference signals have to be sent.
- **Capacity Adaptation (CAP)** is a method, which does not change the maximum used bandwidth and the number of reference signals. An adaptation to lower load is performed by scheduling only a part of the subcarriers, i.e. limiting the number of scheduled PRBs.

Fig.10 illustrates the differences between BW Adaptation, CAP Adaptation, and Micro DTX and how they utilize the time and frequency radio resources.

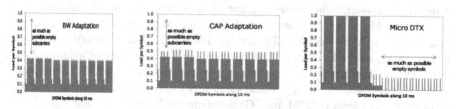

Fig. 10. Illustration of BW Adaptation, CAP adaptation, and Micro DTX

MIMO (Multiple Input Multiple Output), where several antennas are employed at transmitters and receivers, is a natural part of today's wireless systems, e.g. LTE. It is applied for maximized spectral efficiency, but leads to an energy efficiency penalty especially in low load situations. Hence, in certain situations it is beneficial from an energy efficiency point of view to down-scale to single-antenna transmission, as illustrated in Fig.11. **Antenna Muting** refers to fast deactivation of some antennas and the related transceiver components in situations of reduced traffic load. As traffic load varies quickly in a mobile broadband network, the optimization timescale of antenna muting must be in the range of milliseconds to prove beneficial. Luckily this lies within the limits of what the EARTH hardware can do. With this approach, base stations designed for highest throughput can be operated in energy efficient way also when the traffic load drops.

The energy efficient use of **beamforming** techniques, in which an advanced antenna is utilized to direct the transmitted signal in a narrow direction, has also been analysed by EARTH. Slow beamforming based on reconfigurable antennas, exploits medium/long term variations of traffic in order to save energy. Fast beamforming, on the contrary, is immediately following the traffic distribution and can therefore potentially save more energy. Slow beamforming based on reconfigurable antennas is also an enabler for certain network management solutions as used for Integrated Solutions.

5   Network Level Solutions

5.1   Network Deployment Recommendations

EARTH has investigated optimal cell sizes. The surprising results are somewhat counterintuitive and contradict statements found in the literature, where it often is assumed that the lower transmit power of small cells will result in smaller power consumption of the networks. However, EARTH has shown that with realistic power models reflecting state of the art of base station hardware (see Fig.5) smaller cell sizes increase the total power consumption. Therefore, traditional macro network planning, where the distance between base stations (BSs) is adjusted to the maximum inter-site distance (ISD) that provides the requested system performance and capacity, is cost efficient and also energy efficient at the same time.

For areas with ultra-high traffic demand in city hotspots, EARTH also investigated heterogeneous deployments of large macros with an underlay of small cells (heterogeneous networks). It turned out that for such localized high traffic demand, heterogeneous deployments are more efficient than a densification of the macro cell deployment. Moreover, heterogeneous deployments with femto cells are especially beneficial for indoor solutions (13% saving). The results clearly showed that for such heterogeneous networks it is key that the macro cells can turn the offloading of their traffic into reduced energy consumption, e.g. by using adaptive EARTH BS hardware.

EARTH also studied the in practical cases very relevant scenario where operator's build on existing legacy (GSM and 3G) deployments. It turned out that a good strategy is that legacy systems will mainly provide the coverage and low-traffic demanding services in a multi-radio access technology (multi-RAT) scenario, while LTE will serve the increased capacity needs. This fact is in line with the energy consumption optimization, so the multi-RAT networks can be efficiently utilized in heterogeneous networks, as well. As a matter of fact, reality is complex so it was also identified that adopting more energy efficient RATs should be carefully balanced with the constraints coming from the forecast of capacity demand, terminal capabilities, coverage, emission limits, etc. As a relevant energy saving enabler it was estimated that site co-location could result in reduction in power consumption up to around 5% due to better cooling efficiency.

Relaying, the well-known technique often used in many wireless technologies to improve data transmission at cell-edge or to provide coverage in new areas, has also energy saving merits in certain network scenarios. Relays have the potential to be energy efficient because they benefit from shorter transmission hops and from the additional receive or transmit diversity. So with efficient future relay hardware, installation of new relay nodes over a macro-only network will be more energy efficient than the deployment of additional macro nodes to serve increasing traffic demands. From the transmission point of view, several relaying techniques have been compared, and results showed that two-hop half-duplex relaying with hybrid DF/CF forwarding provides considerable gains in large macro cells. This hybrid technique is, however, not supported by current standard releases. Rooftop relays for indoor users can provide energy saving compared to macro indoor coverage.

Beyond the above described techniques focusing on densifying the network, coordination of or cooperation between BSs have been investigated as alternative solutions to cope with increased traffic by utilizing better the available bandwidth of the system. We have found that uplink CoMP is more energy efficient than non-cooperative system for cell edge communication and small cell deployment. Using more than three BSs for cooperation is unlikely to be beneficial and energy efficiency can mainly be achieved via improvement in spectral efficiency as a result of macro-diversity. The most effective technology for backhaul is PON (Passive Optical Network) for today's network and AON (Active Optical Network) is a good candidate for future networks, where bandwidth requirement per BS is getting closer to Gbps.

5.2   Network and Radio Resource Management

The strong requirements on low latency and high system throughput result in that resources on average are not fully utilized and networks will keep using only a small fraction of their capacity [8] [14] (see Fig.6 for illustration). Therefore a key lever to obtain high savings of energy is to dynamically adapt by management the network configuration, e.g., by dynamically reducing the number of active network elements to follow adaptively the daily variation of the traffic. There is a multifold of ways to achieve such network reconfigurability for energy efficiency investigated in EARTH (see Fig.11 for illustration).

Here are some remarkable results. In urban networks, adaptive (de)sectorization of base stations can provide 30-60% energy saving without considerable impact on coverage and cell edge user throughput. Furthermore, in case of dense BS deployment, not only sectors but complete BSs can be switched off in low traffic hours providing 15-20% energy saving in single layer networks and 20-25% in vehicular scenarios. Heterogeneous networks (Hetnets) are the target of network modernization especially in densely populated urban environments as also discussed in Section 5.1. We have found that the idea of adaptive cell on/off in heterogeneous networks (even in multi-RAT environment) can provide 35-40% energy saving meanwhile improving the user experience especially in indoor scenarios and in the uplink direction.

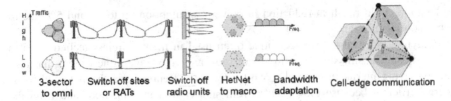

Fig. 11. Base station cooperation and traffic adaptive network reconfiguration for adaptation to traffic variation

Going further below the above timescales during the analysis of mobile systems, the goal of traditional RRM techniques should be rephrased to secure the minimal energy consumption when serving a given traffic demand with special focus on low traffic situations. RRM can support sleep modes and utilize all dimensions of RRM by finding balance between time, frequency and radiated power.

6   Integrated Solutions

EARTH has developed a number of different solutions for improving energy efficiency. They are ranging from base station and antenna hardware improvements, over radio interface techniques, up to solutions acting on the network level such as network management and scheduling. The solutions are developed for the 3GPP Long Term Evolution (LTE) radio technology, also known as 4G. However, some of them are general in their nature and can also be applied to other radio standards. Many of the improvements are pure implementation that can be achieved within the current standard releases, while others may need additional standard support in order to prove beneficial.

Fig.12 provides a high level overview of the relation between the different solutions. As can be seen there is an enable/utilize relation between them. At the bottom are the hardware solutions that provide certain features. The radio interface techniques in the middle level utilize these features. Finally, the network level solutions on top make use of the different radio interface techniques.

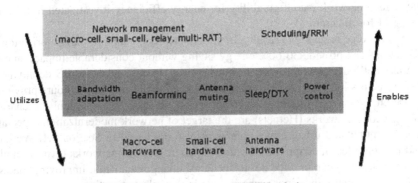

Fig. 12. Relations between EARTH solutions

It is important to realize that the collection of solutions developed and studied in EARTH should be seen as a toolbox, and not "the" solution that should be implemented everywhere. For example, one individual solution may provide good gain in dense urban scenarios but not be attractive for the rural case. Other solutions may be suited in busy hour but detrimental during the night. Therefore, in a network, energy saving solutions should be implemented selectively.

In order to keep analysis and optimization of an entire network tractable, it is practical to consider the system to operate on different time scales, where key parameters of the network can be altered and corresponding characteristics can be changed. Typically, those changes happen on the orders of weeks & days, hours & minutes, and seconds & milliseconds and energy saving solutions developed within EARTH fall into the corresponding categories Deployment & Hardware, Network Management, and Radio Resource Allocation.

Both energy efficiency as well as energy consumption of a wireless network is governed by the strategies chosen on each time scale as depicted in Fig.13. In this regard, deployment strategies determine on the long range the number and types of equipment that are potentially active in the network. Network management techniques adapt to the daily variations of traffic and set the average activity levels of the equipment. Radio resource allocation techniques adapt network operation to variations in the channel quality as well as to small time scale variations in the traffic, in particular to idle periods of only seconds or milliseconds.

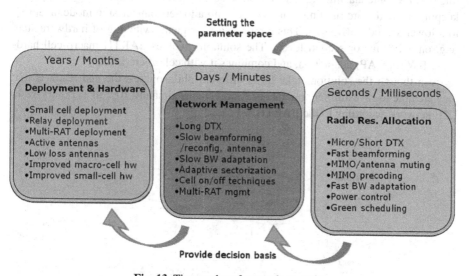

Fig. 13. Time scales of network operation

In the following, we denote by integrated solution a collection of three strategies in the area of deployment, network management, and radio resource allocation, where a strategy refers to the collection of algorithms or techniques that govern the network's characteristic behaviour on a time scale. In particular, a strategy may comprise one or more individual solutions.

As a matter of fact, not all strategies that could be adopted on different time scales are compatible in the sense that their individual improvements in energy efficiency or energy consumption directly accumulate. As a very simple example, note that any equipment can only be sent to sleep mode once, i.e., the savings obtained from a micro sleep technique during longer idle periods can obviously not be harnessed if deep sleep mode is already activated on network management level. In general, strategies on a slower time scale define or set the parameter space and degrees of freedom for strategies on the faster scale: The deployment sets the scene for network management, whose decisions then define the degrees of freedom for resource allocation in individual cells. On the other hand, the average performance of strategies on the faster time scale is used as input or decision basis for strategies on slower time scales as depicted in Fig.13.

Based on extensive work in the project, a number of integrated solutions are defined in [15]. We will here briefly present two of them. Both solutions involve hardware solutions, radio interface techniques, as well as network level solutions. The main difference between these integrated solutions is the philosophies "deactivation" versus "adapting". The first one is deactivating sectors, antennas and timeslots when traffic can be served with less equipment running. With a very agile hardware (on PRB or OFDM symbol level) this can handle bursty traffic like file download always with full peak rate. The solution hence combines EARTH macro-cell hardware, cell micro DTX, antenna muting, and adaptive sectorization. The second philosophy is keeping the hardware running, but switches into a lower transmission mode, adapting to a lower served traffic rate. This requires less frequent switching of hardware state (e.g. on a 100 ms or second level). The solution involves EARTH macro-cell hardware, BW (or CAP) adaptation, and combines it with cell micro DTX.

Even though the solutions take these different philosophies, the end result is that they are able to save similar amounts of energy, approximately 70% in a country-wide LTE network according to the EARTH E^3F, see Fig.14.

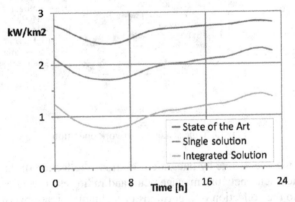

Fig. 14. Example energy saving over the day with an integrated solution

7   Disruptive Approaches Beyond Today's Networks

Looking further ahead in time and beyond today's existing system standards and typical deployments, there are several promising design options and technology solutions that may enable enhanced energy efficiency in future mobile radio systems. The conclusion is that future systems / radio interfaces (beyond ~2020) should be designed to minimize idle mode transmissions such as signalling, reference signals, etc. In particular, a concept where transmissions of data and system information are logically decoupled from each other (see Fig.15), can open the possibilities to more efficient sleep modes by eliminating the high signalling overhead (especially in low load) and provide 85-90% energy saving potential compared to today's systems.

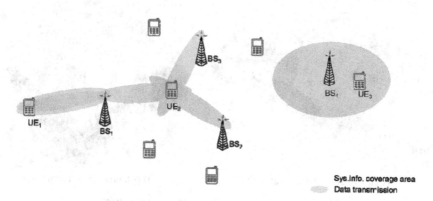

Fig. 15. Decoupling data and system information

8   Validation of Results

The EARTH project has realized several solutions for experimental evaluation at network deployment and management level as well as on hardware and radio interface level to demonstrate the feasibility and the proof of concepts of some key solutions in the EARTH concept. The solutions have been integrated in an operator's test plant or in hardware prototyping platforms and several measurement campaigns have been carried out in order to validate the solutions under realistic operation conditions.

Here we will briefly present these activities, while the details of the validation scenarios, setups and validation test results are found in [16].

8.1   Validation of Hardware Concepts by Transceiver Prototypes

The novel hardware solutions developed by EARTH are key enablers for many of the other EARTH concepts for energy efficient mobile systems. These hardware solutions have been realized for macro-cell and pico-cell transceivers and have been evaluated by measurements. Examples of these prototypes are shown in Fig.16. The obtained power characteristics (see Section 4.1) delivered the instantaneous behaviour for different signal levels and allowed the validation of the base station power models used in the project for system level simulations. By means of realistic LTE signals, the dynamic performance of the hardware components could be studied. The transition times during the deactivation of different components with maximum 10μs for high power amplifiers and much lower for components operating at lower power level, demonstrated that component deactivation can be applied for LTE signals even in short time slots of 2 or 3 successive symbols. This has been validated even with regard to the spectral signal performance by a successful transmission of LTE signals when operating the component adaptation or deactivation features.

    (a) Adaptive small signal transceiver   (b) Adaptive power amplifier

Fig. 16. Pico-cell transceiver prototype components

8.2   Validation of Network Level Solutions in an Operator Test Plant

One of the key solutions of radio access network management proposed by the EARTH project is the possibility to switch a cell on and off in order to adapt the network configuration to traffic demand. Therefore it was identified as important to validate and demonstrate the feasibility to do this. The cell on/off scheme is mainly based on a network management software tool designed and developed by EARTH to reduce the network power consumption at all the levels of traffic loads, with a proper focus on low traffic loads. Its main objective is to reduce the power consumption, on the basis of the number of users registered and attached inside an area of radio coverage and of the corresponding traffic demands, by switching off and on a single cell. Energy savings are possible by redistribution of the users over the cells of a base station and by enabling to switch off cells that are not serving users. The cell on/off scheme has been implemented and validated by setting up in Telecom Italia test plant a proper test scenario and by performing real measurements with the cell on/off scheme in operation.

    The experimental study carried out has shown that it is feasible to implement such a scheme on a commercial base station, and that energy savings indeed are possible.

The experimental studies carried out have shown that already the application of a specific EARTH network management solution in a network made up by commercial base station allows for daily savings in the order of 15%. This is very well in line with the savings predicted by simulations and confirms that integrating such solution with the EARTH hardware and the other EARTH solutions has really the potential to provide the >50% savings as predicted by simulations (see Section 6).

9 Summary and Conclusion

The EARTH project had the ambition to pioneer the research on sustainability and energy efficiency of mobile broadband. Indicators that EARTH was successful in this are listed in the following bullet points:

- EARTH developed a methodology, E^3F, for assessment of RAN energy consumption and energy efficiency. The methodology has been adopted also outside the project in other research initiatives and provides foundations in standardization towards characterizing network energy efficiency, e.g., in ETSI Eco-environmental Product Standards.
- EARTH developed key solutions for improved energy efficiency of such infrastructure. It found ways to integrate hardware, deployment and management solutions efficiently into an Integrated Solution that allows decreasing energy consumption by more than 50%.
- EARTH implemented key constituents of its solutions in hardware and software prototypes, illustrating the feasibility and proving validity of the developed novel solutions and of their foreseen savings in an operator's testbed under realistic operation conditions. So EARTH ensured that its theoretical savings will be also practical savings.
- EARTH analysed for the first time the impact of Future Internet on sustainability and energy demands of mobile communications infrastructure. It showed that the EARTH Integrated Solution allows avoiding an increase of CO_2e emissions and energy demands whilst expanding the mobile infrastructure to satisfy the future traffic demands. EARTH results are therefore pivotal for a sustainable and environment friendly growth of mobile broadband communications as needed to bridge the digital divide and allowing for smart growth enabled by mobile infrastructure.

The EARTH project was committed to have a high impact. Fig.17 depicts how the EARTH results bring about impact in the different areas.

Furthermore, EARTH also had impact in standards and in the scientific community as well as among the general public. For example, the EARTH white paper "Challenges and Enabling Technologies for Energy Aware Mobile Radio Networks" published in IEEE communication Magazine [17] was in the top ten list of papers downloaded in November 2010 [18]. EARTH also was awarded the 4th Future Internet Award at the Aalborg's edition of FIA in 2012 [19], for its enabling contributions to sustainable and environment friendly growth of mobile broadband infrastructure, bridging the digital divide and supporting smart growth. The European Commission

Vice President Neelie Kroes commented: "The ICT sector is growing but its carbon footprint should not follow. I congratulate the partners of the EARTH project who have found ways to deliver the services we need while reducing CO_2 emissions and cutting down on energy bills." [20].

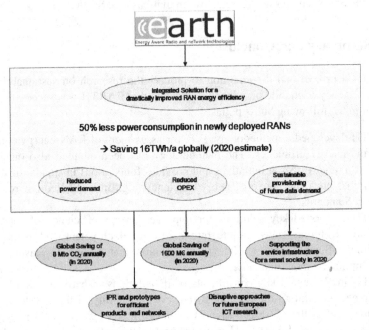

Fig. 17. EARTH results and the resulting savings bring about their socio-economic impact

For further information and details on EARTH, we refer to the comprehensive public website (**https://www.ict-earth.eu/**) which contains all relevant information about the project, such as the project vision and objectives, the relation of the project to the funding program and other projects in the same domain and the EARTH consortium details. Also the public deliverables of the consortium are available for download at this site.

Acknowledgements. The research leading to these results has received funding from the European Community's Seventh Framework Programme FP7/2007-2013 under grant agreement n° 247733 – project EARTH.

The authors would like to thank all the EARTH partners for the fruitful joint work leading to the results presented in this chapter.

References

1. http://www.ict-earth.eu
2. The Europe 2020 strategy, http://ec.europa.eu/europe2020/europe-2020-in-a-nutshell/priorities/index_en.html
3. SMART2020 report with respect to footprint of mobile networks. Technical report, GeSI - Global e-Sustainability Initiative, http://www.gesi.org/Reports Publications/Smart2020/tabid/192/Default.aspx
4. EU Commissioner Calls on ICT Industry to Reduce Its Carbon Footprint by 20% as Early as 2015. Press release, MEMO/09/140 (2009)
5. Fehske, A., Fettweis, G., Malmodin, J., Biczók, G.: The Global Footprint of Mobile Communications: The Ecological and Economic Perspective. IEEE Communications Magazine 49(8), 55–62 (2011)
6. Energy Efficiency of Wireless Access Network Equipment. Technical specification, ETSI Environmental Engineering (EE), ETSI TS 102 706 V1.2.1 (2011), http://www.etsi.org/deliver/etsi_ts/102700_102799/102706/
7. An Energy Efficiency Benchmarking Service for Mobile Network Operators. Technical report, GSMA (2011), http://www.gsmworld.com/mee
8. Auer, G., Vito, G., Desset, C., Gódor, I., Skillermark, P., Olsson, M., Imran, M.A., Sabella, D., Gonzalez, M.J., Blume, O., Fehske, A.: How much Energy is needed to run a Wireless Network? IEEE Wireless Communications 18(5), 40–49 (2011)
9. Environmental Engineering (EE); Principles for Mobile Network level energy efficiency. Technical report, ETSI TR103117
10. Green Touch Initiative, Mobile Communications Working Group, http://www.green touch.org/index.php?page=mobile-communications-working-group
11. Desset, C., Debaillie, B., Giannini, V., Fehske, A., Auer, G., Holtkamp, H., Wajda, W., Sabella, D., Richter, F., Gonzalez, M.J., Klessig, H., Gódor, I., Olsson, M., Imran, M.A., Ambrosy, A., Blume, O.: Flexible power modelling of LTE base stations. In: IEEE WCNC 2012, Paris, pp. 2858–2862 (2012)
12. Base station power model. Technical report, 3GPP TSG-RAN WG1 #67, R1-114336, DOCOMO, Ericsson, Alcatel-Lucent, Telecom Italia
13. http://www.umts-forum.org
14. Mobile internet phenomena report. Technical report, Sandvine (2010), http://www.sandvine.com/downloads/documents/2010%20Global%20 Internet%20Phenomena%20Report.pdf
15. Olsson, M. (ed.): Deliverable 6.4: Final Integrated Concept. Technical report, INFSO-ICT-247733 EARTH (Energy Aware Radio and NeTworkTecHnologies) (2012)
16. Tomaselli, W. (ed.): Deliverable 5.3: Report on Validation. Technical report INFSO-ICT-247733 EARTH (Energy Aware Radio and NeTworkTecHnologies) (2012)
17. Correia, L., Zeller, D., Blume, O., Ferling, D., Jading, Y., Gódor, I., Auer, G., Van Der Perre, L.: Challenges and Enabling Technologies for Energy Aware Mobile Radio Networks. IEEE Communications Magazine 48(11), 66–72 (2010)
18. http://www.comsoc.org/topten/november-2010-top-ten
19. Earth Project Wins Aalborg Future Internet Competition (May 2012), http://www.cefims.eu/2012/05/earth-project-wins-aalborg-future-internet-competition/
20. Digital Agenda: EU research breakthrough will cut 4G / LTE mobile network energy use in half. Press release, EC, http://europa.eu/rapid/press-release_MEMO-12-327_en.html

An Internet-Based Architecture Supporting Ubiquitous Application User Interfaces

Heiko Desruelle[1], Simon Isenberg[2], Dieter Blomme[1],
Krishna Bangalore[3], and Frank Gielen[1]

[1] Ghent University – iMinds,
Dept. of Infomation Technology – IBCN, Ghent, Belgium
{heiko.desruelle,dieter.blomme,frank.gielen}@intec.ugent.be
[2] BMW Forschung und Technik GmbH, Berlin, Germany
simon.isenberg@bmw.de
[3] Technische Universität München, Garnich, Germany
krishna.bangalore@in.tum.de

Abstract. Maintaining a viable balance between development costs and market coverage has turned out to be a challenging issue when developing mobile software applications. The diversity of devices running third-party developed software applications is rapidly expanding from PC, to mobile, home entertainment systems, and even the automotive industry. With the help of Web technology and the Internet infrastructure, ubiquitous applications have become a reality. Nevertheless, the variety of presentation and interaction modalities still limit the number of targetable devices. In this chapter we present webinos, a multi-device application platform founded on the Future Internet infrastructure. Hereto we describe webinos' model-based user interface framework as a means to support context-aware adaptiveness for applications that are executed in such ubiquitous computing environments.

Keywords: ubiquitous web, model-driven user interfaces, adaptation.

1 Introduction

The diversity of personal computing devices is increasing at an incredible pace. In result, people are often using a multitude of consumer electronic devices that have the ability to run third-party developed applications. Such devices can range from desktop PC, to mobile and tablet devices, to home entertainment and even in-car units. However, the fragmentation of devices and usage contexts makes it for applications particularly difficult to target a broad segment of devices and end-users. From a development perspective, the greatest common denominator amongst the available multi-device approaches is the Web. By adopting the Web as an application platform, applications can be made available whenever and wherever the user wants, regardless of the device type that is being used.

Nevertheless these clear advantages, existing Web application platforms are generally founded on the principles of porting traditional API support and operating system aspects to the Web. The evolution towards large-scale distributed

A. Galis and A. Gavras (Eds.): FIA 2013, LNCS 7858, pp. 272–283, 2013.

service access and sensor usage is often not supported [1]. In result, the true immersive nature of ubiquitous web applications is mostly left behind. To enable developers to set up Web applications and services that fade out the physical boundaries of a device, the webinos platform has been proposed. Webinos is a virtualized application platform that spans across the various Web-enabled devices owned by an end-user. Webinos integrates the capabilities of these devices by seamlessly enabling the distribution of API requests.

In this chapter, we elaborate on the webinos platform's innovation and in particular its ability to dynamically adapt application user interfaces to the current delivery context. The remainder of this chapter is structured as follows. Related work and background on adaptive user interfaces are covered in Section 2. Section 3 provides a high-level introduction to the webinos platform, as well as a more in-depth discussion of its adaptive user interface approach. Section 4 highlights the proposed approach via a use case on dynamic adaptation of an application's navigation structure. Finally, our conclusions and future work are presented in Section 5.

2 Model Based User Interfaces

Model driven engineering (MDE) aims to accommodate with high-variability aspects of software systems. This development methodology is characterized by the separation of concerns, as it embodies a well accepted technique to reduce the engineering complexity of a software system [2]. A vast number of Web engineering approaches incorporate partial support for model-based development (e.g., UWE, WSDM, HERA, WebML, etc.). With a model driven engineering approach, software development is started with an abstract platform independent model (PIM) specification of the system [3]. A transformation model is in turn applied to compile the PIM to a platform-specific model (PSM). The transformation process is at the heart of the methodology's flexibility. For this purpose, MDE can use transformation languages such as the Query-View-Transformation standard (QVT) or the ATLAS Transformation Language (ATL) for specifying model-to-model transition rules [4].

Recent research on model driven engineering has been particularly active in the domain of user interface (UI) engineering. The CAMELEON Reference Framework (CRF) defines an important foundation for this type of approaches [5]. The framework specifies a context-sensitive user interface development process, driven by an intrinsic notion of the current user context, the environment context, as well as the platform context. According to the CRF approach, an application's user interface development consists of multiple levels of abstraction. Starting from an abstract representation of the interface's task and domain model, a PSM of the user interface is subsequently generated by means of a chained model transformations based on contextual knowledge. A number of major UI languages have adopted CRF, e.g., UsiXML [6], and MARIA [7]. Moreover, the World Wide Web Consortium (W3C) charted the Model-Based UI Working Group (MBUI-WG) as part of its Ubiquitous Web Activity (UWA) to investigate the standardization of context-aware user interface authoring [8]. Its goal is to work on standards that enable the authoring of context-aware user interfaces for web applications. The MBUI-WG aims to achieve this type of adaptivity by means of a model driven design approach. In this context, the semantically structured aspects of HTML5 will be used as key delivery platform for the applications' adaptive user interface.

The CAMELEON Reference Framework, more specifically, relies on a model driven approach and structures the development of a user interface into four subsequent levels of abstraction:

- Specification of the task and domain model, defining a user's required activities in order to reach his goals.
- Definition of an abstract user interface (AUI) model. The AUI model defines a platform-independent model (PIM), which expresses the application's interface independently from any interactors or modalities within the delivery context's attributes.
- Definition of a concrete user interface (CUI) model, a platform-specific model (PSM) which generates a more concrete description of the AUI by including specific dependencies and interactor types based on the delivery context.
- Specification of the final user interface (FUI), covering the code that corresponds with the user interface in its runtime environment (e.g., HTML, Java, etc.).

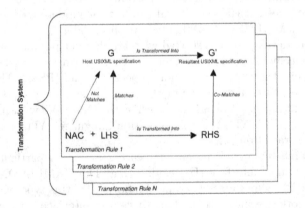

Fig. 1. Model-to-model transformation approach for the adaptation of a model-based user interface [6]

As documented by Schaefer, various approaches can be used to express the adaptation of a model-based user interface [9]. In essence, three types of adaptation approaches can be distinguished: model-to-model transformations, transformations on the XML representation of models, and code transformations. The model-to-model approach relies on the fact that most MBUI models can be designed based on a directed graph structure. In result, adaptations between two models are specified with model mappings by means of graph transformation rules. As depicted in Fig. 1, transformation rules consist of a Left Hand Side (LHS) condition matching the current UI model represented by graph G [6]. To add expressiveness, one or more Negative Application Condition (NAC), which should not match G, can be defined. Based on the matching of these conditions a Right Hand Side (RHS) defines the transformation result by replacing LHS occurrence in G with RHS. This substitution operation results in an adapted UI model represented by graph G'.

Furthermore, for UI models represented with XML, XSLT transformations can be used as a more declarative way to define adaptations [10]. The transformation process takes a XML based document as input together with an XSLT stylesheet module containing the transformation rules. Each transformation rule consists of a matching pattern and an output template. Patterns to be matched in the input XML document are defined by a subset of the XPath language [11]. The output after applying the appropriate transformations can be standard XML, but also other formats such as (X)HTML, XSL-FO, plain text, etc.

3 Multi-Device Adaptive User Interfaces

3.1 The Webinos Platform

To enable application developers to set up services that fade out the physical boundaries of a device, we propose the webinos platform. Webinos defines a federated Web application platform and its runtime components are distributed over the devices, as well as the cloud. Fig. 2 depicts a high-level overview of the platform's structure and deployment. The system's seamless interconnection principle is cornered around the notion of a so called Personal Zone.

The Personal Zone represents a secure overlay network, virtually grouping a user's personal devices and services. To enable external access to and from the devices in this zone, the webinos platform defines a centralized Personal Zone Hub (PZH) component. Each user has his own PZH instance running in the cloud. The PZH is a key element in this architecture, as it contains a centralized repository of all devices and contextual data in the Personal Zone. The PZH keeps track of all services in the zone and provides functionality to enable their discovery and mutual communication. This way, the PZH facilitates cross-device interaction with personal services over the Internet. Moreover, PZHs are federated, allowing applications to easily discover and share data and services residing on other people's devices. Webinos achieves this structure by incorporating two service discovery abstraction mechanisms. On a local level, webinos supports various fine-grained discovery techniques to maximize its capability to detect devices and services (e.g., through multicast DNS, UPnP, Bluetooth discovery, USB discovery, RFID/NFC, etc.). Secondly, on a remote level, the local discovery data are propagated within the Personal Zone and with authorized external PZHs. Based on webinos' aim for flexible Personal Zones in terms of scalability and modifiability, the overlay network is designed in line with the callback

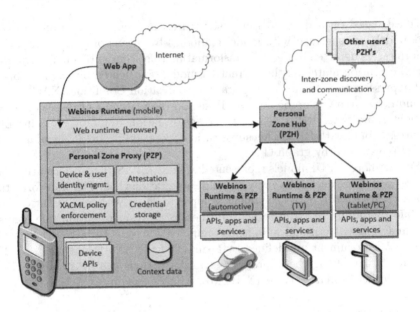

Fig. 2. High-level overview of webinos' ubiquitous application platform

broker system pattern [12]. With this pattern, the availability of locally exposed services is communicated throughout the Personal Zone via a service broker in the PZH. Moreover, the platform's high-level communication infrastructure is founded on a direct handle tactic via JSON-RPC (JavaScript object notation - remote procedure call), which is invoked over HTTP and WebSockets.

On the device-side, a Personal Zone Proxy (PZP) component is deployed. The PZP abstracts the local service discovery and handles the direct communication with the zone's PZH. As all external communication goes through the PZP, this component is responsible for acting as a policy enforcement point and managing the access to the device's exposed resources. In addition, the PZP is a fundamental component in upholding the webinos platform's offline usage support. Although the proposed platform is designed with a strong focus on taking benefit from online usage, all devices in the Personal Zone have access to a locally synchronized subset of the data maintained by the PZH. The PZP can thus temporarily act in place of the PZH in case no reliable Internet connection can be established. This allows users to still operate the basic functionality of their applications even while being offline and unable to access the Internet. Through communication queuing, all data to and from the PZP are again synchronized with the PZH as soon as the device's Internet access gets restored.

The Web Runtime (WRT) represents the last main component in the webinos architecture. The WRT can be considered as the extension of a traditional Web render engine (e.g., WebKit, Mozilla Gecko). The WRT contains all necessary components for running and rendering Web applications designed with standardized Web technologies: a HTML parser, JavaScript engine, CSS processor, rendering engine, etc. Furthermore, the WRT maintains a tight binding with the local PZP. The WRT-PZP binding exposes JavaScript interfaces, allowing the WRT to be much more powerful than traditional browser-based application environments. Through this binding, applications running in the WRT are able to securely interface with local device APIs and services. In addition, the PZP also enables the runtime to connect and synchronize with other devices in the Personal Zone through its binding with the PZH.

3.2   Adaptive User Interface Framework

Within webinos, the process for adapting user interfaces to the active delivery context is regulated by the local PZP. For this particular purpose, the PZP contains an Adaptation Manager component (see Fig. 3). The Adaptation Manager aggregates all available adaptation rules, analyzes them, and feeds them to a Rule Engine for evaluation. In turn, the Rule Engine aims to match the applicability of each rule by comparing its conditions with the context data exposed by the PZP's internal services. Once an applicable rule is identified, the adaptation process is fired by sending its transformation instruction to the Web runtime. Moreover, by applying the RETE algorithm for executing the reasoning within the Rule Engine, the worst case computational complexity of this process remains linear

$$O\left(R \cdot F^C\right),\tag{1}$$

with R the average number of rules, F the number of facts in the knowledgebase that need to be evaluated, and C the average number of conditions in each rule [13].

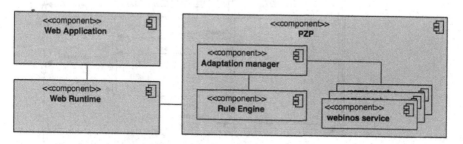

Fig. 3. Component diagram of webinos' UI adaptation framework

In order to accommodate webinos with support for dynamically triggered adaptations based on at runtime contextual changes, the used rule syntax complies with the Event Condition Action (ECA) format. The structure of an ECA rule consists of three main parts.

$$\text{on } [event] \text{ if } [conditions] \text{ do } [action]\tag{2}$$

The event part specifies the system signal or event that triggers the invocation of this particular rule. The conditions part is a logical test that, if evaluated to true, causes the rule to be carried out. Lastly, the action part consists of invocable JavaScript instructions on the resource that needs adaptation. In result, adaptation requirements can be expressed in terms of events or other context changes which might occur during the application's life cycle (see the case study in Section 4 for elaborating examples on adaptation rules).

For each ECA rule, the Adaptation Manager analyzes the rule's trigger event. Based on the event type, it subsequently feeds the rule to a dedicated instance of the Rule Engine, which is registered with the appropriate webinos services for a callback so it can launch the condition evaluation when the event occurs. For rules triggered by the *application.launch* event, the Rule Engine instance is initiated right away. The active instance matches the rules' conditions based on context properties fetched from webinos services such as the Device Status API [14].

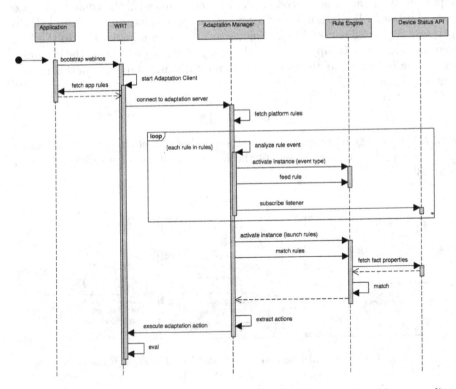

Fig. 4. Sequence diagram for the lookup of applicable UI adaptation rules at application launch

The sequence diagram in Fig. 4 provides a more detailed overview of how the adaptation process is handled. By bootstrapping webinos at the launch of an application, a communication interface is established between the Web runtime environment and the local PZP. This interface allows for the injection of an Adaptation Client component in the WRT. The Adaptation Client executes all the UI adaptation instructions it receives from the PZP's Adaptation Manager. As the Adaptation Client runs within the WRT, it has access to the application's DOM (Document Object Model) [15]. Moreover, this component is thus able to access and adapt the application's content, structure and style via the manipulation of DOM structures and properties.

4 Case Study: Adaptive Navigation Bar

This section elaborates on a case study for using webinos' UI framework to dynamically adapt the presentation of an application's navigation structure. For this adaptation case study, the HTML skeleton code in Listing 1.1 will serve as a sample application. This basic application is semantically enhanced with HTML element attributes to guide the adaptation process. The application skeleton contains a navigation menu component and a number of application specific subviews. As shown in Fig. 5 and Fig. 6, the presentation of this application's navigation component can be optimized based on various parameters such as the device's operating system, input modalities screen size, screen orientation, etc. Taking these contextual characteristics into account is necessary in order to ensure the adaptive usability requirements of a multi-device ubiquitous application, but also, e.g., for meeting existing safety regulations regarding user distraction in-vehicle applications [16].

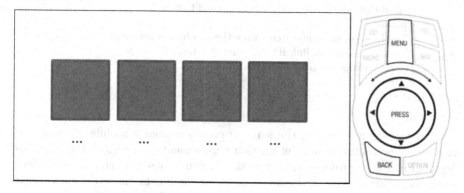

Fig. 5. Application navigation bar adaptation for an in-vehicle infotainment setup

For such an in-vehicle infotainment (IVI) system, adaptation rules can be set to display the application's navigation bar fullscreen (see rule in Listing 1.2). This can be done on application startup (i.e., *application.launch* event trigger combined with an IVI-based system as rule condition). All other UI elements are hidden to further decrease the risk for user distraction. Moreover, based on the specific interaction modalities provided by an IVI system, displaying the application's navigation bar can also be triggered by pressing the MENU button on its controller module. The interaction controller depicted in Fig. 5 is BMW's iDrive controller, which internally maps to the combination of a jog dial and four-way scroller device.

Listing 1.1. Sample HTML application skeleton

```
1   <body>
2       <div class="menu">
3           <!-- list menu items -->
4       </div>
5       <div class="page" id="home">
6           <!-- home screen content -->
7       </div>
8       <div class="page" id="settings">
9           <!-- settings screen content-->
10      </div>
11      ...
12  </body>
```

Listing 1.2. Vehicular adaptation rule

```
1   <rule description="vehicular menu">
2       <event>application.launch</event>
3       <condition>device.type == "ivi"</condition>
4       <action>
5           <!-- spread menu items over the headunit's screen -->
6           <!-- map and link iDrive controller buttons -->
7           <!-- hide all page elements -->
8       </action>
9   </rule>
```

However, when accessing the same application from a mobile or tablet device, other presentation and interaction requirements come into play. The case depicted in Fig. 6 provides an adaptation example based on changes a device's screen orientation (i.e., landscape or portrait mode). In the event of a touchscreen device that is being rotated to landscape mode, adaptation rules are set to transform the navigation bar in a vertically organized list that is moved to the lefthand side of the display. Moreover, on the right side of the screen only one page element is shown. All other page elements can be accessed via its appropriate link in the navigation bar (see rule in Listing 1.3). In case the device is rotated to portrait mode, the navigation bar is reduced to a collapsible UI element located on the top of the screen. Finally, a running multi-device prototype of this case is depicted in Fig. 7.

Listing 1.3. Touch-based adaptation rule

```
1   <rule description="touch−based menu landscape">
2       <event>device.orientationchange</event>
3           <condition>
4               device.inputtype == "touchScreen" &&
5               screen.orientation == "landscape"
6           </condition>
7       <action>
8           <!−− resize menu items to fit the screen's height −−>
9           <!−− move menu to the lefthand side −−>
10          <!−− hide all page elements but the active −−>
11      </action>
12  </rule>
```

Fig. 6. Application navigation bar adaptation for mobile and tablet devices based on screen orientation

Fig. 7. Running multi-device prototype of the application navigation case

5 Conclusion

In this chapter we presented the webinos application platform and its aim to enable immersive ubiquitous software applications through adaptive user interfaces. Webinos does so by leveraging the fundamental cross-platform opportunities offered by the Web as well as the Future Internet infrastructure. With the introduced Personal Zone concept, applications developers are enabled to create software that transcends the executing device's physical boundaries by simultaneously accessing the capabilities of multiple devices. In order to ensure users a comparable and intuitive quality in use throughout all their devices, the presentation and interaction modalities of the applications' user interface can be adapted accordingly. Based on the contextual knowledge available in the webinos Personal Zone, rule-based adaptation decisions can be made as a means to dynamically optimize the applications user interfaces to the executing device's characteristics.

The developed webinos technology aims to influence the Future Internet architecture and its related frameworks. Collaboration has hereto been established with various Future Internet projects such as FI-WARE and FI-CONTENT. Future work for the webinos project includes further exploring the possibility to use the webinos platform as a generic enabler for these initiatives and to seamlessly connect ubiquitous devices on an application level [17].

Acknowledgments. The research leading to these results has received funding from the European Union's Seventh Framework Programme (FP7-ICT-2009-5, Objective 1.2) under grant agreement number 257103 (webinos project). The authors thank all Webinos project partners, as this chapter draws upon their work.

References

1. Desruelle, H., Lyle, J., Isenberg, S., Gielen, F.: On the challenges of building a Web-based ubiquitous application platform. In: 14th ACM International Conference on Ubiquitous Computing, pp. 733–736. ACM, New York (2012)
2. Dijkstra, E.W.: A Discipline of Programming. Prentice Hall, Englewood Cliffs (1976)
3. Moreno, N., Romero, J.R., Vallecillo, A.: An overview of model-driven Web engineering and the MDA. In: Rossi, G., Pastor, O., Schwabe, D., Olsina, L. (eds.) Web Engineering: Modelling and Implementing Web Applications. Human-Computer Interaction Series, pp. 353–382. Springer, London (2008)
4. Koch, N.: Classification of Model Transformation Techniques used in UML-based Web Engineering. IET Software 1(3), 98–111 (2007)
5. Calvary, G., Coutaz, J., Thevenin, D., Limbourg, Q., Bouillon, L., Vanderdonckt, J.: A Unifying Reference Framework for Multi-Target User Interfaces. Interacting with Computers 15, 289–308 (2003)
6. Limbourg, Q., Vanderdonckt, J., Michotte, B., Bouillon, L., López-Jaquero, V.: USIXML: A language supporting multi-path development of user interfaces. In: Bastide, R., Palanque, P., Roth, J. (eds.) EHCI-DSVIS 2004. LNCS, vol. 3425, pp. 200–220. Springer, Heidelberg (2005)
7. Paterno, F., Santoro, C., Spano, L.D.: MARIA: A universal, declarative, multiple abstraction-level language for service-oriented applications in ubiquitous environments. ACM TOCHI 16(4), 19 (2009)
8. Cantera, J.M. (ed.): Model-Based UI XG Final Report. W3C Incubator Group Report (2010), http://www.w3.org/2005/Incubator/model-based-ui/XGR-mbui
9. Schaefer, R.: A Survey on Transformation Tools for Model Based User Interface Development. In: Jacko, J.A. (ed.) HCII 2007, Part I. LNCS, vol. 4550, pp. 1178–1187. Springer, Heidelberg (2007)
10. Kay, M. (ed.): XSL Transformations (XSLT) Version 2.0. W3C Recommendation (2007)
11. Berglund, A., Boag, S., Chamberlin, D., Fernandez, M.F., Kay, M., Robie, J., Simeon, J. (eds.): XML Path Language (XPath) 2.0 (Second Edition). W3C Recommendation (2010)
12. Buschmann, F., Meunier, R., Rohnert, H., Sommerlad, P., Stal, M.: Pattern-oriented software architecture: A system of patterns. John Wiley & Sons, West Sussex (2001)
13. Forgy, F.: On the efficient implementation of production systems. PhD thesis, Carnegie-Mellon University (1979)
14. Webinos Device Status API, http://dev.webinos.org/specifications/new/devicestatus.html
15. Le Hors, A., Le Hegaret, P., Wood, L., Nicol, G., Robie, J., Champion, M., Byrne, S. (eds.): Document Object Model (DOM) Level 3 Core Specification. W3C Recommendation (2004)
16. Faily, S., Lyle, J., Paul, A., Atzeni, A., Blomme, D., Desruelle, H., Bangalore, K.: Requirements sensemaking using concept maps. In: Winckler, M., Forbrig, P., Bernhaupt, R. (eds.) HCSE 2012. LNCS, vol. 7623, pp. 217–232. Springer, Heidelberg (2012)
17. Allott, N.: Collaboration Opportunities: FIWARE and webinos, http://www.webinos.org/blog/2012/11/14/collaboration-opportunities-fiware-and-webinos/

Cooperative Strategies for Power Saving in Multi-standard Wireless Devices

Firooz B. Saghezchi, Muhammad Alam,
Ayman Radwan, and Jonathan Rodriguez

Instituto de Telecomunicações
Campus Universitário de Santiago, 3810-193 Aveiro, Portugal
{firooz,alam,aradwan,jonathan}@av.it.pt
http://www.av.it.pt/4tell/

Abstract. 4G is a promising solution for the future mobile Internet through integrating heterogeneous radio access technologies (RATs) based on the Internet Protocol (IP) where multi-standard wireless devices allow mobile users to experience ubiquitous connectivity by roaming across different networks and connecting through the RAT that best suits their traffic requirements. However, holding multiple active interfaces incurs significant power consumption to the wireless devices. This necessitates investigating disruptive techniques for decreasing the power consumption of the 4G wireless devices. In this paper, we demonstrate how cognitive radio and cooperative communication can be integrated in 4G networks to conduct wireless devices to either perform vertical handover or execute relaying by exploiting their available short range interfaces (e.g., WiMedia, Bluetooth, etc) to reduce their power consumption while still enabling the required QoS. Simulation and experimental results validate that 4G wireless devices can double their battery lifetime by adopting the proposed strategies.

Keywords: 4G, power saving, multi-standard wireless devices, cognitive radio, cooperative strategies, short range relaying, context-aware.

1 Introduction

4G is a new paradigm for cellular architecture that not only supports traditional voice service but also promises broadband and ubiquitous Internet for the future. Unlike previous generations of cellular systems that possess a specific air interface and primarily support voice traffic, 4G is based on Internet Protocol (IP) and aims to bring together the evolving radio access technologies (RATs) to allow mobile users to connect anywhere with better QoS. A 4G user particularly relies on a multi-standard wireless device to stay connected through the heterogeneous radio access network. The device connects through the best interface at any time considering a number of parameters such as the available RATs, user's mobility, traffic type, etc. For instance, if the user wants to make a phone call while travelling with vehicular speed, it can connect through its LTE or WiMax

A. Galis and A. Gavras (Eds.): FIA 2013, LNCS 7858, pp. 284–296, 2013.

interface. On the other hand, if the user is static or experiences nomadic mobility in an indoor scenario such as a coffee shop or a shopping mall and wants to browse a webpage, it can connect through its WiFi interface.

Energy is becoming a critical resource for the emerging multi-standard wireless devices. Holding multiple active interfaces requires higher power consumption for a wireless device that normally relies on a limited battery for power supply. Furthermore, advanced imaging features (e.g., camera, high-definition display, etc) and GPS/Galileo receivers will increase considerably the power demand of 4G wireless devices. On the other hand, mobile battery capacity is finite and the progress of battery technology is very slow, with capacity expected to make little improvement in the near future [1]. As a consequence, there exists a continuously growing gap between the energy consumption of the emerging wireless devices and what can be achieved by the battery technology evolution. Indeed, one could imagine that the future wireless devices may lose their freedom to have "true mobile experience" due to becoming restricted in the proximity of power outlets.

As an attempt to reduce the power consumption of the emerging wireless devices, the European Union (EU) has initiated the C2POWER project [2]. This project introduces a novel approach that exploits the advantages achieved by cognitive radio and cooperative communication to prolong the battery lifetime of multi-standard wireless devices. Cognitive radio and cooperative communication have widely been investigated for efficient spectrum usage and improving the wireless link capacity, respectively. However, research and development to apply these techniques for power saving is still at an early stage.

C2POWER assumes that any wireless device is equipped with two radio interfaces: a long range (LR) interface (e.g., LTE, WiMAX, WiFi, etc) and a short range (SR) interface (e.g., WiMedia, Bluetooth, etc). A wireless device always senses the radio environment and communicates with neighbour devices or networks by exchanging context information. Thanks to this context exchange, wireless devices become aware of their environment (e.g., available networks, channel qualities, nearby wireless devices, their battery levels, etc), so they can react appropriately to reduce their power consumption. To this end, a wireless device either performs vertical handover (VHO) to the RAT demanding the least power consumption or joins a nearby cluster and adopts cooperative relaying using a power efficient SR interface. Specifically, in the later case, nearby wireless devices form an ad-hoc network to be embedded with the infrastructure network. This type of network with mixed nature is known as hybrid ad-hoc network (HANET) or multi-hop cellular network (MCN) in the literature.

In the rest of this paper, we address the C2POWER strategies to reduce the power consumption of multi-standard wireless devices highlighting its contributions and achievements. Section 2 illustrates the scenarios; section 3 presents our architecture for context exchange; section 4 discusses power saving strategies and provides a mathematical model based on coalitional game theory; section 5 discusses the simulation results; finally, section 6 concludes the paper.

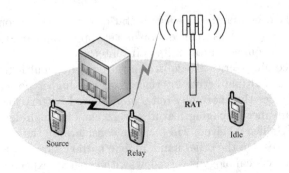

Fig. 1. Scenario 1: A wireless device located in a deep shadowing area relays its traffic through a cooperative SR link. The black link depicts a SR link, while the gray one depicts a LR link.

2   C2POWER Scenarios

C2POWER targets three scenarios for power saving. In this section, we illustrate these scenarios.

2.1   Scenario 1: SR Relaying in Homogeneous RATs

This scenario addresses a hybrid combination of infrastructure architecture and short range ad-hoc network. As illustrated by Fig. 1, some mobile devices located in the proximity of each other decide to form a cooperative cluster, motivated by power saving strategy or economic incentive. Mobile devices in the same cluster can communicate directly with each other using SR technology. Thanks to the spatial proximity and spatial diversity within a group of cooperative mobiles, there is a high potential for power saving. A particular use case of this scenario is a cooperative strategy where one wireless devices sacrifices part of its energy to instantiate the power saving strategy of the cooperative cluster motivated by a pay-off or other incentives based on a business model.

2.2   Scenario 2: VHO in Heterogeneous RATs

This scenario, which is illustrated by Fig. 2, considers that several RATs are available in the location of a multi-standard wireless device. Through this scenario C2POWER investigates strategies and algorithms that assist a system to switch among these interfaces, each with diverse radio characteristics and ranges, to save power. It is pivotal to have efficient handover strategies in place conserving the optimal QoS in addition to reducing the energy consumption. As part of this scenario, C2POWER also considers handover between macro and femtocells. This use case contemplates the specificities of femtocells and handover to/from these cells as well as the improvements that can be achieved by introducing context information (e.g., user location, habits, expected indoor movement, cell coverage, etc).

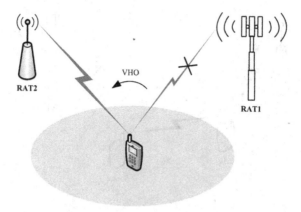

Fig. 2. Scenario 2: A wireless device experiencing bad channel quality to RAT1 performs VHO to RAT2

2.3   Scenario 3: SR Relaying and VHO in Heterogeneous RATs

Scenario 3 is a merger of power saving features from Scenario 1 and Scenario 2, allowing cooperation among heterogeneous RATs. As shown by Fig. 3, the source node is initially connected to RAT1 where it is experiencing bad channel quality and demanding a service (e.g., video streaming) which entails high power consumption when offered by RAT1. Using context-aware capabilities, this node detects a relay node that has access to RAT2 in its SR coverage. This RAT fulfills better the QoS required by the source node and additionally requires less power consumption. Thanks to a low-power SR interface, the source node invites the relay node to establish cooperation. After some negotiation—motivated by a payment or a reputation mechanism—the relay node agrees and a cooperative cluster is established. The relay node then connects to RAT2 and relays to the source node the required traffic over the low-power SR link. The overall power consumption of the cooperative cluster decreases due to this strategy; the amount of power gain depends on the energy efficiency of the cooperative link.

3   Context-Aware Architecture

A number of alternative definitions have been applied to the term *Context* in the literature. For instance, [3] defines context as "any information that can be used to characterize the situation of an entity. An entity is a person, place, or object that is considered relevant to the interaction between the user and the application, including the user and the applications themselves". In [4], *context-aware* is defined as "location identities of nearby people, objects and changes to those objects".

A number of EU projects have explored context-aware aspects, especially focusing on advantages offered by the context information in wired and wireless communication. Examples are MobiLife [5], SPICE [6], and OPUCE [7], C-CAST

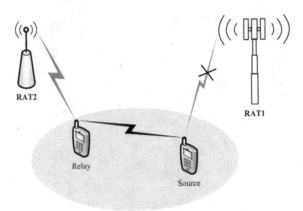

Fig. 3. Scenario 3: A wireless device experiencing bad channel quality to RAT1 performs VHO to RAT2 through a cooperative SR link

[8]. Integration of context aware systems with mobile multimedia delivery technologies are explored in [9]. A detail of the advantages offered by context and context-aware systems is reported in [10]. In [11], the context is divided and structured into mobile and network context: network context is structured into security, polices, coverage and QoS, while mobile terminal context is related to its capabilities, mobility, application in use, energy and user preferences.

Fig. 4 illustrates the proposed context-aware architecture for the context management and utilization in the cognitive engine of the wireless devices. Each device is exposed to the outer world to acquire context information related to other entities (i.e., wireless devices and networks) and feed this information to the context provider. The context provider not only holds the external context but also collects the wireless device's internal context. The context accumulated in the context provider is mostly the raw data which is passed to the context reasoner and filter. The way context provider interacts with the rest of the system depends on whether it is deployed on the network side or on a wireless device. For example, in case of cooperative communication, the context provider receives the data related to nearby wireless devices or available RATs and passes it to the context reasoner. The context reasoner filters, processes, and aggregates the raw data it receives from the context provider and results processed information that is stored in the context repository for future queries. The processed context can also be passed to the context negotiator to exchange with other interested or subscribed wireless devices or networks. Based on publish/subscribe paradigm, the context negotiator gets data via one-time queries to the context repository and to other entities' context negotiators. Thus, context negotiator acts as mediator between two entities (wireless device and network). The processed context information, which is received from the context reasoner, is stored in the database. The context database is then accessed for different purposes via queries. The stored context is useful information to assist wireless devices in decision making while interacting with other entities. The decision engine can access the stored

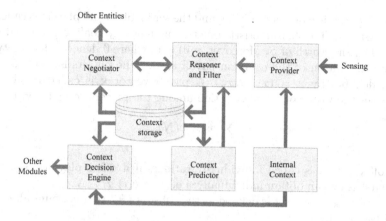

Fig. 4. Context-aware architecture

context and also the internal context to run the decision algorithm. The decisions are based on user preference and the network policies. The outcome of the decision engine can be suggestions for VHO, cooperative SR relaying, etc.

The context predictor provides predictions about future utilization of the context in different cases. Predictions can be made about future battery level for a particular application usage, or it can be related to a wireless device's location after a specific time. The prediction module can be applied to the network side also. For instance, this component can predict location information for disconnected or sleep devices as well as the expected network load in short and medium terms. The context predictor provides this information to the data base through the context reasoner via queries.

4   Power Saving Strategies

Utilizing the context information, a cognitive device evaluates the energy cost of all its alternative links to access the network in terms of Joule/Bit and chooses the one that requires the minimum energy while satisfying the required QoS. For a single-hop link, the cost is evaluated by the ratio of the required transmit power to the achieved data rate (i.e., $c = P_t/R$), and for a two-hop link, it is evaluated as the sum of three terms: the first term is the cost of transmitting through the SR interface for the source; the second term is the cost of receiving through the SR interface for the relay; and the third term is the cost of forwarding through the LR interface for the relay. In the rest of this section, we provide a mathematical model for cooperative SR relaying based on coalitional game theory.

4.1   Coalitional Game Theory

A coalitional game in characteristic function form is defined as $\langle N, v \rangle$ where N and v denote the set of players and the characteristic function, respectively [12].

Any subset of N is called a coalition, and the set involving all players is called the grand coalition. The characteristic function assigns any coalition S a real value $v(S)$, called the worth of S. Moreover, $v(\emptyset) = 0$, where $\emptyset$ denotes the empty set.

Any distribution of the common payoff among the players is called a payoff vector, denoted by $\mathbf{x} = (x_1, ..., x_n)$. A payoff vector $\mathbf{x}$ is called feasible if it distributes the worth of grand coalition among the players completely; i.e.,

$$\sum_{i \in N} x_i = v(N). \tag{1}$$

A payoff vector $\mathbf{x}$ is called individually rational if it offers players more payoff than what they can obtain individually; i.e, $x_i \geq v(i) \; \forall i \in N$.

The pre-imputation set is defined as the subset of $\mathbb{R}^n$ that contains all feasible payoff vectors; i.e.,

$$PI(v) = \left\{ \mathbf{x} \in \mathbb{R}^n \mid \sum_{i \in N} x_i = v(N) \right\}. \tag{2}$$

The imputation set is defined as the subset of $\mathbb{R}^n$ that contains all feasible and individually rational payoff vectors; i.e.,

$$I(v) = \left\{ \mathbf{x} \in \mathbb{R}^n \mid \sum_{i \in N} x_i = v(N) \; and \; x_i \geq v(i), \; \forall i \in N \right\}. \tag{3}$$

Solution of a coalitional game provides a payoff vector that satisfies the stability of the game. Based on different stability criteria, different solution concepts have been introduced in the literature, namely *core*, *Shapley value*, *stable set*, *bargaining set*, and *kernel*. For example, core is defined as the set of payoff vectors that are feasible and cannot be improved upon by any coalition. That is,

$$c(v) = \left\{ \mathbf{x} \in \mathbb{R}^n \mid \sum_{i \in N} x_i = v(N) \; and \; \sum_{i \in S} x_i \geq v(S) \; \forall S \subset N \right\}. \tag{4}$$

4.2 Coalitional Game Model

For any coalition of wireless devices $S \subset N$, we define the characteristic function as the maximum amount of energy saving that the wireless devices in S can obtain by adopting the cooperative SR relaying strategy. To determine the worth of coalitions, let us partition an arbitrary cluster C into two mutually exclusive sets, namely relays and sources; denoted by M and N, respectively. We define a mixed coalition as a subset of C that involves both types of players (relays and sources). For an arbitrary coalition $S \subset N$, if S involves only one player, the worth of coalition is zero since, in such coalitions, the player will find no other player to cooperate with. Generally, if $S \cap M = \emptyset$ or $S \cap N = \emptyset$, the worth of coalition is zero since, in a coalition composed merely of sources (relays), there is no relay (source) to cooperate with and hence there is no opportunity for energy saving. Finally, we determine the worth of a mixed coalition by solving an optimization problem with the objective function of maximizing the energy saving of the coalition subject to the resource constraints. For example, for the case of two-hop relaying, this optimization problem can be expressed as follows:

$$Maximize\ v(S) = \sum_{i \in S} \sum_{\substack{j \in S \\ j \neq i}} x_{ij} v(\{i, j\})$$

Subject to :

$$\sum_{j \in N} x_{ij} \leq 1 \ \forall i = 1, ..., m \qquad (5)$$

$$\sum_{i \in M} x_{ij} \leq 1 \ \forall j = 1, ..., n$$

$$x_{ij} \in \{0, 1\} \ \forall i, j$$

where x_{ij} is a binary decision variable indicating whether relay i should relay source j or not, and $v(\{i, j\})$ is the potential energy saving from cooperation of relay i and source j. There are two constraint inequalities: the first one indicates that any relay can relay at most one source, while the second one indicates that any source can either communicate directly or utilize at most one relay to reach the access point. The latter is resulted from the two-hop constraint, which governs that any cooperative link utilizes at most one intermediate relay node.

Once the characteristic function of the game is determined, we can apply one of the solution concepts such as the core solution defined by (4) to solve the game. Solution of the game indeed provides a fair distribution of the common energy saving among the wireless devices within the cooperative cluster so that every player is satisfied—this way the cooperation evolves. Further discussion on this topic is available in [13].

4.3   Cooperation Enforcement

In a cooperative cluster, the saved energy is nontransferable. That is, only source nodes enjoy power saving, while relays are incurred some extra power consumption for relaying. Consequently, even if the cooperation can reduce the aggregate power consumption of the cluster, a relay will be reluctant to cooperate unless it is assured that any effort will be compensated. Although reciprocal altruism can be adopted by players to settle this problem, it suffers from lack of trust among players, rendering it highly vulnerable to potential free riding attempts from malicious nodes. Therefore, a mechanism should exist to incentivize cooperative players and avert potential threats of the selfish players; otherwise, the cooperation will collapse. There are two main approaches to address this problem, namely *reputation* and *virtual currency*. We apply the latter using a similar approach as in [14] where a virtual central bank (VCB) is adopted to assess the trustworthiness of the players. In this scheme, any wireless device has an energy account in the VCB, with some initial credit, where its efforts are fully recorded

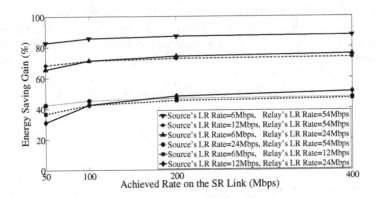

Fig. 5. Energy saving gain from theoretical analysis

and tracked. The VCB rewards cooperative nodes by energy credits, the amount of which is determined by the solution of the game. Moreover, the VCB compensates the relays by rewarding them while charging their corresponding sources by means of energy credit. Receiving a cooperation request from a source device, the VCB checks the device's energy account and entitles it to benefit from others' help if there is enough credit in its account. Finally, to be trustable by all players, the VCB should be implemented in the infrastructure side. Further discussion on this topic is available in [15].

5   Results and Discussion

For numerical validation, we focus on Scenario 1 with WiFi and WiMedia interfaces. We define energy saving gain as the ratio of the achieved energy saving from cooperation to the required energy for direct communication. A comprehensive quantitative analysis has been conducted in [16] considering different SR-LR use cases (i.e., WiMedia-WiFi, WiFi-WiMax, and WiFi-WiFi). As a result of this study, Fig. 5 illustrates the achievable energy saving gains for the case of WiFi-WiMedia. As can be seen in this figure, wireless devices can achieve more than 50% energy saving on average which can even surpass 80% in some cases when the source node and the relay node possess 6Mbps and 54Mbps LR channels, respectively. Although, this study is a theoretical analysis and overlooks any possibility of establishing the required SR channel between the source and relay nodes, it can shed light on the achievable energy saving limits.

As a first attempt to study the impact of SR and LR channels, a simulation was conducted in [15] for a coffee shop scenario with 5 sources and 5 relays with simplistic Euclidian distance channel models. This study, which considers the WiFi-WiMedia use case, reports an average energy saving gain of 38.8% with standard deviation 16% and maximum 76.6%.

To study the energy saving gain in more realistic scenarios, we conducted simulations with stochastic channel models in [17]. In this study, for SR channels,

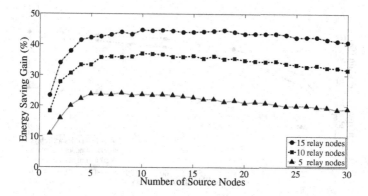

Fig. 6. Energy saving gain for three different numbers of relay nodes when the number of source nodes varies from 1 to 30

we assume line-of-sight (LOS) model with path loss exponent 1.7, while for LR channels, we assume non line-of-sight (NLOS) model with path loss exponent 5, shadowing standard deviation 8dB, and with flat Rayleigh fading. Fig. 6 illustrates the energy saving gain for three different populations of relays as the number of sources varies between 1 and 30. As can be seen from this figure, for a given number of source nodes, the energy saving gain increases as the population of relays increases. Moreover, when we introduce more source nodes in the simulation area, although the energy saving gain increases in the early stages, it saturates soon after introducing few sources.

To study the impact of relays' density, we vary the total number of nodes from 10 to 100 for three different densities of relay nodes, namely 20%, 50%, and 80%., Fig. 7 depicts the result of this simulation. As can be seen from this figure, when the percentage of relays increases from 20% to 50%, energy saving gain increases significantly; however, the gain improves slightly when the percentage of relays increases from 50% to 80%. Moreover, the curves are fairly steep until reaching 50 nodes in total, yet their gradients start to decline afterwards. The result indicates that the energy saving gain depends not only on the total population of the nodes but also on the percentage of relays. Furthermore, to avoid intractable relay selection algorithm in terms of running time and context overhead while ensuring a reasonable energy saving gain, appropriate cluster size is estimated in the order of 30–50 nodes. Finally, as an instance, for a cluster of 50 nodes with 50% relay density, the result indicates that the cooperative SR relaying strategy can reduce the power consumption of the wireless devices by 50%.

For further validation, a demonstrative testbed was designed and implemented within C2POWER project. The demonstrative showcase is dedicated to test SR cooperative strategies for power savings. The testbed consists of C2POWER nodes, which allows the power and energy efficiency to be measured in heterogeneous environment. Each node has two interfaces, namely WiFi and WiMedia. The testbed also includes a WiFi AP. The nodes can connect to the AP either

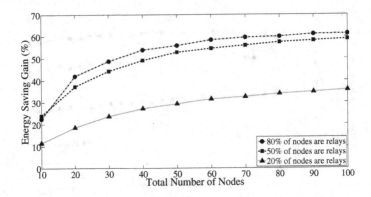

Fig. 7. Energy saving gain for three different densities of relay nodes when the total number of nodes vary from 10 to 100

directly using WiFi connections, or through SR cooperative connections using WiMedia. The testbed was originally designed in a wired environment to provide reliability, stability and reproducibility, but was upgraded to integrate wireless front-end module developed within C2POWER. The testbed has demonstrated good proof of the concept, achieving energy savings, which can reach up to 75%. The testbed is available and was demonstrated at different venues. Due to space limitations, the testbed and its associated results are not fully detailed here.

6   Conclusion

The energy required to keep wireless devices connected to the network over extended periods of time dissipates quickly, while the battery technology is not sufficiently mature to anticipate existing and future demands. Without new approaches for energy saving, 4G mobile users will relentlessly be searching for power outlets rather than the network access, and becoming once again bound to a single location. To avoid this problem and to help wireless devices become more environment friendly, this paper addresses strategies to reduce power consumption of multi-standard wireless devices, enabling users to experience true mobile Internet.

We discussed context-aware power saving strategies. These strategies allow the cognitive engine to make the right decision whether or not to initiate cooperative communication based on the foreseen trade off between cooperation cost and potential energy saving. Simulation results validate that wireless devices can reduce their power consumption by 50% by adopting the proposed strategies. Experimental results through the implemented testbed within C2POWER project also demonstrate the efficiency of the proposed strategies to reduce the power consumption of wireless devices by 75%.

Acknowledgments. The research leading to these results has received funding from the European Community's Seventh Framework Programme [FP7/2007-2013] under grant agreement n° 248577 [C2POWER] and from the grant of the Fundacão para a Ciência e a Tecnologia (FCT-Portugal), with the reference number: SFRH/BD/79909/2011.

References

1. Anderson, C., Freeman, D., James, I., Johnston, A., Ljung, S.: Mobile Media and Applications, From concept to Cash: Successful Service Creation and Launch. Wiley (2006)
2. C2POWER: ICT-FP7 research project, http://www.ict-c2power.eu/
3. Dey, A.K., Abowd, G.D.: A Conceptual Framework and a Toolkit for Supporting Rapid Prototyping of Context-Aware Applications. J. Human-Computer Interactions 16(2-4), 97–166 (2001)
4. Weiser, M.: The Computer for the 21st Century. Readings in Human-Computer Interaction: Toward the Year 2000, pp. 933–940. Morgan Kaufmann, San Francisco (1995)
5. MobiLife: IST-FP6 Research Project, http://www.ist-mobilife.org
6. SPICE: Service Platform for Innovative Communication Environment, FP6-IST Project, http://www.ist-spice.org
7. OPUCE: Open Platform for User-Centric Service Creation and Execution, FP6-IST Project, http://www.opuce.eu/
8. C-CAST: Context Casting, FP7-ICT Project, http://www.ict-c2power.eu/
9. C-MOBILE: FP6-IST Project, http://c-mobile.ptinovacao.pt/
10. Baldauf, M., Dustdar, S., Rosenberg, F.: A Survey on Context-Aware Systems. International Journal of Ad Hoc And Ubiquitous Computing 2(4), 263–277 (2007)
11. Alam, M., Albano, M., Radwan, A., Rodriguez, J.: Context Parameter Prediction to Prolong Mobile Terminal Battery Life. In: Rodriguez, J., Tafazolli, R., Verikoukis, C. (eds.) Mobimedia 2010. LNICST, vol. 77, pp. 476–489. Springer, Heidelberg (2012)
12. Myerson, R.B.: Game Theory Analysis of Conflict. Harvard University Press (1991)
13. Saghezchi, F.B., Nascimento, A., Albano, M., Radwan, A., Rodriguez, J.: A Novel Relay Selection Game in Cooperative Wireless Networks based on Combinatorial Optimizations. In: Proceedings of IEEE 73rd Vehicular Technology Conference (VTC Spring), Budapest (2011)
14. Zhong, S., Chen, J., Yang, Y.R.: Sprite: A Simple, Cheat-Proof, Credit-Based System for Mobile Ad hoc Networks. In: Proceedings of IEEE INFOCOM 2003, San Francisco (2003)

15. Saghezchi, F.B., Radwan, A., Nascimento, A., Rodriguez, J.: An Incentive Mechanism based on Coalitional Game for Fair Cooperation of Mobile Users in HANETs. In: Proceedings of IEEE 17th International Workshop on Computer Aided Modeling And Design of Communication Links and Networks (CAMAD), Barcelona (2012)
16. Radwan, A., Rodriguez, J.: Energy Saving in Multi-standard Mobile Terminals Through Short-Range Cooperation. EURASIP Journal on Wireless Communications and Networking, 1–15 (2012)
17. Saghezchi, F.B., Radwan, A., Rodriguez, J.: Energy Efficiency Performance of WiFi/WiMedia Relaying in Hybrid Ad-hoc Networks. Submitted to IEEE 3rd International Conference on Communications and Information Technology (ICCIT), Beirut (2013)

Counting the Cost of FIRE:

Overcoming Barriers to Sustainable Experimentation Facilities

Michael Boniface[1], Philip Inglesant[2], and Juri Papay[1]

[1] University of Southampton IT Innovation, United Kingdom
[2] 451 Group, United Kingdom
`mjb@it-innovation.soton.ac.uk, philip.inglesant@451research.com,`
`{jp@it-innovation.soton.ac.uk}`

Abstract. Sustaining European experimental facilities for Future Internet research is a significant challenge for testbed providers, funding bodies, and customers who depend on their long-term availability. To date, sustainability plans for experimental facilities have been dominated by abstract notions of business value and unclear business models. We argue that this fails to recognise that cost accountability is the critical element necessary to drive efficiency, irrespective of whether revenue is provided from public or commercial sources. Only through cost accountability can facilities make operational management decisions that are aligned with performance metrics and assess the financial viability of business plans. In this paper we demonstrate how cost modelling and usage accounting can be used to support operational and sustainability decisions for a federated cloud experimentation facility.

Keywords: Future Internet Socio-Economics, sustainability, cloud, Future Internet Research and Experimentation, business modelling.

1 Introduction

The research and development of products and services for the Internet is an increasingly complex endeavour. This is especially true for disruptive technologies that impact current Internet business models. Investigating new ideas and verifying and validating systems as they grow in maturity from the laboratory to commercial deployments requires resources that are diverse, distributed, and of sufficient scale to test hypotheses and assumptions. The European Future Internet Research and Experimentation (FIRE) initiative offers a novel approach to European testbed provision that moves away from project- and industry-specific facilities to general purpose, reusable, experimentation platforms [1]. Facilities are being created across Europe to support a range of technical domains, from sensor networking to cloud computing and social and networked media [2][3][4]. More complex federations of testbeds supporting system-level research are also being explored [5]. FIRE projects bring together largely existing national assets and establishes advanced mechanisms to access and use those assets on a European scale. In essence, the investment creates a European

A. Galis and A. Gavras (Eds.): FIA 2013, LNCS 7858, pp. 297–309, 2013.

dimension for national facilities, enhancing their potential through new types of use and a broader range of users.

A common challenge for all facilities is to sustain a service offering to European researchers beyond the lifetime of the project funding. Sustainability requires a business model that can attract sufficient revenues to pay for the costs associated with a service over a target period. This does not imply a commercial business or "self-sustainability" where revenues are exclusively acquired from paying customers. Previous attempts to establish commercially-operated FIRE testbeds have been explored [6] but, to date, no such service has been launched. We recognise that research infrastructures such as FIRE cannot be operated purely on a commercial basis due to their complex and federated nature and the need to support fundamental research [7]. The challenge of sustainability is not unique to the FIRE programme; for example, EGI has developed funding structures to ensure long-term European-scale continuity [8].

Until now, the sustainability debate is almost exclusively focused on a qualitative assessment of business models: Who are the customers? Who is going to pay? What do customers want? The FIRE roadmap comments on financial aspects at a superficial level but fails to provide a cost structure or quantify costs in any way [9]. However, no business model can be investigated unless financial aspects such as cost structures and revenue models are developed, quantified and explored. Managing the cost performance of a business is an essential element, irrespective of whether it is commercially or publicly funded. We argue that the lack of cost accountability and operational performance monitoring is a major barrier to sustainability because:

- budget holders and potential investors do not have the necessary information to assess viability of business plans; and
- testbed providers do not have the decision-making tools to control costs and achieve satisfactory levels of operational performance to meet their targets

In this chapter we present a method to demonstrate that cost accountability, operational performance and business-planning tools deployed within the lifetime of a FIRE project can provide valuable insight into sustainability beyond the lifetime of the project. The work is being conducted in the BonFIRE project, which offers a multi-site experimentation service for research and development of novel cloud and networking products and services. In Section 2 we describe the value propositions for a cloud experimental facility and a strategy for transitioning revenue flows from investment to demand-driven payments. In Section 3 we describe the cost model for Testbed-as-a-Service (TaaS) and then how the model is used to build a cost accounting system for a federated facility. In Section 4, we show how the cost accounting model can be used to support operational performance decisions for the facility. Finally, in Sections 5 and 6 we describe our future work and conclusions.

2   A Value Proposition for a Cloud Experimentation Facility

The BonFIRE value propositions have been studied using value chain analysis in conjunction with Ostewalder & Pigneur's Business Model Canvas [10]. The primary proposition is an outsourced on-demand testbed infrastructure offering four key capabilities: control, observability, usability and advanced cloud/network features (including cross-site elasticity, bandwidth on-demand). Uniquely, the facility offers capabilities to allow customers to explore cross-cutting effects of applications, clouds and networks, and to control and observe the behaviour of physical and virtualised infrastructure in ways that are not offered by existing public cloud providers. Capabilities are designed for testing and experimentation, rather than production runs, aimed at customers who do not have sufficient capital or requirement for long-term investment in dedicated testbed facilities. This includes SMEs, academic researchers, and research collaborations. As such, the facility is not a "mass" market service, but most users are largely self-supporting and the service is not tailored for each customer; this makes for an efficient use of the public investment in these research infrastructures.

We have developed a number of value propositions and analysed them to understand how value is created and flows from service providers to customers. The service delivery models are all built on the rapid-provisioning and self-service paradigm of cloud computing (Table 1).

Table 1. BonFIRE Service Delivery Models

Value Proposition	Description
Testbed-as-a-Service (TaaS)	Multi-site cloud service with testbeds centrally controlled by a broker
Infrastructure-as-a-Service (IaaS)++	The BonFIRE capability as a value-added service to existing IaaS services.
3rd Party Testbed Provision (3PTP)	Multi-site cloud service with testbeds hosted on 3rd party commercial clouds and public funded facilities
Experiment-as-a-Service (EaaS)	Test and development service providing experiment design, running, and analysis using BonFIRE facilities

Although business model generation [10] and value chain analysis offer effective high-level thinking tools to explore the general attributes of a business model and to prioritise across different scenarios, they do not provide the *quantitative* analysis necessary to monitor and investigate the operating and financial performance of a facility. Facilities need to develop and operate cost accounting systems to explore internal operating dynamics of experiment costs, capacity planning, product mix, investment and, potentially, pricing, so that they can:

- account for, and predict, the total cost for a product (e.g. experiment or test); and
- determine either the level of investment is required from public funding to maintain a certain level of service or to explore possible profit margins if considering commercial business models.

An important challenge is that the investment cost reflected in the price to a customer is generally above what they would pay on the commercial market, and under these business drivers, facilities must constantly find was to control and reduce costs. This

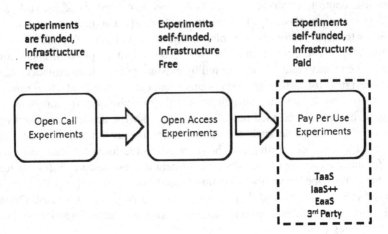

Fig. 1. Three-phase strategy, shifting the revenue flows

is not something most experimental facilities consider in their operations. Facilities need to understand how costs behave and how they respond to changes in volume, price and product mix.

In the remainder of this chapter we describe the BonFIRE cost accounting system and initial results for the TaaS service delivery model (as described in Table 1). The system is being deployed during BonFIRE's "open access" offer, in which facilities are available to selected users without cost but also without funding, as part of Bon-FIRE's three-phase strategy (Fig. 1) towards sustainability; this phase provides the opportunity to conduct a business investigation to understand in practice the operating dynamics of an experimental facility.

3   Cost Modelling and Accounting

In a *cost model*, costs are classified into categories, can be organised into fixed and marginal, and are allocated to business activities [11]. For the TaaS service delivery model, testbed providers offer both infrastructure and software services to customers. A testbed provider makes capital investments in infrastructure for compute servers, storage servers, networking equipment and connectivity. They then develop and operate software services supporting the capabilities of a testbed (provisioning, monitoring, etc.). The general activities of a TaaS provider would include: software development, maintenance and support; experiment training and support; infrastructure management; management of partnerships and suppliers.

A cost model, like most models of real world processes, is based on assumptions where ground truth data is not available. In a funded facility project, accurate data is not always available about the resources of each partner. However, we have developed a working model based on initial assumptions, which can be refined either through actual data collections or deeper dialog with domain experts; this enables us to start quantitative discussion about sustainability with related stakeholders.

Table 2. Site specific model parameters

Site Specific Parameters	Site A	Site B	Site C	Site D	Site E	Site F	Total
Site Core Hrs capacity (per year)	908544	1118208	279552	838656	1345344	419328	4909632
Site Storage GB-Months capacity	305952	60 000	3 840	80 400	144000	14 400	608592
% network hardware	0.20	0.20	0.20	0.20	0.20	0.20	0.20
% hardware maintenance	0.10	0.10	0.10	0.10	0.10	0.10	0.10
KW rating	16.60	13.40	3.60	8.80	16.00	5.60	10.67
KW hrs per year	145 018	117 062	31 450	76 877	139 776	48 922	559 104
Power Usage Effectiveness (PUE)	1.80	1.80	1.80	1.80	1.80	1.80	1.80
Cost per KWhr €	0.09	0.09	0.10	0.08	0.11	0.09	0.09
% of marginal cost allocated to compute	0.60	0.60	0.60	0.60	0.60	0.60	0.60
% of marginal cost allocated to storage	0.20	0.20	0.20	0.20	0.20	0.20	0.20
% of marginal cost allocated to network	0.20	0.20	0.20	0.20	0.20	0.20	0.20
Systems admin rate €	52 844	52 844	52 844	52 844	52 844	52 844	52 844
Number of servers supported per admin	50	50	50	50	50	50	50
Number of servers deployed	19	33	9	14	18	6	99
Number of admin FTE's needed	0.38	0.66	0.18	0.28	0.36	0.12	1.98
Software developer €	59 061	59 061	59 061	59 061	59 061	59 061	59 061
Number of developers FTE	0.50	0.50	0.50	0.50	0.50	0.50	3.00
Support staff rate €	43 518	43 518	43 518	43 518	43 518	43 518	43 518
Number of users per support staff	20	20	20	20	20	20	20
Number of users expected	10	10	10	10	10	10	60
Number of support FTE's needed	0.50	0.50	0.50	0.50	0.50	0.50	3.00

The cost model we have developed (Table 2 & Table 3) is based on the annualised total cost of ownership for the cloud infrastructure. An inventory of fixed hardware assets is created for each site with depreciation period of three years, costed either based on information from the testbed provider or mid-range market prices. We assume that the total cost of the hardware has to be met by the testbed providers, as this is representative of starting a commercial business. In practice, there are cases where fixed assets are already partially or fully depreciated before entering service in the testbed. Network hardware is assumed at 20% of server costs.

We then consider other fixed costs for operating hardware infrastructure and facility services for each site. Hardware maintenance is assumed at 10% of initial server costs, power is calculated based on a function of nameplate rating, assumed data centre efficiency rating [12] and industrial energy costs for each European country [13]. Network connectivity is assumed at 500Mbps symmetrical leased line for each site. Space costs are assumed to be zero, because testbed providers already operate data centres. Operating system costs are assumed to be zero as the facility only supports Linux/Open Source operating systems.

Staff costs are incurred for systems administration, software development and support. Support costs are estimated at 1 FTE per month for each 20 users and vary depending on usage. Staff salary rates are assumed at market rates. Overhead costs are

Table 3. Annualised facility costs (Capital Depreciated over 3 years)[1]

Cost Category	Site A	Site B	Site C	Site D	Site E	Site F	Total
Compute Hardware	7 000	7 497	1 030	3 251	1 353	566	20 698
Storage Hardware	2 777	829	21	2 850	1 036	249	7 761
Network Hardware	1 955	1 665	210	1 220	478	163	5 692
Total Hardware	*11 732*	*9 992*	*1 261*	*7 321*	*2 868*	*978*	*34 151*
Hardware Maintenance	3 520	2 997	378	2 196	860	293	10 245
Op. System	0	0	0	0	0	0	0
Space	0	0	0	0	0	0	0
Power	23 858	19 259	5 474	10 420	28 355	7 652	95 019
Systems admin	20 081	34 877	9 512	14 796	19 024	6 341	104630
Software development	29 530	29 530	29 530	29 530	29 530	29 530	177182
User Support	21 759	21 759	21 759	21 759	21 759	21 759	130555
Data Transfer	7 460	7 460	7 460	7 460	7 460	7 460	44 762
Total operational	*106208*	*115883*	*74 114*	*86 162*	*106989*	*73 037*	*562393*
Total Costs	117941	125875	75 375	93 483	109856	74 015	596544

---

[1] We emphasise that these are illustrations and do not represent actual costs of BonFIRE sites.

allocated to compute, storage, and networking on the basis of 60% of operational costs (excluding capital) are allocated to compute 20% to storage and 20% to networking[2]. The annualised costs for a facility with six sites offering a total of 4.9 Million Core hours and 608600 GB-Months storage per year total €596K (Table 3).

We can see from the cost model assumptions that the headline cost could be subject to significant error and variation between sites. However, the existence of the model allows us to explore the relationships between different cost categories and to help improve the assumptions. Firstly, in the current model almost all costs are fixed costs - the only cost which varies by usage relates to the number of staff needed to support variable numbers of users. Secondly, hardware costs are small in comparison to the staff costs required to operate the service; this is typical of most facilities, and means that, when combined with the self-service model of BonFIRE, the facility can scale (e.g. increasing compute/storage capacity) without incurring significant increase in staff costs. At this level the cost model is useful for long term (annual) business planning, but becomes even more powerful when linked to facility usage data.

Each site maintains a set of physical servers, and each physical server can offer compute and/or storage resources to experimenters. Each compute server has a set of CPU's offering a number of cores. When an experimenter requests compute resources they ask for either a predefined or custom instance type. Each instance type defines a number of cores, the number of vCPUs presented to the guest image, and memory (Mbytes) for each core. An experimenter can allocate a single, multiple, or fractions of a core. Each VM is considered a compute resource and consumes a proportion of the overall capacity.

The *resource model* defines the types of resources and how they are characterised in terms of metrics; currently, we define basic usage metrics: Core hours and Storage GB-months. For example, a VM running for 3 hours with 50% of a core incurs a usage of 1.5 core hours. Having defined our cost model and resource model, we are able to develop tools to analyse and improve the operational performance of the facility.

4   Operational Performance Management

Operational performance management is concerned with tracking, analysing and planning facility operations in a way that maximises efficiency and the value delivered to customers. Service managers need information that can assist them in day- to-day decision-making as they work towards the facility's key performance indicators (KPIs). Key questions for a FIRE facility would include:

- What are the facilities' utilisation targets and have they been met?
- What are the facilities' expected demand patterns over the next month and do we have enough capacity?
- Where should we invest more resources?
- How much will an experiment cost?

---

[2] Currently, network usage is not measured. We have allocated network costs to compute costs in our calculations.

Table 4. Weekly snapshot of facility performance using a box score chart

KPI	Site A	Site B	Site C	Site D	Site E	Site F	Total
Operational							
Core Hours Used	2306.63	2785.83	115.869	5458.03	2995.47	0.000	13661.8
Storage Hours Used	5289.05	0.000	0.000	21797.4	21179.3	0.000	48265.9
Core Utilisation	13.202	12.955	2.155	33.842	11.578	0.000	14.47
Storage Utilisation	0.123	0.000	0.000	1.937	1.051	0.000	0.566
# Site Allocations	104	36	9	188	138	0	475
Capacity							
Site Core Capacity	17472	21504	5376	16128	25872	8064	94416
Permanent Core Capacity	17472	21504	5376	16128	25872	8064	94416
Site Storage Capacity	4283328	840000	53760	1125600	2016000	201600	8520288
Permanent Storage Capacity	4283328	840000	53760	1125600	2016000	201600	8520288
Finance							
Cost per core hr	0.78	0.70	10.05	0.26	0.56	0.00	0.67
Cost per storage GB month	63.75	0.00	0.00	12.93	14.87	0.00	34.97
Cost for network	N/A	N/A	N/A	N/A	N/A	N/A	N/A
Costs allocated to core	1806.19	1959.02	1164.06	1411.56	1681.20	1137.67	9159.70
Costs allocated to storage	461.89	461.65	285.45	386.19	431.42	285.69	2312.30

To answer such questions, a facility must define KPIs and relate them to the cost and resource model, whilst continuously tracking KPIs during facility operations. We use a technique from lean accounting called the Box Score Chart to provide a weekly

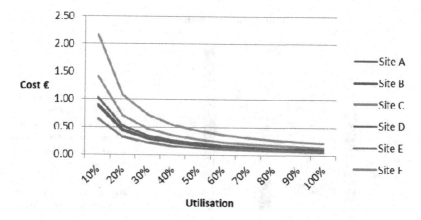

Fig. 2. Core hour cost vs. utilisation for each testbed site

snapshot of the facility performance [14]. The box score chart incorporates operational, capacity and financial KPIs.

At the centre of the chart (Table 4) we calculate the capacity of each site for the weekly reporting period, for example, Site A offers 17.4K core hours and 4.2 million Storage GB-hours. We can optionally track capacity that is productive (online) and unproductive (offline) due to failures or planned maintenance. We then define operational KPIs including core hours and storage hours used and as a proportion of total capacity. We know from the costs allocated to compute and storage for a given period and therefore we can calculate the cost for core and storage during the week. For Site A, core usage is 2306 core hours, capacity is 17422 core hours and costs of €1.8k, giving 13.2% utilisation for the week at a cost of €0.78 per core hour.

Understanding the utilisation KPIs is a powerful tool to maximise the efficient use of facilities, reducing the cost of experiments and moving to sustainability of the facility. Matching capacity to demand is essential because resources that are not used are a cost. A clear way to see this is from the high level utilisation targets as shown in Fig. 2. Here we see that costs vary between sites largely due to economies of scale,

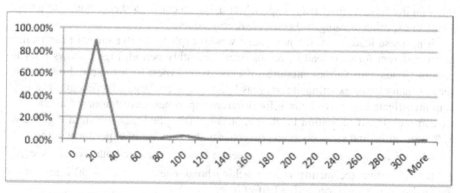

Fig. 3. Experiment cost distribution for observed experiments in one week

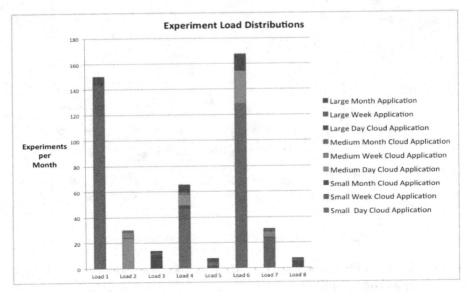

Fig. 4. Monthly forward loads with different distributions of experiment types

where Site C offers less capacity than Site E. We also see that core hour costs reduce significantly between 10% and 40% utilisation but there is a diminishing return for the increase in utilisation beyond 60%. Commercial providers operate at utilisation above 70%, but FIRE facilities are not expected to achieve this.

By incorporating dynamic costs into the model we can calculate per-experiment costs and investigate how these costs change from week to week with the variation in utilisation. Fig. 3 shows a distribution of costs for 400 experiments run in a weekly reporting period. We can see that 95% of experiments cost less than €50.

The previous discussion has focused on the current performance of the facility, but to verify the viability of a business model, "what if" scenarios are needed to explore different future operational conditions. We use business model simulation to investigate the relationship between experiment types, forward loads, utilisation, cost, and revenue.

To do this, we first defined a set of experiment types with varying size and duration ranging from a small 1-day experiment using 10 cores (240 core hours) to a large 1-month experiment using 100 cores (73K core hours).

Using these load types, the next stage was to explore the dynamics of the facility under different forward load scenarios over a monthly period. Fig. 4 shows a set of possible loads with various mixtures of experiment types: for example, Load 1 consists of many small experiments whereas Load 3 is a few large experiments. The goal is to investigate how costs behave for different experiment distributions; for example, we can set a target utilisation level, say, 30% or 70% (the loads shown in Fig. 4 give 30% utilisation) and show costs and revenues under each set of experiment loads.

In Fig. 5 we show the costs and the revenue at €0.15 per core hour. We can see that at 70% utilisation the facility is approaching break-even whereas at 30% utilisation the facility is not even recovering half of its costs.

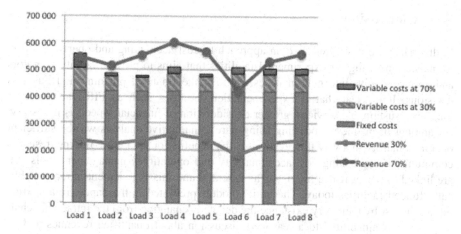

Fig. 5. Modelled revenue and costs assuming €0.15 per core hour in loads of 70% & 30%

Of course, this is still a very simple model and only shows revenue from pay-per-use; however, it is indicative of our approach and of the choices that will be necessary to place the testbeds on a sustainable basis.

5 Future Work

The initial model has been applied to our Testbed-as-a-Service value proposition, that is, BonFIRE's current operational setup. The model assumptions will be continuously validated and improved using actual data collected throughout the open access period of the project to improve the accuracy of results. The model will also be extended to include value-added services such as brokering, elasticity-as-a-service and bandwidth-on demand. The advanced cloud features offered by the facility at the end of the project need to be evaluated in terms of cost of maintenance and value to customers, so as to prioritise the capabilities based on the demand of customers.

All-in-one services such as TaaS are familiar to research centres and academic providers, who tend to operate with high levels of mutual trust and where universal service for a target research community is often a key requirement. However, the TaaS model presents challenges for commercial operators in terms of both the balance of control between the broker and testbeds, and the distribution of revenues. Our next steps are to extend the model to explore the commercially oriented value propositions, IaaS++ and 3rd party test-site provision. We are working closely with a commercial cloud provider, Wellness Telecom, who offer a BonFIRE site to explore infrastructure on demand from a 3rd party. This work will explore the balance between permanent and on-demand capacity. Finally, the work will be taken forward in the EC Fed4FIRE project, which will include to a diverse set of infrastructure resources including sensor and wireless networks, presenting the challenge of specialised assets and fewer of economies of scale.

6   Conclusions

In this paper we have presented an approach to cost accounting and operational performance modelling for experimental facilities that aims to provide facility operators and investors with information necessary to make financial planning and business decisions. It is clear that if experimentation facilities such as FIRE are to offer long-term sustainable services, greater consideration of financial aspects is necessary. No amount of business modelling using purely qualitative analysis will be sufficient operate a facility in a way that maximises the benefits for the Future Internet research community. Establishing cost accountability and operational management tools that are linked to performance metrics is an essential and missing element in many publically funded facilities today. The initial models presented in the paper are a starting point, but just by their very existence the debate is changing from the intractable challenge of "sustainability" to a reasoned discussion about quantified revenues and an understanding of ways in which specific levels of investment can deliver a level of capacity and service.

References

1. FIRE Brochure (2011),
   http://www.ict-fire.eu/fileadmin/publications/
   FIRE_brochure2011_screen.pdf
2. Hernández-Muñoz, J.M., Vercher, J.B., Muñoz, L., Galache, J.A., Presser, M., Hernández Gómez, L.A., Pettersson, J.: Smart cities at the forefront of the future internet. In: Domingue, J., et al. (eds.) Future Internet Assembly. LNCS, vol. 6656, pp. 447–462. Springer, Heidelberg (2011)
3. Hume, A.C., et al.: BonFIRE: A Multi-cloud Test Facility for Internet of Services Experimentation. In: Korakis, T., Zink, M., Ott, M. (eds.) TridentCom 2012. LNICST, vol. 44, pp. 81–96. Springer, Heidelberg (2012)
4. EC ICT EXPERIMEDIA Project, http://www.experimedia.eu
5. EC ICT FED4FIRE Project, http://www.fed4fire.eu/
6. PanLab Techno Socio-economic Analysis Report, http://www.panlab.net/
   fileadmin/documents/PII-Deliverables/D1.4-Techno-Socio-
   Economic_Analysis_Report_v1.0.pdf
7. http://www.ictresearchinfrastructures.eu/communicraft-cms-
   system/uploads/Report_on_the_Event_20_june_2012.pdf
8. Newhouse, S.: EGI Sustainabilty Plan,
   https://documents.egi.eu/public/RetrieveFile?docid=313&versi
   on=11&filename=EGI-D2.7-final.pdf

 9. FIRE Roadmap - Sharing, sustainability, federation and interoperability among FIRE testbeds
10. Osterwalder, A., Pigneur, Y.: Business model generation: a handbook for visionaries, game changers, and challengers. Wiley (2010)
11. Stickney, C.P., et al.: Financial accounting: An introduction to concepts, methods, and uses. South-Western Pub. (2009)
12. http://www.datacenterknowledge.com/archives/2011/05/10
13. Europe's Energy Portal, http://www.energy.eu
14. Maskell, B.H., et al.: Practical lean accounting: a proven system for measuring and managing the lean enterprise. Productivity Press (2011)

User Involvement in Future Internet Projects

Anne-Marie Oostveen[1], Eric T. Meyer[1], and Brian Pickering[2]

[1] Oxford Internet Institute, University of Oxford, United Kingdom
{anne-marie.oostveen,eric.meyer}@oii.ox.ac.uk
[2] University of Southampton IT Innovation Centre, United Kingdom
jbp@it-innovation.soton.ac.uk

Abstract. To determine actual attitudes and practices of those in the Future Internet industry towards user involvement, delegates at the 2012 FIA participated in a focus group and a survey. Continuous user involvement is highly valued and expected to maximise the societal benefits of FI applications. However, just over half of the FI projects apply a user-centred approach, and a large number of survey respondents admitted to being not very knowledgeable about standard user-centred design tools or techniques.

Keywords: Future Internet, user involvement, user-centred design tools, SESERV.

1   Introduction

The design of socio-technical environments, such as the evolving Internet, cannot solely be based on technical considerations or they risk experiencing a cascade of unintended consequences as the technical systems enter use in-the-wild. Social Informatics researchers have identified the exclusion of people who will be using a system from the design process as one major cause of system failures. Many designers develop tacit scenarios of the ways they imagine that people will use systems that often differ significantly from actual conditions and uses [1]. Unless there is integration of the requirements of users and technology "there is the risk that researchers and designers invent something that only a few people need, want to use, or are able to use" [2]. Extrapolating from current trends, the Future Internet (FI) will almost certainly have more users, a greater diversity of users and support a greater diversity of Internet applications. End-users are increasingly active participants, not just passive recipients in the online value chain. Only through identification of user requirements will it be possible to achieve the customer satisfaction that leads to the success of any commercial system.

In this chapter we address user involvement in the Future Internet community. We were interested to find out whether current FI projects support user-led innovation and in this way empower ordinary people, citizens and non-commercial entities. To determine actual attitudes and practices of those working in the Future Internet industry towards user-centricity, the authors, as part of the SESERV FI support action (www.seserv.org) involved participants at the 2012 Future Internet Assembly

A. Galis and A. Gavras (Eds.): FIA 2013, LNCS 7858, pp. 310–322, 2013.

(FIA) in Aalborg, Denmark by organising a focus group and by distributing a survey on user-centricity.

2   Methodology

During the first year of the SESERV project, eight major societal topics of interest to FI projects were identified, mainly as a result of a survey and a workshop held at the University of Oxford in 2011 [3]. The workshop brought together technologists, policy makers and experts across various Challenge 1 ICT and socio-economic projects. In SESERV's second year another survey asked respondents to rank these eight topics along with seven network-economic issues in order of relevance and interest to identify appropriate topics for focus groups. The highest ranking topic showed that the most significant societal issue according to the respondents is the need for more user-centricity and control in the design and use of online services.

Furthermore, one of the major themes that emerged from discussion between those building and those studying the Future Internet was the fact that users are now more than just consumers of services and content: they have become participants in the Internet and in consequence there is a real need for user-centricity in design and discussion. At a SESERV workshop in Athens, it was acknowledged that user behaviour presents challenges for operators [4]. Even more than that, users are now savvy technology adopters whose opinions are ignored at the operator's peril. Furthermore, at a SESERV workshop in Brussels it was very clear that technology is now everywhere and regarded as a commodity, not so much a "must-have" but a "so-what's-next" where innovation is driven by the users. The transition is very clear and not unknown in the business innovation literature: what starts as a technology push ends up being market demand, if not user drive [5].

In order to investigate users' motivations and to understand their needs, desires, and fears it is recommended that designers and engineers involve users continuously throughout the development process. We organised a focus group and distributed a survey at the 2012 Future Internet Assembly to investigate the *actual* attitudes and practices of those working in the Future Internet industry towards user involvement. Both the focus group participants and the survey respondents were recruited from the 500 registered delegates during the two-day FIA meeting.

Using a small number of participants, the *focus group* discussed in what way end-users could or should shape the Future Internet. It investigated whether current Future Internet projects are user-centric and what kinds of methods are used to give users an active role – a voice – not just as commentators on new developments, but as innovators and shapers of technology. The focus group discussed whether FI projects need to assign as much importance to the needs of ordinary users as to the requirements of industrial players. We asked what is more important: user needs or technical possibilities. We also examined whether involving users stifles creativity and innovation. Throughout the chapter, verbatim quotes from participants will appear in *italics*.

The *survey*, which was distributed among the delegates at the Aalborg FIA, asked similar questions as the focus group. The survey consisted of three parts. In the first part the respondents were asked some background questions (gender, age, area of work, FI project involved in, etc.). The second part asked about respondents' opinions about user involvement in general, while the third part of the survey asked about user involvement in the respondents' own FI project.

The survey was completed by 55 respondents (four female) working on 35 different FI projects. The age distribution is shown in Figure 1. Half of the respondents worked in academia, mostly in the fields of computer science or engineering. A quarter of the respondents worked in the technology industry, while the remaining respondents worked in government and policy units, as IT and data service providers, or as project managers in telecommunications. On average the respondents have worked in their current field for about 11 years (ranging from 1 to 40 years).

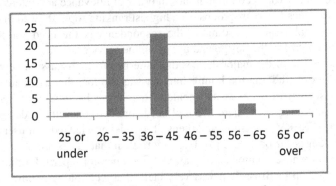

Fig. 1. Age distribution of the survey respondents

3   User Involvement in General

Overall, the survey respondents have a positive attitude towards user involvement. About 93% agree or agree strongly with the statement that continuous user involvement throughout the development process will result in higher adoption rates of new Future Internet technologies. Users should be seen as active research partners according to 82%. Almost all respondents (95%) agree that involving end-users will maximise the societal benefits of Future Internet infrastructures and applications. The majority (69%) feels that the quality of information obtained through user involvement is high and they would recommend (80%) that other development teams spend effort on user-centred design activities. Three quarters of the respondents feel that the expenses incurred by such activities are offset by savings elsewhere in the development process or life-cycle of the product.

The 2010 'Towards a Future Internet' (TAFI) report [6] explains that in the early days, a specialized technical community oversaw the internet's development, while today major commercial internet players have a stronger influence, especially within the context of the committees that agree open standards. The report argues that the future should see a strengthened role for the end-user and user-led design. We asked the FI community who they think is currently driving the development of internet technology. Their opinion supports the TAFI report findings with 56% stating that commercial players dominate, 25% claiming that technical developments drive the technology and 9% saying that end-user innovation is the main driving force. When asked what *should* be driving the development of internet technology in the future 35% say end-user innovation, 29% say technical developments, 14% say large commercial players, while 22% indicate that there should be a balance between the three players.

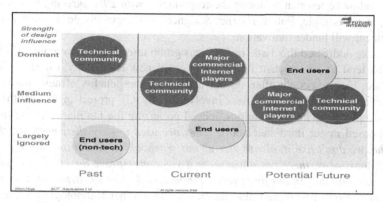

Fig. 2. Who influences the evolution of the internet? (Source: [6])

The focus group participants pointed out that what guides or controls technology development is often a political issue, and may be becoming one of the most important political issues. There is considerable debate about privacy, surveillance and similar issues, which is really about where the technology will go. The political frameworks, such as whether technology is developed in a setting with high or low government regulation, the global distributional production, and so on, set a role for what kind of technology can be developed. Funding models are also seen to have an impact on who sets the agenda. One participant did not agree with the 'current' situation depicted in Figure 2:

> *I would say that the major commercial players are not so dominant in coming up with new ideas. Rather, to some extent end-users and primarily lead user types, so different types of technically fluent end-users and to some extent new start-ups. It could be commercially driven but it's not the major players who come up with the new ideas. I mean, it is the start-ups that then get bought by some of the major players after a year or two. But the major innovation is not within the big players.*

Although it is acknowledged in both the focus group and the survey that end-users need to be involved in the development of the Future Internet, two-thirds of the respondents agree that users do not always know what they want and that they frequently make bad choices. So, does it follow from this that end-users are seen to be hindering innovation? We asked the survey respondents to indicate how much they agreed or disagreed with three statements about this. First we asked whether end-user involvement hinders innovation because end-users have too limited skills to understand the technical possibilities and constraints of Future Internet applications. Only 10% agreed with this statement. We then wanted to know whether end-user involvement hinders innovation because a 'user-centric design focus' creates sameness and therefore stifles creativity. Again only 15% agreed with this statement. Finally, we wanted to know whether end-user involvement hinders innovation because end-users tend to be conservative in their tastes, preferring the familiar over the innovative. This statement found more resonance among the respondents with 29% agreeing to it. Overall though, in our sample, Future Internet designers and engineers do not feel that user involvement will hinder innovation.

When we addressed this issue in the focus group three reasons were identified why end-users tend to be reluctant in the adoption of new technology, especially in the workplace. Firstly, people often do not understand the benefits of new innovations. One participant explained that users involved in an ICT project in the health sector were not open to technical solutions, indeed preferring the familiar over the innovative (as posed in our third statement): *They are used to have their methods, their...* *"ICT, no, we don't like it, please give us our notebook"... And it took some time but we said, look, okay, there are advantages if you can improve the efficiency, you can do this, this, and this. In our first project I think it took one year before we understood each other'*. From this remark the question arose whether technologists are actually listening to what users want and are taking their needs serious, or whether it becomes a case of technology push where the believe in the own product or system is so high that the end-users need to be convinced at all costs. An interesting discussion ensued in which it was argued by the participants that end-users often need to be informed about new technologies as they don't understand what they are or what they can do for them:

> *But then, if you try to explain it to them and if you develop an application so that it is tailored to their activities, after some time they see "yes, we can have advantages, yes, it's not that bad".*

Secondly, people seem to be reluctant to accept new technologies when they feel they are imposed upon them against their will. It was argued that when innovations are imposed top-down there can be issues which are not optimal, making users feel that they end up having to work harder because the technology has not been well thought out. One participant argued that developers often take the following position:

> *"Hey, it can be so much smarter, it's just a matter of explaining and convincing them, they're so stupid they won't understand." That means they[the developers] are not interested in their [the end-users'] world. "Oh, we have this new system for you, it will make life easier". "Yeah... Right".*

A third reason why end-user may be reluctant or even resistant to adopt new technologies has been noted before by many researchers and relates to the power balances within organisations. New innovations can upset traditional power balances. When a system is introduced, people will make projections about the consequences of its use.

> *I actually don't think that it has so much to do with fear of technology or technical things. I think it often has a lot to do with organisational things. That if*

people, for example in a health organisation, feel that the change comes from above, this is the bosses who have decided it should be this way, and if you are a nurse or something and have a paper notebook you can use it in informal ways. You can write things in the margin or something that is not really sanctioned from above. If you have a computer programme, maybe the fear is that this will be precisely controlled by the way the administration think the work is done, while in their perspective they always have to find ways to work around it to actually make it work. We must acknowledge that if you introduce new technology in organisations, say healthcare or something like that, then it's not only the technology change. I mean it always comes with organisational change and power balances, and all these other things that you must acknowledge and recognise, which perhaps are not made explicit.

This last comment reflects a situation where participatory design could be applied as a successful user-centred method. After all, participatory design is one of the efforts to democratize technical change, where people who will be using a system or application are providing a voice in the process of design, evaluation and implementation [7]. As Ehn [8] points out: "Participatory design raises questions of democracy, power, and control in the workplace".

When asked about their knowledge of user-centred design tools, 44% of the respondents admit to having little awareness of standard tools. 45% indicate that they have never attended a user test session, and 56% have never helped to conduct a user test session. The following section gives more detail about user involvement respondents' projects.

4   User Involvement in Future Internet Projects

Of the 55 respondents, 32 indicated that their Future Internet project applied a user-centred approach. Of these 32 respondents, 17 (53%) said that it had been easy to identify the end-users in their project, while 12 (38%) disagreed with that. In the focus group one participant argued that the term 'user' is becoming less clearly defined:

The term 'user' already presupposes a certain technical configuration, where you have on the one hand someone who develops the technology, manages it, owns it, controls it, and then you have the end-user who then maybe can feed back into this but is not really in control. If you compare it to free software, then the distinction between who is the developer and who is a user is kind of arbitrary. There was a project out there about community owned internet infrastructure, where you also have no distinction really between the managers and the users. I think it's important to be a bit careful with this term, and maybe you can involve users so much that they cease being users and become something else.

Deciding how many users to involve in a project is another issue developers have to deal with, varying from a handful to well over a hundred. Usually it boils down to a pragmatic issue; projects only have a limited amount of time and money. Then again it is also related to the kind of research questions being asked, as pointed out in the focus group:

> *I mean is it something where you want statistical relevance, where you are really comparing one system to another to show that this is so much better with some significant thing for instance? Or is it a more general enquiry into understanding what are the possibilities, because then it is a more qualitative investigation, and then you apply different types of methods. So you need to understand what you are looking into, what kinds of approaches are relevant. What are the research questions that you are investigating? And then apply appropriate methodology.*

Overall, the survey respondents that had experience with user involvement in their project were positive about the impact. In the relevant projects, 84% had made user involvement a priority. It was felt by most of the respondents to have been effective (84%), to have made the project more innovative (78%), leading to major new insights (69%). User involvement seems to have had a real practical impact, with 59% of the respondents who had experience of it claiming it had changed the developed technology.

> *We have applied observations and interviews in the real home environment or the real context where people actually are, and found that quite useful, and then also different levels of co-creation or participatory design to some extent, where we actually make sure the people who we were working with understand the general issue of what we are trying to do. Once they are used to that to some extent then we can introduce ideas, and based on the feedback we can suggest technical ideas that address the needs that they express, and then have an ongoing discussion in a quite agile or iterative way, and develop new technical ideas and try them out and have this kind of process.*

Only 15% of the respondents were of the opinion that user involvement had been a hindrance, and that it just created more work and was too expensive.

Between technologists and users, often sits an additional layer: the user researcher and UX (user experience) designer. Depending on the skills of this team – whether they pick up the important aspects that users express and how they communicate what they discover to the technologists – designers and engineers will have different experiences with user involvement. We asked the survey respondents whether the user researchers/UX designers in their projects were able to clearly communicate the user needs to the people developing the technology. Only one person felt that they were not able to communicate their findings clearly due to 'speaking a different language'. About 66% felt that there are some difficulties translating the user requirements into technological terms. A quarter of the respondents thought that the user researchers were able to pick up on the important user aspects and explained them well to the technologists. In the focus group we saw a similar result:

> *In many cases we do interviews. Well not me, but the people from the social sciences. They have their methods. So we are not bothering with them. We are*

together in a project and at the beginning of a project they will organise with different types of users, they do many interviews, and this is the approach they follow. They try to create persona, and then they make a kind of summary page for each persona, to understand how their life is organised and what they expect, so we understand those people. We don't have to participate in this interview but at the end of these interviews, we - the technical persons - understand what they are expecting and we take that into account. Then we come to more technical requirements, so what is expected from the system. And then the technical people get involved and create the architectures and concepts and things like that. Then the user, at least not in healthcare, you cannot involve Alzheimer's patients, but nurses stay involved in the project and follow up what is happening, are also involved in these technical proof of concepts, but there sometimes you see that it's a bit too technical for them. There is sometimes a mismatch.

From the survey we learn that the projects that apply a user-centric approach have many different methods to give end-users an active role. Figure 3 gives an overview of all the methods used by the Future Internet projects represented in the survey.

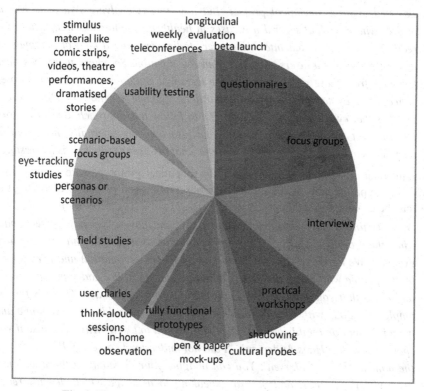

Fig. 3. User-centred design tools used in Future Internet projects

The most popular user-centred design tools are interviews, questionnaires, focus groups, usability testing and field studies. But fully functional prototypes, practical workshops, and scenario-based focus groups are also used frequently. Less common are methods such as shadowing, in-home observation, and user diaries. This might be because these methods are very labour-intensive and time-consuming (either on the part of the researchers or on the part of the end-users). Relatively novel methods based on stimulus materials such as comic strips, theatre performances or dramatised stories are not very common but might increase in popularity over time, however, in comparison to the more popular methods they are in general very expensive.

The participants in the focus group also applied a rich set of methods in their projects. They were of the opinion that if you use the classical waterfall design (business requirements, functional requirements, and functional design) it separates the developers from the outside world so they don't need to understand why a function is needed. In the more agile types of development, however, it is much more common for developers to talk directly with users (themselves or through an intermediary), and that way they really hear what the users are saying. One participant illustrated the user involvement in her project as follows:

> In earlier projects the focus was still more on the technical, and also the industry expected a purely technical project. But now this is evolving. We once had a project where we had several use cases in healthcare, things like that, where we really had very nice and interesting user studies, creating a kind of personas to understand what the users expected from our solution. So where there was peer feedback from these requirements to the technical solutions it was greatly appreciated, also by technical industrial partners, and we see now in more recent projects that even industrial partners like to follow this approach, and take more into account the needs from the user and also applying internally these kind of techniques to match their products more to what the user needs. This is interesting.

Again, interviews, field studies, and fully functional prototypes are popular methods, but the participants also used in-home observation and personas. Involving the users can be challenging though:

> When testing a fully functional prototype, it can have a very negative impact when the prototype does not immediately function as it should. I have a very nice example. We had a system which worked by speech recognition and it was used by the people who check the tickets in public transport. We had some speech interface so that you could look up information from a database. There is for example somebody without a valid ticket, and then they could speak the name and have information on this person. They didn't want to use it. Why? Because if you spoke a name... 'Hans Andersen'. "I did not understand correctly. Please restate the name." 'Hans Andersen'. You can imagine yourself standing there with this guy, with his friends, and you are speaking to a device which doesn't react, which doesn't work. You are a complete loser. They didn't want to use it, because the image that they created by using this was so negative.

Another participant had the same experience with failing tests:

> We also try to go to a kind of field test. But this is not always the case, and again I said earlier, you have to be careful, in the beginning we did more field tests. But then if a field test fails, if it is not working for the first time, if you have to come for example at home several times to fix it they really don't like that. If it goes wrong when you test it for the first time with real users that is really a bad thing, while we as technical people say, "Look, yes, it can happen. We do it again and then it's okay". But you can't do this with users because they expect it to work from the beginning. If you go to the field, you should be shown that it is working from the first time, otherwise you will, even if it is a good solution, people, they don't trust it anymore and they are sceptical.

The duration of a project has an impact on both the success of user involvement and a successful outcome. Typical two-year projects are seen as too short to accomplish anything beyond a mere technical proof of concept, possibly leading to a mismatch in expectations of the involved end-users. They should be followed-up by product development projects.

> A two-year project is not that long if you have to do the whole cycle of having requirements and development and implementation and proof of concept. And what we see sometimes at the end, that users are a bit disappointed about the technical solutions we offer, which is not really the technical issues that are a problem, but we are making a research proof of concept, and users are expecting a fully integrated project with a nice design and form factor and everything, and then they say "Oh, this is not a nice thing".

From the conversations it appears that particularly in the domain of eHealth, going beyond 'proof of concept' or prototypes is difficult due to the funding models.

> In healthcare if the government is not coming into play... The involvement of the government is very low in this kind of project... at least it is in Belgium. But the industry, as long as it is not supported by the government it will say look, it costs too much, we will not have enough customers. So there are several parties and in Belgium what we believe in this area is missing is the involvement of policy makers and government and things like that. They are not involved, we involve the users, we involve the technical people, but we do not involve the policy makers.

In general, the problem is that projects often stop after the first iteration because of a lack of money and time. This is why applications which would be highly appreciated by the end-users do not come to be a final product. There are however alternative ways to go beyond the actual duration of a project, as one participant points out:

> Instead of the project coming in with something and then after a project ends, leave, let's say you have to find some caretakers of what the project is about, and you are sort of helping them to grow. You make the project through them, or let's say, I don't know, if you want to improve a neighbourhood in some way you find some organisation that's there and you just improve something there but they

can continue afterwards. It's not always possible to do, but that's just one way that...if you do that then you can make sure there is some kind of continuation.

Another participant shows that this is indeed a viable solution by giving an example of such a project:

Here the community is so strong that you just only have to give them small bits of information, and of course you have to find some funding, etc., but then they take it out of your hands while you're working at it. And I think that is one illustration of, if you have a strong local community and you have to invest a lot of time in it and in discovering what it would really need, and you have to find people who are enthusiastic, the caretakers, then well it just keeps on running, then you just have to feed in the correct technical infrastructure and they will take care of it. You sort of help them create rather than create for them. But well, this project that I was sketching, that's the only project that I know of which works this way, completely bottom-up. And I have invested an awful lot of time in it.

5   Conclusions

In the debates between those who develop and those who study the Future Internet, user-centricity was raised as one of the most significant themes across all the socio-economic workshops organised by SESERV. This chapter has presented the attitudes and experiences of computer scientists, engineers and IT providers working on the Future Internet with regards to user involvement. Overall, the research participants value continuous user involvement, arguing that it will maximise the societal benefits of Future Internet solutions. However, a large number of survey respondents admitted to being not very knowledgeable about standard user-centred design tools and just over half of the FI projects they work on apply a user-centred approach. Those who do employ such an approach consider it to have a positive impact on the project's output, often leading to major new insights which influence the final product. A number of tools and techniques are used to obtain valuable input from end-users, making them active participants in the shaping of an innovation (Figure 3).

Although in our sample only 15% of the developers who were involved in user-centred projects were of the opinion that user involvement is more of a burden than a benefit, this number might not be representative of all FIA delegates, painting a rosier picture than reality. A limitation of our study was the self-selection of both the survey and focus group participants which makes it possible that engineers and designers with either no interest in, or a more negative view of, user involvement did not take part in our research. While it is common knowledge in the HCI field that user involvement correlates both with higher acceptance of new technologies as well as with better designed devices, it is important to recognize that some technologists are of the opinion that user involvement is a hindrance which creates more work, stifles creativity and innovation, or is too expensive [9]. It is therefore essential to first of all *create awareness* of the benefits of user-centred design within the Future Internet community to persuade developers of the advantages of adopting such principles; this paper tries to make that contribution. The positive experiences of those who do engage users in their research, design and innovation processes provide evidence of the value of conducting extensive user-centred research. User involvement can identify new and significant needs, leading to fundamentally changed concepts of devices and applications and improved end-products. User-driven innovation will help developers to understand the context of use of their applications, and user expectations. To achieve this it is recommended that user-centred design begins early and continues throughout development [10].

Addressing the practicalities of user involvement is the next step in making the Future Internet community more user-centred. There is a need for practical guidance and advice on how developers should conduct user-centred design. Furthermore, there is a need to "create easy and context-specific access to common technical and non-technical resources and capabilities that can be shared for complex experimentation and innovation projects" [11] integrating for instance FI testbeds and Living Lab environments. The challenge remains to move beyond the idea of the 'user' as a problem or barrier, and instead to investigate ways to work effectively with technology users and consider them as key stakeholders and co-creators in the design of the Future Internet.

Acknowledgements. The SESERV project (FP7-2010-ICT-258138-CSA) was funded by the European Commission.

References

1. Oostveen, A., Van den Besselaar, P.: User Involvement in Large-Scale eGovernment Projects: Finding an Effective Combination of Strategies and Methods. In: Folstad, A., Krogstie, J., Oppermann, R., Svanaes, D. (eds.) User Involvement in e-Government development projects, pp. 11–18 (2005)
2. Steen, M., Kuijt-Evers, L., Klok, J.: Early user involvement in research and design projects - A review of methods and practices. In: 23rd EGOS Colloquium (2007)
3. Oostveen, A.-M., Hjorth, I., Pickering, B., Boniface, M., Meyer, E.T., Cobo, C., Schroeder, R.: Cross-disciplinary lessons for the future internet. In: Álvarez, F., et al. (eds.) FIA 2012. LNCS, vol. 7281, pp. 42–54. Springer, Heidelberg (2012)
4. See webcasts Bob Briscoe and Falk von Bornstaedt (2012), http://www.seserv.org/athens-ws-1
5. Astebro, T., Dahlin, K.: Opportunity Knocks. Research Policy 34(9), 1404–1418 (2005)
6. Blackman, C., Brown, I., Cave, J., Forge, S., Guevara, K., Srivastava, M., et al.: Towards a Future Internet: Interrelation between Technological, Social and Economic Trends. EC, Brussels (2010), http://www.internetfutures.eu/wp-content/uploads/2010/11/TAFI-Final-Report.pdf
7. Van den Besselaar, P.: Technology and Democracy, the limits to steering. In: Henderson Chatfield, R., Kuhn, S., Muller, M. (eds.) Broadening Participation -5th PDC, pp. 1–10. CPSR, Seattle (1998)

8. Ehn, P.: Scandinavian design: On participation and skill. In: Schuler, Namioka (eds.) Participatory design: Principles and practices, pp. 41–77. Hillsdale, New Jersey (1993)
9. Brian-Davies, E.: (2011),
   `http://www.seserv.org/panel/videos-interviews`
10. Schaffers, H., Komninos, N., Pallot, M., Trousse, B., Nilsson, M., Oliveira, A.: Smart Cities and the Future Internet: Towards Cooperation Frameworks for Open Innovation. In: Domingue, J., et al. (eds.) Future Internet Assembly. LNCS, vol. 6656, pp. 431–446. Springer, Heidelberg (2011)
11. Schaffers, H., Sallstrom, A., Pallot, M., Hernandez-Munoz, J., Santoro, R., Trousse, B.: Integrating Living Labs with Future Internet Experimental Platforms for Co-creating Services within Smart Cities. In: Proceedings of the 17th International Conference on Concurrent Enterprising (2011)

Design and Implementation of Cooperative Network Connectivity Proxy Using Universal Plug and Play

Raffaele Bolla[1], Maurizio Giribaldi[2], Rafiullah Khan[1], and Matteo Repetto[3]

[1] DITEN Dept. University of Genoa, Via Opera Pia 13, 16145 Genoa, Italy
{raffaele.bolla,rafiullah.khan}@unige.it
[2] Infocom s.r.l, P.zza Alessi 2/7, 16128 Genoa, Italy
maurizio.giribaldi@infocomgenova.it
[3] CNIT, University of Genoa Research Unit, Via Opera Pia 13, 16145 Genoa, Italy
matteo.repetto@cnit.it

Abstract. Reducing the network energy waste is one of the key challenges of the Future Internet. Many Internet-based applications require preserving network connectivity for getting incoming remote service requests or confirming their availability and presence to remote peers by sending periodic keep-alive or heart-beating messages. Billions of dollars of electricity is wasted every year to keep idle or unused network hosts fully powered-up only to maintain the network connectivity. This paper describes a new approach to design and implement the cooperative Network Connectivity Proxy (*NCP*) for reducing energy waste in the ever-growing future Internet. The *NCP* is implemented using Universal Plug and Play (*UPnP*), that uses a set of protocols to allow seamless discovery and interaction between the network hosts and the *NCP*. The *NCP* allows all registered network hosts to transition into the low power sleep modes and maintains the network connectivity on their behalf. It handles basic network presence and management protocols like *ICMP*, *DHCP*, *ARP* etc on behalf of the sleeping network hosts and wakes them up only when their resources are required. Depending on the network hosts time usage model, the *NCP* can provide about 60 to 70% network energy savings.

Keywords: Green networking, energy efficiency, power proxy, power measurement, Universal Plug and Play.

1 Introduction

Green technology is one of the key challenges of the Future Internet to step into a sustainable society with reduced CO_2 footprint. The Environmental Protection Agency (*EPA*) estimated that PCs in US consumes about 2% of the overall US electricity requirement [1]. For a typical household, a single 80W PC that remains powered-up 24/7 will add about 6.5% to the utility bill [2], [3].

A. Galis and A. Gavras (Eds.): FIA 2013, LNCS 7858, pp. 323–335, 2013.

Beyond PCs, the number of other Internet connected edge devices like smart-phones, tablets, IP-phones, set-top boxes, game consoles, network based multi-media equipments etc are increasing at a rapid rate. Thus, reducing the energy waste of *ICT* is becoming primarily important due to the ever increasing cost of electricity, rapid increase in the Internet connected edge devices, rapid development of the Internet-based applications, high data rates, increase in the number of services offered by the telcos and Internet Service Providers (*ISP*) and environmental concerns [4].

A recent study by Lawrence Berkeley National Laboratory (*LBNL*) has revealed that about 60% of the office computers are left powered-up 24/7 with existing power management features disabled only to maintain the network connectivity for remote access, Voice-over-IP (*VOIP*) clients, Instant Messaging (*IM*) and other Internet-based applications [5]. Normally, the Internet-based applications require preserving network connectivity for getting incoming remote service requests or receiving/responding to periodic heart-beat messages. Failing to generate/respond heart-beat messages will drop the network connection and results in the application state loss [6]. Thus, much of the energy consumed by the Internet connected edge devices is wasted as these applications don't transmit real data most of the time but just the periodic heart-beat messages [1].

This paper describes the design and implementation of cooperative Network Connectivity Proxy (*NCP*) using Universal Plug and Play (*UPnP*) protocol. The *NCP* performs key network presence and management tasks on behalf of the network hosts and allows them to sleep as long as their resources are not required [4]. The *UPnP* can be well suited approach for the design of *NCP* due to its increasing popularity and automatic seamless configuration ease that it offers. Also, *UPnP* is well suited for the residential networks and can be implemented on network based devices e.g., PCs, printers, Internet gateways, Wi-Fi access points, mobile devices etc for offering their services and communicate in a seamless way [7], [8]. Thus, the *UPnP* based *NCP* uses a set of protocols that allows the network hosts to seamlessly discover and take advantage of the services offered by the *NCP*. The implementation of *NCP* inside a residential Home Gateway (*HG*) e.g., *ADSL* switch/router that will perform the basic network based activities on behalf of sleeping network hosts is also one of the key objectives of this work.

The rest of the paper is organized as follows. Section 2 briefly presents the related work. Section 3 describes briefly the *UPnP* protocol. Section 4 describes the *NCP* concept and its possible modes of operation. Section 5 presents the design of cooperative *NCP* using *UPnP*. Section 6 describes the practical implementation of *NCP*. Section 7 presents the measurements and observations. Finally, section 8 concludes the paper.

2   Related Work

K. Christensen can be probably the first to propose the *NCP* concept for reducing the network energy waste [2]. His initial work focuses on the *NCP* design for on-board *NIC* and *LAN* scenarios. He also analyzed the network traffic in university dormitory during idle and busy periods to forecast the *NCP* importance [1]. The *NCP* design on host's *NIC*, application specific wake-up, preserving *TCP* connections and strategies to increase the host's sleep period are addressed in [5]. The concept of proxy server that manages the *TCP/IP* connections on behalf of sleeping clients is proposed in [3]. The state of art work pointing key challenges in the *NCP* design is presented in [4]. It also addresses future possibilities for extending the *NCP* functionalities and capabilities.

Some preliminary work on embedding *NCP* functionalities within the host's *NIC* is proposed in [1]. Agarwal et al. proposed a low power *USB* based architecture called Somniloquy that embeds a low power processor in the PC's network interface and runs an embedded *OS* [9]. The Somniloquy uses application specific stubs to maintain the presence of applications. The proxy designs for applications like Gnutella *P2P* file sharing and Jabber clients are proposed in [10] and [11], respectively.

S. Nedevschi et. al. in [12] have classified *NCP* into four types based on its treatment to network traffic from different protocols and applications. They also presented the energy savings achieved by different proxies in home and office environment. The concept of *Selective Connectivity* was introduced in [13] that defines several degrees of connectivity, ranges from disconnection to full connection. Further, the fast and efficient hardware based packet classification that can easily sustain on high data rate links is proposed in [6].

This paper proposes the design of cooperative *NCP* that is well suited for the *LAN* scenario. It uses *UPnP* protocol to achieve auto configuration and seamless communication between the *NCP* and its clients. Our *UPnP* based approach can also be quite useful to easily extend the *NCP* functionalities for other network devices e.g., copiers, printers, scanners etc.

3   Overview of UPnP

The *UPnP* technology is designed to support zero-configuration, invisible networking and automatic discovery of the network devices. It has the potential to be widely deployed in the residential networks and will get its full penetration in home network devices in near future [7]. The *UPnP* Device Architecture (*UDA*) classify the devices into two general categories: controlled device (*CD*) (or simply 'device') and control point (*CP*) [8]. A *CD* in a broad sense performs the role of a server and responds to the request sent by the *CP*. Both the *CP* and the *CD* can be implemented on any platform like PCs and embedded systems. Fig. 1 shows the generic *UPnP* scenario. The generic work flow consists of six steps: *(i) Addressing:* The *UPnP* device gets an *IP* address. *(ii) Discovery:* The *CP* and *CD* use Simple Service Discovery Protocol (*SSDP*) to advertise/discover their presence. *(iii) Description:* The *CP* retrieves the *CD*'s description from the *URL* provided by the *CD* in the discovery message. *(iv) Control:* The *CP* sends action to the services offered by the *CD*. *(v) Eventing:* The action performed by the *CD* may cause changes in state variables value which represent the *CD* current status. The service publishes updates to the *CP* about these changes using eventing messages. *(vi) Presentation:* The *CP* can retrieve the *CD* page from the presentation *URL* of the *CD* and load it into a browser.

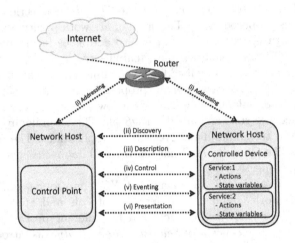

Fig. 1. Generic *UPnP* communication scenario

4   Network Connectivity Proxy

The *NCP* uses a low power entity that can maintain the network presence for high power devices and smartly make the high power devices to transition into low power sleep and active modes [4]. The *NCP* encourages the devices to enter into low power modes during idle periods that would otherwise be left powered up by the users only to maintain the network presence. The *NCP* allows automatic waking up of the devices from low power modes only when it is truly necessary [5].

4.1   Overview of NCP

The network host transfers its proxiable state information to the *NCP* before entering into sleep mode. The *NCP* starts functioning by generating/responding to the routine network traffic on behalf of sleeping host. It impersonates the sleeping host as long as a packet or new *TCP* connection request is received that requires host resources. It wakes up the sleeping host by sending Wake On LAN (*WOL*) packet (also known as magic packet) and transfers the presence state back to the host [2]. Generally, the *NCP* performs three basic tasks on behalf of sleeping host: (i) *NCP* maintains the *MAC* level reachability by generating/responding to the *ARP* requests that are intended for the sleeping network hosts. (ii) *NCP* maintains the network level reachability of sleeping host by maintaining the presence of its *IP* address in the network. It accomplishes this task by sending periodic

DHCP lease requests and responding to network presence messages e.g., *ICMP* ping requests etc. (iii) *NCP* maintains the application-level reachability for the sleeping network host. It accomplishes this task by allowing to establish new *TCP* connections and generating/responding to the network-based applications periodic heart beat messages.

4.2   NCP Types

There are two different modes of operation for the *NCP* [14].

1. *Invisible NCP:* The *NCP* doesn't advertise its presence in the network. It invisibly guesses about the power state of network hosts from the traffic analysis. Invisible *NCP* does not require any changes to the hosts and/or application servers. Since it doesn't communicate with the hosts, it cannot verify the host presence in the network while sleeping.
2. *Cooperative NCP:* Cooperative *NCP* announces its presence in the network and communicates directly with the network hosts. Thus, cooperative *NCP* requires a software on the hosts that can be used for the communication with the *NCP*. The *NCP* and host exchange two types of messages: application specific and power state messages. Application specific messages contain information about the application connections and routine heartbeat messages while power state messages include wakeup and sleep notifications.

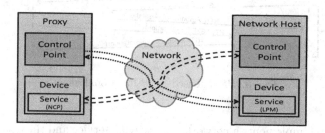

Fig. 2. *UPnP* based *NCP* generic view

5   Design of Cooperative Network Connectivity Proxy

This section describes the design of cooperative *NCP* using *UPnP*. The generic *UPnP* scenario consists of *CP* and *CD* implemented on two different network entities. The *CP* sends control messages to invoke a specific action provided by the services inside *CD*. The *CD* state variables value may change as the result of action performed. The *CD* informs all registered *CPs* about the changes in state variables value. The generic design of *UPnP* based *NCP* is shown in Fig. 2 and basic functional view is shown in Fig. 3. Both, the proxy and network host implement *CP* as well as *CD* with logical services. The proxy is implemented on the residential *HG* and has the capability to maintain the network presence for high power devices in the Home Area Network (*HAN*).

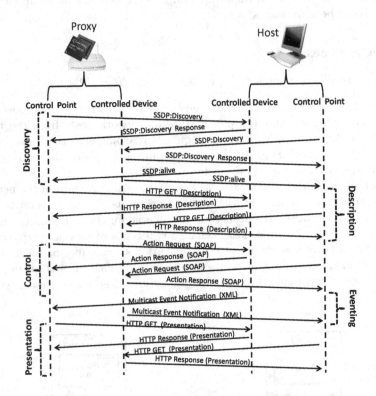

Fig. 3. *UPnP* based *NCP* functional view

Proxy's *CD* implements a network connectivity service and the network host's *CD* implements a Low Power Management (*LPM*) service. Proxy's *CP* can invoke an action defined by the power management service inside the host's *CD*. The result of these actions will change the power state of the network host. Similarly, network host's *CP* can invoke an action defined by the network connectivity service inside the proxy's *CD*. The result of these actions will define different network presence and management capabilities, that will automatically activate when the network host enters into sleep mode. These actions include:

1. *Wake-On-Connection:* Wake up the sleeping network host when a new connection attempt at the specific protocol and port is received.
2. *Wake-On-Packet:* Wake up the sleeping network host on receiving a specific packet.
3. *Send-Reply-On-Packet:* Send reply on receiving the specified packet e.g., responding to heartbeat messages.

Fig. 4 shows the flow-chart of *NCP* functionality. Since we have designed cooperative *NCP*, the proxy and the network host exchange power state information and *UPnP* control messages. Before the host enters into sleep mode, it registers the proxying request along with the required actions at the proxy. The proxy examines the power state of network host and enables packet sniffing and proxying as soon as the host enters into sleep mode. Fig. 4 also depicts the functionality of packet processing unit that performs appropriate action on each received packet addressed to the sleeping host.

6   Implementation of the NCP

The cooperative *NCP* was implemented in linux operating system on a standard PC. The *NCP* software was written in *C++* programming language using *QT* libraries. The *QT* libraries provide rich set of functions to easily perform network programming. The *UPnP CPs* and *CDs* were implemented using Herqq *UPnP* (*HUPnP*) libraries that is compliant with *UPnP* specification v1.1. The key component of *UPnP* based *NCP* is the design of services and actions. Actions work on state variables that represents the state of the *CD* at runtime. Our cooperative *NCP* requires two-way *UPnP* implementation. Thus, the network host and proxy, both contains *CP* as well as *CD*. On the proxy side, *PCAP* libraries were also used to sniff packets intended for the sleeping network hosts.

A linux kernel module was developed for the network hosts to automatically detect changes in their power state. This kernel module communicates the power state changes to the network host's *CD* that modify the corresponding state variables. The host's *CD* keeps the proxy's *CP* updated about the state variables value using *UPnP* event notification messages. The host's *CP* is used to register desired actions at the proxy's *CD*. The proxy starts proxying and creates packet sniffers based on registered actions as soon as the host enters into sleep mode.

The proxy implemented *ARP* spoofing functionality that broadcast gratuitous *ARP* reply packets to bind its *MAC* address with the sleeping host's *IP* address in the *ARP* tables of network hosts/routers. The proxy forwards the sniffed packets intended for the sleeping network hosts to the packet processing unit. The packet processing unit analyses the packet and determines the appropriate action. The proxy implemented response packets for basic network presence and management protocols like *ARP*, *ICMP* echo etc. The proxy also implemented *WOL* packet that is sent to the sleeping host when proxy sniffs a packet that requires host's resources e.g., new *TCP* connection attempt etc.

One of the objectives of this research is to implement *NCP* inside residential *HG* e.g., *ADSL* switch/router etc. Switch/Router can be the optimum place for proxy implementation and don't cause any significant increase in network energy consumption as it remains powered up 24/7. Our experiment was successfully conducted on Lantiq XWAY VRX288 (PSB 80920) v1.1 evaluation board that uses embedded linux 2.6.20. This XWAY VRX288 board embeds a 32 bit Microprocessor without Interlocked Pipeline Stages (*MIPS*) processor and has *CPU* frequency of 500 MHz, 32 KB boot *ROM*, and 16 bit DDR-2 32MB memory.

The *NCP* software was cross compiled for Lantiq evaluation board using cross compiler tool chain generated for *MIPS32* processor. The *NCP* functionalities were successfully evaluated on XWAY VRX288 board in our LAB environment.

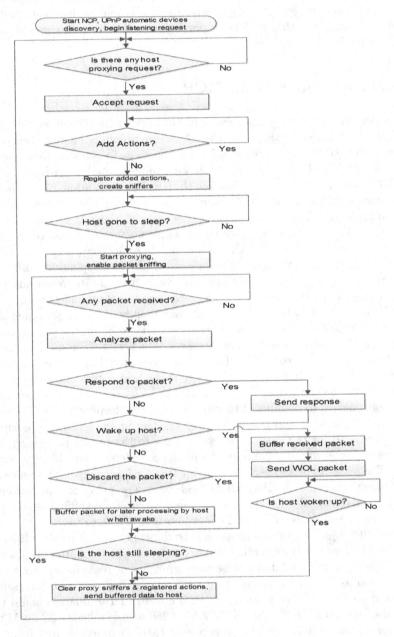

Fig. 4. *NCP* functional flow-chart

7   Measurements and Observations

Some benefits of the *NCP* and its impact on network performance and applications is presented in [12]. This paper presents the performance of *NCP* in different realistic scenarios and addresses its network overhead due to UPnP signalling. Table 1 presents the Wireshark statistical results to evaluate the network overhead. The test was performed for duration of 712 seconds considering only one *NCP*'s client that announces it presence periodically, gets registered with *NCP*, registers Wake-On-Connection action, transitions into sleep and wake-up states and finally de-registers with *NCP*. From Table 1, it can be observed that most of the packets are exchanged during steady state condition while average packet size is the smallest which are mostly the *CD*'s periodic advertisements. The avg. packet size is quite large during discovery phase as *CPs* on both sides download the *CD*'s *XML* description file.

Table 1. Traffic overhead due to *UPnP* signaling

Event Type	No. of Packets Exchanged	Total Bytes Exchanged	Avg. packet size [Bytes]
Discovery & Description	130	34678	266.75
Steady State	650	68154	104.85
Action Registration	46	5976	129.91
Power State Notification	43	4929	114.62
De-registration	80	17508	218.85

The *NCP* performance was evaluated considering two different realistic scenarios, (i) *Scenario 1: NCP* application on the *HG* covers for its sleeping client while third party host located in the same *HAN* tries to access *NCP*'s client. (ii) *Scenario 2: NCP* application on the *HG* covers for its sleeping client while third-party host tries to access *NCP*'s client from outside *HAN* (*NCP* lies between its client and third-party host). The *ICMP* echo test results averaged over 3 trials are shown in Table 2. Few packets are lost during wake-to-sleep (*WTS*) and sleep-to-wake (*STW*) transitions in scenario 1 as packets diversion through gratuitous *ARP* takes some time to update *ARP* caches of network devices. There is no loss in scenario 2 as *NCP* lies in path between its client and third-party host (No traffic diversion required). Similar considerations also hold for packet duplication. The *NCP*'s client takes some time to inform *NCP* about wake-up and stop *NCP* service, thus resulting in few *PING* packets replied by both *NCP* and its client. The Wake-On-Connection test results are also shown in Table 2 in which *NCP* client registers a wake-up request at *NCP* for Secure SHell (*SSH*) remote connection application (*TCP* port 22). The *NCP* latency is calculated as the time *NCP* takes to send *WOL* packet after receiving new *SSH* connection request for its client. The *SSH* response time is evaluated as the time when *NCP* receives and buffers the first *SSH* request packet to the time when *SSH* response is sent by the *NCP*'s client after wake-up. The *NCP* forwards the buffered *SSH* requests as soon as it's client wakes-up. While host wake-up time represents the time interval between sending *WOL* packet and first update packet sent by host after wake-up. Scenario 1 values are a bit smaller as the host receives another *SSH* request from third-party host before it receives buffered *SSH* requests from *NCP*. Whereas, *NCP* buffers continuously *SSH* requests in scenario 2 until it receives wake-up notification from its client.

Table 2. Experimental Results

	ICMP Echo Tests				Wake-On-Connection Tests		
	No. of lost PING responses		No. of duplicate PING responses		SSH response time	Host wake-up time	NCP latency
	WTS	STW	WTS	STW	(seconds)	(seconds)	(milliseconds)
Scenario 1	4	2	0	0	6.35	5.88	0.71
Scenario 2	0	0	1	4	10.89	10.69	0.74

Table 3. Power level measurements in ACPI S0 and S3 states

Network Host	Power Requirement (W)	
	ACPI S0 state	ACPI S3 state
PC1: Motherboard SuperMicro X8DAH+-F, two CPU Intel Xeon X5650, 6 GB RAM	146	8
PC2: Motherboard P5QPL-M, Intel CPU E5400 and 4 GB RAM	55	3
PC3: Intel Atom D510, 1 GB of RAM	22	3
Notebook1: Dell Inspiron 910	19	1.2
Notebook2: Dell Latitude D531	23.5	2
Notebook3: Toshiba Satellite A205	21.4	1.46

Table 3 represents the power measurements performed for three desktop computers and notebooks in *ACPI* S0 and S3 states. It is obvious that both desktop computers and notebooks consume much less energy in sleep state (S3:suspended to *RAM*) compared to powered-up state(S0). Table 4 shows the expected energy savings by considering average values from Table 3. It is obvious that future deployment of *NCP* in the network can provide on average 438 kWh/year energy savings for a desktop computer and 102 kWh/year energy savings for a notebook that correspond to the savings of 96.36 Euro/year and 22.5 Euro/year, respectively. The calculations were performed using 22 cent/kWh as the average cost of electricity in Europe. An organization with 10,000 PCs will be able to save about 0.96 million Euro/year for desktop computers and 0.225 million Euro/year for notebooks. Also, table 4 provides energy savings for the whole world using an estimate of 815 million in use desktops and 164 million in use notebooks during the year 2008. Table 4 does not consider increase in power consumption due to running the *NCP* service on *HG*. Table 5 presents the Lantiq XWAY VRX288 experimental *HG* power consumption in different cases by considering two hosts connected to it. It can be observed that the *NCP* service causes negligible increase in *HG's* power consumption. Thus, *NCP* has the potential to provide billions of Euro savings every year in the world.

Table 4. Estimated energy savings

Measurements/Estimates	Desktop	Notebook
'ON' Power (W)	80	22
'Sleep' Power (W)	5	2
Power savings (W)	75	20
Actual usage (hour/day)	8	10
Actual usage (hour/year)	2920	3650
Full time 'ON' (hours/year)	8760	8760
Full time 'ON' (kWh/year)	700.8	192.72
Actual use + sleep when idle(kWh/year)	262.8	90.52
Savings for 1 (kWh/year)	438	102.2
Savings for 1 (Euro/year)	96.36	22.5
Savings for 10,000 (Million Euro/yr)	0.96	0.225
Worldwide savings (Billion Euro/yr)	78.5	3.7

Table 5. Home gateway power consumption

No host connected (NCP inactive)	Hosts connected (NCP inactive)	Hosts connected (NCP active)	Hosts connected, one sleeping (NCP active)	Hosts connected, one sleeping (NCP active & managing PING)
4.78 W	5.50 W	5.55 W	5.04 W	5.07 W

8 Conclusions

The *NCP* is a useful approach that allows high power network hosts to sleep when idle while maintaining their virtual presence using a low power network entity. This paper has addressed the generic structure of *NCP*, its basic functionalities and described a new approach for the design and implementation of *NCP* using *UPnP* protocol. The *UPnP* is in fact a well suited approach to implement the *NCP* for *HAN*. Furthermore, the *UPnP* based *NCP* concept for PCs can be easily extended for the power management of other local network devices e.g., *UPnP* printers, copiers and scanners etc. To achieve maximum possible energy savings, this paper has addressed the *NCP* implementation inside *HGs* (routers/switchs).

The future work will focus on the development of *NCP* that will also embed the capabilities to preserve open *TCP* connections on behalf of sleeping network hosts. Also, due to large number of network based applications with different type of heart-beat messages, the future work will also focus on the development of application independent *NCP*. The *NCP* has potential of providing great economic savings in the ever-growing future Internet.

Acknowledgment. This work was partially supported by the European Commission in the framework of the *FP7 ECONET* (low Energy COnsumption NETworks) project (contract no. INFSO-ICT-258454).

References

1. Christensen, K., Gunaratne, P., Nordman, B., George, A.: The Next Frontier for Communications Networks: Power Management. Computer Communications 27(18), 1758–1770 (2004)
2. Jimeno, M., Christensen, K., Nordman, B.: A Network Connection Proxy to Enable Hosts to Sleep and Save Energy. In: IEEE International Conference on Performance, Computing and Communications Conference, IPCCC (December 2008)
3. Christensen, K., Gulledge, F.: Enabling Power Management for Network-Attached Computers. Int. Journal of Network Management 8(2), 120–130 (1998)
4. Khan, R., Bolla, R., Repetto, M., Bruschi, R., Giribaldi, M.: Smart Proxying for Reducing Network Energy Consumption. In: IEEE International Symposium on Performance Evaluation of Computer and Telecommunication Systems, SPECTS (July 2012)
5. Gunaratne, C., Christensen, K., Nordman, B.: Managing Energy Consumption Costs in Desktop PCs and LAN Switches with Proxying, Split TCP Connections, and Scaling of Link Speed. Int. Journal of Network Management 15(5), 297–310 (2005)
6. Sabhanatarajan, K., Gordon-Ross, A., Oden, M., Navada, M., George, A.: Smart-NICs: Power Proxying for Reduced Power Consumption in Network Edge Devices. In: IEEE Computer Society Annual Symposium on VLSI, ISVLSI 2008 (April 2008)
7. Goland, Y., Cai, T., Leach, P., Gu, Y.: Simple Service Discovery Protocol/1.0 Operating without an Arbiter, in draft-cai-ssdp-v1-03.txt, IETF Draft (October 28, 1999)
8. UPnP forum (2012), http://www.upnp.org
9. Agarwal, Y., Hodges, S., Chandra, R., Scott, J., Bahl, P., Gupta, R.: Somniloquy: Augmenting Network Interfaces to Reduce PC Energy Usage. In: 6th ACM/USENIX Symp. on Networked Systems Design and Implementation (NSDI 2009), Boston, MA, USA (April 2009)
10. Jimeno, M., Christensen, K.: A Prototype Power Management Proxy for Gnutella Peer-to-Peer File Sharing. In: Proceedings of the IEEE Conference on Local Computer Networks, Dublin, Ireland, October 15-18 (2007)
11. Werstein, P., Vossen, W.: A Low-Power Proxy to Allow Unattended Jabber Clients to Sleep. In: Ninth International Conference on Parallel and Distributed Computing, Applications and Technologies, PDCAT 2008 (December 2008)

12. Nedevschi, S., Chandrashekar, J., Liu, J., Nordman, B., Ratnasamy, S., Taft, N.: Skilled in the Art of Being Idle: Reducing Energy Waste in Networked Systems. In: Proceedings of the 6th USENIX Symposium on Networked Systems Design and Implementation (NSDI). USENIX Association, Berkeley (2009)
13. Allman, M., Christensen, K., Nordman, B., Paxson, V.: Enabling an Energy-Efficient Future Internet Through Selectively Connected End Systems. In: Sixth Workshop on Hot Topics in Networks, HotNets-VI (November 2007)
14. Nordman, B., Christensen, K.: Improving the Energy Efficiency of Ethernet-Connected Devices: A Proposal for Proxying. Ethernet Alliance White Paper (September 2007)

Book Sponsoring Projects Overview

3DLife - Bringing the Media Internet to Life

Qianni Zhang[1], Noel E. O'Connor[2], and Ebroul Izquierdo[1]

[1] Queen Mary University of London, UK
[2] CLARITY: Centre for Sensor Web Technologies, Dublin City University, Ireland

Abstract. The 3DLife EU FP7 Network of Excellence focuses on stimulating joint research and integrating leading European research groups to create a long-term integration of critical mass for innovation of currently fragmented research addressing media Internet. It fosters the creation of sustainable and long-term relationships between existing national research groups and lay the foundations for a Virtual Centre of Excellence in 3D media Internet - EMC^2. This is a summary of 3DLife's missions as well as its achievements in the last three years.

1 Summary of Project Objectives and Achievements

3DLife: Bringing the Media Internet to Life [1], is an FP7 Network of Excellence (started 01 Jan 2010) that brings together leading European and Korean research groups across a variety of different technology areas in order to address important issues affecting the long-term development of the media Internet. The consortium is formed of seven members:

- Queen Mary University of London (UK)
- Dublin City University (Ireland)
- Groupe des Ecoles des Telecommunications (France)
- Heinrich Hertz Institute, Fraunhofer (Germany)
- University of Geneva (Switzerland)
- Informatics and Telematics Institute (Greece)
- Korean University (KU)

The research agenda underpinning 3DLife focuses on novel technologies for generating 3D information from a variety of content sources so that this information can be used to drive forward novel media Internet applications. The research domains covered by 3DLife include:

- **Media analysis for 3D data generation** i.e. tools that integrate image and audio processing techniques to robustly extract 3D data ranging from coarse-grained 3D information to fine-grained human motion analysis;
- **3D computer graphics** techniques for the generation of virtual worlds, objects and most importantly humans targeting new levels of realism;
- Tools for the creation of **distributed immersive virtual worlds**, including **media networking technologies**, targeting re-creation of existing locations from users' personal content and creation of new imaginary locations.

A. Galis and A. Gavras (Eds.): FIA 2013, LNCS 7858, pp. 339–341, 2013.

The 3DLife work programme is designed to support collaboration across these areas by providing a range of supports for integrating complementary expertise. Activities include short and long-term research fellowships, resource optimization and sharing and the collection and maintenance of freely accessible research resources. In the past three years of the project, a total of 19 PhD exchanges via short-term fellowships and 15 exchanges of senior researchers have been supported by 3DLife. 3DLife has designed and installed a technical infrastructure to enable and facilitate human and technical integration activities. It provides support to share and exchange research resources among partners, including equipment, teaching resources, tools, interfaces and test data. By the end of year 2012, the integration framework wiki lists 24 software tools from various areas of interest, as well as 14 datasets with more than 23.4 hours of recorded audio and video.

The long term sustainability of 3DLife has been addressed via the establishment of a dedicated centre of excellence. **EMC^2: Excellence in Media Computing and Communication** [2], has been established as a non-for-profit legal entity with offices in Queen Mary University of London. It is supported by the similarly named EMC^2 Coordination and Support Action. EMC^2's mission is to bring together partners' capabilities, knowledge and expertise to facilitate R&D through cooperative projects, joint research publication and technology transfer, including (i) Academia industry matchmaking to enable technology transfer, particularly to SMEs; (ii) Mentoring, coaching and training of the entrepreneurs of the future; (iii) Formation of PhD courses on the MC^2 field with entrepreneurial focus; and (iv) Shaping national and European research agendas.

The need to reach beyond the existing founding projects and associated consortium members was well recognised both by 3DLife and EMC^2. A key joint objective, originally initiated by 3DLife but with a view to being continued by EMC^2, was to reach out to the broader community in order to raise awareness and stimulate interaction between both academic and industrial players. The ACM Multimedia Grand Challenge series, then a new initiative in the community, was considered to be the ideal vehicle for this. The idea of the ACM Multimedia Grand Challenge series arose within ACM Multimedia, the premier conference in the field of multimedia. In the series, a set of forward-looking technical challenges for the future of multimedia (with a horizon of 3-5 years) are formulated and proposed to the research community.

3DLife has organised and co-sponsored three challenges in this series:

- 3DLife/Technicolor Grand Challenge 2009-2010 on Sports Activity Analysis in Camera Networks;
- 3DLife/Huawei Grand Challenge 2010-2012 on Realistic Interaction In Online Virtual Environments;
- 3DLife/Huawei Grand Challenge 2013 on 3D reconstruction of moving human bodies from multiple active and passive sensors.

3DLife project has been working closely with industry sponsors to jointly define challenges so that 3DLife project partners could then dedicate project resources towards creating the required data set. To facilitate the Grand Challenge, project partners captured a comprehensive and unique data set consisting of multimodal recordings of participants, captured at different sites with different pieces of equipment.

As with any exercise of this nature, a key challenge is providing useful data sets that are sufficiently interesting to the community in terms of carrying out high-quality research. Creating such data sets can require a significant amount of effort that may surpass the ability of an industry sponsor to provide. For this reason, it was decided within the 3DLife project to work closely with industry sponsors to jointly define challenges so that 3DLife project partners could then dedicate project resources towards creating the required data set. This relieves the industry partner of this burden but ensures that representative data is available to enable research by the broader community. To facilitate the Grand Challenge, project partners captured a comprehensive and unique data set consisting of multimodal recordings of Salsa dancers, captured at different sites with different pieces of equipment. There have been 72 requests to download the various datasets, with 18 of these requests coming from outside the EU.

Numerous activities were conducted during the first three years of the project, aiming at spreading the Network's Excellence in integrative efforts, technology transfer, scientific results, and training. The dissemination actions are focused on the three groups of people, namely, academics, industry/business, and the non-specialist. 3DLife website and the overall 3DLife online community have been well maintained and gained significant visibility. 3DLife partners have participated in various exhibitions, EC activities and other events with venues spread over Europe, Asia, America and Africa and with audiences from both academic and industry.

References

1. 3DLife NoE, http://www.3dlife-noe.eu (accessed in 2013)
2. Excellence in Media Computing and Communication,
   http://www.emc-square.org (accessed in 2013)

CONCORD Project Management of the Future Internet

Ilkka Lakaniemi

Aalto University, Helsinki, Finland
Ilkka.lakaniemi@aalto.fi

Abstract. CONCORD is the Facilitation and Support action for the EU-funded Future Internet Public-Private Partnerships (FI PPP) programme. CONCORD coordinates FI PPP cross-project activities. It facilitates knowledge transfer and co-creation across projects as well as with related external groups. It focuses on future-oriented strategic planning for FI PPP and on bringing a valuable contribution via unbiased outsider attention to FI PPP structures and processes.

The current Internet is a story of evolving relationships between public and private sector activities. Some of these activities have been results of pragmatic plans and policies, but in many occasions the current networked world of Inter-net-enabled services is based on individual inventions and innovations pasted together without holistic planning.

As the Internet and other information and communications technologies (ICTs) are having an ever-increasing role in many economic and social activities, it is obvious that there has been and continues to be a need to create holistic planning for European Internet-related activities. For this purpose and to follow the public-private sector co-operative mode akin to the early Internet, the European Commission launched in 2011 the Future Internet Public-Private Partnership Programme (FI-PPP).

The original primary objective of the FI-PPP was to advance a shared vision for European-scale technology platforms and their implementation, as well as the integration and harmonization of the relevant policy, legal, political and regulatory frameworks to allow for the widest impact in European Internet-related market developments.

As the FI-PPP is entering its second phase in 2013, the original primary objective is even more imperative as Europe continues to look at technology innovations to set anew its global competitive advantage, innovation capacity and its internal capability to meet the societal challenges arising in the next decade.

During its first phase 2011-2013, the FI-PPP has produced deliverables and various outcomes from eleven technology platform, use case-driven and cross-FI-PPP projects: CONCORD, ENVIROFI, FI-CONTENT, FI-WARE, FINEST, FINSENY, INFINITY, INSTANT MOBILITY, OUTSMART, SAFECITY and SMARTAGRIFOOD.

These deliverables and other outcomes have provided insights for market creation in specific European Future Internet-enabled services, developed common technology enablers for future use and created greater awareness among European business and research communities on Future Internet-based joint opportunities. Examples of these outcomes range from developing sets of generic Future Internet-technology enablers

A. Galis and A. Gavras (Eds.): FIA 2013, LNCS 7858, pp. 342–343, 2013.

to Future Internet-enabled case studies in European food chain development to logistics and providing for safer urban environments.

The first phase has in general met with the FI-PPP primary objective of setting the technology and policy frameworks in place, yet at the same time revealed challenges that continue to be addressed in the second phase of the FI-PPP to create further opportunities for technology implementation and go-to-market planning.

It is noteworthy that many of the challenges and opportunities identified in FI-PPP are not necessarily new in terms of technology development, the most innovative thinking is required to develop novel ways of putting together the existing elements for Future Internet-enabled services in Europe and creating an enabling business environment for getting the most economic value out of the European innovations in the field of Future Internet.

Reference

1. CONCORD Facilitation and Support Action, http://www.fi-ppp.eu, http://www.fi-ppp.eu/concord/

FLAMINGO NoE Project Management of the Future Internet

Sebastian Seeber

University of Munich, Germany
sebastian.seeber@unibw.de

Abstract. The FLAMINGO project will strongly integrate the research of leading European research groups in the area of network and service management, strengthen the European and worldwide research in this area, and bridge the gap between scientific research and industrial application.

1 Introduction

FLAMINGO [1] has several objectives, such as to lead the scientific network and service management community, to organize conferences and workshops, develop open source software, establish joint labs, jointly supervise Ph.D. students, develop educational and training material, interact with academia and industry as well as to contribute to (IETF and IRTF) standardization. There are three major and federating challenges which will be investigated: At first the Network and service monitoring, based on flow-based techniques, enabling scalable monitoring systems to share collected data and feed the knowledge plane and decision algorithms of the Future Internet (FI). Next is automated configuration and repair, based on self-* features and frameworks, enabling billions of devices and managed objects to manage themselves in a fully distributed and autonomic way. Last the economic, legal, and regulative constraints, which do border management systems and operational solutions of the FI.

2 Key Issues and Problems

The FLAMINGO project is focused around three key research activities (see Figure 1 below). Before any management decision can be taken, it is essential to first monitor the managed objects (networks, services, traffic, devices etc.). The output of the monitoring process is than used to automatically configure and repair the managed objects. Monitoring as well as the automated configuration and repair should be performed within the boundaries of the economic, legal and regulative constraints.

Monitoring: To make informed network and service management decisions, it is essential to have a thorough understanding of the traffic. The FLAMINGO consortium will focus on new flow-analysis techniques, propose novel distributed techniques to capture and analyse management data, and develop new query languages to detect flow patterns. These novel approaches will be validated for the purpose of security management and privacy awareness.

A. Galis and A. Gavras (Eds.): FIA 2013, LNCS 7858, pp. 344–345, 2013.

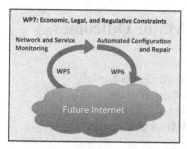

Fig. 1. Interaction between the different Workpackages

Automated Configuration and Repair: Due to the billions of objects that need to be managed, and the resulting scalability problems, it is necessary to rethink existing management approaches. A centralized and hierarchical approach can no longer address these challenges adequately. What we need is automated configuration and repair of managed objects, such that these objects react to their environment in an adaptive way, according to certain rules. These novel concepts will be investigated and validated by the application in content-aware networking, optical networks, cloudbased services, personal and wireless sensor networks.

Economic, Legal, and Regulative Constraints: The Future Internet will see management decisions to be taken and optimized, based not only on technological, but also on commercial deployment and economic viability concerns. Therefore a crossdisciplinary approach is needed, taking into account a) costawareness, b) incentives for service provisioning, c) fulfilment schemes, d) business policies, and e) legal/regulative aspects. These aspects are complemented by legal and regulative constraints, which have to be evaluated to ensure that contracts concluded will be legally valid and provider-dependent cost models as well as accounting models are legally compliant with regulations.

3   Expected Results

The impact of the FLAMINGO Network of Excellence will be a strong European position in the field of network and service management. To achieve this, FLAMINGO creates training material to facilitate researchers within industry to keep up with the latest developments in this field. The project develops network management course material and makes such material available to universities worldwide. It will develop technologies for future generations of European high speed networks, in particular scalable monitoring techniques and network components that operate autonomically. FLAMINGO will contribute to standardization, in particular within the IETF to the evolution of the NETCONF and YANG standards, as well as several other working groups. FLAMINGO also organizes prestandardization in this area within the IRTF Network Management Research Group.

Reference

1. FLAMINGO NOE Project, European Framework Program 7,
   http://fp7-flamingo.eu

The GEYSERS Concept and Major Outcomes

Anna Tzanakaki[1], Sergi Figuerola[2], Joan A. García-Espín[2],
Dimitra Simeonidou[3], Nicola Ciulli[4], Philip Robinson[5], Juan Rodríguez[6],
Giada Landi[4], Bartosz Belter[7], Pascale Vicat-Blanc[8], Matteo Biancani[9],
Cees de Laat[10], Eduard Escalona[2], and Artur Binczewski[7]

[1] Athens Institute of Technology
atza@ait.gr
[2] i2CAT Foundation
[3] University of Bristol
[4] Nextworks
[5] SAP Ireland
[6] Telefónica I+D
[7] Poznan Supercomputing and Networking Center
[8] Lyatiss
[9] Interoute Italy
[10] University of Amsterdam

1   Introduction

Large-scale computer networks supporting both communication and computation are extensively employed to deal with a variety of existing and emerging demanding applications. These high-performance applications, requiring very high network capacities and specific IT resources, cannot be delivered by the current Best Effort Internet. Optical networking is offering a very high capacity transport with increased dynamicity and flexibility through recent technology advancements including dynamic control planes etc. The European project GEYSERS (Generalised Architecture for Dynamic Infrastructure Services) proposed a novel architecture capable of provisioning "Optical Network and IT resources" for end-to-end service delivery. The proposed approach adopts the Infrastructure as a Service (IaaS) paradigm. The GEYSERS architecture presents an innovative solution to enable infrastructure operators to virtualize their optical network + IT physical resources and offer them as a service based on the user/application requirements. The adoption of Virtual Infrastructures (VIs) facilitates sharing of physical resources among various virtual operators, introducing new business models that suit well the nature and characteristics of the Future Internet and enables new exploitation opportunities for the underlying Physical Infrastructures (PIs).

The GEYSERS architecture (figure 1) is based on a layered model that introduces two novel layers, the enhanced Network Control Plane (NCP+) and the Logical Infrastructure Composition Layer (LICL), and leverages on existing solutions to represent a Service Middleware Layer (SML) and the PI. The PI layer comprises optical network + IT resources from different providers. These resources are virtualized by the LICL and composed into VIs using dynamic on-demand planning mechanisms. On top of LICL, GEYSERS deploys the NCP+, a control plane based on the Generalised

A. Galis and A. Gavras (Eds.): FIA 2013, LNCS 7858, pp. 346–349, 2013.

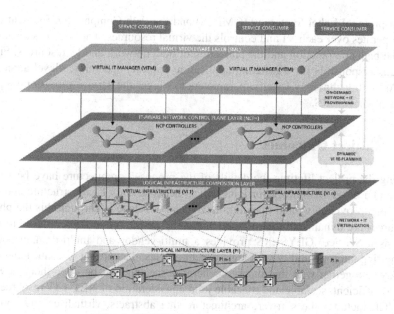

Fig. 1. GEYSERS layered architecture

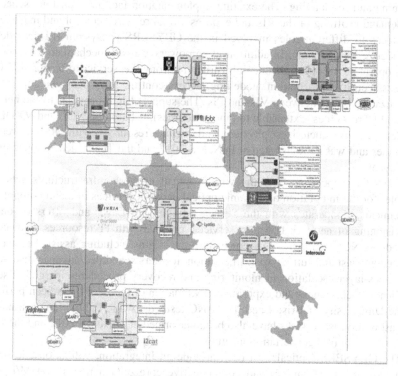

Fig. 2. GEYSERS testbed

Multi-protocol Label Switching (GMPLS) and the Path Computation Element (PCE) that operates over each VI and controls the virtual resources. The NCP+ is responsible for the path computation and the allocation of both network and IT resources. Finally, SML is responsible for translating application requests and service level agreements (SLAs) into technology specific parameters to trigger the service provisioning procedures of GEYSERS.

2   Project Outcomes

During the project lifetime the details of the proposed architecture have been specified and a novel framework for joint optical network and IT infrastructure automated planning, provisioning and operation have been developed. Through this the physical resources are dynamically partitioned and composed in VIs and are offered to operators as a Service. GEYSERS provides a multi-vendor and multi-domain solution, supporting interoperability with legacy technologies, decoupling of control and physical layers together with the required coherence mechanisms between them as well as energy-efficient, scalable and trustable joint consideration of NET + IT resources.

LICL includes the software architecture that abstracts, virtualises and composes optical Network and IT infrastructure resources, and enables dynamic infrastructure planning and re-planning. The existing implementation facilitates custom, scheduled, on-demand profiling of the VIs and exposes virtual resource control and management interfaces to different roles involved in the GEYSERS ecosystem (PI provider, VI provider & VI operator). In addition, it empowers a novel mechanism to allow telecom operators to decouple the infrastructure from the service offering. LICL addresses security, information modelling, access control, SLA management and synchronization issues between VIs and PIs. The support LICL provides to the networking and IT resources (extensible to other resources), is based on NDL and VXDL data models and parameterizes physical and virtual resources with all the required attributes and was demonstrated at FuNeMS 2012 and the Telefonica I+D Dissemination event.

The NCP+ operating over the virtual optical network infrastructures acts as an enabler for the integration of dynamic optical network services in cloud computing. It dynamically cooperates with the Service Middleware Layer and offers on-demand provisioning of network transport services, coupled with IT resources connected to the edges. NCP+ supports new connection paradigms including assisted unicast, restricted anycast and full anycast. In addition, it offers scheduled/advance reservations and cross-layer escalation of monitoring and recovery procedures for global service resilience. Deployment and experimental validation of the NCP+ has been performed at the Uninversity of Bristol and the PSNC testbeds, while Public demonstrations of unicast & anycast services have also been performed at FuNeMS 2012 and the Future Networks 10th FP7 concertation meeting.

The GEYSERS Optical Test-beds provide an integration, validation and demonstration platform (figure 2) and comprise five core optical nodes (WDM/DWDM, OTN and fibre switces) interconnected with high speed links over GÉANT, GLIF and

CBF infrastructures and IT Nodes, offering computing clusters and other IT facilities, attached to the core nodes through 1 GE link. The IT resources (servers, PC clusters and Storage elements) are provided through eight cloud nodes. Examples of experiments performed using the test-bed include: application of virtualization paradigms to optical infrastructure resources and validation of seamless and efficient infrastructure composition from IT and network resources, experiments with on-demand provisioning of enhanced network connectivity services tailored to specific applications requirements over a VI.

To facilitate GEYSERS outcomes to complement existing products and services and be able to be integrated with existing systems, GEYSERS has focused on playing an active role in standardization bodies such as the Internet Engineering Task Force (IETF), the TeleManagement Forum (TMF), the Distributed Management Task Force (DMTF), the Open Grid Forum (OGF), the National Institute of Standards and Technologies (NIST) and the VXDL forum.

iCore: A Cognitive Management Framework for the Internet of Things

Raffaele Giaffreda

CREATE-NET, Trento, Italy
raffaele.giaffreda@create-net.org

Abstract. iCore is an EU FP7 Integrated Project aimed at leveraging on the use of cognitive technologies for empowering the Internet of Things to deliver on the current expectations which see it as one of the main pillars of the Future Internet. The project brings together a strong set of industrial Partners, mostly from Europe but spanning also China and Japan which collaborate with research centers and universities to deliver solutions that address heterogeneity and reusability of IoT objects while striving for self-management capabilities that keep low complexity as the numbers of interconnected objects increase exponentially.

1 Key Issues and Objectives

iCore is an EU FP7 project in the Internet of Things (IoT) domain. The project aims to address some of the numerous challenges posed by the "7 trillion devices for 7 billion people" paradigm, namely the technological heterogeneity that derives from such vast amounts of heterogeneous interconnected objects and the complexity this future vision entails.

In order to achieve these objectives iCore proposes a cognitive management framework for the Internet of things which on the one hand investigates the means to virtualise interconnected objects, while on the other aims to leverage on the use of cognitive technologies to achieve self-management of these objects while considering the needs and requirements of the application / user to be supported.

iCore solutions will contribute to the ability of the Internet of Things to achieve its full potential providing architectural and technology foundations that foster the easy creation of innovative applications and exploit the increasingly widespread fabric of sensing and actuating IoT objects.

Obvious beneficiaries of such innovation, besides end-users, are expected to be manufacturers of objects that thanks to solved interoperability issues can promote re-use of their devices in many different application contexts. iCore solutions will also open-up new opportunities for all stakeholders traditionally associated with smart-cities scenarios (energy, water, traffic, waste etc.), which will have to face the challenge of homogeneous interactions with and the ability to extract relevant and compartmentalised knowledge from ubiquitous sensing capabilities of IoT.

A. Galis and A. Gavras (Eds.): FIA 2013, LNCS 7858, pp. 350–352, 2013.

2   Technical Approach

To achieve these objectives iCore proposes a cognitive framework comprising three levels of functionality, exposing well defined interfaces which make the functionality therein reusable for various and diverse applications.

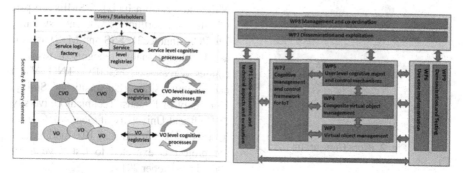

Fig. 1. iCore Cognitive Framework and work-package structure

Starting from the bottom of Fig. 1, the first level is the Virtual Object (VO) level, dedicated to the characterisation of the VO abstraction, meant to address interoperability and heterogeneity issues of IoT. Part of this abstraction also foresees the semantic enrichment of the description of Real World Objects, according to an RDF model, therefore contributing to the issue of automatic re-use of objects in diverse application contexts.

The next level up is dedicated to the set of functional blocks that realise the Composite Virtual Object (CVO) concept, whereby individual VOs are mashed-up to provide more composite functionality that dynamically binds the requirements of the Service Level to the continuously changing availability of underlying IoT resources. In this way the CVO level contributes to an iCore platform the ability to maintain "system knowledge".

The top level, called Service Level, is the one that exposes interfaces towards applications or users, as it's meant to translate Service Requests from outside the iCore platform into actions that, starting from service templates dynamically deploy, bind and run the set of processes that satisfy the request. This level is also responsible for maintaining and growing so called "real world knowledge" within the platform, to ensure that the knowledge supporting iCore autonomic decisions is indeed representative of the actual and changing application / user situation contextual background.

These three levels are developed in three separate work-packages, while the cross-cutting concerns at architectural, cognitive management and security & privacy and level are factored out in a separate technical coordination work-package.

The proposed solutions are to be validated through three further work-packages, one dedicated to socio-economic and business aspects, one to the implementation of four use cases (ambient assisted living, smart office, smart transportation, and supply chain management) and one dedicated to the implementation of demonstration trials.

iCore profile

The iCore Consortium consists of 21 partners with a strong industrial component represented by 8 ICT manufacturers, telecom operators, software vendors, system integrators,

software service/end users (Siemens, Thales, Alcatel-Lucent, Fiat, Atos, Software AG, NTT and Telecom Italia). 5 SMEs are part of the consortium (Ambient systems, ZIGPOS, Innotec21, SSS and M3S) as well as 4 internationally recognised research centres (Create-net, EC JRC, TNO, VTT) and 4 universities (University of Surrey, University of Piraeus, Technical University of Delft and University of Genova). Overall iCore size is 8.7 mEur of EU funding and the project is expected to last 3 years (it started in October 2011).

Fig. 2. iCore Consortium

3   Expected Impact

iCore solutions enable a variety of stakeholders to take part in the easy creation and delivery of value-add IoT services which can be dynamically tailored to the users situation and needs.

The iCore technology is designed to be managed and used by multiple stakeholders, driven by different business models and various interests, from platform operators to device manufacturers, to SMEs concentrating on bespoke services around their core IoT business. iCore will allow an adequate level of interoperability, so that innovative and competitive cross-domain systems and applications can be developed. In fact infrastructure and concepts are aimed at being agnostic of the application domain in which they will be used and this is where the strength of its solutions lies from an impact perspective.

The interconnection of physical objects and VOs in iCore will amplify the profound effects that large-scale networked communications are having on our society, gradually resulting in a genuine paradigm shift. Future Internet and IoT are becoming more and more a vital resource to economy and society, as vital processes in society, be it energy distribution, traffic management and (food) logistics are being coordinated by and thus heavily depend on means of telecommunication networks.

Reference

1. iCoreProject WebSite, http://www.iot-icore.eu

IoT6 Project in a Nutshell

Sébastien Ziegler and Cedric Crettaz

Mandat International, Geneva, Switzerland
{iot6,sziegler}@mandint.org

Abstract. IoT6 aims at exploiting the potential of IPv6 and related standards to overcome current shortcomings and fragmentation of the Internet of Things. The main objectives of the project are to research, design and develop a highly scalable IPv6-based Service-Oriented Architecture to achieve interoperability, mobility, cloud computing integration and intelligence distribution among heterogeneous smart things components, applications and services.

Keywords: IoT, M2M, IPv6, CoAP, architecture, interoperability, building automation.

The Internet of Things is exponentially growing towards an ecosystem interconnecting tens of billions of smart things. Simultaneously, the Internet is facing a significant transformation by moving to a new Internet protocol: the Internet Protocol version 6 (IPv6), which is scaling up the Internet to an almost unlimited number of globally reachable addresses.

IoT6 [1] is a 3 years FP7 European research project on the Internet of Things that started in October 2011 and will finish in September 2014. It aims at researching and exploiting the potential of IPv6 and related standards (6LoWPAN [2], CoAP [3], etc.) to address current needs of the Internet of Things. Its main challenges and objectives are to research, design and develop a highly scalable IPv6-based Service-Oriented Architecture. Its potential will be researched by exploring innovative forms of interactions such as:

— Provide generic techniques and interfaces to bridge different technologies to ensure communication over IPv6
— Information and intelligence distribution, with concepts such as "smart routing", exploiting IPv6-related features to enable a distributed data transmission management between a high number of IoT components and services.
— Multi-protocol interoperability with and among heterogeneous devices using all kinds of IP and non-IP communication protocols.
— Device mobility and the role of mobile phones in providing ubiquitous access to smart things
— Cloud computing integration with a focus on Software as a Service (SaaS) interconnected with smart things.

A. Galis and A. Gavras (Eds.): FIA 2013, LNCS 7858, pp. 353–355, 2013.

— IPv6 - Smart Things Information Services (STIS) innovative interactions, by exploring the potential of IPv6 to locate, identify and provide information on all kind of smart things.

The main outcomes of IoT6 will be recommendations on IPv6 features exploitation for the Internet of Things and an open and well-defined IPv6-based Service Oriented Architecture enabling interoperability, mobility, cloud computing and intelligence distribution among heterogeneous smart things components, applications and services, including with business processes management tools. It is exploring both horizontal (cross-domain) and vertical (IoT – cloud) integrations.

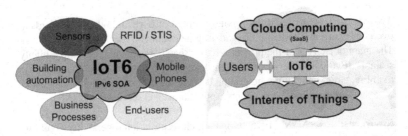

The project has already designed and developed most of its targeted IPv6-based IoT architecture taking the existing work done in ETSI M2M, IoT-A [5], and FI-WARE [6] as the basis. The initial integration with sensors, building automation components, tags, mobile phones and software as a service has been demonstrated. The project has also developed an innovative lookup and discovery system, named "Digcovery" [7]. More detailed information is provided in the Chapter "IoT6 – Moving to an IPv6-based future IoT". Finally, the project has organized several events and workshops in cooperation with other European research projects in order to synergize efforts and align their visions on IPv6 exploitation for the future Internet of Things. IoT6 members have also been elected to chair the new IoT TC Subcommittee of IEEE Communication Society [8], giving Europe a leading role and responsibility.

References

1. IoT6, http://www.iot6.eu
2. IPv6 over Low-Power Wireless Personal Area Networks (6LoWPANs), https://tools.ietf.org/html/rfc4919
3. Constrained Application Protocol (CoAP), draft-ietf-core-coap-11 (July 16, 2012), https://datatracker.ietf.org/doc/draft-ietf-core-coap/
4. ETSI M2M Communications, http://www.etsi.org/website/technologies/m2m.aspx

5. Internet of Things Architecture, IoT-A, http://www.iot-a.eu
6. FI-WARE, http://www.fi-ppp.eu/about-us/projects/fi-ware/
7. Jara, A.J., Martinez-Julia, P., Skarmeta, A.F.: Light-weight multicast DNS and DNS-SD (lmDNS-SD): IPv6-based resource and service discovery for the Web of Things. In: International Workshop on Extending Seamlessly to the Internet of Things (2012)
8. IEEE Communications Society, SubCommitee on the Internet of Things, http://www.comsoc.org/about/committees/emerging

Mobile Cloud Networking:
Mobile Network, Compute, and Storage as One Service On-Demand

Almerima Jamakovic[1], Thomas Michael Bohnert[2], and Georgios Karagiannis[3]

[1] University of Bern,
Communication and Distributed Systems Group,
Institute of Computer Science and Applied Mathematics,
Neubrückstrasse 10, CH-3012 Bern, Switzerland
jamakovic@iam.unibe.ch
[2] Zurich University of Applied Sciences,
ZHAW/ICCLab,
Institute of Information Technology,
Obere Kirchgasse 2, CH-8400 Winterthur, Switzerland
thomas.bohnert@zhaw.ch
[3] University of Twente,
Design and Analysis of Communication Systems Group,
Faculty for Electrical Engineering, Mathematics and Computer Science,
P.O. Box 217, 7500 AE Enschede, The Netherlands
karagian@cs.utwente.nl

Abstract. The Future Communication Architecture for Mobile Cloud Services: Mobile Cloud Networking (MCN)[1] is a EU FP7 Large-scale Integrating Project (IP) funded by the European Commission. MCN project was launched in November 2012 for the period of 36 month. In total top-tier 19 partners from industry and academia commit to jointly establish the vision of Mobile Cloud Networking, to *develop a fully cloud-based mobile communication and application platform*.

1 Introduction

Today's Cloud Computing is confided to data centres and one of the weakest points of the established Cloud Computing value proposition is that it does not support the seamless integration of cloud computing services in the mobile ecosystem. Another observation is that infrastructure sharing, enabled by virtualisation and seen as one of the most fundamental enablers of Cloud Computing, does exist in the Mobile Telco industry ever since the emergence of the Mobile Virtual Network Operator (MVNO). However, the principles of Cloud Computing are neither used nor supported by Mobile Networks and this regardless of the fact that many of today's network components are intrinsically cloud-ready and could be hosted on top of a Cloud Computing platform. These facts create a unique opportunity for the European Telco industry to provide a novel, distinct, and atomic (i.e., all services as one bundle) Mobile Cloud Networking

---

[1] http://www.mobile-cloud-networking.eu

A. Galis and A. Gavras (Eds.): FIA 2013, LNCS 7858, pp. 356–358, 2013.

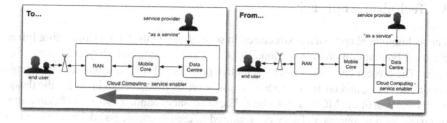

Fig. 1. Vision and Scope of Mobile Cloud Networking

service, that is: Mobile Network plus Decentralised Computing plus Smart Storage offered as One Service On-Demand, Elastic and Pay-As-You-Go. The MCN project will investigate, implement and evaluate a fully cloud-based mobile communication and application platform for Mobile Cloud Networking services.

2 Main Objectives

The top-most objectives of the MCN project are to: a) extend the concept of Cloud Computing beyond data centres towards the mobile End-User, b) to design an 3GPP Log Term Evolution (LTE) compliant Mobile Cloud Networking Architecture that exploits and supports Cloud Computing, c) to enable a novel business actor, the MCN Provider, and d) to deliver and exploit the concept of an End-to-End MCN for Novel Applications and Services. The MCN architecture will define and implement an architecture that meets real-time performance requirements of Mobile Network functions on top of a high-performance Cloud computing framework. It will further support efficient and elastic use and sharing of both, radio access and mobile core network resources between operators. Mobile network functionalities, such as baseband unit processing, mobility management and QoS control, will run on the enhanced mobile cloud platform leveraging commodity hardware. This requires extensions towards higher decentralisation of Mobile Network functions and enhancing those functionalities to enable elastically scaling up and down according to the load. In addition, the end-to-end control and management will orchestrate infrastructure and services across several technological domains: wireless, mobile core and data centres, providing an entirely novel mobile cloud application platform and thus novel revenue streams for telco operators. This platform will bridge Cloud Computing and the Mobile Network domains by integrated solutions such as end-to-end SLAs, monitoring, AAA, Rating, Charging, and Billing. Besides the technological aspects, MCN will identify and evaluate overarching novel business models that support the exploitation of the Mobile Cloud Networking in various multi-stakeholder scenarios. The MCN architecture will be evaluated in realistic scenarios and with a set of concrete use-cases, based on applications such as MCN-enabled Digital Signage. The evaluation will be done from diverse viewpoints, exploiting the well-balanced and representative consortium, including leading industry from the Telecommunication as well as the Cloud Computing segments.

3 Technical Approach

The technological approach is structured in several segments; Cloud Computing Infrastructural Foundation, Wireless Cloud, Mobile Core Cloud, and Mobile Platform Services. The project baseline is a representative portfolio of mobile cloud services, application scenarios, and business models. These serve as fundamental input for the design and evaluation of the MCN architecture. The necessary foundational, Cloud Computing infrastructural resources and services required to create, enable and deliver fully virtualised end-to-end MCN services are based on the popular OpenStack framework and respective extensions to be developed. On top of this framework mobile network extensions are foreseen, namely to enable the concept of Wireless Cloud and Mobile Core Network Cloud. This will address in particular a novel mobile network cloud concept in support of on-demand and dynamic deployment of wireless access and mobile core network services in a Cloud Computing environment. The project will also design and develop a mobile platform for end-to-end mobile-aware service deployment including SLA management, AAA, Content Distribution Services, Rating, Charing, and Billing. The ultimate objective is to specify, implement, evaluate, and standardize a complete Mobile Cloud Networking and Service platform.

4 Key Issues

The key research and innovation issues that the MCN project is expected to tackle are the following: a) how to virtualise the Radio Access Networks (RAN), b) how to design a cross-domain Infrastructure-as-a-Service (IaaS) control plane, c) how to upgrade virtualisation and Cloud Computing middleware to support highly demanding, real-time network applications and services, d) how to design, deploy, and operate 3GPP LTE software components to attain and fully benefit from Cloud Computing attributes, e) how to ensure a good QoE with advanced content and service migration mechanisms for mobile cloud users, and f) how to support multiple cross-domain aspects that must service a multitude of business actors and stakeholders.

5 Expected Impact

MCN innovations will enable European Mobile Telco providers to enter the Cloud Computing domain with a strategic advantage, which is the ownership of the mobile network. The enabler for this is an MCN architecture that seamlessly integrates the domains, cloud computing, mobile networks, and respective support services for application development and commercialization.

The SmartenIT STREP Project:
Socially-Aware Management of New Overlay Application Traffic Combined with Energy Efficiency in the Internet

Burkhard Stiller

University of Zürich, Department of Informatics, Communication Systems Group CSG
On behalf of the project partners: Athens University of Economics and Business,
University of Würzburg, Technische Universität Darmstadt, AGH University of Science and
Technology, Intracom S.A. Telecom, Solutions, Alcatel Lucent Bell Labs France
Instytut Chemii Bioorganiczej PAN, Interoute Spa, Telekom Deutschland GmbH

1 Main Objectives

The Internet has seen a strong move to support overlay applications, which demand a coherent and integrated control in the underlying heterogeneous networks in a scalable, resilient, and energy-efficient manner. A tighter integration of network management and overlay service functionality can lead to cross-layer optimization of operations and management, thus, being a promising approach to offer a large business potential in operational perspectives for all players involved.

Therefore, SmartenIT [1] targets an incentive-compatible cross-layer network management for providers of overlay-based applications (*e.g.*, cloud applications, content deli-very networks, and social networks), for network providers, and for end-users to ensure QoE-awareness (Quality-of-Experience), by accordingly addressing load and traffic patterns or special application requirements, and exploiting at the same time social awareness (in terms of user relations and interests). Moreover, the energy efficiency with respect to both end-user devices and underlying networking infrastructure is tackled to ensure an operationally efficient management. Incentive-compatible network management mechanisms for improving metrics in all layers and on an inter-domain basis for internet service and telecommunication providers serve as the major means to deal with real-life scenarios. Such metrics and mechanisms encompass:

1) Inter-cloud communication through many operators where applications demand for dedicated Quality-of-Service (QoS) levels.
2) An integrated and energy-aware traffic management considering limited energy resources of mobile devices accessing the cloud.
3) The exploitation of meta-information by network operators for the purpose of socially aware traffic management.

Selected scenarios are ported into test-beds, in which the effectiveness of appropriate traffic management mechanisms, integrated in an innovative architecture, is demonstrated. This will lead to benefits in cost and service quality for various stakeholders, including network, overlay application providers, and end-users – all of which are relevant players in Europe and world-wide.

A. Galis and A. Gavras (Eds.): FIA 2013, LNCS 7858, pp. 359–360, 2013.

2   SmartenIT Requirements and Goals

The three SmartenIT requirements encompass:

1) Detailed understanding of overlay-based applications' management demands in terms of traffic, QoE, and user behavior.
2) Network management support for cloud-based applications being seamlessly integrated into heterogeneous network management approaches of existing networks.
3) Cross-layer, operational, incentive-compatible, and efficient network management mechanisms for dealing with inter-domain ISPs functionality.

The design, implementation, and evaluation of networking functionality for improving this management support of massively adopted applications generating large traffic volume, *e.g.*, content delivery, can be achieved by exploiting cloud computing and social networking principles. In turn, key SmartenIT requirements have led to the SmartenIT key design goals:

1) Incentive-compatible network management mechanisms for end-users, overlay service providers, and network providers, being based on an open protocol like ALTO and support an operational framework for agile connectivity, distributed management, and a better control of heterogeneous networks.
2) QoE-awareness by monitoring key influence factors like end-user equipment capabilities or traffic load (including bursty traffic situations, congestion cases) and social awareness, especially awareness of user relations and interests.
3) Energy efficiency with respect to networking infrastructure as well as wireless and wired end-user devices, including flexibility in terms of adaptability to changing application requirements.

SmartenIT starts with major scenarios, which are driven by technology demands: (a) Energy-aware Traffic Management — by addressing the trade-off between energy efficient computation in the cloud and energy consumption on mobile end-user devices; (b) Social-aware Traffic Management — by exploiting meta-information extracted from online social networks by network operators; (c) Inter-cloud Communications — through many operators, where applications demand for dedicated traffic quality levels.

3   Expected Outcomes

The set of outcomes SmartenIT plans to develop include appropriate management mechanisms to qualify and quantify the selected use cases, which will be dependent on those scenarios as outlined above. They will be demonstrated as an implemented prototype for the proof-of-concept.

Reference

1. EU ICT STREP SmartenIT Project: FP7-ICT-2011-317846,
   http://www.smartenit.eu

The SmartSantander Project

José M. Hernández-Muñoz[1] and Luis Muñoz[2]

[1] Telefonica I+D, Madrid, Spain
jmhm@tid.es
[2] Universidad de Cantabria, Santander, Spain
luis@tlmat.unican.es

Abstract. The SmartSantander project has deployed during the past two years a unique in the world city-scale experimental research facility in support of typical applications and services for a smart city. This facility is sufficiently large, open and flexible to enable horizontal and vertical federation with other experimental facilities, and to stimulate the development of new applications by end-users. Besides, it provides support to the experimental advanced research on IoT technologies, and allows a realistic assessment on new services by means of users' acceptability tests. The facility already counts with more than 10,000 IoT devices (March 2013), and by the end of 2013 it will comprise of more than 12,000. The core of the facility is being installed in the city of Santander (Spain), the capital of the region of Cantabria situated on the north coast of Spain, and its surroundings. Besides Santander, other deployments have been placed in Lübeck (Germany), Guilford (UK) and Belgrade (Serbia). SmartSantander will enable the Future Internet of Things to become a reality.

Keywords: SmartCity, IoT, IoS, testbed, Future Internet.

1 The Service/Experimentation Duality

The testbed has being designed and implemented to operate in a scalable, heterogeneous and trustable way, thus becoming a flexible large-scale real-world experimental facility. Besides providing support to scientific experimentation, SmartSantander is also granting benefits of the massive IoT infrastructure deployed to the citizenship by providing support to end-user services in the framework of the city. The deployment into a realistic environment will not only secure sustainability through direct value generation for its users, but also drive the facility to evolve and dynamically adapt to the changing conditions of the everyday life in the city.

2 A Real-Life, Large-Scale Facility

One of the main objectives of the project is to fuel the use of the facility among the scientific community, end users and service providers in order to reduce the technical and societal barriers that prevent the IoT paradigm to become an everyday reality.

To attract the widest interest and demonstrate the usefulness of the SmartSantander platform, a key aspect has been from the very beginning the inclusion of a wide set of

A. Galis and A. Gavras (Eds.): FIA 2013, LNCS 7858, pp. 361–362, 2013.

applications areas. With this principle in mind, a number of key use cases have been selected based on their potential impact to the citizenship as well as their ability to exhibit the diversity, dynamics and scale that are essential in advanced protocol solutions. The high oversubscription experimented in the two open calls released so far have demonstrated that the ability to evaluate technologies and use cases by means of the platform is highly attractive for all involved stakeholders: industries, communities of users, other entities that are willing to use the experimental facility for deploying and assessing new services and applications, and Internet researchers to validate their cutting-edge technologies (protocols, algorithms, sensor platforms, etc.).

Some details of the experimental facility corresponding to the parking management scenario, where sensors have been deployed in one of the streets parallel to the sea and close to Santander downtown, are show in Fig. 1.

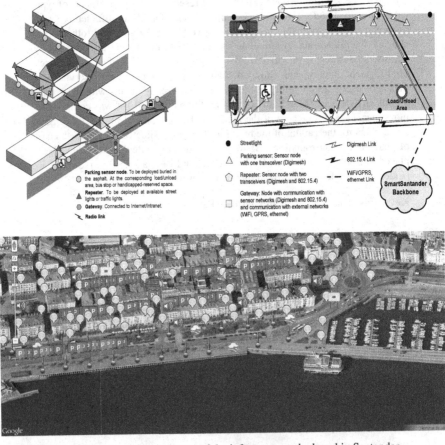

Fig. 1. Overview of a small part of the infrastructure deployed in Santander

UniverSelf, Realizing Autonomics for Future Networks

Laurent Ciavaglia

Alcatel-Lucent
Laurent.Ciavaglia@alcatel-lucent.com

Abstract. Despite undeniable progress in the field of autonomic networking, the need for techniques enabling the transformation of operational models, and the evolution towards more flexible networks, real-world deployments of self-managing networks are still limited. Most efforts have been focused on solving manageability bottlenecks in a given technological domain, while communication services extend anywhere, regardless of the technological boundaries (e.g. wireline/wireless). The FP7 UniverSelf project is developing an end-to-end and modular framework based common management substrates and network empowerment mechanisms, following a reference trust assurance process to foster large-scale deployment and adoption by the ICT actors.

1 Four Challenging Objectives

UniverSelf is an FP7 IP project that addresses autonomic networks and the interoperability of their parts in a holistic manner, i.e. including both wireline and wireless parts of the network. This project is vital because the operational complexity in an operator's network is growing, because the cost structure of the current management model is not sustainable, and because the already existing management architecture is no longer adapted. Correspondingly, the four main objectives of UniverSelf are:

— Design a Unified Management Framework for the different existing and emerging architectures that is cross-technology (i.e. wireless and wireline) and will serve as a common platform for both systems and services.
— Design the functions that will enable self-managing networks and embed these functions directly within the systems and elements that comprise the network infrastructure and support service delivery.
— Demonstrating the potential for deployment of autonomic solutions in carrier grade networks with an eye towards stimulating further research in Europe towards application and commercialization.
— Generate confidence in the viability and use of autonomic technologies in telecommunication networks by defining "certification" parameters for autonomic networking products.

2 An Impactful Experimentation Strategy

UniverSelf aims at demonstrating the feasibility and efficiency of the project solutions, mechanisms and algorithms in a proof-of-concept environment comprising

A. Galis and A. Gavras (Eds.): FIA 2013, LNCS 7858, pp. 363–366, 2013.

simulation modules and prototyping activities, together with testing and assessment capabilities. The experiments are organized according to the timeline shown in Figure1. The validation part of this activity addresses feasibility aspects, as well as assessment of key performance or stability, scalability etc. indicators and works especially on the integration of the solutions in and via the Unified Management Framework (UMF). Experimentation can be seen as a concrete methodology for the production of validation results close to real life scenarios. Experimentation and validation activities focus on the collection and analysis of metrics related to the achieved performance and optimization benefits, QoS in service provisioning, the end-to-end coherence of management actions, the system's stability and responsiveness, the realized compliance to the imposed policies and profiles, the CAPEX and OPEX gains etc... The main capabilities targeted for the federated framework for the experimental facilities, are the computation resources, the incorporation of heterogeneous wired and wireless systems and network management operations (emphasis on the autonomic aspects). Moreover, issues related to the business sustainability and user acceptance and trust in autonomic solutions are also addressed.

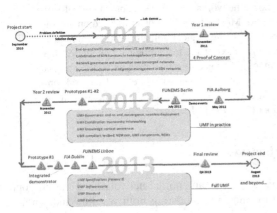

Fig. 1. UniverSelf experimentation timeline

3   An Integrated Portfolio

The aim of the project portfolio is to provide a comprehensive and consistent view about the solutions and technologies developed within the UniverSelf project, their constituting elements, their relationships and respective development levels. The portfolio presents an overall and integrated view about the solutions. The project portfolio is a tool useful to show the industry impact, feasibility, and relevance. The portfolio is structured around three dimensions: the capability levels (of a NEM or core mechanism), the development lifecycle, and the application domain(s). The UniverSelf project produces two essential pieces of solutions tightly related: the Unified Management Framework (UMF) and the Network Empowerment Mechanisms (NEM). These elements constitute the base of the project portfolio. The various combinations (or packaging) of these elements (UMF core functions and mechanisms, NEMs) constitute the project integrated solutions. As example, UMF core functions, mechanisms and specific NEMs are combined together to provide an integrated solution to the use case 1 on self-diagnosis and self-healing for VoIP and VPN services. Similar examples exist for the other project use cases, and infinity of variations can be imagined to address the different problems and use cases.

The solutions developed are modular, composable, extensible, interoperable, and can interwork with legacy systems. The IT/telco environments where they can be deployed have been evaluated, tested, and benchmarked, Examples of interworking and deployment (options) are also described as part of the project portfolio documentation together with other elements (or views) related to the different solutions such are the applicable business reference use case(s), problems...

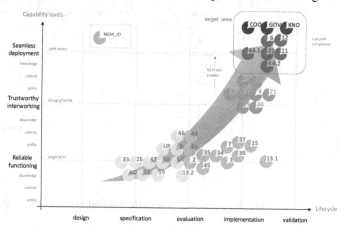

Fig. 2. UniverSelf portfolio (Spring 2013)

4   The Unified Management Framework (UMF)

A NEM achieves a self-management function (a closed control loop), with a specific purpose: an operational problem to solve with a defined performance objective in specific technological domain. Examples are for instance the use of Bayesian inference for fault diagnosis in FTTH environments, or the use of genetic algorithm for interference coordination in LTE networks.

When a NEM is deployed within an operator infrastructure, it has to deal with its environment composed by the operator, the network/service equipments, the legacy management systems and also the other NEMs. To realize a seamless deployment and trustworthy interworking of a large number of NEMs, we need a unified framework to manage them. This UMF shall be composed by:

— Tools to deploy, drive and track progress of NEMs which highlight the need for Governance/Human-to-Network tools.
— Tools to avoid conflicts ensure stability and performance when several NEMs are concurrently working which highlight the need for Coordination/Orchestration mechanisms.
— Tools to make NEMs find, formulate and share relevant information to enable or improve their functioning which highlight the need for Knowledge management.
— Tools to allow NEMs getting monitoring data and enforcing configuration actions at equipment level which highlight the need for specific adaptors.

These areas outline the core functional decomposition of the Unified Management Framework, as depicted in Figure 3.

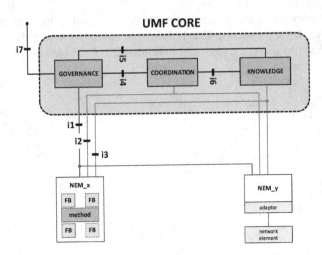

Fig. 3. Functional view of the Unified Management Framework

5   Summary of Main Achievements

The main achievement the UniverSelf project is the design, specification, demonstration and standardization a Unified Management Framework (UMF) capable of managing any kind of intelligent/autonomic functions over heterogeneous network technologies. The UMF provides operators and vendors with inter-operable (standardized), reliable and trustworthy (tested and certified), seamlessly deployable (unified, end-to-end, and cross-technology) autonomic functions (NEM - Network Empowerment Mechanisms). The UMF CORE is composed of 3 main functional blocks: GOVERNANCE, COORDINATION and KNOWLEDGE designed to manage the large number of NEMs, by providing:

The project provides both written specifications (to be channeled into standards) and readily available and validated software solutions (UMF software/libraries, NEM skin as an accelerator for NEM developers to make them UMF-compliant to support operators and vendors in the development and deployment of these new autonomic functions. In the time frame of the project, three releases of the UMF are/will be developed (currently 3rd release in under specs/development) and multiple autonomic functions (35+) are also specified, developed, tested and validated in real-world conditions. These functions covers both fixed and wireless technologies like several 3GPP/LTE SON functions, IP/MPLS traffic engineering, software-defined networks, learning and prediction algorithms, diagnosis, cloud mobility... The project also demonstrates its solutions on the basis of 6 use cases (based on problems and technologies identified by operators participating in the project (Orange, Telefonica, Telecom Italia, NTT)).

The project results are available on the UniverSelf project website at http://www.univerself-project.eu

Author Index